The Testimony
of JOHN the
BELOVED

Sidney B. Sperry

Other volumes in the Sperry Symposium Series
from Deseret Book Company:

Voices of Old Testament Prophets
The Doctrine and Covenants, a Book of Answers
Nurturing Faith through the Book of Mormon
The Apostle Paul: His Life and His Testimony
Thy People Shall Be My People
The Heavens Are Open
Doctrines of the Book of Mormon
The Lord of the Gospels
A Witness of Jesus Christ
Doctrines for Exaltation

The Testimony
of JOHN the
BELOVED

The 27th Annual
Sidney B. Sperry Symposium

Deseret Book Company
Salt Lake City, Utah

Library of Congress Cataloging-in-Publication Data

Sperry Symposium (27th : 1998)
    The testimony of John the Beloved : the 1998 Sperry Symposium on the New Testament.
       p.   cm.
    Includes bibliographical references and index.
    ISBN 1-57345-448-6
    1. Bible. N. T. John—Criticism, interpretation, etc.—
Congresses.   2. Bible. N. T. Epistles of John—Criticism,
interpretation, etc.—Congresses.   3. Bible. N. T. Revelation—
Criticism, interpretation, etc.—Congresses.   4. Church of Jesus
Christ of Latter-day Saints—Doctrines—Congresses.   5. Mormon
Church—Doctrines—Congresses.   I. Title.
BS2601.S62   1998
226.5'06—dc21   98-30963
                                                            CIP

Printed in the United States of America   72082 - 6421

10 9   8   7   6   5   4   3   2   1

CONTENTS

PREFACE

The writings of John the beloved apostle contain some of the most profound events, specific prophecies, and significant doctrines recorded in all of ancient scripture. Although they provide limited historical detail, it is clear from the writings of John that his primary purpose was to bear testimony that "Jesus is the Christ, the Son of God" (John 20:31). The Joseph Smith Translation of the title of John's Gospel, "The Testimony of St. John," provides an accurate description of what the reader will find in all of John's writings, not only in the Gospel account but in the epistles of John and the book of Revelation as well.

John's writings include descriptions of the premortal Jehovah and panoramic prophecies of the Savior's second coming, millennial reign, and eternal dwelling in celestial glory. With the exception of the apostle Paul, John the Revelator contributed more books to the New Testament canon than any other writer.

More than 90 percent of the Gospel of John is unique, containing information that is not found in the other three Gospel accounts. The Gospel of Matthew was written specifically to the Jews, the Gospel of Mark to the Gentiles, and the Gospel of Luke to the Greeks. It is clear that John's Gospel was written to all faithful members of the Lord's Church. The LDS Bible Dictionary tells us: "John's account does not contain much of the fundamental information that the other records contain, and it is evident that he was writing to members of the Church who already had basic information about the Lord. His primary purpose was to emphasize the divine nature of Jesus as the Only Begotten Son of God in the flesh" (683).

The book of Revelation underscores the theme found throughout scripture "that there will be an eventual triumph on this earth of God over the devil; a permanent victory of good over evil" (LDS Bible Dictionary, 762). In addition to emphasizing the incarnation of Jesus and the centrality of love, John's epistles warn the reader of false teachings and of the antichrists who espouse them. How blessed we are to have the writings of John the beloved apostle and revelator, "the disciple whom Jesus loved" (John 13:23).

To commemorate the meritorious service of Dr. Sidney B. Sperry, this volume provides both insight and understanding to students and teachers of the New Testament. Building on previous New Testament Sperry Symposiums, which have focused on the Gospels and on the writings of the apostle Paul, this volume on the writings of John will add to the reader's appreciation of the New Testament. We sincerely hope this diverse collection of perceptive and inspirational essays will bless the reader "that ye might believe that Jesus is the Christ, the Son of God; and that believing ye might have life through his name" (John 20:31).

We would like to acknowledge Patty Smith from the Religious Education Faculty Support Center at Brigham Young University for her assistance in the organization of the Sperry Symposium and in helping to prepare this volume. Special thanks go to Suzanne Brady and her colleagues at Deseret Book Company for their fine work in editing and coordinating the publication of *The Testimony of John the Beloved.*

We also wish to thank Dee Richard Darling of the Church Educational System and Randy Hayes from the Department of Religion at Ricks College for their dedicated service on the Sperry Symposium Committee.

Daniel K Judd

Craig J. Ostler

Richard D. Draper

CHAPTER ONE

JOHN THE BELOVED: A SPECIAL WITNESS OF THE ATONEMENT

KENT R. BROOKS

Every prophet who has ever lived on this earth has received the sure witness of the divinity of the Son of God. As recorded in holy scripture—ancient and modern—their testimonies declare that Jesus is the Christ, the Savior and Redeemer of the world, and salvation is available only through him. One of those prophets, John the Beloved, taught about the redeeming and enabling powers of the Atonement in his writings: the Gospel of John, 1 John, 2 John, 3 John, and the book of Revelation.

Jesus declared, "I am come in my Father's name" (John 5:43). Jesus was foreordained by the Father and given the authority to act in his name and to be the Savior of the world. John taught that "as many as received him, to them gave he power to become the sons of God" (John 1:12). In this passage, the English word *power* is used to translate the Greek word *exousia,* which literally means authority, right, or privilege. By believing on Christ, we are given the power, or authority, to become the sons of God: even though we are not sons of God the Father in the flesh, we are given the privilege to become such through adoption into the family of Christ. We become co-heirs with the Only Begotten to all that the Father has. No one can claim such honor unto himself without proper authority from the Savior, who received it from the Father.

Kent R. Brooks is a member of the Religious Education faculty at Ricks College.

1

JOHN, A SPECIAL WITNESS OF JESUS CHRIST

"We believe that a man must be called of God, by prophecy, and by the laying on of hands by those who are in authority, to preach the Gospel and administer in the ordinances thereof" (Articles of Faith 1:5). John, a fisherman by trade, was called by the Lord and given the *power*, the authority, the right, and the privilege to be one of the Twelve Apostles, or special witnesses, of Jesus Christ. Upon his call, John "immediately left [his] ship and [his] father, and followed [Jesus]" (Matthew 4:22). When one is called by proper authority and acts "in the power of the ordination wherewith he has been ordained" (D&C 79:1), it does not matter what his background or experience is, for "whom the Lord calls, the Lord qualifies."[1] Under the divine tutelage of the Savior, John was qualified as one of the "special witnesses of the name of Christ" (D&C 107:23) to "bear witness to his doctrine [and] of its effect upon mankind."[2]

What is the doctrine of Christ, of which John was to be a special witness? The doctrine of Christ is the doctrine of the Father. Jesus taught, "My doctrine is not mine, but his that sent me. If any man will do his will, he shall know of the doctrine, whether it be of God, or whether I speak of myself" (John 7:16–17). "For I came down from heaven, not to do mine own will, but the will of him that sent me" (John 6:38; see also 4:34; 5:30). The doctrine of Christ is that we come unto him through faith, repent of our sins, receive the Holy Ghost, and endure to the end (see 2 Nephi 31:17–21; 3 Nephi 11:29–41). Jesus said, "I am the way, the truth, and the life" (John 14:6). "I am the door of the sheepfold. . . . By me if any man enter in, he shall be saved, and shall . . . find pasture" (JST John 10:7; KJV John 10:9). John stated that his whole purpose in writing was that "ye might believe that Jesus is the Christ, the Son of God; and that believing ye might have life through his name" (John 20:31).

John wrote of the premortal Christ, the "Word" who was "with God, and, was . . . God," by whom "all things were made" (John 1:1–3). He recorded the Savior's testimony that "before Abraham was, I am" (John 8:58). He was an eyewitness of the postmortal, resurrected Christ. Within the first eight days following his resurrection, Jesus visited the Twelve on at least two occasions. His special witnesses were privileged to see and feel the nail prints in his hands and feet (see John 20:19–20, 26–29; 1 John 1:1). After those visits, Jesus appeared to John and other disciples at the Sea of Tiberius or the Sea of Galilee (see John 21:1–2). On numerous other occasions during his forty-day ministry, they were taught many "things pertaining to the kingdom of God" and received "many infallible proofs" of the living Christ (Acts 1:3). Later, while living in exile on the isle of Patmos, John was personally visited by the risen Lord. Jesus testified, "I am the first and the last: I am he that liveth, and was dead; . . . behold, I am alive for evermore" (Revelation 1:17–18).

As a witness of the mortal Christ, the "only begotten of the Father," who "was made flesh, and dwelt among [men]" (John 1:14), John drew upon the powerful imagery the Savior used in his sermons to teach his doctrine. Jesus spoke of himself as the "living water" (John 4:11), the "bread of life" (John 6:35, 48), the "light of the world" (John 8:12), and the "good shepherd" (John 10:11, 14), all of which bore witness that life and salvation are to be found only in Christ. John related the tender story of Lazarus, a disciple whom Jesus loved (see John 11:5, 36), for whom he wept (see John 11:35), and whom he raised from the dead (see John 11:43–44), a vivid testimony that Jesus is the "resurrection, and the life" (John 11:25). To emphasize that it is only "by grace that we are saved, after all we can do" (2 Nephi 25:23), Jesus taught the parable of the vine and the branches, testifying, "I am the true vine . . . ye are the branches . . . without me ye can do nothing" (John 15:1, 5). John was the only one of the Gospel writers who preserved the metaphorical allusions to Jesus as the Living Water, the Bread of Life, the Good Shepherd, and the True Vine.

The mission of Christ was to "bring to pass the immortality and eternal life of man" (Moses 1:39) through the Atonement, the supreme act of love. It was his love for the Father (see John 14:31) and his love for all of us (see John 15:13), that moved Jesus to finish the work the Father gave him to do (see John 17:4). John the Beloved testified, "For God so loved the world, that he gave his only begotten Son, that whosoever believeth in him should not perish, but have everlasting life" (John 3:16), in what Elder Bruce R. McConkie called "perhaps the most . . . powerful single verse of scripture ever uttered." Elder McConkie said that this one verse "summarizes the whole plan of salvation, tying together the Father, the Son, his atoning sacrifice, that belief in him which presupposes righteous works, and ultimate eternal exaltation for the faithful."³

No one but Christ had the ability to atone for the sins of all mankind. John taught two reasons for this. First, the Atonement had to be performed by one who was sinless—one who had been perfectly obedient to the laws of God (see 1 John 3:5). Only the unblemished "Lamb of God" qualified (John 1:29). Second, the Atonement had to be performed by one who had power over life and death. From his mortal mother, Christ inherited the power to lay down his life; from his immortal Father, he inherited the power to take up his life again (see John 5:26). In perfect submission to the will of the Father, Jesus chose to lay down his life voluntarily (see John 10:17–18). John testified that this act of matchless love could not have been completed without the shedding of blood (see 1 John 1:7; Revelation 1:5, 5:9). Christ's sinless and voluntary self-sacrifice provided a redemptive and enabling power to all mankind.

THE REDEMPTIVE POWER OF THE ATONEMENT

The fall of Adam brought into the world both physical death, which is the separation of the spirit from the body (see James 2:26), and spiritual death, which is separation or alienation from righteousness or the things of God (see Alma 12:32). The atonement of Christ redeems, or ransoms, us from the effects of the fall. "Redemption," Elder Bruce R. McConkie taught, "is of two kinds: conditional and unconditional."⁴

Unconditional redemption provides two free gifts to mankind. The first unconditional gift is that all who ever have or ever will live in mortality will be redeemed from physical death through the resurrection, because Jesus "taste[d] death for every man" (Hebrews 2:9). John recorded the Savior's own testimony that all "shall come forth; they who have done good, in the resurrection of the just; and they who have done evil, in the resurrection of the unjust" (JST John 5:29). Whether just or unjust, all will be raised with an immortal body, never again subject to death or the pains, sicknesses, and fatigues of the mortal body (see Alma 11:41–45). I came to appreciate that blessing when I was a teenager. My father suffered from the effects of diabetes, going completely blind during the last two years of his life. Though I felt a great loss when he died during my senior year in high school, I felt peace in knowing that his spirit would one day be reunited with a perfect physical body that would be free from the suffering he had experienced in this life. I rejoiced to know that his passing had restored his sight again and that he could see his family for the first time in more than two years. "And Jesus said, For judgment I am come into this world, that they which see not might see" (John 9:39).

The second unconditional blessing of the Atonement is expressed in our second Article of Faith: "We believe that men will be punished for their own sins, and not for Adam's transgression." Although each of us is certainly influenced by the fall of Adam (that is, we all experience pain, suffering, sickness, and death), the infinite mercy of Christ prevents us from being punished for Adam's transgression or the sins of anyone else. We may suffer because of the sins of another, but that suffering does not occur as a punishment imposed by God. For God to punish one person for the sins of another would not be just. John recorded the words of Jesus: "The Father . . . hath committed all judgment unto the Son" (John 5:22) and "my judgment is just" (John 5:30).

Redemption from physical death is unconditional, but redemption from spiritual death is not. "Conditional redemption," Elder McConkie said, "is synonymous with exaltation or eternal life. It comes by the grace of God coupled with good works and includes redemption from the effects of both the temporal and spiritual fall."[5] We alienate ourselves from God and die spiritually through sin. And because all sin, John reasoned, all have need of the Atonement (see 1 John 1:8, 10). John further explained that the Atonement provides redemption from spiritual death upon conditions of repentance and subsequent obedience and makes spiritual rebirth possible (see John 3:3–5; 8:51; 1 John 1:9, 2:29; JST 1 John 3:9; 5:18; Revelation 2:11; 20:6). John testified, "But if any man sin and repent, we have an advocate with the Father, Jesus Christ the righteous; and he is the propitiation for our sins: and not for ours only, but also for the sins of the whole world" (JST 1 John 2:1; KJV 1 John 2:2). Here the English word *advocate* is used to translate the Greek word *parakletos,* which means intercessor, helper, or comforter. If our hearts are broken, our spirits contrite, and we exercise faith unto repentance, Jesus will intercede at the final judgment as our advocate with the Father (see Moroni 7:28). And "no man," Jesus said, "cometh unto the Father, but by me" (John 14:6).

The word *atonement* means literally to reconcile or to set at one, one with God.[6] Jesus mediates a reconciliation between God and us whereby we are "brought again into communion with [the Father], and [are] made able to live and advance as a resurrected being in the eternal worlds."[7] By so doing, Jesus, the "author and finisher of our faith" (Hebrews 12:2), answers "the ends of the law" (2 Nephi 2:7), thus bringing about our eternal happiness, which is the "end" or the "object and design of our existence."[8]

The word *propitiation* is used to translate the Greek word *hilasmos,* which means an appeasing, or the means of appeasing. We are accountable for how we exercise our agency and what we do with the laws of God. According to the law of justice, if we obey the laws of God, we automatically receive the blessings associated with those laws (see D&C 82:10). In a sense, we get what we deserve. But if we violate the laws of God, we will also get what we deserve because the penalty of sin automatically follows (see D&C 130:20–21). "That," Elder Dallin H. Oaks said, "is an outcome I fear. I cannot achieve my eternal goals on the basis of what I deserve. Though I try with all my might, I am still what King Benjamin called an 'unprofitable servant' (see Mosiah 2:21). To achieve my eternal goals, I need more than I deserve. I need more than justice. . . . [I need mercy through] the atonement of Jesus Christ. . . . Mercy signifies an advantage greater than is deserved. This could come by the withholding of a deserved punishment or by the granting of an undeserved benefit. . . . If justice is exactly [the punishment] one deserves, then mercy is *more* benefit than one deserves. . . . *The Atonement* is the means by which justice is served and mercy is extended."[9]

President J. Reuben Clark Jr. said: "I believe that our Heavenly Father wants to save every one of his children. . . . I believe that in his justice and mercy he will give us the maximum reward for our acts, give us all that he can give, and in the reverse, I believe that he will impose upon us the minimum penalty which it is possible for him to impose."[10] If we accept the terms of conditional redemption, then "mercy can satisfy the demands of justice, and encircles [us] in the arms of safety" (Alma 34:16). John testified that "the Lamb . . . shall feed [us], and shall lead [us] unto living fountains of waters: and

God shall wipe away all tears from [our] eyes" (Revelation 7:17). If we let him, the Good Shepherd will free us from the entanglements of sin and bring us safely back to the fold.

To qualify fully for that conditional redemption requires that we repent fully of all our sins. And the repentance that brings about complete forgiveness requires suffering. President Spencer W. Kimball said: "There can be no forgiveness without real and total repentance, and there can be no repentance without punishment."[11] The unrepentant sinner must pay the full price of sin. Alma taught that "he that exercises no faith unto repentance is exposed to the whole law of the demands of justice; therefore only unto him that has faith unto repentance is brought about the great and eternal plan of redemption" (Alma 34:16). If the unrepentant sinner is exposed to the full extent of the demands of justice, then what about the repentant sinner? Jesus said: "For behold, I, God, have suffered these things for all, that they might not suffer if they would repent; but if they would not repent they must suffer even as I" (D&C 19:16–17). Can the repentant sinner escape suffering entirely, or is he still subject to part of the demands of justice? Can the repentant sinner satisfy the demands of justice by his own suffering, by his own works of repentance?

Elder Dallin H. Oaks answered these questions. He said: "Do these [verses] mean that a person who repents does not need to suffer at all because the entire punishment is borne by the Savior? [No, they mean] that the person who repents does not need to suffer 'even as' the Savior suffered for that sin. Sinners who are repenting will experience some suffering, but, because of their repentance and because of the Atonement, they will not experience the full . . . extent of [suffering] the Savior [did] for that sin. . . . The suffering that impels a transgressor toward repentance is his or her own suffering. But the suffering that satisfies the demands of justice for all repented transgressions is the suffering of our Savior and Redeemer. . . . Some transgressors . . . [ask] 'Why must I suffer at all? . . . Now that I have said I am sorry, why can't you just give me mercy and forget about this?' . . . The object of God's laws is to save the sinner, not simply to punish him. . . . The repentant transgressor must be changed, and the conditions of repentance, including confession and personal suffering, are essential to accomplish that change. To exempt a transgressor from those conditions would deprive him of the change necessary for his salvation."[12]

Only through Christ's suffering and Christ's grace, John testified, can we receive the "fulness" of the Father, "even immortality and eternal life" (JST John 1:16). Lehi taught that "there is no flesh that can dwell in the presence of God, save it be through the merits, and mercy, and grace of the Holy Messiah" (2 Nephi 2:8). Nephi said that the fulness of the Father is available only to those who have unshaken faith in the words of Christ, "relying wholly upon the merits of him who is mighty to save" (2 Nephi 31:19). The word *merits* is used six times in the scriptures. Five of those references are in the Book of Mormon (see 2 Nephi 2:8; 31:19; Alma 24:10; Helaman 14:13; Moroni 6:4), and one is in the Doctrine and Covenants (see D&C 3:20). All six references refer to the merits of Christ.

We must do our part, but no matter how hard we try, no matter how fully we repent, no matter how many good works we do, we simply cannot bring about our own redemption. John recorded the words of Jesus: "As the branch cannot bear fruit of itself, except it abide in the vine; no more can ye, except ye abide in me" (John 15:4). Elder Dallin H. Oaks said: "Man unquestionably has impressive powers and can bring to pass great things by tireless efforts and indomitable will. But after all our obedience and good works, we cannot be saved from the effect of our sins without the grace extended by the atonement of Jesus Christ."[13]

THE ENABLING POWER OF THE ATONEMENT

In the October 1995 general conference of the Church, President Boyd K. Packer said: "[Except for] the very few who defect to perdition, there is no habit, no addiction, no rebellion, no transgression, no apostasy, no crime exempted from the promise of complete forgiveness. That is the promise of the atonement of Christ."[14] Clearly, the Atonement has the power to redeem us from sin and from the effects of the Fall. But the Atonement also has the power to enable us. To *enable* means "to make able; give power, means, or ability to; make competent."[15] The redemptive power of the Atonement makes us clean. The enabling power of the Atonement, which is activated by faith in Jesus Christ, makes us powerful, able, competent, and holy. It is the power that compensates when we do our best and still fall short. It is the power that magnifies our abilities, allowing us to do things beyond our own natural capacity. It is the power that enables us to keep trying even when we feel like giving up. It is the power by which we are "born again" (John 3:3) and become perfect (see John 17:23).

Our goal is not just to become clean. Our goal is to become like God! We cannot do that by ourselves. C. S. Lewis said: "When I was a child I often had toothache, and I knew that if I went to my mother she would give me something which would deaden the pain for that night and let me get to sleep. But I did not go to my mother . . . till the pain became very bad. . . . I did not doubt she would give me the aspirin; but I knew she would also do something else. I knew she would take me to the dentist next morning. I could not get what I wanted out of her without getting something more, which I did not want. I wanted immediate relief from pain: but I could not get it without [also going to the dentist].

"Our Lord is like the dentist. Dozens of people go to Him to be cured of some one particular sin which they are ashamed of . . . or which is . . . spoiling daily life. . . . Well, He will cure it all right: but He will not stop there. That may be all you asked; but if you once call Him in, He will give you the full treatment. . . . 'Make no mistake,' He says, 'if you let Me, I will make you perfect. The moment you put yourself in My hands, that is what you are in for. Nothing less, or other, than that. You have [your agency], and if you choose, you can push Me away. But if you do not push Me away, understand that I am going to see this job through. . . . I will never rest, nor let you rest, until you are literally perfect—until my Father can say without reservation that He is well pleased with you, as He said He was well pleased with Me.'

"And yet—this is the other and equally important side of it—this Helper who will, in the long run, be satisfied with nothing less than absolute perfection, will also be delighted with the first feeble, stumbling effort you make tomorrow to do the simplest duty. . . . As a great Christian writer (George Macdonald) pointed out . . . 'God is easy to please, but hard to satisfy.' [So], on the one hand, God's demand for perfection need not discourage you in the least in your present attempts to be good—or even in your present failures. Each time you fall He will pick you up again. And He knows perfectly well that your own efforts are never going to bring you anywhere near perfection. On the other hand, you must realize from the outset that the goal toward which He is beginning to guide you is absolute perfection; and no power in the whole universe, except you yourself, can prevent Him from taking you to that goal."[16]

Like the redemptive power of the Atonement, the enabling power is made possible because of the grace of God. We can, by our sins, spiritually disable ourselves. But we cannot, without his help, be enabled. He is the source, the "outlet," of the power. If we accept his atonement and let our will be swallowed up in his, we can "plug into" that unfailing source of power and strength.

John wrote of the enabling power of the Atonement. Recorded in John 15:7 are the words of the Savior that "if ye abide in me, and my words abide in you, ye shall ask what ye will, and it shall be done unto you." John bore witness that "whatsoever we ask, we receive of him, because we *keep his commandments,* and *do those things that are pleasing in his sight*" (1 John 3:22; emphasis added). "And this is the confidence that we have in him, that, if we ask any thing *according to his will,* he heareth us" (1 John 5:14; emphasis added). Those who are obedient to that counsel will truly discover that "with God nothing *can* be impossible" (JST Luke 1:37; emphasis added). There is no weakness, no bitterness, no pain, no sickness, no trouble, no habit, no hurt we cannot overcome with his help. There is no attribute of godliness we cannot develop, no righteous desire we cannot achieve through his enabling power. The Bread of Life can supplant what we lack. The Living Water can bring further growth "after all we can do" (2 Nephi 25:23).

For example, we may feel we cannot forgive another who has hurt us, cannot love someone who seems unlovable, cannot pray for those who despitefully use us (see Matthew 5:44), cannot again trust one who has violated our trust, or cannot keep trying when we are weary of well-doing or feel we are not succeeding. Through faith, the enabling power can help us forgive when we can't find forgiveness within ourselves, love when we feel no love, pray when we do not feel like praying, trust when trust seems impossible, and press forward in spite of the press of life. The enabling power of the Atonement can help us overcome all things (see D&C 63:47) because "all things are possible to him that believeth" (Mark 9:23).

John taught that those who overcome through the enabling power of the Atonement will become "kings and priests" (Revelation 1:6, 5:10), will gain eternal life (see Revelation 2:7), will avoid the second spiritual death (see Revelation 2:11), will inherit the celestial kingdom (see Revelation 2:17), will be made rulers over many kingdoms (see Revelation 2:26–28), will retain their names in the Lamb's book of life (see Revelation 3:5), will become the sons of God (see Revelation 21:7), endowed with the power, the authority, the right, and the privilege to reign forever in celestial splendor (see Revelation 22:3–5). "And God shall wipe away all tears from their eyes;" John said, "and there shall be no more death, neither sorrow, nor crying, neither shall there be any more pain: for the former things are passed away" (Revelation 21:4).

In the words of the beautiful hymn, "More Holiness Give Me,"[17] we find a wonderful expression of what the enabling power can bring to us:

> More holiness give me,
> More strivings within,
> More patience in suff'ring,
>
> . . . .
>
> More faith in my Savior,
> More sense of his care,
> More joy in his service,
> More purpose in prayer.
>
> More gratitude give me,
> More trust in the Lord,
>
> . . . .
>
> More hope in his word,
>
> . . . .
>
> More meekness in trial,
> More praise for relief.
>
> More purity give me,
> More strength to o'ercome,
>
> . . . .
>
> More blessed and holy—
> More, Savior, like thee.

President Ezra Taft Benson said that "men and women who turn their lives over to God will discover that He can make a lot more out of their lives than they can. He will deepen their joys, expand their vision, quicken their minds, strengthen their muscles, lift their spirits, multiply their blessings, increase their opportunities, comfort their souls, raise up friends, and pour out peace. Whoever will lose his life in the service of God will find eternal life."[18]

The enabling power of Christ can do all that and more. Alma taught: "And [Jesus] shall go forth, suffering pains . . . of every kind; and . . . he will take upon him the . . . sicknesses of his people . . . and . . . their infirmities, that his bowels may be filled with mercy, according to the flesh, that he may know according to the flesh how to succor his people according to their infirmities" (Alma 7:11–12; see also Matthew 8:17).

Elder Jeffrey R. Holland noted that the word *succor* literally means "to run to. . . . Even as he calls us to come to him and follow him, he is unfailingly running to help us."[19] Such is the love of the Good Shepherd. As John so beautifully recorded: "The sheep hear his voice: and he calleth his own sheep by name, and leadeth them out. . . . And . . . he goeth before them, and the sheep follow him: for they know his voice" (John 10:3–4). Jesus understands perfectly every feeling, every temptation, every pain, every weakness, every sickness, every infirmity, every difficulty known to man. He knows us. He loves us. He desires to help us. And he can enable us to do all things, if we will but let him.

Bruce C. Hafen, now a member of the Quorum of the Seventy, spoke of the enabling power of the Atonement. He said: "A sense of falling short or falling down is not only natural but essential to the mortal experience. . . . The Savior's victory can compensate not only for our sins but also for our inadequacies; not only for our deliberate mistakes but also for our sins committed in ignorance, our errors of judgement, and our unavoidable imperfections. . . . I grieve for those who . . . believe that, in the quest for eternal life, the Atonement is there only to help big-time sinners, and that they, as everyday Mormons who just have to try harder, must 'make it' on their own. The truth is not that we must make it on our own, but that he will make us his own. . . . As we [hold onto the iron rod], we are likely to find that the cold rod of iron will begin to feel . . . [like the] loving hand of one who is literally pulling us along the way. He gives us strength enough to rescue us [and] warmth enough to tell us that home is not far away. . . . Sometimes we talk about how important it is to be on the Lord's side. Perhaps we should talk more about how important it is that the Lord is on *our* side."[20]

Is it any wonder that John, the "disciple whom Jesus loved" (John 21:7, 20; 13:23; 19:26–27; 20:2), spoke so often and with so much tenderness of the love of the Son of God. He said that Jesus loved the Twelve "unto the end" (John 13:1). As a special witness of that love, John wrote: "[I] have seen and do testify that the Father sent the Son to be the Saviour of the world. . . . [I] have known and believed the love that God hath to [me.] God is love . . . [and] there is no fear in love; but perfect love casteth out fear. . . . [I] love him, because he first loved [me]" (1 John 4:14, 16, 18–19). The amazing thing is not that *we* could love *him,* a being who is perfect and who has done so much for us. No, what causes each of us to "stand all amazed" is that he was willing

> to rescue a soul so rebellious and proud as mine,
> That he should extend his great love unto such as I, . . .
> Oh, it is wonderful that he should care for me
> Enough to die for me!
> Oh, it is wonderful, wonderful to me![21]

The Prophet Joseph Smith taught: "Would it be possible for a man to exercise faith in God, so as to be saved, unless he had an idea that God was love? He could not; because man could not love God unless he had an idea that God was love, and if he did not love God he could not have faith in him."[22] Without God's perfect love for us, we could not be saved. Without our faith in that perfect love and our determination to love and serve God with all our "heart, . . . might, mind, and strength" (D&C 59:5), we could not be saved. But through his perfect love, his atoning sacrifice, we can be redeemed from the fall and be enabled to return home, back to the presence of our Heavenly Father, where, John testified, we will forever "have right to the tree of life" (Revelation 22:14) and the love of God (see 1 Nephi 11:21–22), and we can "take the water of life freely" (Revelation 22:17).

"When, at last, we are truly pointed homeward," Elder Neal A.

Maxwell said, "then the world's pointing fingers of scorn can better be endured. As we come to know to Whom we belong, the other forms of belonging cease to mean very much. Likewise, as Jesus begins to have a real place in our lives, we are much less concerned with losing our places in the world. When our minds really catch hold of the significance of Jesus' atonement, the world's hold on us loosens. (See Alma 36:18.)"[23]

John declared of his writings, "These are written, that ye might believe that Jesus is the Christ, the Son of God; and that believing ye might have life through his name" (John 20:31). Blessed by the testimony of this special witness, our knowledge of and our faith in the redeeming and enabling powers of the Atonement are strengthened. With gratitude we exclaim "Oh, sweet the joy this sentence gives: 'I know that my Redeemer lives!'"[24]

Notes

1. Thomas S. Monson, *Ensign,* May 1988, 43.

2. David O. McKay, *Gospel Ideals* (Salt Lake City: Improvement Era, 1953), 251.

3. Bruce R. McConkie, *Doctrinal New Testament Commentary,* 3 vols. (Salt Lake City: Bookcraft, 1965–73), 1:144.

4. Bruce R. McConkie, *Mormon Doctrine,* 2d ed. (Salt Lake City: Bookcraft, 1966), 623.

5. McConkie, *Mormon Doctrine,* 623.

6. Boyd K. Packer, *Ensign,* May 1988, 69.

7. James E. Talmage, quoted in Hugh B. Brown, *The Abundant Life* (Salt Lake City: Bookcraft, 1965), 315.

8. Joseph Smith, *Teachings of the Prophet Joseph Smith,* sel. Joseph Fielding Smith (Salt Lake City: Deseret Book, 1976), 255.

9. Dallin H. Oaks, *Sins, Crimes, and Atonement* (address to CES religious educators), 7 February 1992 (Salt Lake City: The Church of Jesus Christ of Latter-day Saints), 2.

10. J. Reuben Clark Jr., in Conference Report, October 1953, 84.

11. Spencer W. Kimball, *Ensign,* May 1975, 78.

12. Oaks, *Sins, Crimes, and Atonement,* 5–6.

13. Dallin H. Oaks, *Ensign,* November 1988, 67.

14. Boyd K. Packer, *Ensign,* November 1995, 20.

15. *Webster's Encyclopedic Unabridged Dictionary of the English Language* (New York: Gramercy Books, 1989), 469, s.v. "enable."

16. C. S. Lewis, "Perfection," from *The Joyful Christian* (New York: Macmillan,1977), 77–78.

17. *Hymns of The Church of Jesus Christ of Latter-day Saints* (Salt Lake City: The Church of Jesus Christ of Latter-day Saints, 1985), no. 131.

18. Ezra Taft Benson, *Teachings of Ezra Taft Benson* (Salt Lake City: Bookcraft, 1988), 361; see Matthew 10:39.

19. Jeffrey R. Holland, "Come unto Me," *Ensign,* April 1998, 22; see also D&C 112:13.

20. Bruce C. Hafen, *The Broken Heart* (Salt Lake City: Deseret Book, 1989), 20, 22.

21. "I Stand All Amazed," *Hymns,* no. 193.

22. *Lectures on Faith* (Salt Lake City: Deseret Book, 1985), 3:47.

23. Neal A. Maxwell, *Ensign,* November 1992, 66–67.

24. "I Know That My Redeemer Lives," *Hymns,* no. 136.

CHAPTER TWO

WHAT THE LATTER-DAY SCRIPTURES TEACH ABOUT JOHN THE BELOVED

JONN D. CLAYBAUGH

When I was eighteen years old, my best friend and I drove from southern California to Salt Lake City, where he was to enter the mission home. Along the way we stopped to visit his grandmother, a saintly old woman who fed us a delicious meal and told wonderful stories of her life. I was especially impressed by her account of once being alone and stranded in a potentially dangerous place. There was a telephone, but she had no coins. As she prayed for divine guidance, a stranger appeared. He spoke kind words, gave her a dime, and then disappeared. She made a phone call and was rescued. She spoke her conviction that the answer to her prayer had come in the person of John the Beloved, the ancient apostle of the Lord. I had heard similar accounts of appearances of the Three Nephites, but the idea of John the Revelator fulfilling this role was new to me. I should have been a better student of the scriptures.

The apostle John is the second most prolific author of New Testament scripture, and his writings in that sacred book provide special knowledge and inspiration. But, additionally, the Book of Mormon and the Doctrine and Covenants provide further understanding about John the Beloved, including a confirmation of the authenticity of John's work and writings, information about his status and mission as a translated being, information about his role in

Jonn D. Claybaugh is an institute director in the Church Educational System in Fresno, California.

the latter-day restoration of the gospel, numerous historical and doctrinal clarifications of his New Testament writings, and his yet-future contributions, including both writings and ministry.

MODERN REVELATION CONFIRMS THE TRUTH OF JOHN'S NEW TESTAMENT WRITINGS

It is important to affirm the truth and value of John's ancient writings, especially his Gospel and the book of Revelation. From scriptures revealed through the Prophet Joseph Smith, we know that John really did exist, that he really did write the New Testament books attributed to him, and that the existing text of the Gospel of John and the book of Revelation are true and reliable. Unfortunately, there are scholars in the world who doubt and devalue much of what we consider to be sacred text, including the writings of John. For example, the *Interpreter's Dictionary of the Bible* points out: "There has been much controversy about [the Gospel of John's] authorship, place of origin, theological affiliations and background, and historical value. Already in the late second century certain conservative and otherwise orthodox Christians . . . denied its apostolic authorship."[1] And in the *Anchor Bible Dictionary* we read, "The storm of controversy around the gospel [of John] in the nascent centuries of Christianity continues in recent times, and the question of its interpretation is still not settled."[2] Another commentary says of the book of Revelation: "Although chs. 1–3 are plainly Christian, . . . chs. 4–22 show little evidence of being a truly Christian work."[3] Regarding the author of Revelation, we read, "In the third century . . . an African bishop named Dionysius compared the language, style and thought of the Apocalypse (Revelation) with that of the other writings of John and decided that the book could not have been written by the apostle John."[4] And this is from Dummelow's commentary: "An Asiatic sect of the end of the 2nd cent., known as the 'Alogi,' rejected all the writings of St. John, and among them Rev. They did not appeal to any knowledge or tradition as to the authorship, but said that they found the book unprofitable. . . . Its reception in modern times has not been so unqualified as that of the rest of the New Testament."[5]

As Bible scholarship advances in modern times, faith among scholars seems to decline, as evidenced in a recent report in *Bible*

Review, telling of a new multicolor edition of the Gospels. This particular work presents the sayings of Jesus in four different colors. Red print means Jesus really did say it; pink is for things that surely sound like what Jesus might have said; gray means maybe he said it; and black signifies "there's been some mistake." The things in gray and black are assumed to be the product of the early Christian movement, not of Jesus himself. A team of Bible scholars who analyzed, discussed, and then voted, made the color determinations on each of Christ's purported utterances. What is most shocking is the list of statements that they have declared are not the voice of Jesus. This list includes all passages that speak of Jesus having an exalted status, passages in which such words as *Messiah, Son of God, light of the world, bread of life,* and so forth are used, plus "all passages that speak of Jesus' dying for the sins of the world; all the end-of-the-world or 'second coming' passages; and essentially *all of the Gospel of John.*"[6]

We know, of course, that John's biblical writings are in the same category as the rest of the Bible, being "the word of God as far as [they are] translated correctly" (Articles of Faith 1:8). But, thankfully, we do not have to consider whether or not to throw out the beloved books of John and Revelation. Affirmation of John's authorship of both, and evidence that they are true scripture, is expressed in various ways in modern scriptures. For example, the prophet Nephi saw in vision that an old-world apostle would see and write the remainder of Nephi's vision, which writing would be "just and true" and would be contained in the book which Nephi saw proceed out of the mouth of the Jews, meaning the Bible. The angel even informed Nephi that "the name of the apostle of the Lamb was John" (1 Nephi 14:23, 27).

Additionally, several revelations in the Doctrine and Covenants came as a result of Joseph Smith's study of John's New Testament writings, giving further support to their validity and value. For example, section 76 was received after Joseph Smith and Sidney Rigdon pondered John 5:29 (regarding the resurrection), and the Lord revealed section 77 as an "explanation of the Revelation of St. John" (D&C 77, heading). There are also in the Doctrine and Covenants several places where the Lord himself specifically refers to John's writings, such as 88:3: "Wherefore, I now send upon you another Comforter . . . which other Comforter is the same that I promised unto my disciples, as is recorded in the testimony of John" (see John 14:16). Also: "The ordinance of washing feet is to be administered . . . according to the pattern given in the thirteenth chapter of John's testimony concerning me" (D&C 88:140–41).

We see that the Lord validated the writings of John the Beloved by using John's ancient scriptural words as an inspirational springboard for some of Joseph Smith's modern scriptural words. Joseph followed this same pattern in Doctrine and Covenants 128, in which he stated, "I want you to remember that John the Revelator was contemplating this very subject in relation to the dead, when he declared, as you will find recorded in Revelation 20:12 [followed by John's vision of the dead being judged out of the books]" (D&C 128:6).

Further help comes from the Joseph Smith Translation, in the first chapter of Revelation. Verse 1 in the King James Version begins, "The Revelation of Jesus Christ, which God gave unto him, to shew unto his servants"; the Joseph Smith Translation reads, *"The Revelation of John,* a servant of God, which was given unto him of Jesus Christ" (emphasis added). The Joseph Smith Translation adds the following to the beginning of verse 5: "Therefore, I, John, the faithful witness, bear record of the things which were delivered me of the angel, and from Jesus Christ." There is no mention of John in Revelation 1:5 in the King James Version.

It is also helpful to note that the New Testament writings of John have been quoted and applied by modern prophets and apostles from Joseph Smith to the present day without the slightest hint of suspicion regarding their authenticity and value. Indeed, John's writings have been widely used and revered throughout the history of The Church of Jesus Christ of Latter-day Saints. Elder Bruce R. McConkie eloquently expressed our esteem for the writings of John when he commented upon the relative value of the various books of the Bible. His statement could also be taken as a response to those who dismiss the writings of John. Speaking about the Bible at a gathering of religious educators, he taught: "The words are sacred. Insofar as they have come down to us as originally penned, they were inspired by the Holy Ghost. They are to be read over and over again as long as we live. But they are not all of equal worth. The gospels, particularly the gospel of John, are worth their weight in gold. . . .

The writings of Peter and James, plus 1 John, rank as though written by angels. . . . For those with gospel understanding, Revelation is a foundation of divine wisdom that expands the mind and enlightens the soul."[7]

Thus, one of the most significant contributions of modern scripture to our understanding of John's writings is the simple affirmation that they are true.

CONTRIBUTIONS OF THE BOOK OF MORMON TO OUR KNOWLEDGE OF JOHN AND HIS WRITINGS

The Book of Mormon teaches us about the apocalyptic revelation that John saw, about what John would write, what happened to John after the resurrection of Christ, and how we can qualify to receive more of John's writings, which the Lord has thus far withheld.

After his father, Lehi, had received a vision of the tree of life (see 1 Nephi 8), Nephi prayed and was given his own vision (see 1 Nephi 10:17; 11:1–3). This vision is recorded in 1 Nephi 11:8 through 14:17. After the vision, the angel of the Lord told Nephi that John the Beloved was to write "the remainder of these things" (1 Nephi 14:21), meaning the remainder of the vision of Nephi. Nephi recorded at least forty things, beginning with the tree of life, Jerusalem and Nazareth, and the virgin Mary, and ending with wars and rumors of wars among all nations, the destruction of the great and abominable church, and the commencement of the fulfilling of the Father's covenants with the house of Israel.[8]

Let us consider what might constitute the "remainder" of the things that the angel said John would write. Nephi tells us in 1 Nephi 14:28 that he himself wrote "but a small part" of the things he saw, and the angel told Nephi that in addition to the remainder of Nephi's vision, John would write "many things which have been" and things "concerning the end of the world" (1 Nephi 14:21–22). Although the book of Revelation certainly contains things which had been and things which would yet be at the end of the world, we cannot expect the Bible to contain everything the angel said John would write. One reason is that the angel taught Nephi that the things which John would write would be "plain and pure, and most precious and easy to the understanding of all men" (1 Nephi 14:23). Even though the Prophet Joseph Smith said that Revelation was "one of the plainest books God ever caused to be written,"[9] it can hardly be said of Revelation today that it is "easy to the understanding of all men." Either something is missing from Revelation, or something is changed, or both.

There is another reason our current book of Revelation cannot contain all of the things that Nephi saw John write. Speaking of the things he saw that John and other prophets would write, Nephi said: "They are sealed up to come forth in their purity, according to the truth which is in the Lamb, in the own due time of the Lord" (1 Nephi 14:26). Thus, our search for all of the remainder of Nephi's vision among John's writings is probably futile. Instead, we may one day expect to receive more of the visions of Nephi and John.

Another insight from the Book of Mormon is what the angel told Nephi: "The things which this apostle of the Lamb shall write are many things which thou hast seen" (1 Nephi 14:24). Therefore, we can expect some duplication between the writings of Nephi and the writings of John that we already have. There are at least twelve themes that Nephi recorded which also appear in the book of Revelation, including the tree of life, the rod of iron, the fountain of living waters, the persecution of the apostles and the New Testament church, the establishment of the great and abominable church, the corruption of nations, the latter-day restoration of the gospel, the worldwide dominion of the great and abominable church, the gathering of the wicked to fight against the Saints of God, wars and rumors of wars among all nations, the destruction of the great and abominable church, and the fulfilling of the Father's covenants with the house of Israel. Plus, there are other things in Nephi's vision that John saw and wrote about in his Gospel, including the ministry of John the Baptist, the life and mission of Jesus Christ, and the work of the apostles.

Finally, Nephi was privileged to see the things John would write but that he, Nephi, was forbidden to write, for the angel told Nephi, "And behold, the remainder shalt thou see. But the things which thou shalt see hereafter thou shalt not write; for the Lord God hath ordained the apostle of the Lamb of God that he should write them" (1 Nephi 14:24–25). Themes of the book of Revelation that are not found in Nephi's writings, and therefore constitute at least a portion of the "remainder" that was promised by the angel, include John's magnificent writings regarding the premortal life, the second coming of Jesus Christ, the Millennium, and the celestial kingdom.

Another contribution of the Book of Mormon to our understanding of John comes from the book of 3 Nephi. It tells us what happened to John after the deaths of the rest of the apostles, straightening out the potentially confusing passages at the end of John's Gospel. In John 21, after the Savior spoke of Peter's death, Peter asked what would happen to John. Jesus responded, "If I will that he tarry till I come, what is that to thee? Follow thou me." The following verse reads, "Then went this saying abroad among the brethren, that that disciple should not die: yet Jesus said not unto him, He shall not die; but, If I will that he tarry till I come, what is that to thee?" (John 21:22–23).

When the Savior told Peter, "If I will that [John] tarry till I come," he provoked centuries of speculation and disagreement over what his statement meant. For example, the *New Bible Commentary* teaches that Jesus' statement was incorrectly interpreted to mean that John would never die, which misunderstanding the author of the Gospel seeks to correct, for John had already passed away.[10] Another commentator says, "The slow-hearted disciples misconstrued [Jesus'] words, taking them to mean that John would not die but would live on until the Lord returned in His glory. The idea seemed reasonable enough in early days when it was believed that the Second Advent was imminent; and it was confidently believed. . . . Even after [John] had actually died, it still persisted."[11] *The Interpreter's One-Volume Commentary on the Bible* states that it is clear that the beloved disciple (whoever he might have been, it says) had died. But in an attempt to draw a useful metaphor from the passage, the author continues, "But in a sense the beloved disciple does not die; he remains until Jesus comes again. In every generation, from the time of Jesus' resurrection until the end of the world, disciples whom Jesus loves and who love Jesus in return shall remain with us."[12]

We should not condemn this misunderstanding, for such conclusions were reached without the benefit of modern revelation, which we enjoy. Apparently there was even a disagreement between the Prophet Joseph Smith and Oliver Cowdery about John's fate, which led to the answer that is recorded in section 7 of the Doctrine and Covenants.[13] It was April 1829 when Joseph and Oliver inquired through the Urim and Thummim about John, but they would also have learned the answer to their question a short time later, when translating chapter 3 Nephi 28.

In any case, the Savior's statement in 3 Nephi 28 ends all controversy. In response to the unspoken request of three of the Nephite disciples for the privilege of remaining on earth to minister until the Second Coming, Jesus said, "Ye have desired the thing which John, my beloved, who was with me in my ministry, before that I was lifted up by the Jews, desired of me" (3 Nephi 28:6). From what follows, we learn that John and the Three Nephites are more blessed because of their desire, were granted their desire by Jesus, will never taste of death nor endure the pains of death but will live to behold all the doings of the Father until the Second Coming, will be changed at the Second Coming from mortality to immortality, have no pain nor sorrow except for the sins of the world, help bring souls unto Christ, and will have fulness of joy and sit down in the Father's kingdom (see 3 Nephi 28:7–10).

Thus is clarified the seeming contradiction in John 21 that John would tarry till Christ's return but somehow would also die, for we see that John would indeed tarry until Jesus' second coming, bringing souls unto Christ, and he would also die, for at the coming of Christ translated beings die and are resurrected in the "twinkling of an eye" (3 Nephi 28:8).

The next Book of Mormon reference to John is brief but full of promise. Moroni recorded the Lord's teachings regarding our acceptance or rejection of the Book of Mormon. He invites us to come unto Christ and to see "how great things the Father hath laid up for [us], from the foundation of the world" (Ether 4:14). We have not yet received these things because of unbelief, wickedness, hardness of heart, and blindness of mind. But when we rend the veil of unbelief, calling upon the Father with broken hearts and contrite spirits, we shall "know that the Father hath remembered the covenant which he made unto [our] fathers," which Jesus followed by promising, "Then shall my revelations which I have caused to be written by my servant John be unfolded in the eyes of all the people" (Ether 4:14–16).

Moroni was writing after the New Testament ministry of John had ended, but the promise the Lord gave through Moroni is similar to the promise spoken by the angel to Nephi more than a thousand years earlier, before the days of John. The angel revealed that the writings of John and others "are sealed up to come forth in their purity . . . in the own due time of the Lord, unto the house of Israel" (1 Nephi 14:26). As great as our appreciation is of John's biblical writings, the Book of Mormon gives us an elevated vision of his work and writings, with an open invitation from the Lord to qualify ourselves to receive John's writings that have been sealed up.

CONTRIBUTIONS OF THE DOCTRINE AND COVENANTS TO OUR KNOWLEDGE OF JOHN AND HIS WRITINGS

Just as the Book of Mormon expands our vision of John's past, present, and future, so does the Doctrine and Covenants enlarge our view of John's ministry and our comprehension of his writings. From various revelations to the Prophet Joseph Smith that draw upon the work and writings of John, we gain valuable insights regarding angelic ministrations, the keys and ordinances of the priesthood, the life and mission of the Savior Jesus Christ, the role of the Comforter, and events of the last days, the Second Coming, the Millennium, the Resurrection, and the Judgment.

In April 1829, Joseph Smith and Oliver Cowdery learned through the Urim and Thummim that John had made a record on parchment and hidden it up. Although we do not know if Joseph and Oliver ever possessed or otherwise saw the parchment, we do know that Doctrine and Covenants 7 is a translation of part or all of it. From the translation we learn at least the following points:

1. After Jesus was resurrected, He asked John what he desired.

2. John requested power over death, to tarry on earth until Christ's second coming.

3. By being translated, John would be able to do at least four things: to bring souls unto Christ; to prophesy before nations, kindreds, tongues, and people; to do an even greater work among men than he had previously done; and to minister for those who are heirs of salvation who dwell on the earth. In these things John was to become a "flaming fire" and a "ministering angel."

These four purposes obviously require personal interaction between John and people on earth and perhaps on other planets as well. Jesus' statement to the apostles in Matthew 16:28 seems to foreshadow John's postmeridian ministry: "Verily I say unto you, There be some standing here, which shall not taste of death, till they see the Son of man coming in his kingdom." Luke's version of this statement has a helpful addition in the Joseph Smith Translation: "There are some standing here who shall not taste of death, until they see the kingdom of God coming in power" (JST Luke 9:27), an obvious reference to the Second Coming. Revelation 10:8–11 also speaks of John's future ministry, as confirmed by the chapter heading, which states that John "is commissioned to participate in the restoration of all things."

One example of John's participation was related by Elder Heber C. Kimball, who said that after certain ordinances of anointing had been performed in the Kirtland Temple, those in attendance "responded to it with a loud shout of Hosanna! Hosanna! etc. While these things were being attended to, the beloved disciple John was seen in our midst by the Prophet Joseph, Oliver Cowdery and others."[14]

Joseph Smith clarified the doctrine of translation when he taught that translated personages are reserved for "future missions." They are not yet taken into the presence of God, nor into resurrection or their eternal fulness but remain in a "terrestrial order." They are to be ministering angels unto many planets, participating in a prolonged labor of the ministry. They are free from the tortures and sufferings of the body but will eventually undergo a change equivalent to death.[15] Apparently John's terrestrial state is similar to some of the conditions in the Garden of Eden before the fall of man, for there Adam and Eve were not subject to physical pain, sickness, disease, nor death.[16]

4. John tells us that Jesus had also asked Peter what he desired, and Peter asked to speedily come into the Lord's kingdom, after his death. This request was granted.

5. Peter, James, and John possess the keys of the Savior's ministry until the Second Coming. This cross-dispensational role of the ancient First Presidency seems to be confirmed by what we learn from the Lord's statement in Doctrine and Covenants 27:13, verifying that the Lord had committed to Peter, James, and John "the keys of [his] kingdom, and a dispensation of the gospel for the last times; and for the fulness of times." An additional witness comes from the

heading for Doctrine and Covenants 13 (and Joseph Smith–History 1:72, in the Pearl of Great Price), which states that John the Baptist ordained Joseph Smith and Oliver Cowdery to the Aaronic Priesthood "under the direction of Peter, James, and John, the ancient apostles, who held the keys of the higher priesthood." In Doctrine and Covenants 128:20 Joseph Smith recounts the appearance of Peter, James, and John to restore the Melchizedek Priesthood, saying that they came "declaring themselves as possessing the keys of the kingdom, and of the dispensation of the fulness of times!"

6. From John's parchment we gain a great insight into the character of a divine Personage, as the Lord granted unto both Peter and John the things which they desired, without comparison nor condemnation, recognizing that both took joy in that which they desired.

Next is Doctrine and Covenants 20:35. In this verse, after reciting a long and glorious list of doctrines and beliefs pertaining to the true gospel and the latter days, the Lord said, "And we know that these things are true and according to the revelations of John, neither adding to, nor diminishing from the prophecy of his book." This is an apparent reference to the much-quoted but often misused warning at the end of Revelation regarding the curses that will come upon those who "add unto" or "take away from" the words of the book (Revelation 22:18–19).

Most Latter-day Saints have heard these verses quoted in an attempt to disprove the divinity of the Book of Mormon and other modern scripture. Of course we know that John was speaking only of the book of Revelation itself, and it may be that the Lord was pre-emptively brushing aside this misguided argument against modern revelation. Indeed, the Lord next announced his intention to continue giving us "revelations of God which shall come hereafter by the gift and power of the Holy Ghost, the voice of God, or the ministering of angels" (D&C 20:35).

Next, Doctrine and Covenants 27 confirms the role of Peter, James, and John in restoring the Melchizedek Priesthood to the earth. Additionally, it names these three as participants in the future ordinance of the sacrament that will involve the Savior and the prophets of all dispensations, another evidence of John's future ministry (vv. 5–14).

Doctrine and Covenants 61 is another place where modern revelation confirms what John wrote and its possible application in today's world. The Lord declares that in the last days he has "cursed the waters" by the mouth of John. Several passages in the book of Revelation tell us how and why the waters are cursed in our day. For example, speaking of the destruction preceding the Second Coming, John wrote concerning a great mountain burning with fire, which will be cast into the sea. As a result, one-third of the sea will become blood (red?, poisonous?), one-third of sea life will be killed, and one-third of the ships will be destroyed (see Revelation 8:8–9). Volcanic activity, earthquakes, tsunami waves, torrential oceanic storms, or some combination of these things could bring about these cataclysmic events.

Next, John saw a great burning star fall from heaven (perhaps a dying planet or some other gigantic meteorite), which falls upon the third part of the rivers and fountains of waters. This causes the deaths of many men, presumably by poisoning (see Revelation 8:10–11). Later, John describes the sea becoming "as the blood of a dead man" (dark and clotted), this time causing the death of every living thing in the sea. The angel tells John that this curse will come because men have shed the blood of Saints and prophets (see Revelation 16:3–6).

In John's vision of the two prophets who will minister and be slain in Jerusalem in the last days, he saw that they would have power to shut heaven so that it does not rain for an extended time. A heaven-caused drought may be a different turn on the idea of the waters being cursed, but the result upon mankind can be just as devastating as other water-related curses. In addition, John said that the two prophets will have power to turn waters to blood and to smite the earth with all plagues (see Revelation 11:6).

Finally, John saw a connection between the waters and the great and abominable church, saying, "I will shew unto thee the judgment of the great whore that sitteth upon many waters. . . . The waters which thou [seest], where the whore sitteth, are peoples, and multitudes, and nations, and tongues" (Revelation 17:1, 15). Here, the waters appear to be figurative, rather than literal, but the resulting spiritual plague upon the world is equally destructive.

In Doctrine and Covenants 76 is another amplification of the writings of John. Joseph Smith and Sidney Rigdon, while working on the revision of the Bible, came upon John 5:28–29, which speaks of the resurrection. Their questioning led to their reception of what can be considered one of the greatest visions of our day: the vision of the degrees of glory. This revelation greatly expands our understanding of the next life, for in the Bible (and even in the Book of Mormon), the concept of salvation or damnation receives great attention, with hardly any mention of a middle ground or of kingdoms and gradations. The rendering of John 5:29 in Doctrine and Covenants 76:17 differs from the King James Version of the Bible in that it changes "the resurrection of life" and "the resurrection of damnation" to "the resurrection of the just" and "the resurrection of the unjust" (this change is also reflected in the Joseph Smith Translation). The Prophet's inspired change relates the idea of two different categories of resurrection, which can include varying levels or degrees, rather than two inflexible conditions of "life" and "damnation."

Another helpful resource the Lord has given us for understanding John's writings is Doctrine and Covenants 77. Although we may wish for the Lord's interpretive commentary on every verse of Revelation, the fifteen questions and answers in this section are a wonderful beginning and are a key to understanding the rest of the book. Some of the great truths we learn from section 77 include the following: animals will be saved in God's kingdom; this earth will have a temporal existence of seven thousand years (from the fall of Adam to the end of the Millennium); the 144,000 men that John saw are high priests who will minister salvation to all nations in the last days; the Second Coming will not occur until after the beginning of the seventh thousand-year period and the completion of the events in Revelation 9 (perhaps making the date of the Second Coming later than many have supposed); the apostle John will participate as an "Elias" in the gathering of the tribes of Israel;[17] and, before the Second Coming the Jews will gather in Jerusalem, rebuild the city, and be blessed by the ministry of two prophets.

The Prophet worked on the inspired revision of the New Testament during the same time period that he received section 77, making it possible that Joseph's questions recorded in section 77 may have derived from his work on the translation. Even though Joseph made inspired changes to 83 of the 404 verses in the book of Revelation (amounting to 21 percent), none of the verses addressed in section 77 are changed in ways that reflect the additional truths revealed in the Lord's fifteen answers.[18] A simple explanation is that we know Joseph did not consider his work on the inspired revision of the Bible to be complete. Also, there are other passages in the Bible that do not reflect truths that Joseph taught elsewhere, but in the Joseph Smith Translation these verses remain untouched. Perhaps the Prophet did not have the time, or through economy of effort did not feel the need, or both.

In Doctrine and Covenants 88 the Lord teaches us about the other Comforter that he promised his disciples at the Last Supper, as recorded by John (see John 14:16). Commentators on these verses, both in John and in Doctrine and Covenants 88, teach that the meaning of "another Comforter" is either the Second Comforter, in other words, a personal appearance of the Lord Jesus Christ, to proclaim one's calling and election to be sure,[19] or that it refers to the reception of the Holy Ghost and its "stamp of approval" upon our obedience and our ordinances (otherwise known as the "Holy Spirit of Promise)."[20]

We also gain another great insight from Doctrine and Covenants 88. John the Beloved recorded the Lord's actions and teachings regarding the washing of his disciples' feet at the Last Supper (see John 13:4–15). At the end of Doctrine and Covenants 88, we learn that the Savior was performing a priesthood ordinance, which is to be administered by the presiding elder, or president of the Church (or, presumably, under his direction).

Others have spoken and written extensively on this topic,[21] from which we learn that the washing of feet belongs to the higher ordinances of the priesthood and the temple, being a step in our progression toward eternal life. The Prophet Joseph Smith was particularly anxious to extend the administration of this ordinance to the Twelve and beyond, requiring the building of the temple.[22] Underscoring the eternal importance of this ordinance, we note the Lord's words to Peter when in humility Peter insisted that the Lord would never wash his feet. Jesus responded, "If I wash thee not, thou hast no part with me" (John 13:8).

Doctrine and Covenants 93 is one of modern scripture's greatest contributions to our understanding of the writings of John, especially as they relate to the Savior Jesus Christ. When the Lord said in

Doctrine and Covenants 93:6, "And John saw and bore record of the fulness of my glory, and the fulness of John's record is hereafter to be revealed," he left open the question of whether he spoke of John the Baptist or John the Beloved. Various commentators insist this John is John the Baptist; others are certain it is John the Beloved. The index of the LDS triple combination contains entries for John the Baptist and John the Beloved, both of which send the reader to these verses of Doctrine and Covenants 93. Perhaps the most satisfying conclusion is that both Johns are involved. In other words, the John who "saw and bore record" is the Baptist, whose testimony John the Beloved recorded (either by copying from the Baptist's own written record or by originally recording it in his Gospel). The record which the Lord says "is hereafter to be revealed" could be that of either one or both of these faithful disciples. It is similar to what we see in the first chapter of the Gospel of John, in which the writer, John the Beloved, is quoting the speaker, John the Baptist, and both are testifying of Christ.

Among the great truths we learn from (or have confirmed by) these verses in Doctrine and Covenants 93 are that Christ was in the beginning before the world was; the worlds and all things were made by Christ; he is the life and light of men; the Savior did not receive of a fulness of knowledge, power, and glory at the first but received grace for grace; Jesus eventually received all power, both in heaven and on earth; and, if we are faithful, we shall receive the fulness of the record of John.

In the epistle to Church members that became section 128 of the Doctrine and Covenants, the Prophet Joseph Smith teaches that when John the Revelator saw in vision the dead standing before God, he (John) was contemplating the work of the salvation of the dead. Joseph implies that Latter-day Saints are to take an active part in the work that John was contemplating, which we do through family history and temple work. The "books" that John saw, from which the dead are to be judged, include the scriptures, the records of the Church, and "the record kept in heaven of the names and righteous deeds of the faithful."[23]

Later in Doctrine and Covenants 128 Joseph Smith again testifies of the appearance of Peter, James, and John—an apparent reference to the 1829 restoration of the Melchizedek Priesthood. We learn from this verse that this manifestation occurred "in the wilderness between Harmony, Susquehanna county, and Colesville, Broome county, on the Susquehanna river."

We learn another truth relating to John's writngs in the absorbing "items of instruction" that the Prophet Joseph Smith gives in Doctrine and Covenants 130. He makes reference to John 14:23, wherein John recorded one of the Savior's statements at the Last Supper: "If a man love me, he will keep my words: and my Father will love him, and we will come unto him, and make our abode with him." Joseph taught that the Lord was referring to a personal appearance, stating that the idea of the Father and the Son dwelling in a man's heart is "an old sectarian notion, and is false" (D&C 130:3).

So what is this personal appearance? Joseph taught that it is the "other Comforter." The first Comforter is the gift of the Holy Ghost, and a recipient of this gift who will "continue to humble himself before God, hungering and thirsting after righteousness, and living by every word of God, . . . the Lord will soon say unto him, Son, thou shalt be exalted." This is what happens when a person has his or her calling and election made sure, Joseph taught, saying, "then it will be his privilege to receive the other Comforter, which the Lord hath promised the Saints, as is recorded in the testimony of St. John, in the 14th chapter, from the 12th to the 27th verses. . . . It is no more nor less than the Lord Jesus Christ Himself."[24]

Finally, Elder John Taylor wrote an impassioned report of the martyrdom of Joseph and Hyrum Smith, which became Doctrine and Covenants 135. In his conclusion, Elder Taylor wrote that the "innocent blood" of Joseph and Hyrum would join with the innocent blood of the early Christian martyrs, to cry unto the Lord for vengeance, as seen by John the Beloved in Revelation 6:9: "I saw under the altar the souls of them that were slain for the word of God, and for the testimony which they held." Elder Taylor's reference to this verse in Revelation implies that John had envisioned the future martyrdom of the Prophet and Patriarch, for John also said of the meridian-day martyrs: "And they cried with a loud voice, saying, How long, O Lord, holy and true, dost thou not judge and avenge our blood on them that dwell on the earth? And white robes were given unto every one of them; and it was said unto them, that they should rest yet for a little season, until *their fellowservants* also and their brethren, *that should be killed as they were,* should be fulfilled" (Revelation 6:10–11; emphasis added).

CONCLUSION

From latter-day scripture, we learn that John the Beloved did indeed compose the biblical writings credited to him and that they are true scripture. We have also received invaluable amplification and clarification of many of John's New Testament writings. We know that we can one day receive more of his writings, which shall be among the greatest truths ever recorded. And we know that John has been privileged to continue his sacred ministry as a translated being, including key roles in the restoration of the gospel and the ongoing work of the dispensation of the fulness of times. We are greatly blessed to have this additional knowledge and inspiration regarding John the Beloved that comes from modern revelation. The Lord's promise to John that he would become "as flaming fire and a ministering angel" (D&C 7:6) truly has been and continues to be fulfilled.

As we move into the twenty-first century, contemplating and preparing for the second coming of our Savior, we can be eternally grateful for the immeasurable and ongoing contributions of John the Beloved. His lifetime and his ministry cross dispensations as well as planetary boundaries. His writings and his work touched the meridian-day Saints just as they do Latter-day Saints. He has taught and testified to the Jews and to the lost tribes,[25] to Gentiles and to modern Israel. John's simple desire was to continue to bring souls unto Christ. He has shown us how to turn our desires to the Lord and his work, to do our own part in bringing souls unto the Savior.

NOTES

1. *The Interpreter's Dictionary of the Bible,* 4 vols. (Nashville: Abingdon Press, 1962), 2:932.

2. David Noel Freeman, ed., *The Anchor Bible Dictionary,* 6 vols. (New York: Doubleday, 1992), 3:912.

3. J. Massyngberde Ford, *Revelation,* vol. 38 of *The Anchor Bible* (Garden City, New York: Doubleday, 1975), 12.

4. Kenneth Barker, ed., *The NIV Study Bible* (Grand Rapids, Mich.: Zondervan Bible Publishers, 1985), 1923. See also *The Interpreter's Dictionary of the Bible,* 4 vols. (Nashville: Abingdon Press, 1962), 4:60.

5. J. R. Dummelow, ed., *A Commentary on the Holy Bible* (New York: Macmillan, 1966), 1068–69.

6. Marcus J. Borg, "Jesus in Four Colors," *Bible Review* 9, no. 6 (December 1993): 10; emphasis added.

7. Bruce R. McConkie, *Doctrines of the Restoration: Sermons and Writings of Bruce R. McConkie,* ed. Mark L. McConkie (Salt Lake City: Bookcraft, 1989), 284.

8. My full list is as follows:

The tree of life

Jerusalem and Nazareth

The virgin Mary

The birth of Christ

The mortal ministry of Christ

The rod of iron

The fountain of living waters

The ministry of John the Baptist

The baptism of Christ

The twelve disciples of the Old World

Healings and others miracles performed by the Savior

The rejection of Jesus by the people

The trial and crucifixion of Christ

The persecution of the apostles and the New Testament church

The great and spacious building

The future of the Nephite/Lamanite civilizations

The destruction in the Americas at the time of the crucifixion of Christ

The ministry of Christ among the Nephites

The twelve Nephite disciples

The fountain of filthy water

The mists of darkness

The wars among the Nephites and Lamanites

The end of the Nephite society

The dwindling of the Lamanites

The establishment of the great and abominable church among the nations of the Gentiles

The voyage of Christopher Columbus to the New World

The colonization of the New World

The scattering of the seed of the Lamanites

The prosperity of the Gentiles upon the American continent

The war between the American colonies and Great Britain

The removal of many plain and precious parts from the Bible

The diffusion of the Bible among the Gentiles

The corruption of the Gentile nations

The coming forth of the Book of Mormon and other latter-day scripture

The latter-day restoration of the gospel

The worldwide dominion of the great and abominable church

The gathering of the wicked to fight against the Saints, who are armed with power

Wars and rumors of wars among all nations

The destruction of the great and abominable church

The commencement of the fulfilling of the Father's covenants with the house of Israel

9. Joseph Smith, *Teachings of the Prophet Joseph Smith,* sel. Joseph Fielding Smith (Salt Lake City: Deseret Book, 1976), 290.

10. F. Davidson, ed., *The New Bible Commentary* (Grand Rapids, Mich.: Wm. B. Eerdmans, 1956), 896. See also Raymond E. Brown, *The Gospel According to John (xiii-xxi),* vol. 29A of *The Anchor Bible* (Garden City, N. Y.: Doubleday, 1970), 1118–19.

11. David Smith, *The Days of His Flesh,* 518–19, as cited in Sidney B. Sperry, *Doctrine and Covenants Compendium* (Salt Lake City: Bookcraft, 1960), 66–67.

12. Charles M. Laymon, ed., *The Interpreter's One-Volume Commentary on the Bible* (Nashville: Abingdon Press, 1971), 728.

13. See Joseph Smith, *History of The Church of Jesus Christ of Latter-day Saints,* ed. B. H. Roberts, 2d ed. rev., 7 vols. (Salt Lake City: The Church of Jesus Christ of Latter-day Saints, 1932–51), 1:35–36.

14. *Life of Heber C. Kimball,* 91–92, as cited in Daniel H. Ludlow, *A Companion to Your Study of the Doctrine and Covenants,* 2 vols. (Salt Lake City: Deseret Book, 1978), 1:87.

15. Smith, *Teachings of the Prophet Joseph Smith,* 170–71, 191.

16. Bruce R. McConkie, *Mormon Doctrine,* 2d ed. (Salt Lake City: Bookcraft, 1966), 634.

17. See LDS Bible Dictionary, 663, s.v. "Elias."

18. The Reorganized Church of Jesus Christ of Latter Day Saints has published *Joseph Smith's "New Translation" of the Bible* (Independence, Mo.: Herald Publishing House, 1970), which is a side-by-side comparison of Joseph Smith's inspired revision of the Bible (the Joseph Smith Translation, or JST) and the King James Version. It shows that Joseph made changes in every book of the New Testament, except 2 John and 3 John. By simply counting the verses that are changed in the Joseph

Smith Translation, I learned the following: of the 879 verses in the Gospel of John, 238 are changed, or 27 percent; of the 105 verses in 1 John, sixteen are changed, or 15 percent; of the 404 verses in Revelation, 83 are changed, or 21 percent. Overall, of the 1,415 New Testament verses written by John, 337 are changed, or 24 percent.

19. Smith, *Teachings of the Prophet Joseph Smith*, 150–51; Marion G. Romney, Conference Report, October 1965, 21; *Ensign*, May 1977, 144–45; Bruce R. McConkie, *Doctrinal New Testament Commentary*, 3 vols. (Salt Lake City: Bookcraft, 1965–73), 2:494; 3:340.

20. Joseph Fielding Smith, *Doctrines of Salvation*, ed. Bruce R. McConkie, 3 vols. (Salt Lake City: Bookcraft, 1954), 1:55; Daniel H. Ludlow, ed., *Encyclopedia of Mormonism*, 4 vols. (New York: Macmillan, 1992), 2:651–52; Robert J. Matthews, "The Olive Leaf," in Robert L. Millet and Kent P. Jackson, eds., *Studies in Scripture, Volume One: The Doctrine and Covenants* (Sandy, Ut.: Randall Book, 1984), 341–42.

21. Smith, *Teachings of the Prophet Joseph Smith*, 90; Smith, *History of the Church*, 1:322–24; 2:287, 308–9; 428–31, 475; Bruce R. McConkie, *The Mortal Messiah: From Bethlehem to Calvary*, 4 vols. (Salt Lake City: Deseret Book, 1979), 4:36–41; *Doctrinal New Testament Commentary*, 1:707–10; *Mormon Doctrine*, 829–31; James E. Talmage, *Jesus the Christ*, 3d ed. (Salt Lake City: Deseret Book, 1916), 595–96.

22. *History of the Church*, 2:308–9.

23. McConkie, *Doctrinal New Testament Commentary*, 3:578.

24. Smith, *Teachings of the Prophet Joseph Smith*, 150–51.

25. In June 1831 the Prophet Joseph Smith stated that "John the Revelator was then among the ten tribes of Israel . . . to prepare them for their return from their long dispersion to again possess the land of their fathers" (*History of the Church*, 1:176).

CHAPTER THREE

THE APOCALYPTIC
WITNESS OF THE MESSIAH

RICHARD D. DRAPER

The book of Revelation is not easy reading. As one New Testament authority observed, the book either finds a man mad or leaves him that way.[1] I must admit that I can sympathize with that sentiment, even though it is overstated. Anyone who has spent time trying to decode John's message knows the difficulties involved in extracting its meaning. One major problem is that some passages can be understood on more than one level or in more than one way. Consider the first line of the first verse: "The Revelation of Jesus Christ." What does the phrase mean? Does the revelation belong to Jesus, or does the revelation disclose him? The context suggests the first idea is correct. John expressly states that "God gave [it] unto him, to shew unto his servants things which must shortly come to pass" (Revelation 1:1). Still, as we look at the book's prophetic message, we cannot doubt that the great revelation emphasizes the work of the Savior in its full cosmic scale. So, though Revelation belongs to Jesus, it is also the revelation that discloses him.

THE REVELATION OF THE SAVIOR IN THE FIRST VISION (REVELATION 1)

In the very first chapter of the book of Revelation, John records the Savior's testimony of himself: "I am Alpha and Omega, the beginning and the ending, saith the Lord, which is, and which was, and which is to come, the Almighty" (v. 8). That the Lord introduced

Richard D. Draper is an associate professor of ancient scripture at Brigham Young University.

himself with these elements suggests that they form the framework of what he wants to disclose about himself. The Lord begins that disclosure by identifying himself with the first and last letters of the Greek alphabet. In doing so he stresses his overarching role in the process of salvation. The Lord begins as "Alpha" by giving people the "light of Christ" (Moroni 7:19; D&C 88:7–13) by which they are able to discern and live the way of God. As they respond to their new understanding—by entering into and keeping covenants with him—he is able to finish their perfection as "Omega" by bringing them to the Father (see Moroni 10:31–32; D&C 84:46–47). Thus, salvation begins and ends in him.[2]

Jesus describes himself further as "the Lord, who is, and who was, and who is to come" (JST Revelation 1:8). The descriptive title is a paraphrase of the name of God given to Moses in Exodus 3:14–15 as translated in the Septuagint (the Hebrew Bible translated into Greek sometime between 300 and 100 B.C.).[3] The Greek phrase, as written by John, begins with *apo*, "from," which takes the genitive case but here is followed by three nominative phrases linked by the connective *kai*, "and." By keeping the form in the nominative, John emphasizes the idea that the Savior is always the subject. He holds the initiative. From the beginning, "He ordered all things according to the council of His own will."[4] Men do not force his hand. Everything they do, even in their rebellion, works according to his plan.[5] We can understand the phrase as an indeclinable noun, a rephrase of the tetragrammaton, *YHWH*, "he who is."[6] This rephrase of Jehovah's name reminds the reader that Jehovah is eternally existent. As he said to Moses, "Endless is my name; for I am without beginning of days or end of years; and is not this endless?" (Moses 1:3).[7]

The title "Endless" does more. It brings the Endless One onto the stage of history. He alone stands as the Lord of the past, the present, and the future. He "contemplated the whole of the events connected with the earth, pertaining to the plan of salvation, before it rolled into existence, or ever 'the morning stars sang together' for joy; the past, the present, and the future were and are, with Him, one eternal 'now.'"[8] Jesus, by virtue of his eternal existence, exercises power and fulfills his purposes throughout the course of history.

The last title the Lord uses to describe himself is "the Almighty" (Revelation 1:8). The appellation emphasizes his power over and throughout history. The Greek word used here, *pantokrator,* is not a synonym for the omnipotent: those who have power to do all things. Rather, it designates one who holds together and regulates all things.[9] In this title, "Almighty," we see the central message of Revelation, which is reiterated in modern scripture: he "ascended up on high, as also he descended below all things, in that he comprehended all things, that he might be in all through all things, the light of truth" (D&C 88:6). It is this "light which is in all things, which giveth life to all things, which is the law by which all things are governed" (D&C 88:13). Thus, the Savior oversees the sun, the moon, and even the stars with all their world systems. He rules world history and determines humankind's destiny. As will be shown, nothing goes beyond the limits he sets. He is indeed God, the Almighty.

This auditory witness was the beginning of John's understanding of the nature of the Lord. Within moments the Savior parted the veil and appeared to his beloved disciple. With powerful imagery, John records his encounter with Christ, the Second Comforter. As the vision opened, the prophet saw in the midst of seven lamp stands "one like unto the Son of man, clothed with a garment down to the foot, and girt about the paps with a golden girdle" (Revelation 1:12–13).[10] The phrase "Son of man," found in all the standard works, usually refers to the Savior, though in the Old Testament it is used to distinguish mortals from Gods—especially in the context of judgment (see Numbers 23:19; Psalm 8:4; Isaiah 51:12). The book of Moses gives another dimension to the title. There the name is capitalized, "Son of Man," making it a proper name or title. According to that passage, "in the language of Adam, Man of Holiness" is the name of God, "and the name of his Only Begotten is the Son of Man, even Jesus Christ, a righteous Judge" (Moses 6:57). In this context, the name designates him who is the Son of the Man of Holiness.

John's culture gives the title a further dimension. The term can be found in a number of writings during the first century after Christ.[11] Though scholars are still unsure about its full meaning, the term designated a supernatural figure who was to act as the vice-regent of God at the close of the age.[12] It is noteworthy that Jesus first applied the term to himself when his dual power to heal physical and spiritual illness proved his divinity (see Luke 5:18–26). The ancient definition of supernatural being and God's vice-regent seems to fit much of the profile of the Savior.[13] The implications of the title would have been obvious to John's readers.

The imagery John uses to describe the Lord reveals much. His appearance, along with the lamp stands, ties the vision to the temple. The words John uses to describe the Lord's robes are the same as those used in the Septuagint for the vestments of the high priest (see Exodus 28:4; 29:5; Daniel 10:5). The golden girdle, or clasp, worn at breast level, marked royalty.[14] Thus, the Lord presents himself as both king and priest, offices associated with the temple and the fulness of the priesthood. The revelation foreshadows his standing at the head of the patriarchal order, presiding as Eternal Father, king, and priest.

John goes on to describe the Lord's countenance as that of the sun shining in its strength, his hair "white like wool, as white as snow; and his eyes . . . as a flame of fire." Fire also surrounded his feet and legs, "as if they burned in a furnace" (Revelation 1:14–16). John's vision mirrors that of Joseph Smith and Oliver Cowdery. When they saw the Lord, "His eyes were as a flame of fire; the hair of his head was white like the pure snow; his countenance shone above the brightness of the sun; and his voice was as the sound of the rushing of great waters, even the voice of Jehovah" (D&C 110:3). Both visions emphasize the celestial, almost overwhelming glory associated with the Lord.[15]

There is a dramatic difference between the two visions, however. In John's, "a sharp twoedged sword" issues from the Lord's mouth (Revelation 1:16). The image is a bit startling, but like much in John's visions, the symbolism is meant not for the eye but for the mind. In other words, John means to teach us something through his imagery, not to have us draw it. The King James Version translates two Greek words as "sword": *machaira* and *rhomphaia*. Both terms refer to swords in general, but a *machaira* also described a butcher's knife and a surgeon's scalpel. Not so the *rhomphaia*, the word John used. It specifically designated a Thracian broadsword but was sometimes used to denote a lance or spear with a broad, double-edged head.[16]

The symbolism echoes Isaiah 11:4: "He shall smite the earth with the rod of his mouth" (the Septuagint replaces *rod* with *word*), and 49:2: "He hath made my mouth like a sharp sword." The sword makes an excellent symbol for the executive and judicial powers of the Lord: that which severs, cuts, opens, and reveals. It stands as a perfect symbol of the word of the Lord, which is "quick and power-ful, . . . to the dividing asunder of the joints and marrow, soul and spirit; and is a discerner of the thoughts and intents of the heart" (D&C 33:1).

Before giving John his commission, the Lord revealed one more fact about himself: "[I] have the keys of hell and of death" (Revelation 1:18). Many find that phrase surprising, feeling that Satan possesses those keys. Revelation, however, has it right. Keys give access or control; they symbolize authority. The Greek word translated "hell" (*hades*) denoted, in its Christian context, the world of spirits where the rebellious await the Day of Judgment in torment. The Lord holds power over spirit prison as well as paradise. The wicked, consigned to hell, feel "a certain fearful looking for of judg-ment and fiery indignation, which shall devour the [Lord's] adver-saries" (Hebrews 10:27). Alma testified that "this is the state of the souls of the wicked, yea, in darkness, and a state of awful, fearful looking for the fiery indignation of the wrath of God upon them" (Alma 40:14). The Lord's judgment places the wicked in torment so they will repent, be purged, and prepared through the fire for a king-dom of glory and happiness.

The Lord's power over death and hell come through the Atonement and the resurrection. Peter testified that the Lord's descent into spirit prison made it possible for the souls there to be taught the gospel that they might be judged with the same judgment as men in the flesh (see 1 Peter 3:18–20; 4:6). The Savior's descent was that of a conquering hero come to liberate the prisoners. His ministers declared "liberty to the captives who were bound, even unto all who would repent of their sins and receive the gospel" (D&C 138:31). It was, however, through the power of the resurrection that the Lord fully demonstrated his complete authority. Indeed, one day, through the twin keys that belong to him alone, all hell and every tomb will stand empty.

THE MESSAGE OF THE FIRST VISION

From the very first vision, Revelation shows Jesus not only as king and priest but as caretaker and director as well—a God immediate, intimate, and cognizant. "I know your doings," he assured the ser-vants of the seven churches (see Revelation 2:2, 9, 13, 19; 3:1, 8, 15;

the KJV "works" translates the Greek quite well, but "doings" is somewhat better).

John's Lord stood not outside history but at its very core. He was the mover and shaker. "I can stretch forth mine hands and hold all the creations which I have made; and mine eye can pierce them also," he assured Moses (Moses 7:36). He warned the seven churches to mend their ways or he would take away their candlesticks. The Lord reveals himself as caring and compassionate, yet exacting and unyielding.

THE REVELATION OF THE SAVIOR IN THE SECOND VISION (REVELATION 5)

As a prelude to the second appearance of the Lord in Revelation, John was invited to see the celestial kingdom with God sitting upon his throne surrounded by cherubim and elders. In the Father's hand was a scroll. It was the book of destiny, for in it was recorded "the revealed will, mysteries, and the works of God; the hidden things of his economy concerning this earth during the seven thousand years of its continuance, or its temporal existence" (D&C 77:6). John understood that someone had to execute God's will. John also recognized a problem: the heavens could find no one worthy to do the job. Indeed, no one "was able to open the book, neither to look thereon" (Revelation 5:3). The earth stood in danger of not having the will of God executed because no one "was able." The Greek word (*dunamai*) suggests that no one had the power or ability in or of himself to do the task, not even the angels of heaven.

John's reaction was instant and heartfelt: "I mourned deeply." His sorrow, however, was short lived, for one of the elders assured him that "the Lion of the tribe of Juda, the Root of David, hath prevailed" and could, therefore, open the scroll (Revelation 5:5). Both titles come from Jewish messianism. The first echoes Genesis 49:9–10, in which Judah is called a "lion's whelp" and is promised that the scepter would not depart from him "until Shiloh [i.e. the Messiah] come." The second title suggests Isaiah 11:1, which refers to the root of Jesse, the future ideal king of David's line, who was to usher in the millennial era of peace. Both combine to reveal the Savior as the true king of Israel, the sovereign of heaven and earth ready to bring in his millennial reign. John turned to look, but he did not see the majestic figure of a regal lion. Instead, he saw a lamb "in the midst of the throne." The phrase gives the lamb a position nearest the throne, sharing, as it were, the central place. In this way, the Father symbolized a principal reality. The Lamb is the center of all things, preeminent over all his creations.

The Lamb, though living, bore the marks of a violent death. The Greek verb used to describe the wound, *sphazo,* "slaughter," refers to the act of sacrificing. John could have had the paschal lamb in mind. If so, his imagery echoed the celebration of the Passover with its ritual slaughtering of a lamb. That would have reminded his Jewish readers of the ultimate victory and freedom from death they gained through Jehovah, the Lamb of God. This powerful symbol also emphasized a central biblical theme: victory through sacrifice.[17] The Lamb prevails not by sovereign might but by sacrifice grounded in love (see John 16:33). He derives his worthiness by purchasing God's people with its own blood (see Ephesians 1:7; Titus 2:14). The Seer's metaphor emphasizes both the high value of those he purchased, costing him his blood and his life, and the universality of the Lord's action in redeeming all the faithful from death and hell.[18]

John described the Lamb as having seven eyes and seven horns. Again, the image created suggests symbolic interpretation rather than visual reconstruction. The eyes depict knowledge, the horns represent power, and the number seven suggests fulness or completeness.[19] Christ possesses with his Father the powers of omnipotence and omniscience; he has "the power of God, and the wisdom of God" (1 Corinthians. 1:24). To these the Seer adds, through the symbolism of the "seven Spirits of God," the fulness of administrative authority. Each image shows the Lord's connection to earthly government, which he is about to assume in his redemptive role as "slain."

Through "the seven Spirits of God sent forth into all the earth" (Revelation 5:6), John represents the omnipresent nature of the Lamb. The Joseph Smith Translation provides an additional insight. There the Lamb has twelve horns and twelve eyes, "which are the twelve servants of God, sent forth into all the earth" (JST Revelation 5:6). The text defines the nature of the power of the Lamb. Twelve symbolizes the priesthood, and the Joseph Smith Translation seems to be teaching that all priesthood centers in and flows from the Lamb. The Doctrine and Covenants notes that at one time "it was called *the Holy Priesthood, after the Order of the Son of God.* But out of respect or reverence to the name of the Supreme Being, to avoid the too frequent repetition of his name, they, the church, in ancient days, called that priesthood after Melchizedek, or the Melchizedek Priesthood" (D&C 107:3–4; emphasis added). Further, "The Melchizedek Priesthood holds the right of presidency, and has power and authority over all the offices in the church in all ages of the world, to administer in spiritual things" (D&C 107:8). All this power centers in the Lamb and flows from him to his leaders, especially his apostles. By its authority the Savior acted to bring about the Atonement and continues to minister its saving power in the world. This is the central deed in the scroll of destiny, for all history pivots on this one act. It alone allowed for the complete fulfillment of the Father's will.

THE MESSAGE OF THE SECOND VISION

The imagery in which God chose to clothe the revelation of his Son in this vision manifests the Redeemer's role as the slain or sacrificed Lamb. But though the wound is horrible, it does not dominate the metaphor. The Lamb's horns and the eyes stand out. The image draws the reader's mind to those elements that explain why the Lamb prevailed to open the scroll and why he could act when no one else "was found worthy to open the book, neither to look thereon" (Revelation 5:4). Remember that John could clearly see the scroll from where he was standing, but he could not "look" on it. The Greek word John chose (*blepo*) suggests not just viewing but reading, understanding, or comprehending. This he could not do. It took more power and knowledge than he had to comprehend the will, economy, and mystery of God as it played out in the world's history. The Lamb possessed those powers. He received them, we must remember, because of the wound. It was the sacrifice that made the Lamb "worthy to open the book, and to loose the seals thereof" (Revelation 5:2). The imagery of the vision brings the reader's mind to an even higher understanding. The horns and eyes do indeed invest the Savior with the attributes of deity, but, more importantly, the whole image—the Lamb, the eyes, the horns, and especially the wound—force a new definition of omnipotence. Often used to describe God's power of unlimited coercion, the Seer reveals its true nature as the power of infinite persuasion, the invincible strength of self-sacrificing love.[20]

THE REVELATION OF THE SAVIOR IN THE THIRD VISION (REVELATION 14)

As the next vision opened, John saw the Savior standing with 144,000 of the Saints of God. These represent those whom the Savior has sealed unto eternal life. We do not need to take the number literally. The Doctrine and Covenants states "that those who are sealed are high priests, ordained unto the holy order of God, to administer the everlasting gospel; for they are they who are ordained out of every nation, kindred, tongue, and people, by the angels to whom is given power over the nations of the earth, to bring as many as will come to the church of the Firstborn" (77:11). Note that this scripture does not specify a number. Instead, it says that they are high priests who have a special calling "to administer the everlasting gospel," and "to bring as many as will come to the church of the Firstborn."

Joseph Smith associated the 144,000 with the temple.[21] The symbolic meaning of the number supports this association. Twelve represents the priesthood. Biblical people squared a number to amplify its symbolic meaning. Thus, 144 suggests a fulness of priesthood authority. But the Lord was not satisfied with that. He gives the image a superlative quality by multiplying 144 by a thousand, representing completeness. In this way he shows the strength and breadth of the priesthood in the latter days, in this dispensation, which is, indeed, the dispensation of the fulness of times. During this period complete priesthood authority will operate. It is little wonder that as the world spurns this authority, it will be condemned.

It is these people who have built the New Jerusalem and established the foundation of Zion. It is here, John understands, where the Lord will dwell before the great and dreadful day overtakes the rest of the earth. The presence of the Lord prepares the Saints against the judgments he is about to unleash against the rest of the world.

The momentum of John's vision up to this point has prepared the reader for the onset of a great battle, but, as usual, God throws in a twist. He does not disclose the figure standing on Mount Zion as a terrible warrior-king garbed in battle array but instead as a lamb, the symbol of meekness and peace. Further, harmony and joy reign over the entire scene. These people do not know worry or distress; they seem unconcerned about the war clouds gathering over the whole earth. The harmony of sweet music fills the region and reaches from earth to heaven, where it ignites a rhapsody expressing itself as a new song—new not only because it has never been sung before but because it could never have been sung before. It signals a total victory which only now becomes possible. For this reason, only the 144,000—representing the sealed, those who have won the battle—are able to sing it. The Doctrine and Covenants provides the setting for the song and its content. In it the Lord states:

"For I, the Almighty, have laid my hands upon the nations, to scourge them for their wickedness.

"And plagues shall go forth, and they shall not be taken from the earth until I have completed my work, which shall be cut short in righteousness—

"Until all shall know me, who remain, even from the least unto the greatest, and shall be filled with the knowledge of the Lord, and shall see eye to eye, and shall lift up their voice, and with the voice together sing this new song, saying:

"The Lord hath brought again Zion;
The Lord hath redeemed his people, Israel,
According to the election of grace,
Which was brought to pass by the faith
And covenant of their fathers.

"The Lord hath redeemed his people;
And Satan is bound and time is no longer.
The Lord hath gathered all things in one.
The Lord hath brought down Zion from above.
The Lord hath brought up Zion from beneath.

"The earth hath travailed and brought forth her strength;
And truth is established in her bowels;
And the heavens have smiled upon her;
And she is clothed with the glory of her God;
For he stands in the midst of his people.

"Glory, and honor, and power, and might,
Be ascribed to our God; for he is full of mercy,
Justice, grace and truth, and peace,
Forever and ever, Amen" (D&C 84:96–102).

In these verses, the Lord reveals the triumphant nature of the song. It celebrates the time when the plagues of judgment will cleanse the earth. Only the redeemed will remain. God and his Saints will win the day, and Zion will stand supreme.

Chapter 14 explains the underpinnings of the song, allowing us to understand why it can be sung. In the dramatic closing scene, John beholds "one like unto the Son of man" seated upon a white cloud. The imagery is taken from Daniel 7:13–14 and appears to be a reference to the resurrected Lord coming in the fulness of his power. On his head sits a golden wreath. The King James Version describes it as a "crown," but the Greek word (*stephenos*) does not refer to a diadem, the mark of civil rule, but rather to a wreath, a sign of the highest athletic achievement or of a great military victory. In his hand, he readies the sickle of judgment and begins to harvest the wheat fields. The day of judgment has fully come, "for the harvest of the earth is ripe" (Revelation 14:15). It is the ripeness that determines the timing of the reaping. The Lord expresses this idea in a parable of harvest: "But behold, in the last days, even now while the Lord is beginning to bring forth the word, and the blade is springing up and is yet tender—behold, verily I say unto you, the angels are crying unto the Lord day and night, who are ready and waiting to be sent forth to reap down the fields; but the Lord saith unto them, pluck not up the tares while the blade is yet tender (for verily your faith is weak), lest you destroy the wheat also. Therefore, let the wheat and the tares grow together until the harvest is fully ripe; then ye shall first gather out the wheat from among the tares, and after the gathering of the wheat, behold and lo, the tares are bound in bundles, and the field remaineth to be burned" (D&C 86:4–7).

The first harvest, the harvest of the Lord, is the ingathering of the wheat. That time is now, and the time is urgent. To his Saints the Lord declared: "For verily, verily, I say unto you that ye are called to lift up your voices as with the sound of a trump, to declare my gospel unto a crooked and perverse generation. For behold, the field is white already to harvest; and it is the eleventh hour, and the last time that I shall call laborers into my vineyard" (D&C 33:2–3).

It is in this light that the Lord admonishes: "Whoso desireth to reap let him thrust in his sickle with his might, and reap while the day lasts, that he may treasure up for his soul everlasting salvation in the kingdom of God" (D&C 11:3). Now is the time when the wheat must be gathered in. Those who participate are the Lord's sickle. The Lord will reward the effort of his laborers with the security and peace of Zion.

Through the efforts of the laborers, the world will hear the gospel. But when the world openly rejects goodness and turns against God's people, then another sickle will begin to do its terrible work.[22] That will be the day when the voice of God will utter "out of the heaven, saying: Hearken, O ye nations of the earth, and hear the words of that God, who made you. O, ye nations of the earth, how often would I have gathered you together as a hen gathereth her chickens under her wings, but ye would not! How oft have I called upon you by the mouth of my servants, and by the ministering of angels, and by mine own voice, and by the voice of thunderings, and by the voice of lightnings, and by the voice of tempests, and by the voice of earthquakes, and great hailstorms, and by the voice of famines and pestilences of every kind, and by the great sound of a trump, and by the voice of judgment, and by the voice of mercy all the day long, and by the voice of glory and honor and the riches of eternal life, and would have saved you with an everlasting salvation, but ye would not! Behold, the day has come, when the cup of the wrath of mine indignation is full" (D&C 43:23–26).

The period of the second sickle begins when all peaceful attempts to redeem the world have failed. At that point the warning of the Book of Mormon may again find fulfillment: "For behold, there is a curse upon all this land, that destruction shall come upon all those workers of darkness, according to the power of God, when they are fully ripe" (Alma 37:28). The warning applies not only to the Americas but also to the world at large.

The harvest of ruin will be carried out not by the Lord but by an angel of destruction. His target is not the fields but the vineyards.[23] He is to "gather the clusters of the vine of the earth; for her grapes are fully ripe" (Revelation 14:18). Further, he is to cast the fruit "into the great wine press of the wrath of God" (Revelation 14:19). The destruction will be tremendous and bitter.

THE MESSAGE OF THE THIRD VISION

In the third vision, the Father reveals his Son as the victor, the great general who has met his foe and won. It is out of this victory that the 144,000 sing their song and celebrate both security and peace. But the celebration, in the context of Revelation, seems premature. The actual battle has not commenced, and the enemy still stands strong, arrogant, and undefeated. How then can the Saints celebrate with such surety? There are two reasons: the first is grounded in their absolute faith in the ability of the Lord to overcome. Part of this is based on the redemption he has already won for them. Their absolute confidence echoes the same faith they exhibited during the great war in heaven when "they overcame him [Satan] by the blood of the Lamb, and by the word of their testimony" (Revelation 12:11). The second stems from the fact that the Lord is personally with them, directing affairs and attending to the Saint's needs and assuring their safety. The Lord promised the Saints of America that here "shall be a New Jerusalem. And the powers of heaven shall be in the midst of this people; yea, even I will be in the midst of you" (3 Nephi 20:22). He assured them further that his shall be "a land of peace, a city of refuge, a place of safety for the saints of the Most High God; and the glory of the Lord shall be there, and the terror of the Lord also shall be there, insomuch that the wicked will not come unto it, and it shall be called Zion" (D&C 45:66–67). It is not the Saints who need to fear, but the enemy.

The Lord directs the work of the harvest from Zion. The 144,000 act as the sickle of the Lord moving among the nations to gather out all who will come to Zion. John emphasizes the Lord's saving ministry. Neither he nor any of his people work to destroy the world or its enemies. It was another angel whom John saw that "came out of the temple which is in heaven, he also having a sharp sickle" (Revelation 14:17). It is this one to whom the angel of the altar commands: "Thrust in thy sharp sickle, and gather the clusters of the vine of the earth; for her grapes are fully ripe" (Revelation 14:18). John's point seems to be that, at least at this point, the Lord does not come to destroy the earth nor its people. He comes to save it. Revelation gives credit for destruction to the five angels of the Lord (the four in chapter 7 and the one in chapter 14) on one side and to Satan on the other. The actual work is done by the army described as horsemen with "breastplates of fire, and of jacinth, and brimstone" (Revelation 9:17) and led by one "whose name in the Hebrew tongue is Abaddon, but in the Greek tongue hath his name Apollyon," and in English, the Destroyer, or Perdition (see Revelation 9:11; D&C 76:26).[24] Out of the horsemen's mouths come fire and smoke and brimstone, and "by these three was the third part of men killed" (Revelation 9:18). So what does the Lord do at his coming? John understood perfectly. The Lord comes to "destroy them which destroy the earth" (Revelation 11:18).

The point is that the Savior does just what his name says: he saves. The paradox is that the Lord's destruction becomes his tool of salvation. He uses that tool, however, only when all others have failed. Still, it is a tool of salvation, and for that reason the angels can say, "Lord God Almighty, true and righteous are thy judgments" (Revelation 16:7). The Lord is perfectly prepared to allow his destroying angels and the beasts of Satan a certain destructive power over millions. Some may have trouble with this idea, but Revelation forces upon us a very realistic understanding about death. From the Lord's perspective, all must die. The question is when and how. Ultimate destiny is not determined by the moment or manner of death: it is by the manner of life. Keep in mind that those who are destroyed are not annihilated. They have further existence. For the present, they refuse to play the game by God's rules. They have become mean and violent, and so they are thrown into the penalty box, so to speak, for unnecessary roughness while the game goes on. We must fight against the current idea that mortality is so infallibly precious that, as one scholar put it, "the death which robs us of it must be the ultimate tragedy." Such an idea, he says, "is precisely the idolatry that John is trying here to combat. We have already seen that John calls the enemies of the church 'the inhabitants of earth,' because they have made themselves utterly at home in this transient world order. If all men must die, and if at the end heaven and earth must vanish, along with those whose life is irremediably bounded by worldly horizons, then it is surely in accord with the mercy of God that he should send men from time to time forceful reminders of the insecurity of their tenure."[25]

Besides, John shows us clearly that the purpose of the plagues is to drive those who would not do so otherwise to repentance and, thus, into the protective arms of God. Those who will not repent must be accountable to the fire. What happens to those who refuse to repent leads us to God's next revelation of his Son.

THE REVELATION OF THE SAVIOR IN THE FOURTH VISION (REVELATION 19)

At the beginning of his heavenly revelations, John saw "a door . . . opened in heaven" through which he was able to see the throne of God (Revelation 4:1). Later "the temple of God was opened in heaven," such that the Seer could behold the ark of the testimony (Revelation 11:19). Then the whole temple opened so that the seven angels with the seven bowls could come out (Revelation 15:5). Now John sees the entire expanse of heaven unfold to make way for the Warrior-king and his army prepared to battle the hosts of darkness.[26] The Rider, terrible in majesty upon his white horse, is the Savior, "called Faithful and True" (Revelation 19:11; compare D&C 45:74–75). These names of Christ, as Elder Bruce R. McConkie points out, "signify that he is the embodiment and personification of these godly attributes. Above all his fellows, he was obedient to the will of the Father and true to every trust imposed upon him."[27] John clearly states the rider's purpose: "in righteousness he doth judge and make war" (Revelation 19:11). War results from his just judgment. Evil must be put down even by force when necessary.

John sees the Lord coming with crowns upon his head. These are not wreaths but diadems, the symbol of political rule. The King comes to take back his domain. John deliberately contrasts the King with the dragon and the sea beast met in Revelation 12. Whereas the former two possess seven and ten diadems respectively, the Warrior has "many" diadems (Revelation 19:12). The King's true royalty far surpasses the false sovereignty of Satan and his minion. He now rides as "KING OF KINGS, AND LORD OF LORDS" (Revelation 19:16)— and he has acquired his crowns since John last saw him. Although John had seen him in regal authority early in the revelation (Revelation 3:21; compare 1:5), John mentions no diadem. Here they are prominently displayed. They signify that the "kingdoms of this world are become the kingdoms of our Lord, and of his Christ; and he shall reign for ever and ever" (Revelation 11:15).[28]

The Rider bore a name "that no man knew, but he himself" (Revelation 19:12). Again Elder McConkie gives insight: "As with all glorified beings, our Lord has a new name in celestial exaltation, a name known to and comprehended by those only who know God in the sense that they have become as he is and have eternal life. See Revelation 2:12–17. Thus, Christ's 'new name' shall be written upon all those who are joint-heirs with him (Revelation 3:12), and shall signify that they have become even as he is."[29]

But the Warrior does have a known name: "The Word of God" (Revelation 19:13). John calls him by this same title at the beginning of his gospel (John 1:1–3). In Revelation the name emphasizes that he judges the kings of the world.[30] Among many ancient peoples, a word was not simply a lifeless sound but an active agent bringing into being the intent of the one who spoke.[31] The Savior is the active agent who executes the word (that is, the will) of God. That word is now judgment. Thus, the Rider's vestments are blood red, for the judgment is one of death (compare Isaiah 63:1–6). According to the Doctrine and Covenants, his appearance will cause consternation among the nations. Many will ask: "Who is this that cometh down from God in heaven with dyed garments; yea, from the regions which are not known, clothed in his glorious apparel, traveling in the greatness of his strength? And he shall say: I am he who spake in righteousness, mighty to save. . . . And so great shall be the glory of his presence that the sun shall hide his face in shame, and the moon shall withhold its light, and the stars shall be hurled from their places. And his voice shall be heard: I have trodden the wine-press alone, and have brought judgment upon all people; and none were with me; And I have trampled them in my fury, and I did tread upon them in mine anger, and their blood have I sprinkled upon my garments, and stained all my raiment; for this was the day of vengeance which was in my heart" (D&C 133:46–47, 49–51).

Clearly John depicts the moment of vengeance when the Lord will destroy all wickedness by the brightness of his coming (see D&C 5:19). But he does not come alone. With him comes his army "upon white horses, clothed in fine linen, white and clean" (Revelation 19:14). Against these "the kings of the earth, and their armies, gathered together to make war" (Revelation 19:19), but they will be "slain with the sword of him that sat upon the horse, which sword proceeded out of his mouth: and all the fowls were filled with their flesh" (Revelation 19:21). At this moment all nations will come under his authority, "and he shall rule them with a rod of iron" (Revelation 19:15).

THE MESSAGE OF THE FOURTH VISION

Revelation 19 gives us a clear view of the nature and purpose of the Second Coming. Unlike other accounts in which the glory and burning power of the Redeemer dominate, Revelation stresses the regal and martial authority of the Lord. He appears as the warrior-king at the head of his angelic host to take back his land from the Dark Lord and his legions. Actually, he does not need to take it back, for he has never lost it. His is more of a mopping-up exercise against those that have tried to take his world and failed.

Some may be concerned because the day of the Lord is filled with destruction. But it has its purpose. Nothing unclean (that is, unjustified) can enter into the Lord's presence and survive.[32] Christ is about to sweep the earth with his glory that the millennial era may be established. Therefore, evil must come to an end. By the time the Lord comes, there will be very little evil left to put to an end. Throughout Revelation we have seen the self-destructive nature of wickedness. God cannot allow such self-destruction to act as an impersonal nemesis: an independent, self-operating moral law sweeping away all in its path. To do so would allow the powers of evil to carry all the inhabitants of the earth down with them to utter ruin. God would be left with a hollow, Pyrrhic victory. Because God's victory must also be the Saints' victory, it must be won through righteous human agents exercising faith in God. Evil must be allowed to combine its forces against the Savior's people and then fall back in utter defeat through their faith and trust coupled with the glory of those who come with the Savior.[33]

Because his victory is theirs, they reign with him. As John declared, "I saw thrones, and they [who] sat upon them, and judgment was given to them" (Revelation 20:4). These "lived and reigned with Christ a thousand years" (Revelation 20:4). His coming, then, results in a world over which he will preside with the faithful and without opposition from the dragon. The result will be that his people "shall be priests of God and of Christ, and shall reign with him a thousand years" (Revelation 20:6).

WHAT REVELATION REVEALS ABOUT THE LORD

The book of Revelation contains, as John clearly stated in his introduction, the revelation of Jesus Christ. God the Father chose the imagery and focus of that revelation. Three images eclipse all others. The first is that of Christ as the divine Lamb executing the will of his omnipotent Father. Revelation underscores the work of the Savior as the executor of the Father's will. He is the active God in history. It is true that for much of earth's history the Lamb has chosen to act behind the scenes. That has made it easy for the natural man or woman to attribute the course of history to political, social, and other causes. The naturalistic view, however, will soon prove untenable. Already the great Jehovah is beginning to direct more openly the course of history and manifest more directly his control over the destiny of humankind. An iron curtain has crumbled, the gospel is preached across many lands, and worthy males of all nations can hold the priesthood. Before long, all will see that the Lamb does indeed execute the will of God, whose grasp none can escape.

Tied closely to the image of the Lamb is that of the Almighty God—the one who directs, controls, and orchestrates. John reveals the power of God on two levels. One is through the active voice, by which the prophet attributes direct authority and movement to the Lamb. The other is through the passive voice, by which indirect credit is given to the Lamb. To understand, consider the subtle hope lying behind one of the most frightening chapters in Revelation, chapter nine. John records a vision in which he saw "a star fall from heaven unto the earth: and to him was given the key of the bottomless pit" (Revelation 9:1). God chose a star to represent his rebellious son Satan and the pit to symbolize the source from which powers of hell will be unleashed upon the world in the last days.

Notice, though, that Satan did not possess the key to the pit in the abyss. He had to receive it from someone. Further, John sees that the destructive beasts, described as "locusts," will be "given power, as the scorpions of the earth have power. And it was commanded them that they should not hurt the grass of the earth, neither any green thing, neither any tree; but only those men which have not the seal of God in their foreheads" (Revelation 9:3–4). Something sets limits on these beasts. It gives them power, it tells them what and who they can and cannot hurt, and it dictates how long they shall act: "five months"

(Revelation 9:5). Something even limits the angels of destruction. Their time is set for "an hour, and a day, and a month, and a year," and they can slay but "the third part of men" (Revelation 9:15).

John clearly reveals that something overmasters all that goes on, setting boundaries and establishing limits. What is the power behind history? It is Jehovah. Revelation gives more than a powerful testimony of the prophetic abilities of this God. It shows not only that he knew the end from the beginning and contemplated the whole of earth's history but also that he arranged and continuously orchestrates it. History has moved according to the script he has written, and all movements have stayed within the bounds he has set. He is indeed the Almighty.

The last image through which God reveals his Son is that of the Warrior-king destroying evil with his victorious hosts and reigning with them for a thousand years. Along with the white horse of war, the myriad of diadems atop the king's head dominate the scene. In this way, God set the political aspect of the Lord's power center stage. The millennial era will see true theocracy established and flourishing in preparation for the time when this earth will enter the family of celestial planets. This is the time, as John saw, that "the holy city, the new Jerusalem, . . . [will come] down from God out of heaven, prepared as a bride adorned for her husband" (Revelation 21:2). Then "the tabernacle of God . . . [will be] with men and he will dwell with them, . . . and God himself shall be with them, and be their God" (Revelation 21:3).

It is Christ, the Lamb, the Almighty, the Warrior-king, who shall bring all these things to pass. Little wonder that the angelic hosts will praise his name, singing "the song of Moses the servant of God, and the song of the Lamb, saying, Great and marvelous are thy works, Lord God Almighty; just and true are thy ways, thou King of saints. Who shall not fear thee, O Lord, and glorify thy name? for thou only art holy: for all nations shall come and worship before thee; for thy judgments are made manifest" (Revelation 15:3–4).

NOTES

1. Northrop Frye, "Typology: Apocalypse," in *The Revelation of St. John the Divine,* ed. Harold Bloom (New York: Chelsea House Publishers, 1988), 71.

2. Elohim also uses these same elements as disclosure points. See

Revelation 2:6, wherein he uses the phrase to introduce the reward he will give the faithful. Both the Father and the Son act together to bring eternal life to humankind.

3. Compare Jeremiah 1:6; 14:13; and 32:17 in the Septuagint (LXX).

4. Joseph Smith, *Teachings of the Prophet Joseph Smith,* sel. Joseph Fielding Smith (Salt Lake City: Deseret Book, 1976), 220.

5. See Romans 9:15–18; John 10:18; Ezekiel 38:1–4, 14–22. One of the aspects of apocalyptic literature in general and Revelation in particular is predeterminism. Revelation testifies that all things move in concert toward a divinely predetermined end. Everything is inevitable; nothing is left to chance. The problem of human agency or free will within the context of God's omniscience never surfaces. But there is a tacit insistence that God's ultimate victory is worked out within the framework of human freedom.

6. Josephine Massyngberde Ford, *Revelation,* vol. 38 of *The Anchor Bible* (Garden City, N.Y.: Doubleday, 1975), 376. The Song of the Doves at Dondona speaks of "Zeus who was, Zeus who is, Zeus who will be" (Pausanias, *Asinaria,* 10.12.10). At Sais the shrine of Minerva boasted, "I am that hath been and is and shall be" (Plutarch, *Moralia, De Iside et Osiride,* 9). See Robert H. Mounce, *The Book of Revelation* (Grand Rapids, Mich.: Eerdmans, 1977), 68. For a technical study of the name/title, see R. H. Charles, *A Critical and Exegetical Commentary on the Revelation of St. John,* 2 vols. (Edinburgh: T. & T. Clark, 1920), 1:10.

7. Jesus may well have been speaking by divine investiture of authority as he uttered these words. In that case, it is Elohim who is "Endless" and "Eternal." Revelation 21:6 has Elohim declare that he is "Alpha and Omega, the beginning and the end." Such titles seem to apply to both Father and Son because the perspective of the Father is shared by the Son through the power of the Holy Spirit. According to *Lectures on Faith* 5:1, the Son possesses the same fulness with the Father and "having overcome, received a fulness of the glory of the Father, possessing the same mind with the Father." By sharing the same mind, the Savior can speak from the perspective of the "Endless" and the "Eternal." See Larry E. Dahl and Charles D. Tate Jr., ed., *The Lectures on Faith in Historical Perspective,* vol. 15 of the Religious Studies Center Monograph Series (Provo: Brigham Young University Religious Studies Center, 1990), 84.

8. Smith, *Teachings of the Prophet Joseph Smith,* 220.

9. Bruce R. McConkie, *Doctrinal New Testament Commentary,* 3 vols. (Salt Lake City: Bookcraft, 1965–73), 3:439.

10. The phrase "like unto" seems to suggests that John did not actually see the Savior. Such is not the case. There are a number of scriptures where the phrase "like unto the Son of Man" refers to none other than the Savior. See Abraham 3:27; Revelation 14:14.

11. See James H. Charlesworth, ed., *The Messiah: Developments in Earliest Christianity and Judaism* (Minneapolis: Fortress Press, 1992); for the concept of Messianism in earliest Judaism, see 79–115; on the term "son of man," see 130–44.

12. For discussion see M. D. Hooker, *The Son of Man in Mark* (London: SPCK, 1967), 81–93.

13. Luke spoke previously of the Lord's power (*dunamis*) to heal. Here Luke focuses on his authority (*exousia*) to do so.

14. See Septuagint Exodus 28:4, 5, which indicates that the girdle is connected with the attire of the high priest. His girdle was made of fine-twined linen and embroidered with needlework (see *Septuagint* Exodus 28:36), while the clasp or girdle that gathered together the long robe of the Lord was of gold. Josephus, however, notes that during his time the high priest's girdle was interwoven with gold (*Antiquities of the Jews,* 3.7.2). The golden clasp, or *porpē,* was worn by the king and his associates (1 Maccabees 10:89; 11:58) and so served as a mark of an important office. For further discussion, see Charles, *Commentary,* 1:28; and Mounce, *Book of Revelation,* 77–78.

15. Joseph Smith and Oliver Cowdery may have been echoing the words of Revelation with which they were both acquainted. Even so, those words best described what they experienced.

16. G. Kittel, et al., ed., *Theological Dictionary of the New Testament,* trans. Geoffrey W. Bromily, 10 vols. (Grand Rapids, Mich.: Eerdmans, 1964), s.v. *"machaira"* and *"rhomphaia."*

17. Mounce, *Revelation,* 144.

18. Elizabeth Schussler Fiorenza, *The Book of Revelation: Justice and Judgment* (Philadelphia: Fortress Press, 1985), 73.

19. The possession of seven eyes echoes Zechariah 4:10, in which they are symbols of God's omniscience. The horn is the Old Testament symbol for power. See Numbers 23:22; Deuteronomy 33:17; 1 Samuel 2:1; 1 Kings 22:11; Psalms 75:4; 89:17. Thus, it was the mark of kingly dignity. See Psalms 112:9; 148:14; Zechariah 1:18; Daniel 7:7, 20; 8:3. In 1 Enoch 90.9, the Maccabees are stylized as "horned lambs." See Charles, *Commentary,* 1:141–43.

20. G. B. Caird, *A Commentary on the Revelation of St. John the Divine* (Peabody, Mass.: Hendrickson Publishers, 1966), 75.

21. Joseph Smith, *History of The Church of Jesus Christ of Latter-day Saints,* ed. B. H. Roberts, 2d ed. rev., 7 vols. (Salt Lake City: The Church of Jesus Christ of Latter-day Saints, 1932–51), 6:365; Andrew F. Ehat and Lyndon W. Cook, *The Words of the Prophet Joseph Smith* (Provo: Brigham Young University Religious Studies Center, 1980), 368.

22. Compare 2 Nephi 28:15–20 with Alma 37:30–31, which teaches

that the world is fully ripe when it both rejects and fights against goodness.

23. The *drepanon* was an all-purpose blade used for pruning, cutting clusters of grapes, and harvesting grains. Its roughly foot-long curved blade made it easy to handle, with clean cutting power.

24. The Greek word, a feminine noun, is *apoleia*, which carries the meaning of something that destroys or brings to utter ruin.

25. Caird, *Revelation*, 113.

26. Exodus 15:3 describes Jehovah as a man of war. The idea persists in 2 Maccabees 3:22–30 and in the Qumran scrolls 1QM 12.10–11; 19.2–4.

27. McConkie, *Commentary*, 3:566.

28. Caird, *Revelation*, 241.

29. McConkie, *Commentary*, 3:567.

30. Mounce, *Revelation*, 345–46.

31. Mounce, *Revelation*, 345–46. See, for example, Genesis 1:3, 7, 9; Hebrews 4:12.

32. John 6:46; Moses 7:35.

33. Caird, *Revelation*, 145.

CHAPTER FOUR

THE GREAT INVITATION OF JOHN THE BELOVED

STANLEY E. FAWCETT AND AMYDEE M. FAWCETT

John's great mission, like that of all the Lord's apostles, was to invite any and all who might listen to "come unto Christ" (Jacob 1:7). John's experience with the Lord and with the early Church certainly influenced his approach to delivering this invitation. He had seen the doctrine of Christ mingled with the philosophies of men and witnessed the struggles of the fledgling Church to establish itself on the one true foundation: "Jesus Christ, and him crucified" (1 Corinthians 2:2). Consequently, John made it a point throughout his teachings to provide clear counsel, direction, and encouragement to the members, whom he called "my little children" (1 John 2:1). John's objective was to help them understand exactly what they needed to do to make the Lord's atonement truly effective in their lives and thereby overcome the world.

John's teachings show an understanding that the strait and narrow path back to Heavenly Father's presence is a difficult one to negotiate, even when a well-drawn map is used to guide the journey. John endeavored to provide such a map, complete with a clear vision of the sojourner's ultimate destination: everlasting life. Moreover, because he had already seen competing mapmakers market their own corrupted versions of heavenly maps, John seems to have taken particular care to provide a comprehensive map with a well-marked

---

Stanley E. Fawcett is an associate professor of business management at Brigham Young University. Amydee M. Fawcett is a homemaker, educator, and student of the scriptures.

route that, if followed with real intent, would lead the faithful traveler back to God's presence. John also appears to have been aware that many members of the Church might be enticed, by counterfeit maps and their supposed shortcuts, to look for an easier route. Many members were willing to risk an easier but unknown trail if they could avoid the challenges known to abound on the strait and narrow path. This desire to find a shortcut eventually led the Church down the dead-end path of apostasy.

John's intimate association with the Lord Jesus Christ led him to understand that there are no shortcuts on the strait and narrow path.[1] Because the objective of the journey is to grow and mature en route, the easy paths are precluded. John also knew that all who began the journey would at some point stray from the well-marked path, frequently at the behest of a friend or acquaintance who was following the markings of a counterfeit map. This knowledge led John to provide the encouragement and directions that would lead lost travelers back to safety, if they would only refer back to the map, relying on Christ to light the way. That he had been taught by the Master who built the road and issued the original map made John the Beloved an ideal guide for life's journey. By teaching the flock how to read the map (which is the gospel plan), as well as how to employ it effectively in their individual journeys, John took full advantage of the tutoring he had received from the master mapmaker, Jesus Christ.

REQUIREMENTS FOR EXALTATION: A CORRECT ROADMAP

As a fully licensed guide, John worked dutifully to dispel confusion and to teach the requirements for exaltation. In the early years of John's ministry, divergent views had arisen regarding the answer to the great question: What must a person do to be saved in the kingdom of God? (see John 3:1–5). Much of the divergence in opinion was founded on differing views concerning the efficacy of the Savior's atonement and, then as now, hinged on the interplay between the concepts of faith and works. For some early members of the Church, expressed faith was believed to be sufficient for salvation—the grace of God made behavioral accountability obsolete. For others, including the early Christian sophists, an aggrandized sense of self-reliance superseded the importance of Christ's atoning sacrifice. For still others, a persistent adherence to the dead works of the Mosaic law continued as an important aspect of religious activity. These diverse views regarding the route and way to eternal life are evidenced and illustrated by the writings of John's contemporary apostles, Paul and James, who sought to help their audiences come unto Christ regardless of their ideological position. The epistles of these two apostles, as well as the teachings of John, focused on both the need and the means to make the Savior's atoning sacrifice effective in one's own life.

Indeed, the straitness and the narrowness of the gospel way combined with the diversity of individual experience among the early members of the Church required that each apostle tailor his message to the particular needs of his audience. The following two scriptural passages illustrate how the gospel message was customized in specific instances to teach the principle most needed by distinct groups of people with differing backgrounds and needs:

Ephesians 2:8–9: "For by grace are ye saved through faith; and that not of yourselves: it is the gift of God: not of works, lest any man should boast."

James 2:17–18: "Even so faith, if it hath not works, is dead, being alone. Yea, a man may say, Thou hast faith, and I have works: shew me thy faith without thy works, and I will shew thee my faith by my works."

The reality is that the two apostles are teaching the gospel of Jesus Christ to groups of individuals whose experiences have led them to possess fundamentally different perspectives on both the need for a Savior and his role. When this fact is fully considered, the teachings of these two apostles not only harmonize completely with the teachings of the Lord Jesus Christ but are completely consistent with the Savior's own pedagogy. The Savior emphasized in his teachings faith and works at different times in accordance with the needs of his listeners. For example, speaking to the Jews who followed after him because of his miracles but who had yet to accept him as the Bread of Life, the Savior taught, "Verily, verily, I say unto you, He that believeth on me hath everlasting life. I am that bread of life" (John 6:47–48). The Lord knew that this people needed to receive a witness of his divine calling as the Savior of all mankind. At another time, speaking to his disciples, who had already demonstrated a belief in him as the Savior, the Lord taught, "If ye love me, keep my commandments" (John 14:15). In this instance, the Savior wanted to make sure the disciples understood that their faith and love could be manifest only through obedience to his commandments.

Unfortunately, the sincerity and real intent that led the early apostles to target their message to convincing their audiences to walk after Christ have been distorted to place faith and works in opposition. Certain scriptures, when taken out of context and examined in isolation, suggest somewhat conflicting directions to be used in negotiating the strait and narrow path back to the kingdom of God. John's experiences with the early Church and the confusion introduced by conflicting ideologies appear to have helped him more clearly see mankind's innate tendency to misinterpret the requirements for exaltation. John seems to have recognized that the differing views of faith and works not only provided distinct and competing roadmaps to the kingdom of God but also introduced distractions that made the journey more perilous, introducing detours and hazards at every turn.

Indeed, the clarity with which John integrates his teachings regarding both faith and works suggests that he recognized the dangers inherent in a distorted and exaggerated emphasis on either belief or behavior. Thus, among the four writers of the Gospels, John stands alone in his meticulous effort to place the foundation concepts of belief and behavior in their proper relationship. He alone shares and explicates the teachings of the Savior that demonstrate how faith and works combine to bring us unto Christ. Through John's writings we learn that only by receiving Christ and believing in him can we gain "power to become the sons of God" (John 1:12). With equal conviction, John teaches that to receive, believe, and love Christ, we must do his works (see John 14:12) and "keep [his] commandments" (John 14:15). Moreover, as John teaches that belief and behavior are inseparable, he illustrates the role that each plays in bringing the true believer unto Christ. Ultimately, the sum and integration of John's teachings reveal what we must do to be saved in the kingdom of God.

THE ROLE OF FAITH

The foundation concept of belief or faith—on which so many modern Christian denominations build—is inextricably intertwined with the notion of grace. In this context, it is the grace of God that makes belief in Christ efficacious. In many instances, modernists interchange the words *belief, faith,* and *grace* in their discussions of the requirements for salvation. A true appreciation of the importance of grace and faith in our individual lives can therefore be gained if we answer the following three basic but essential questions: What is grace? From whence does grace come? and Why do we individually need grace? John provides insight into each of these three questions in a single, well-known, and beloved passage of scripture:

"For God so loved the world, that he gave his only begotten Son, that whosoever believeth in him should not perish, but have everlasting life. For God sent not his Son into the world to condemn the world; but that the world through him might be saved" (John 3:16–17).

With simple elegance, John adroitly identifies the saving power of grace as a gift from God—a gift that is given because of God's love for his children. Specifically, the gift of grace through the atonement of the Son saves God's children from condemnation, making it possible that the children perish not but receive everlasting life. As a gift, grace is given because of God's good will and desire, not because his children have done anything of particular merit. Rather, God's love for his children motivates and underlies the gift of grace.

John is equally precise in identifying the source of grace, declaring that the saving power of grace comes from God through his Only Begotten Son. Indeed, it is by the grace of God, which comes by Jesus Christ (see John 1:17), that a sincere belief in the Only Begotten Son makes salvation possible. To assure that no one who possesses real intent of understanding is left in doubt regarding the source of salvation, John reiterated time and time again that the power of salvation comes through the Son of God and his atoning sacrifice. As the needle of the compass points to true north, John always points to Jesus Christ as the source of salvation. The following scriptures illustrate John's consistent message regarding the source of grace and the power of believing:

1. "He that believeth on the Son hath everlasting life" (John 3:36).

2. "He that heareth my [Christ's] word, and believeth on him that sent me, hath everlasting life" (John 5:24).

3. "This is the work of God, that ye believe on him [Jesus Christ] whom he hath sent" (John 6:29).

4. "Every one which seeth the Son, and believeth on him, may have everlasting life" (John 6:40).

5. "He that believeth on me [Jesus Christ] hath everlasting life" (John 6:47).

6. "He that believeth on me [Jesus Christ], . . . out of his belly shall flow rivers of living water" (John 7:38).

7. "Jesus said unto her, I am the resurrection, and the life: he that believeth in me, though he were dead, yet shall he live" (John 11:25).

8. "He that hath the Son hath life; and he that hath not the Son of God hath not life" (1 John 5:12).

9. "He [Christ] is the propitiation for our sins: and not for ours only, but also for the sins of the whole world" (1 John 2:2).

10. "And ye know that he [Christ] was manifested to take away our sins" (1 John 3:5).

Finally, as the preceding scriptures indicate, John is most poignant in affirming that we need the gift of Jesus Christ in our individual lives to avoid everlasting death. In John 3:16, John clearly states that we need God's grace so that we might not perish, but have everlasting life. In John 3:36 and 1 John 5:12, John emphasizes that the failure to believe in Christ brings death: "he that believeth not the Son shall not see life; but the wrath of God abideth on him" and "he that hath not the Son of God hath not life." John appears determined to focus our attention so that we will "behold the Lamb of God, which taketh away the sin of the world" (John 1:29) and choose to come unto him.

Further, it seems reasonable that as a special witness of the Savior, John had been taught the essentials of the gospel such that he understood the relationship between the fall of Adam and the atonement of Jesus Christ. He realized that through the fall of Adam, all men became subject to following after their own will and therefore, at one time or another, would choose to stray from the strait and narrow path. These decisions to transgress the law by deviating from the divinely designated path bring the effects of sin into our individual lives, "for sin is the transgression of the law" (1 John 3:4). The disastrous effect of sin is that we get lost in the wilderness, and, losing sight of our ultimate destination, we lose our inheritance in God's kingdom. As John put it, because of individual sin we "shall not see life," we "ha[ve] not life," and we "perish" (John 3:36; 1 John 5:12; 3:1). John emphasized that universal condemnation comes through the exercise of our own agency when he said, "If we say that we have no sin, we deceive ourselves, and the truth is not in us" (1 John 1:8). There are no exceptions: we all need the Atonement because, except for Jesus only, we all stray from the strait and narrow path. John noted our complete and total dependence on the Savior, whose mission and power were to save us from the effects of sin: "And ye know that he was manifested to take away our sins; and in him is no sin" (1 John 3:5).

John further taught that a singular benefit of grace is that it gives all men hope through the atonement of Jesus Christ. The hope of grace is that through the Atonement the Savior will lift the weight of our sins from our shoulders and make it easier for us to walk back to our Father's presence—as we follow in his footsteps along the pathway for which he is the Light. John specifically encouraged the Saints of his day to rely on the Lord and to look to his saving grace to overcome the effects of sin: "And if any man sin, we have an advocate with the Father, Jesus Christ the righteous: And he is the propitiation for our sins: and not for ours only, but also for the sins of the whole world" (1 John 2:1–2). When we understand that we are totally and absolutely helpless to remove the weight of sin from our lives and that we depend entirely on an Advocate who bought us with a price, we come to more fully appreciate the Savior and his atoning sacrifice unto salvation. This appreciation mingles with the hope of eternal life that is in Christ to motivate us to more fervently "believe on the name of the Son of God" (1 John 5:13).

THE ROLE OF WORKS

If Jesus Christ came into the world to suffer for the sins of mankind—paying the price to make grace available to all those who believe on his name—then what is the role of works? In a sophisticated world, such as we have today, where it is fashionable to presuppose that the grace of Christ obviates the need for personal good works, the answer to this question is critical, especially in the lives of those who seek to live up to God's expectations. Complete confidence in the sufficiency of grace, coupled with the allure and pressures of the world, might easily persuade many good, honest people to live up to a lower standard than has been established by the Lord. The teachings of James demonstrate that this problem was encountered in the early days of the Lord's church. Knowing the people's tendency to rely excessively on expressed faith in Christ to the exclusion of good works and obedience to the commandments, John diligently taught that works matter. Indeed, John clearly and deliberately spelled out the role of works, declaring that, in the resurrection, each of us will reap what we have sowed: "Marvel not at this: for the hour is coming, in the which all that are in the graves shall hear his voice, and shall come forth; they that have done good, unto the resurrection of life; and they that have done evil, unto the resurrection of damnation" (John 5:28–29).

"And I saw the dead, small and great, stand before God; and the books were opened: and another book was opened, which is the book of life: and the dead were judged out of those things which were written in the books, according to their works. And the sea gave up the dead which were in it; and death and hell delivered up the dead which were in them: and they were judged every man according to their works" (Revelation 20:12–13).

That an individual's eternal destiny depends on the works of this life is clearly evidenced by these two passages of scripture. This relationship between works and salvation is a core theme expounded by John. For example, the writings of John reveal that each person who is faithful in obedience "shall never see death," will receive "eternal life; and they shall never perish," "abideth for ever," and obtains the "right to the tree of life" (John 8:51; 10:28; 1 John 2:17; Revelation 22:14). Additionally, a close examination of John's teachings indicates that John viewed good works as an integral thread in the fabric of life, such that works permeate and affect almost every decision made by the faithful disciple of Christ. In fact, the Gospel of John even defines discipleship in terms of obedience and works: "Said Jesus to those Jews which believed on him, If ye continue in my word, then are ye my disciples indeed" (John 8:31). The following scriptures illustrate John's emphasis on works as the thread that binds the disciple to the Master:

1. "Verily, verily, I say unto you, If a man keep my saying, he shall never see death" (John 8:51).

2. "Now we know that God heareth not sinners: but if any man be a worshipper of God, and doeth his will, him he heareth" (John 9:31).

3. "My sheep hear my voice, and I know them, and they follow me: And I give unto them eternal life; and they shall never perish, neither shall any man pluck them out of my hand" (John 10:27–28).

4. "He that believeth on me, the works that I do shall he do also" (John 14:12).

5. "If ye love me, keep my commandments" (John 14:15).

6. "He that hath my commandments, and keepeth them, he it is that loveth me: and he that loveth me shall be loved of my Father, and I will love him, and will manifest myself to him" (John 14:21).

7. "Ye are my friends, if ye do whatsoever I command you" (John 15:14).

8. "He that doeth the will of God abideth for ever" (1 John 2:17).

9. "If ye know that he is righteous, ye know that every one that doeth righteousness is born of him" (1 John 2:29).

10. "And whatsoever we ask, we receive of him, because we keep his commandments, and do those things that are pleasing in his sight" (1 John 3:22).

11. "He that doeth good is of God: but he that doeth evil hath not seen God" (3 John 1:11).

12. "Blessed are the dead which die in the Lord from henceforth: Yea, saith the Spirit, that they may rest from their labours; and their works do follow them" (Revelation 14:13).

13. "Blessed are they that do his commandments, that they may have right to the tree of life, and may enter in through the gates into the city" (Revelation 22:14).

As the preceding scriptures indicate, John is adamant in the belief that it is through works that we develop an intimate relationship with the Lord. For instance, the simple act of believing on the "name of the Son of God" is manifest by, if not predicated on, doing his works (see John 14:12). To be born of Christ requires works of righteousness (see 1 John 2:29). Further, to be a friend of the Lord, the believer must do whatsoever the Lord commands (see John 15:14). Relatively few of those who profess modern discipleship associate obedience and good works with the price of friendship. John points out, however, that to love the Lord is to keep his commandments (see John 14:15). Of greater significance is the notion that both the Father and the Son reciprocate love to those who obey, even to the point that the Savior promises an individual manifestation to the obedient (see John 14:21). John teaches that as we build our relationship with the Father and the Son, we build our eternal mansion (see John 14:2–3). That is, while the Savior is the carpenter's square that is used to assure a properly framed and fitted dwelling, the future resident must—through the labor of good works—construct the edifice. In the end, the Savior's true disciples will enter into his city to rest from their labors and to dwell with him (see Matthew 11:28–29; Revelation 14:13; 24:14). Quite simply, John's teachings reveal him to be firm in his faith that to be of God, a person must do good works (see 3 John 1:11). Christ himself noted that even he, the Savior of the World, was not exempt from this divinely ordained mandate: "I must work the works of him that sent me" (John 9:4).

THE POWER OF GRACE AND WORKS COMBINED

John taught simply and beautifully that grace and works combine synergistically to create great power in the life of the true disciple. Without grace, the penalty of individual sin must be paid individually by all who sin, and that includes every person who lives to the age of accountability. We must remember that the penalty of sin is exclusion from God's kingdom. Without works, our relationship with the Savior must forever remain superficial, for it is through works that belief in, faith in, and love of God are manifest. If we are unwilling to draw near to Christ in this life, becoming his friends in mortality, then we would be terribly out of place living in his presence through endless eternities. Only at the intersection of grace and faith can we gain the power to enter into God's presence.

The inquisitive seeker after truth might readily ask two relevant questions: What exactly is this power that emerges when grace and works interact? and How does this power bring the disciple of Christ back into his presence? John helps us visualize both this great power and its influence in a few brief verses in the third chapter of John: "For God so loved the world, that he gave his only begotten Son, that whosoever believeth in him should not perish, but have everlasting life. For God sent not his Son into the world to condemn the world; but that the world through him might be saved. He that believeth on him is not condemned: but he that believeth not is condemned already, because he hath not believed in the name of the only begotten Son of God. And this is the condemnation, that light is come into the world, and men loved darkness rather than light, because their deeds were evil. For every one that doeth evil hateth the light, neither cometh to the light, lest his deeds should be reproved. But he that doeth truth cometh to the light, that his deeds may be made manifest, that they are wrought in God" (John 3:16–21).

John begins at the focal point of the great plan of happiness—the Savior's atoning sacrifice—and urges those who wish to obtain everlasting life to believe in the Son of God. Through the first two verses, John provides a foundation for confidence and a motivation for belief; after all, it is the love of the Father and the obedience of the Son that make the plan of salvation operative. If we cannot trust a Father and a Savior who both demonstrate unconditional love, then what else could motivate an anxious belief in Christ? With hope through Christ established and the seed of faith hopefully planted, John quickly moves forward to provide instruction that will lead to a bountiful harvest. John fully understood that faith is the principle of all action, the source of real intent, and thus informs us that it is by deeds that the seedling grows toward the light. To use John's words, "he that doeth truth cometh to the light" (John 3:21). Works that are wrought in God truly do make an eternal harvest possible. The message is clear: belief must become behavior before the disciple gains everlasting life.

A closer examination of the final three verses of the above passage of scripture brings further vital insight into the requirements for exaltation in the kingdom of God. John introduces the word *light,* indicating that individuals either hate the light and avoid it to hide their evil deeds or they come to the light by living the truth as it has come forth from God. What is this light that John speaks of that either attracts or repels? That John expects us to associate the light with the Lord Jesus Christ is manifest by John's description of the light in the first verses of his Gospel. In fact, John introduces the Savior as the "light of men" and the "true Light," noting that the "light shineth in darkness; and the darkness comprehended it not" (D&C 88:49). He further points out that John the Baptist "came for a witness, to bear witness of the Light" (John 1:17; see also vv. 4–5, 7, 9). To assure that all might fully comprehend the nature of the light, John quotes the Savior, who said, "I am the light of the world: he that followeth me shall not walk in darkness, but shall have the light of life" (John 8:12). Thus, when John says "he that doeth truth cometh to the light" (John 3:21), he is declaring that those who are obedient and fill their lives with good works come unto the Lord, Jesus Christ.

If we integrate the texts of John 3:21 and John 8:12, John's message might be rendered thus: "he that doeth truth becometh as the light, Jesus Christ." From this perspective, John's invitation is for each of us first to believe in Christ, next to behave as Christ behaved, and ultimately to become like Christ. If we follow the Savior and walk in his light, everlasting life is assured. President Ezra Taft Benson commented on this formula, stating, "Thoughts lead to acts, acts lead to habits, habits lead to character—and our character will determine our eternal destiny."[2] What we become through individual belief and behavior—relying on the Savior's atoning sacrifice to remove the penalty of sin—will determine whether we obtain entrance into the kingdom of God. John teaches that the power of grace and works combined is the power of transformation that can and must occur in the life of every true disciple. As this power is tapped, the disciple of Christ begins to view the Lord's commandments, and the works that result from obedience to them, as an invitation to blessings and an opportunity not only to draw closer to the Master but to become as he is.

Having been instructed by John, we can return to the metaphor of life's journey along the strait and narrow path with a brighter understanding of what we must do to travel safely to our intended destination: the kingdom of God. We now know that works are needed to walk after the Lord and follow in his footsteps. It is by works that we traverse the long miles that make up life's journey, until through a lifetime of faithful obedience to the road signs that singularly mark the safe route, we arrive at the desired destination. Unfortunately, upon arrival, we find that the city gate is closed. A large and hefty toll is required for entry, but we have expended all of our money in making the journey, wasting precious resources on the occasional detour or the costly sightseeing trip. Such is the price of sin—it leaves the sinner without the resources needed to gain entry into the celestial kingdom. Because entry is precluded unless the toll is paid, we are completely helpless at this point in our journey. We must rely on the grace afforded by the Savior's atoning sacrifice to pay the price of admission; otherwise, the journey and all of the effort expended are wasted. Of course, the role of grace extends beyond merely paying the toll. After all, the highway, the roadmap, the signposts, and the light by which we travel are provided by the Lord, as are all other needful things used in the journey. The good news is that by combining grace and works, we not only begin the trip with hope but are able to endure the hazards and the perils of a lifelong journey that will take us back to our Father's presence.

John's Invitation to "Know" God

Through his teachings on grace and works, John the Beloved has provided keen and pertinent insight into the great query: What must a man do to be saved in the kingdom of God? (see Acts 16:30). John clearly answers that both grace and works are needful, that working together, grace and works combine to meet the necessary and sufficient conditions for entry into the city of God. John goes so far as to discuss the roles that grace and works play in making the kingdom of God accessible to all who will diligently seek it. He even turns the attention of the questioner from the original query to the supernal invitation to come unto Christ through faith and works. Having issued this great invitation, John is not satisfied that his work is done; rather, he is determined to testify of Christ and him crucified to all who will listen with the least bit of interest. John is intent on taking this spark of interest and magnifying it into the bright fire of testimony.

Borrowing from another scripture about other dedicated missionaries, we might say that John was "desirous that salvation should be declared to every creature, for [John] could not bear that any human soul should perish; yea, even the very thoughts that any soul should endure endless torment did cause [John] to quake and tremble" (Mosiah 28:3). This burning desire to bless all of God's children led John to seek more earnestly that all might find and walk in the path that leads to everlasting life. To this end, John quoted the Savior who defined eternal life by saying, "And this is life eternal, that they might know thee the only true God, and Jesus Christ, whom thou hast sent" (John 17:3). From this simple statement, we learn that to know God is to qualify for eternal life and thereby obtain the "crown of righteousness" (2 Timothy 4:8) spoken of by Paul.

Because the word *know* has multiple meanings in our language and culture, it is useful to look to John for help in understanding the word and its true importance to our eternal welfare. In the modern world, "to know" is generally associated with the acquisition of facts. To know God would therefore connote that a person had obtained a factual or practical understanding of God and his true nature.[3] Although this "intellectual know" is certainly a prerequisite to real faith and confidence in God and his plan of salvation, it does not require any alteration of an individual's conduct, for the "intellectual know" can easily be reduced to a simple awareness of facts. John's use of the word *know* clearly suggests that the disciple of Christ must graduate from the "intellectual know" to the "experiential know." That is, once we become aware that God exists, we must gain personal experience with God and his laws in order to qualify as a true disciple.

In speaking of the "experiential know," John recognized two distinct connotations. First, an experiential knowledge derives directly from our behavior, accumulating over time as we gain knowledge through experience. The Savior emphasized that behavior is an antecedent to knowledge by extending the following invitation: "If any man will do his will, he shall know of the doctrine, whether it be of God, or whether I speak of myself" (John 7:17). In this light, to know God requires submission to God's will and obedience to God's commandments. John states explicitly that this type of knowledge is a requirement for exaltation: "And hereby we do know that we know him, if we keep his commandments. He that saith, I know him, and keepeth not his commandments, is a liar, and the truth is not in him" (1 John 2:3–4). Our behavior appears either to close or to widen the gap in our knowledge of God. Second, an experiential knowledge suggests personal acquaintance or familiarity. The Savior's reference to himself as the Good Shepherd places experiential knowledge in proper context: "I am the good shepherd, and know my sheep, and am known of mine" (John 10:14). Individual acquaintance is clearly crucial to the relationship between the Savior and his sheep. At another time, the Savior reemphasized the importance of personal familiarity to experiential knowledge: "And the sheep hear his voice:

and he calleth his own sheep by name, and leadeth them out. And when he putteth forth his own sheep, he goeth before them, and the sheep follow him: for they know his voice" (John 10:3–4). These sayings of the Savior, as recorded by John, illustrate that to know God requires an individual acquaintance with him that comes only from following in his footsteps and obeying his commandments.

Even as intellectual knowledge precedes experiential knowledge, John encourages the disciple of Christ to go beyond experiential knowledge. That is, John champions the notion that complete obedience to the Lord's commandments—walking even as he walked—leads us to become like Christ. John stated, "Whoso keepeth his [Christ's] word, in him verily is the love of God perfected: hereby know we that we are in him" (1 John 2:5). The sublime message is that obedience, if it is complete, leads to oneness with Christ. John further emphasized that as God's children, we can become as he is: "Beloved, now are we the sons of God, and it doth not yet appear what we shall be: but we know that, when he shall appear, we shall be like him; for we shall see him as he is" (1 John 3:2). John goes on to point out the means by which this oneness is achieved: "And every man that hath this hope in him purifieth himself, even as he [Christ] is pure" (1 John 3:3). As this purification occurs, the unity and oneness spoken of by the Savior in his great intercessory prayer come to pass: "Neither pray I for these alone, but for them also which shall believe on me through their word; that they all may be one; as thou, Father, [art] in me, and I in thee, that they also may be one in us" (John 17:20–21). That we might understand that we need to seek after this level of knowledge—a knowledge that comes from oneness—was not merely John's desire but was also the Lord's prayer. Indeed, Christ was willing to atone for our sins and be crucified that we might gain this "essential knowledge." John thus rephrased and reiterated his lofty and inspiring invitation to come unto Christ and become as he is.

John's teachings reveal the strait and narrow path back to Heavenly Father's presence in its true character and dimensions. By so doing, John makes our journey more secure by showing how faith and works combine to help us come to know the Lord as we become more like Him. He places the spotlight not only on the path but on the destination—a Christlike life.

NOTES

1. Neal A. Maxwell, *Men and Women of Christ* (Salt Lake City: Bookcraft, 1991), 103.

2. Ezra Taft Benson, *The Teachings of Ezra Taft Benson* (Salt Lake City: Bookcraft, 1988), 275.

3. Merriam-Webster, *Webster's Ninth New Collegiate Dictionary* (Springfield: Merriam-Webster, 1988), s.v. "know."

CHAPTER FIVE

John's Prophetic Vision of God and the Lamb

JOHN L. FOWLES

To understand the significance of John's vision of God and the Lamb in chapters 4 and 5 of the book of Revelation, we have to understand how God called prophets, as recorded in the Old Testament as well as in other ancient literature. The scriptural motif, or pattern, by which prophets were called of God, as it appears throughout ancient writings, may be considered a test of prophetic authenticity. Biblical scholars use several different terms to identify and classify these prophetic scriptural experiences, such as "throne theophanies," "call narratives" or "prophetic motifs."[1] The pattern unfolds in the prophetic calls of Isaiah, Ezekiel, Jeremiah, Micaiah, Amos, and Lehi. John the Revelator's prophetic call from God also fits the pattern of the ancient call narrative. In addition, Joseph Smith's vision of the Father and the Son in the spring of 1820 parallels closely John's vision of God and the Lamb. Joseph Smith's own prophetic authenticity is clear when we examine his experiences in light of the ancient pattern.

PROPHETIC PREPARATION

Isaiah was called by God to be a prophet in the year King Uzziah died—about 740 B.C. Isaiah said he saw in vision, "the Lord sitting upon a throne, high and lifted up, and his train filled the temple"

John L. Fowles is an instructor at the institute of religion at Utah State University in Logan, Utah.

(Isaiah 6:1). Isaiah then describes his vision of the seraphim who worshiped the Lord as they cried, "Holy, holy, holy, is the Lord of hosts" (Isaiah 6:3). Isaiah next expresses his unworthiness to have such a vision because he was a man of "unclean lips" (Isaiah 6:5). As will be seen with other narratives of prophetic calls, Isaiah is purified when one of the seraphim takes a coal from off the altar, lays it upon Isaiah's mouth, and says that his iniquity is taken away (see Isaiah 6:6–7). It then appears that Isaiah is taken back to, or sees in vision, the premortal council in heaven in which he was foreordained to be a prophet. Isaiah, like the Savior, says in that setting, "Here am I; send me" (Isaiah 6:8). The prophetic call continues when Isaiah is told to preach to a group of people who will not understand and will eventually reject his message (Isaiah 6:9–10).

Before Ezekiel is called to instruct his people, he also sees the heavens opened, and therein he sees the throne of God (see Ezekiel 1:26). The record includes Ezekiel's receiving a book or roll which he was commanded to eat (see Ezekiel 3:1–7). Like other books in the pattern of the call narrative, this book contains "lamentations, and mourning, and woe" (Ezekiel 2:10). Ezekiel, like Isaiah, is then sent to the rebellious children of Israel who had transgressed the commandments of God (see Ezekiel 2:3; 4:7).

Jeremiah asks his readers to test whether a person is a prophet by asking whether he has "stood in the counsel of the Lord" (Jeremiah 23:18). Biblical scholars believe the English word *counsel* in this verse should be translated more correctly *council,* deriving from the Hebrew word *sode,* which has the meaning of the heavenly council of the Gods.[2] Jeremiah is saying that if anyone has been truly called of God, they would have had the experience of standing in the "heavenly council of the Lord" and hearing his voice declare their mission.

Micaiah, another Old Testament figure, also experienced a "throne theophany" when he was called to be a prophet. He said, "I saw the Lord sitting on his throne, and all the host of heaven standing by him on his right hand and on his left" (1 Kings 22:19). The Old Testament, as well as other noncanonical literature, records the experiences of prophets in similar ways. Amos states, "Surely the Lord God will do nothing, but he revealeth his secret unto his servants the prophets" (Amos 3:7). Interestingly, in this verse the word which is translated as "secret" comes from the original Hebrew word *sode* which, as already noted, can be translated "council." Joseph Schultz, a non-LDS scholar, summarizes the prophetic call pattern by saying those called of God always seem to have an ascent to heaven, enter a heavenly palace or temple, are received by a high god in his assembly, have a period of purification, and are anointed and given robes or heavenly garments. They then are handed a heavenly book or heavenly tablet bearing revelation, are called with names of honor, are initiated into the heavenly secrets, have an enthronement on God the Father's throne, and are sent forth with a commission or message to instruct the generation.[3]

In the Book of Mormon, Lehi's call from God to lead his family was first prefaced by a "throne theophany" in the first chapter of First Nephi. Nephi tells us that his father, Lehi, was reflecting upon the Lord when he saw "God sitting upon his throne, surrounded with numberless concourses of angels in the attitude of singing and praising their God" (1 Nephi 1:8). Following the ancient pattern, Nephi records Lehi's receiving a book, preaching its message, and being mocked and then the people's seeking the life of Lehi because he testified of their wickedness (see 1 Nephi 1:9–20). Hugh Nibley summarized the prophetic call of Lehi this way:

"The opening chapter of the Book of Mormon emerges as the perfect model and type of those more specialized apocalypses or testaments attributed to individuals that are now taking up their position in the growing procession of early Jewish and Christian Apocrypha. The standard scenario which they follow is the story of the righteous man, distressed by the evils of his time and deeply concerned for the future of his people, for whom he weeps and prays until one day he is carried away in a vision in which he makes a celestial journey culminating with the view of God upon his throne; on his journey he learns the plan of salvation as well as the secrets of the universe, and receives a call, to teach and admonish God's children on earth. Returning to earth, he first bears witness of divine providence to his immediate family, and bestows patriarchal blessings and prophetic warnings on his sons (hence the designation of his story as a "testament"), and then goes forth among the people to preach repentance and warn of judgments to come (that makes the account an apocalypse). Usually his message is rejected and he with a faithful band retires from the scene as destruction descends upon the wicked.

Today we have testaments and apocalypses bearing the name of almost every patriarch, prophet, and apostle from Adam on down, some of them very old, and all of them connected in with each other and with the Bible at crucial points. Hence, we can say without hesitation that the first chapter of the Book of Mormon, the testament of Lehi, has the authenticity of a truly ancient pseudepigraphic writing stamped all over it. It is a well-nigh perfect example of the genre."[4]

Joseph Smith's own story reflects the ancient prophetic motif. He saw the Father and the Son and he received the plates from the angel Moroni before he was sent to instruct his generation. Joseph even specifically records other visions in which he saw God sitting on his throne (see D&C 76:20–21; 137:2–3). On one occasion, Joseph Smith, while reflecting upon the calling of prophets, said, "Every man who has a calling to minister to the inhabitants of the world was ordained to that very purpose in the Grand Council of heaven before this world was. I suppose I was ordained to this very office in that Grand Council."[5]

THE PROPHETIC CALL OF JOHN THE REVELATOR

The Lord declared to the children of Israel, "If there be a prophet among you, I the Lord will make myself known unto him in a vision, and will speak unto him in a dream" (Numbers 12:6). Joseph Smith confirmed this idea when he stated that "John upon the isle of Patmos, saw the same things concerning the last days, which Enoch saw."[6] The apostle John's vision of God and the Lamb fits the ancient pattern of how prophets were called before being sent to the people with a commission or message to instruct their generation. The book seen by John in vision was given, literally, into the hands of Joseph by the angel of the Restoration. Oliver Cowdery wrote that a part of the book was sealed, which, "said he (Moroni), contains the same revelation which was given to John upon the isle of Patmos, and when the people of the Lord are prepared, and found worthy, then it will be unfolded unto them."[7] Joseph Smith eloquently stated on another occasion, "John had the curtains of heaven withdrawn, and by vision looked through the dark vista of future ages, and contemplated events that should transpire throughout every subsequent period of time, until the final winding up scene—while he gazed upon the glories of the eternal world, saw an innumerable company of angels and heard the voice of God—it was in the Spirit, on the Lord's day, unnoticed and unobserved by the world."[8]

As Joseph Smith taught, the book of Revelation records John seeing an open door in heaven and being commanded to come up to see things which would come in the future (see Revelation 4:1).[9] John, like previous prophets, saw a throne set in heaven and "one sat on the throne" (Revelation 4:2). John was privileged to have a vision of God the Father, who seldom appears in the scriptures and usually only to introduce his Son.[10] The first verse in the book of Revelation that specifically says God is on the throne in heaven is in chapter 7. The great multitude, who will come out of the great tribulation period in the last days, cry with a loud voice, "saying, Salvation to our God which sitteth upon the throne, and unto the Lamb" (Revelation 7:10).

According to Richard D. Draper, "John's description . . . keeps the person of God ever hidden. He makes no attempt to portray God's features or form."[11] This is such a sacred experience that John was not allowed to record certain details. Nevertheless, John was permitted to describe God's brilliance, which was "like a jasper and a sardine stone: and there was a rainbow round about the throne, in sight like unto an emerald" (Revelation 4:3). The interpretation of the symbolism of these precious stones varies according to scholars. Robert H. Mounce, for example, states that "various meanings have been attached to the different stones. Jasper suggests such qualities as majesty, holiness, or purity. Sardius is often interpreted as wrath or judgment, and the emerald as mercy."[12] John's description of the throne of God reminds us of Joseph Smith's revelation describing God's throne and his presence as a source of light, "which light proceedeth forth from the presence of God to fill the immensity of space—the light which is in all things, which giveth life to all things, which is the law by which all things are governed, even the power of God who sitteth upon his throne, who is in the bosom of eternity, who is in the midst of all things" (D&C 88:12–13). As the Psalmist said, "Bless the Lord . . . who coverest thyself with light as with a garment: who stretchest out the heavens like a curtain" (Psalm 104:1–2).

John's throne theophany continues as he next sees a "sea of glass" before the throne of God (Revelation 4:6). Joseph Smith interpreted this symbol as the earth in its sanctified, immortal, and eternal state (see D&C 77:1). Another revelation tells us that the sanctified and immortal state or destiny of this earth is to be a celestial kingdom symbolized as a great Urim and Thummim (see D&C 130:8–9). This earth as a "sea of glass" will be made like unto a crystal where revelation will be given to the inhabitants who have the privilege of living thereon (D&C 130:9). John, like prophets before him, saw the destiny of the earth from an eternal perspective.[13]

THE SEALED BOOK

After having the vision of the one sitting on the throne, John sees a sealed book in the right hand of him that sat on the throne (see Revelation 5:1). As we have said, such a book usually contains warnings or other instructions received by those called of God. The book is sealed with seven seals. John's sealed book is specifically interpreted as containing "the revealed will, mysteries, and the works of God; the hidden things of his economy concerning this earth during the seven thousand years of its continuance, or its temporal existence" (D&C 77:6). Because we know from Joseph Smith that John saw what Enoch saw, it is instructive to compare the sealed book spoken of in Doctrine and Covenants 77 (which concerns John's vision) with Enoch's throne theophany found in the Pseudepigrapha book of 1 Enoch 81:1–4. Enoch's account of the sealed book, or written tablet, says:

"Then he said unto me, 'Enoch, look at the tablet(s) of heaven; read what is written upon them and understand (each element on them) one by one.' So I looked at the tablet(s) of heaven, read all the writing (on them), and came to understand everything. I read that book and all the deeds of humanity and all the children of the flesh upon the earth for all the generations of the world. At that very moment, I blessed the Great Lord, the King of Glory for ever, for he has created all the phenomena in the world. I praised the Lord because of his patience; and I wept on account of the children of the people upon the earth."[14]

Enoch weeps on account of the information he received in his vision, just as John weeps because no one is worthy to open the sealed book (see Revelation 5:4). No wonder these prophets weep! These tablets or scrolls are always books of lamentation and woe.

Even the book Lehi read during his vision told of the abomination and destruction of Jerusalem (see 1 Nephi 1:12–13). John weeps not only because at the moment no one was worthy to open the sealed book but because the seals that follow contain the awful destruction that lies ahead for this earth before the Lord returns.[15]

THE OPENING OF THE SEALED BOOK

As John is weeping over the book, one of the elders by the throne tells him to weep not because "the Lion of the tribe of Juda, the Root of David, hath prevailed to open the book and to loose the seven seals thereof" (Revelation 5:5). Both the Lion of Juda and the Root of David are descriptions of Jesus himself (see Revelation 22:16). Jesus is the one worthy or holy to open the seals of human history through his atonement.[16]

The imagery of John's vision shifts at this point from Jesus as the Lion of Judah, or Root of David, to Jesus as the Lamb of God (see Revelation 5:6). The book of Revelation uses the Greek word *arnion,* or "little lamb," to describe Jesus in a sacrificial way. The word is used twenty-eight times in the book of Revelation to describe Christ and only once elsewhere in the New Testament.[17] Jesus is the sacrificial Lamb. The Greek text for "had been slain" is in the perfect tense, which takes on the meaning of past, present, and future (Revelation 5:6). Jesus' sacrifice is meaningful to those in the past, the present, and the future. His atonement will release the seals of the sealed book, "for all history pivots on this one act. It alone allowed for the complete fulfillment of the Father's will."[18]

John' s vision concludes with the four beasts, twenty-four elders, and thousands of angels singing a new song of praise to the Lamb, who was worthy to take the book and open the seals thereof (see Revelation 5:7–14). Indeed every creature was heard by John saying, "Blessing, and honour, and glory, and power, be unto him that sitteth upon the throne (God), and unto the Lamb for ever and ever" (Revelation 5:13).

PRAISE TO GOD AND THE LAMB

The distinction between God and the Lamb appears again in chapter 7: "For the Lamb which is in the midst of the throne shall feed them, and shall lead them unto living fountains of waters: and God shall wipe away all tears from their eyes" (Revelation 7:17).[19] Joseph Smith's visions of God and the Lamb align themselves with John's vision. For example, Joseph Smith and Sidney Rigdon said they "beheld the glory of the Son, on the right hand of the Father, and received of his fulness; And saw the holy angels, and them who are sanctified before his throne, worshiping God, and the Lamb" (D&C 76:20–21). During the dedication of the Kirtland Temple, Joseph Smith prayed "that we may mingle our voices with those bright, shining seraphs around thy throne, with acclamations of praise, singing Hosanna to God and the Lamb!" (D&C 109:79).

SIGNIFICANCE OF JOHN'S VISION

John's vision of God and the Lamb fits the ancient pattern of how God called his prophets. His vision in chapters 4 and 5 of the book of Revelation is consistent with the test of prophetic authenticity. Joseph Smith's own story parallels the prophetic motif. John and Joseph Smith experienced similar visions. John received a sealed book and Joseph received the gold plates, a part of which were sealed. They each saw Heavenly Father and his Son Jesus Christ sitting on the throne surrounded by sanctified beings giving them honor and glory forever and ever, in preparation for their prophetic service to the world.

NOTES

1. See Blake T. Osler, "The Throne-Theophany Prophetic Commission in 1 Nephi," *BYU Studies* 26 (Fall 1986): 67–95; John W. Welch, "The Calling of a Prophet," *The Book of Mormon: First Nephi, the Doctrinal Foundation,* ed. Monte S. Nyman and Charles D. Tate Jr. (Provo: Brigham Young University Religious Studies Center, 1988), 35–54; Stephen Ricks, "The Narrative Call Pattern in the Prophetic Commission of Enoch (Moses 6)," *BYU Studies* 26 (Fall 1986): 97–105; Joseph F. McConkie, "Premortal Existence, Foreordinations and Heavenly Councils," in *Apocryphal Writings and the Latter-day Saints,* ed. C. Wilford Griggs, vol. 13 of the Religious Studies Monograph Series (Provo: Religious Studies Center, Brigham Young University), 182.

2. See McConkie, "Premortal Existence," 185.

3. See McConkie, "Premortal Existence," 182.

4. Hugh Nibley, *Nibley on the Timely and the Timeless,* vol. 1 of the Religious Studies Monograph Series (Provo: Brigham Young University Religious Studies Center, 1992), 3–4.

5. Joseph Smith, *Teachings of the Prophet Joseph Smith,* sel. Joseph Fielding Smith (Salt Lake City: Deseret Book, 1976), 365.

6. Smith, *Teachings,* 84. Compare Enoch's own description in 1 Enoch 81:1–4.

7. Dean C. Jessee, ed., *The Papers of Joseph Smith,* 3 vols. (Salt Lake City: Deseret Book, 1989–), 1:54.

8. Smith, *Teachings,* 247.

9. The Greek word meaning "come up hither" in this verse is an imperative command. The message John is going to receive is extremely important. Joseph Smith said a vision from God was so important that "could you gaze into heaven five minutes, you would know more than you would by reading all that ever was written on the subject." Smith, *Teachings,* 324.

10. See, for example, Matthew 3:17; 17:5; Joseph Smith–History 1:17.

11. Richard D. Draper, *Opening the Seven Seals: The Visions of John the Revelator* (Salt Lake City: Deseret Book, 1991), 45.

12. Robert H. Mounce, *The Book of Revelation: The New International Commentary on the New Testament* (Grand Rapids, Mich.: Eerdmans, 1977), 135.

13. Compare Moses' vision of the world and the ends thereof (Moses 1:8, 27, 28).

14. 1 Enoch 81:1–4, as found in James H. Charlesworth, *Apocalyptic Testaments,* vol. 1 of *The Old Testament Pseudepigrapha* (Garden City, N.Y.: Doubleday, 1983), 59.

15. Revelation 6–9 describes this period of time.

16. The Greek word used in the text of Revelation is *agious,* which means, literally, "holy" or "worthy."

17. See John 21:15; Revelation 5:6, 8, 12–13; 6:1, 16; 7:9–10, 14, 17; 12:11; 13:8, 11; 14:1, 4, 10; 15:3; 17:14; 19:7; 21:14, 22–23, 27; 22:1, 3.

18. Draper, *Opening the Seven Seals,* 57.

19. See also Revelation 14:4, 10; 21:22; 22:1, 3, to see the distinction.

CHAPTER SIX

JOHN'S REVELATION
AND THE RESTORATION OF
THE GOSPEL

ANDREW H. HEDGES

Shortly after publishing the Book of Mormon and organizing The Church of Jesus Christ of Latter-day Saints, Joseph Smith embarked on a project that was to occupy some of his time for the rest of his life: the translation of the Bible. By 7 March 1831, Joseph had worked his way through Genesis 24:42a[1] and had restored, in the process, the book of Moses as contained in the Pearl of Great Price. On that date Joseph received a revelation concerning the last days and the second coming of the Savior. This revelation also contained a charge for him to start translating the New Testament, through which, the Lord told Joseph, more information about the last days and the Second Coming would be made known. The Prophet and Sidney Rigdon began their new project the next day, which resulted not only in the clarification of scores of difficult passages in the Gospels and the Pauline epistles but in the reception of several important revelations that have since been included in the Doctrine and Covenants. The best known of these is the vision of the celestial, terrestrial, and telestial glories (D&C 76). Latter-day Saints have been quick to recognize how revolutionary this revelation was for Joseph Smith's time and how unique our understanding of heaven continues to be when compared with that of other Christian denominations.

Sections 74, 77, and 86 of the Doctrine and Covenants also had

Andrew H. Hedges is an assistant professor of Church history and doctrine at Brigham Young University.

their genesis in Joseph Smith's translation of the Bible. They, too, contain revolutionary ideas about the scriptures and the topics they address, although we may not fully appreciate their significance or realize how revolutionary they are when compared with the way Joseph Smith's contemporaries interpreted and understood the biblical passages upon which they are based. That is especially true of section 77, in which the Lord clarifies several obscure passages in the Revelation of John. In the Prophet's time, scholars and laymen alike dedicated much time and energy to understanding John's revelation, leaving us with a rich record of their ideas concerning the meaning of all that John saw. Significantly, although not unexpectedly, the interpretations the Lord gave through Joseph Smith differ radically from those being offered by his contemporaries.[2] By comparing the Lord's commentary on John's revelation with three highly regarded biblical commentaries that were circulating in America in Joseph Smith's time, we will better understand the role this revelation played in the restoration of precious truths and doctrines to the earth, as well as better appreciate how new and revolutionary these doctrines were on the early American religious scene.

NINETEENTH-CENTURY BIBLICAL COMMENTATORS AND JOSEPH SMITH

The American public's interest in apocalyptic and millennial themes rose to fever pitch during Joseph Smith's lifetime, propelling the Revelation of John—recognized as the primary source of information on those topics—to an unprecedented level of popularity. Those interested in learning how the best minds in England and America interpreted the Revelation had recourse to several excellent commentaries, whose authors systematically examined John's revelation verse by verse and provided their readers with hundreds of pages of notes. Three commentaries commonly used by scholars, ministers, and churchgoers alike in early America were the multivolume sets by Thomas Scott, Adam Clarke, and Matthew Henry. All three authors were university trained scholars; reading only a page or two of their work on the Revelation shows that each was bringing several years' worth of intense research to his study. Scott, for example, makes liberal use of the original Greek in his efforts to arrive at the Revelator's meaning. Clarke goes one step further to use several Hebrew, Greek, Latin, and Syriac versions and manuscripts.[3] All three draw freely on the insights of earlier commentators in their efforts to provide their readers with the most plausible, up-to-date interpretation of the scriptures, and all three commentaries had gone through several revisions and editions by Joseph Smith's time.

Although these commentaries differ on many points contained in the Revelation, there are, nevertheless, many topics upon which they are agreed. All, for example, see many of the various events outlined in the Revelation as having been fulfilled already. Henry sees the entire book as foretelling events that "should come to pass not only *surely*, but *shortly*" after they were revealed to John, meaning the Roman sack of Jerusalem.[4] Clarke views the four angels holding the four winds of the earth, the sealing of the 144,000, and other events of chapter 7 as taking place just before the fall of Jerusalem as well,[5] and he sees the proliferation of locusts from out of the bottomless pit (Revelation 9) as referring to either the Romans or the Muslims.[6] Scott differs slightly by placing the events outlined in Revelation 7 at the time of Constantine[7] but agrees with Clarke that the locusts of chapter 9 refer to "the rise and progress of Mohammed and his successors."[8] Whatever the differences between the three, the commentators agree that the events predicted in chapters 7 and 9 were fulfilled a thousand or more years ago, no more recently than the seventh and eighth centuries after Christ.

Given these authors' unanimity on this point, it is noteworthy that Doctrine and Covenants 77 places the fulfillment of the events outlined in these two chapters much later. When Joseph Smith asks when "the things spoken of in [chapter 7 are] to be accomplished," the Lord responds that "they are to be accomplished in the sixth thousand years, or the opening of the sixth seal" (D&C 77:10). That reference is to the book, which John had seen earlier, that was sealed with seven seals; each seal, the Lord informs us, represents one thousand years of the earth's "temporal existence" (D&C 77:6). The Lord is telling the Prophet that these events will be accomplished sometime during the thousand years prior to the Millennium, and his interpretation of the angels and 144,000 strongly suggests that these were events to be fulfilled as part of the restoration of the gospel in the latter days.[9] The Lord then tells Joseph that the events outlined in chapter 9 would take place "after the opening of the seventh seal, before the coming of Christ" (D&C 77:13), implying, again, some time in the future, immediately preceding the Savior's second coming. Both chapters, in short, deal with events of the last days, some of which were taking shape in Joseph's generation, others of which had yet to transpire.

The same holds true for the events of Revelation 8. Here John sees "seven angels which stood before God," to whom were given seven trumpets (v. 2). The angels then blew their trumpets one at a time; great destruction accompanied the sounding of each horn. The commentators see this as referring to the "confusion, commotions, distresses, and miseries" destined to befall Jerusalem,[10] or perhaps to the prayers of the early Christians calling for the destruction of Rome.[11] Either way, they agree that it was speaking of something that was to happen in John's future but which had already happened long before the nineteenth century. In contrast, again, Joseph sees the chapter as referring to events still to take place, prophetic for the nineteenth century as well as for John's time. Rather than understanding the trumpets as a prelude to the destruction of Jerusalem or Rome centuries ago, Joseph Smith understood them to refer to the Lord's "sanctify[ing] the earth, and complet[ing] the salvation of man . . . in the beginning of the seventh thousand years," preparatory to his coming in his glory (D&C 77:12). The point is this: while the Prophet Joseph's contemporaries were using the Revelation as a window on the past, he was using it as a vision of the future.

In making these comparisons, it is not uncommon to see the commentators treat as relatively insignificant some aspect of John's vision that Joseph Smith and the Lord found worthy of much discussion. The commentators' and the Lord's review of Revelation 4:6 is a good example. In this verse, John, enwrapped in a vision of heaven, finishes describing God's throne by noting that "before the throne there was a sea of glass like unto crystal: and in the midst of the throne, and round about the throne, were four beasts full of eyes before and behind." The commentators treat this part of the vision variously but routinely and unimaginatively. Henry sees the sea of glass as a purifier in which "all those must be washed that are admitted into the gracious presence of God," and the four beasts as signifying "the ministers of the gospel."[12] Clarke sees John's "sea of glass" as referring to "a spacious lucid plain around the throne, from which fiery coruscations were continually emitted,"[13] and the beasts referring to the *"four standards,* or *ensigns,* of the *four divisions* of the tribes in the Israelitish camp," or perhaps to the four Evangelists (Matthew, Mark, Luke, and John) of Christian tradition.[14] Neither Henry nor Clarke, significantly, say anything about the beasts' eyes. Scott interprets the "sea of glass" to be the "'fountain opened for sin and uncleanness,' in which all the spiritual priesthood must wash," and the beasts as representing, "undeniably, . . . some part of the church of redeemed sinners."[15] Scott alone takes notice of the beasts' eyes, which represented, for him, the saints' "vigilance, circumspection, attention . . . and jealous diligence in searching their own hearts."[16] The variations in the interpretations, although present, are small and inconsequential, with the authors agreeing that the "sea of glass" had something to do with purifying the people of God and that the beasts simply represented some of those purified people at various points in sacred history.

In contrast, Joseph and the Lord devote four lengthy verses in Doctrine and Covenants 77—more than one-fourth of the verses in the section—and several verses in section 130 to explaining the sea of glass, the beasts, and their eyes. Far from representing a means of purification, the sea of glass that John saw, Joseph learned, was the earth itself, "in its sanctified, immortal, and eternal state" (D&C 77:1), functioning as a "Urim and Thummim to the inhabitants who dwell thereon, whereby all things pertaining to an inferior kingdom . . . will be manifest to those who dwell on it" (D&C 130:9). The doctrinal implications of these brief statements were revolutionary. The idea that the earth itself is progressing, and will be the eternal dwelling place of the righteous, was unheard of in Joseph's time. Heaven, where God lived and where the righteous would go, was a place above the earth, far removed from the corrupting influences of a physical world. Similarly, the Urim and Thummim was a thing of the past, an instrument used in ancient Israel, not a means of learning in the future. These ideas simply were not part of Joseph's environment—let alone part of the exegetical tradition of the learned divines—and it is small wonder that they do not appear in the commentaries of the time.[17]

Joseph's understanding and interpretation of the four beasts were as unique for his time and place as his views on the sea of glass were.

The beasts were, according to the prophet, "figurative expressions, used . . . in describing heaven, the paradise of God, the happiness of man, and of *beasts,* and of *creeping things,* and of the *fowls of the air* . . . shown to John, to represent the glory of the classes of beings . . . in the enjoyment of their eternal felicity" (D&C 77:2–3). The eyes were "a representation of light and knowledge," suggesting that these various "classes of beings" were "full of knowledge" (D&C 77:3–4). This is a much longer list of what the beasts symbolize than the commentators gave, and it includes the idea that animals as well as people have immortal souls capable of instruction. It also suggests that they, as well as we, will have the opportunity to spend eternity in a state of happiness. Again, this was a novel idea for Joseph Smith's time, and it is instructive to note that two of the commentators, Scott and Clarke, go out of their way to say that the beasts of the vision refer only to people. The whole notion that an animal might actually dwell in heaven "sounds oddly," as Clarke put it,[18] while Scott emphasized that in order to "preserve the truth of the emblem," it was necessary to see the beasts representing "some part of the church of redeemed sinners, *of the human race.*"[19]

The "little book" John sees in the hand of an angel, which he is commanded to eat, elicited a variety of responses from Joseph's learned contemporaries. Henry, whose commentary was the most dated by Joseph's time, sees it as the book John had seen earlier sealed with the seven seals but whose contents, which detailed the destruction about to befall Jerusalem, were now being made known to the apostle.[20] Clarke strikes a far more cautious pose. "Who knows what it means?" he writes. "I do not understand these prophecies; therefore, I do not take upon me to explain them."[21] Daring go no further than to suggest that it means, "probably, some *design* of God long concealed, but now about to be made manifest," Clarke goes on to excoriate those who have been so bold as to suggest a specific interpretation for the "little book" and other phenomena of the Revelation and concludes that "many learned men have mistaken their way here."[22]

Scott, in contrast to Henry, sees the little book as "distinct from the larger book before mentioned" with the seven seals. He introduces his readers to the common idea that the little book contained verbatim various subsequent chapters of the Revelation and offers his own opinion that it was composed of the first fourteen verses of chapter 11, with its discussion of the famous "two witnesses."[23]

Joseph Smith's interpretation of the little book is distinct from all these traditions. Eschewing Clarke's overt cautiousness, the Prophet assigns a very specific meaning to the book, one that is radically different from those proposed by Henry and Scott. "We are to understand that it [the book] was a mission, and an ordinance," Joseph Smith recorded, "for him [John] to gather the tribes of Israel; behold, this is Elias, who, as it is written, must come and restore all things" (D&C 77:14). This mission of John's was a work with which Joseph was well acquainted. Shortly after Oliver Cowdery began working as his scribe in April 1829, Joseph had received a revelation making it clear that John had been translated, with the intent that he would "prophesy before nations, kindreds, tongues and people" until the Lord should come in his glory (D&C 7:3). A little more than a year later, at a conference held in Kirtland, Joseph told those assembled that "John the Revelator was then among the ten tribes of Israel who had been led away by Salmanaser King of israel, to prepare them for their return, from their Long dispersion, to again possess the land of their fathers."[24] With this background, Joseph was able to identify the little book that had excited such speculation over the years as the moment John's call was issued—a call that dealt with events to transpire centuries after it was given, rather than with events surrounding the ancient civilizations of the apostle's day.

Joseph's contemporaries also interpreted the "two witnesses" in a variety of different ways. Henry merely recounts the familiar story of their prophesying, death, and resurrection and seems to suggest that they represent the progress and ultimate triumph of the Lord's church over Satan's forces.[25] Clarke, true to form, pleads his and others' ignorance of the matter. "This is extremely obscure," he says of the passage. "The conjectures of interpreters are as unsatisfactory as they are endless on this point. . . . Those who wish to be amused, or bewildered, may have recourse both to ancients and moderns on this subject."[26]

Without detailing the variety of interpretations others have given over the years, Scott elaborates on Clarke's assessment of the problem. "It would be tedious even to mention the conjectural explications, which have been given of this prophecy concerning the witnesses," he begins, and then he faults them for identifying them with *"private,* and comparatively *little* events . . . as if [they] related to the martyrdom of *individuals,* or partial persecutions, in past times."[27] Trying to set the record straight, he argues that the term *witness* refers not to an individual, but to a *"succession* of men, who, during the period referred to, bore testimony to the truth."[28] Staunch nineteenth-century Protestant that he was, Scott suggests that the first of this long line of witnesses were the reformers who lived during the "darkest ages of popery" and who bore "a decided testimony against the prevailing corruptions of the Roman church."[29] Scott argues that such men were also alive in his day, although not "indeed at present exposed to such terrible sufferings, as in former times." He goes on to suggest that the "great city" where the witnesses will prophesy refers neither to "Rome or Jerusalem *literally,* but to Jerusalem *mystically;* that is, the professing church of God, as possessed by the Gentiles."[30] Breaking with his usual practice of reading the Revelation in terms of past events, Scott then posits a time in the future when the "state of real Christianity" in western Europe will be "exceedingly depressed" by dint of its enemies' attacks, only to revive in some miraculous manner—the witnesses' being restored to life—to triumph over its foes.[31]

The specter of the church at Rome looms large throughout Scott's account, and his interpretation of the two witnesses reflects the rampant anti-Catholicism of his and Joseph Smith's time. Significantly, the Prophet's interpretation includes neither this anti-Catholic bias of his contemporaries nor their tendency to see the witnesses and Jerusalem as symbolic. According to Joseph, the two witnesses prophesying in the "great city . . . where also our Lord was crucified" (Revelation 11:8) are just that: "two prophets that are to be raised up to the Jewish nation in the last days" who will "prophesy to the Jews after they are gathered and have built the city of Jerusalem in the land of their fathers" (D&C 77:15). This brief statement laid the groundwork for a more detailed explanation written in 1837 by Elder Parley P. Pratt—an explanation the Prophet Joseph endorsed when he approved it for publication:

"[John] informs us that after the city and temple are rebuilt by the Jews, the Gentiles will tread it under foot forty and two months, during which time there will be two prophets continually prophesying and working mighty miracles. And it seems that the Gentile army shall be hindered from utterly destroying and overthrowing the city, while these two prophets continue. But . . . they will at length succeed in destroying these two prophets and then overrunning much of the city. . . . But after three days and a half, on a sudden, the spirit of life from God will enter them; they will arise and stand upon their feet, and great fear will fall upon them that see them. And then they shall hear a voice from heaven saying, 'Come up hither,' and they will ascend up to heaven in a cloud, with their enemies beholding them."[32]

This interpretation is unique not only for its straightforward, non-mystical qualities but also for its specific reference to the establishment of a "Jewish nation" in the last days. Though biblical commentators of Joseph's time accepted the idea of a literal gathering of the Jews, most were extremely reticent about suggesting precisely how this gathering would take place and what would be involved.[33] Joseph's confident and straightforward use of the word *nation* contrasts sharply with the cautious, self-deprecating stance his contemporaries took when this subject was raised.

Several other differences should be noted between the inspired interpretations Joseph gave of John's revelation and those given by his contemporaries. Joseph differs with the commentators on virtually every topic he addresses in the Doctrine and Covenants, offering explanations that not only were unique on the American scene but which reintroduced to the world doctrines and visions of the future that had been lost for centuries. It is significant that so many of the doctrines and prophecies that make our Church unique—the immortality of animals, John's mission with the ten tribes, and future events in Jerusalem, to name a few—were couched in the Revelation rather than in other books of the Bible. There they survived for centuries, hidden from the world at large, and brought to light only after the Lord had restored to the earth the same authority that had been on the earth when those doctrines and prophecies were first revealed. When we understand that John's revelation thus became the source for many of our most remarkable doctrines and prophecies, we will better appreciate the prophet who gave his life to making these and other important doctrines known.

NOTES

1. See Scott H. Faulring, "Development of the Joseph Smith Translation (JST), June 1830–July 1833," unpublished manuscript, 1998.

2. This does much to refute the claim some historians are making that Joseph merely promoted and adapted for his own use ideas that were already common in early nineteenth-century America. For examples of this argument, see John L. Brooke, *The Refiner's Fire: The Making of Mormon Cosmology, 1644–1844* (Cambridge: Cambridge University Press, 1994); Brent Lee Metcalfe, ed., *New Approaches to the Book of Mormon: Explorations in Critical Methodology* (Salt Lake City: Signature Books, 1993); and Dan Vogel, ed., *The Word of God: Essays on Mormon Scripture* (Salt Lake City: Signature Books, 1990).

3. Although we do not know how familiar Joseph might have been with the biblical commentaries of his time, we do have evidence that he knew about Clarke's commentary. Emma Smith's uncle, Nathaniel Lewis, who doubted Joseph's use of the Urim and Thummim, owned a copy of Clarke's commentary. At one point, Lewis apparently asked Joseph "if anybody else [could] translate strange languages by the help of them spectacles?" When Joseph allegedly answered in the affirmative, Lewis reportedly responded, "I've got Clarke's Commentary, and it contains a great many strange languages; now if you will let me try the spectacles, and if, by looking through them, I can translate these strange languages into English, then I'll be one of your disciples." Susan Easton Black, "Isaac Hale: Antagonist of Joseph Smith," in Larry C. Porter, Milton V. Backman Jr., and Susan Easton Black, ed., *Regional Studies in Latter-day Saint Church History—New York* (Provo: Brigham Young University Department of Church History and Doctrine, 1992), 104.

4. Matthew Henry, *Commentary on the Whole Bible,* ed. Leslie F. Church (Grand Rapids: Zondervan, 1960), 768. Henry's commentaries on the Old and New Testaments are treated as two separate works in the volume, each with its own pagination. All references in this article to this volume refer to the New Testament, or the second half of the volume.

5. Adam Clarke, *The Holy Bible . . . Containing the Old and New Testaments: With a Commentary and Critical Notes,* 6 vols. (New York: J. Emory and B. Waugh, 1831), 6:946.

6. Clarke, *Holy Bible,* 6:950–51.

7. Thomas Scott, *The Holy Bible; Containing Old and New Testaments, . . . with Explanatory Notes, Practical Observations, and Copious Marginal References,* 6 vols. (London: James Nisbet & Co., 1866), 6:5 D 5.

8. Scott, *Holy Bible,* 6:5 E 4.

9. The angels possessed the "everlasting gospel"; the 144,000 were "high priests, ordained unto the holy order of God, to administer the everlasting gospel"; see D&C 77:9, 11.

10. Clarke, *Holy Bible,* 6:948–49.

11. Scott, *Holy Bible,* 6:5 E.

12. Henry, *Commentary,* 773.

13. Clarke, *Holy Bible,* 6:980.

14. Clarke, *Holy Bible,* 6:939.

15. Scott, *Holy Bible,* 6:5 C 4.

16. Scott, *Holy Bible,* 6:5 C 5.

17. As a further example, nineteenth-century biblical commentators viewed the white stone mentioned in Revelation 2:17 as a reference to "the ancient custom of giving a white stone to those acquitted on trial and a black stone to those condemned" (see Henry, *Commentary,* 770; compare Scott, *Holy Bible,* 6:5 A 8). In contrast, Joseph Smith was taught that the white stone "will become a Urim and Thummim to each individual who receives one, whereby things pertaining to a higher order of kingdoms will be made known" (D&C 130:10).

18. Clarke, *Holy Bible,* 6:939.

19. Scott, *Holy Bible,* 6:5 C 4; emphasis added.

20. Henry, *Commentary,* 776.

21. Clarke, *Holy Bible,* 6:953–54.

22. Clarke, *Holy Bible,* 6:953–54.

23. Scott, *Holy Bible,* 6:5 F.

24. Bruce N. Westergren, ed., *From Historian to Dissident: The Book of John Whitmer* (Salt Lake City: Signature Books, 1995), 69–70.

25. Henry, *Commentary,* 777.

26. Clarke, *Holy Bible,* 6:954.

27. Scott, *Holy Bible,* 6:5 F 4–5, F 5, F 6.

28. Scott, *Holy Bible,* 6:5 F 5.

29. Scott, *Holy Bible,* 6:5 F 5.

30. Scott, *Holy Bible,* 6:5 F 6.

31. Scott, *Holy Bible,* 6:5 F 8.

32. Parley P. Pratt, *Key to the Science of Theology: A Voice of Warning* (Salt Lake City: Deseret Book, 1979), 33.

33. See Andrew H. Hedges, "Isaiah in America, 1700–1830," *Isaiah in the Book of Mormon,* ed. Donald W. Parry and John W. Welch (Provo: Foundation for Ancient Research and Mormon Studies, 1998), 400.

CHAPTER SEVEN

THEMES OF DISCIPLESHIP IN JOHN

JARED W. LUDLOW

"Disciples, like diamonds, are developed in a process of time and heavy pressures, and both the disciple and the diamond reflect and magnify the light that comes through them."[1] We recall this statement by a modern apostle when we consider one of the most tense events depicted in the Gospel of John: Jesus' visit to Jerusalem during the Feast of Tabernacles. While some Jewish leaders were conspiring to capture Jesus, Jesus fervently bore witness of his divine nature and mission to the earth. Among Jesus' discourses, as recorded by John, was a confrontation with some Jews who resisted his invitation to discipleship and in the end took up stones to kill him. By examining this confrontation in John 8:31–59, we see how John presents important teachings on discipleship, many of which have parallels in his other writings. We will see that the figure of Abraham was used to encourage proper discipleship, and Jesus' great humility as an agent of God was emphasized. The rhetorical pattern of these verses reveals important themes of discipleship that also appear in other writings of John.

Throughout the Gospel of John, various confrontation scenes between Jesus and his Jewish listeners are presented. Just in chapter 8, three confrontation scenes occur on the Temple Mount during the Feast of Tabernacles. The encounter we will examine is the third

Jared W. Ludlow is a doctoral candidate in Near Eastern Religions (Second Temple Judaism) at the University of California–Berkeley and the Graduate Theological Union.

episode, which follows Jesus' teaching on water and light and his announcement of his going away.[2] This confrontation provides an excellent example of John's technique of developing discourse through objections on the part of some of the Jewish listeners. Throughout this debate, the motif of Abraham sustains the argument, and there is a feeling of ever-heightening conflict between Jesus and his listeners. At first it is stated that some had begun to believe on Jesus (see v. 31), but at the end they tried to kill him (see v. 59). What happened to these one-time believers? Elder Bruce R. McConkie felt that those who argued with Jesus and tried to kill him were not the same persons as the believers mentioned in verse 31 but rather were unbelievers among the multitude who resisted the word.[3] It is possible to see a continuation in the narrative from verse 21 to the end of the chapter where "at first all are hostile to Jesus, but by the time we reach v. 29 a goodly number are actually won to believe in him, . . . not through miracles, but through the words of warning coupled with grace which these men have just heard. In some way or other, not indicated by John, these believers manifest their change of heart. At once Jesus has a word for them in particular [an invitation to discipleship]. No sooner does he utter it than the hostile crowd of Jews raises further objection. They act just as they did from the start: they pick at some point to which to object (compare v. 22 and 25; also v. 13 and 19). John does not need to say in v. 33 who these objectors are, for we have heard them from the very start, and their objection is of the same type as before."[4]

What becomes evident, therefore, is that as the bitterness increases from some of the multitude, Jesus is attempting "to drive home to formal and casual adherents the meaning of true discipleship. If people in any sense believe in Jesus it is important that they come to see what real faith means."[5] Consequently, Jesus' explanations are full of dualisms (contrasts) which show the difference between true disciples and false ones and help encourage obedience from the listeners. The structure of this confrontation follows a repeatable pattern of, first, a *declaration* by Jesus; second, a *misunderstanding* about Jesus' declaration by the Jewish listeners; and third, further *explanation* by Jesus to clear up the listeners' misunderstanding.[6]

RHETORICAL PATTERN

   I. Truth

      A. Declaration: Truth shall set you free (vv. 31–32).

      B. Misunderstanding: We have never been slaves to anyone (v. 33).

      C. Explanation: Son shall set you free from slavery of sin (vv. 34–37).

   II. Relationship to the Father

      A. Declaration: I do what I have seen in the Father's presence (v. 38).

      B. Misunderstanding: Our father is Abraham (v. 39a).

      C. Explanation: Abraham did not reject truth from God's messengers (vv. 39b–40).

   III. Father's works

      A. Declaration: You do the deeds of your father (v. 41a).

      B. Misunderstanding: We have one father, even God (v. 41b).

      C. Explanation: If God were your Father, ye would love me . . . the devil is your father (vv. 42–45).

   IV. Allegiance to God

      A. Declaration: Can I be convicted of sin? You do not receive God's words because ye are not of God (vv. 46–47).

      B. Misunderstanding: You are a Samaritan and have a devil (v. 48).

      C. Explanation: I do not have a devil but honor my Father (vv. 49–50).

   V. Eternal life

      A. Declaration: If a man keep my saying, he shall never see death (v. 51).

      B. Misunderstanding: Even Abraham and the prophets died. Are you greater? (vv. 52–53).

      C. Explanation: My Father honors me and I know him and keep his saying (vv. 54–55).

   VI. Jesus as Jehovah

      A. Declaration: Abraham rejoiced to see my day (v. 56).

      B. Misunderstanding: You are not yet fifty years old, and have you seen Abraham? (v. 57).

      C. Explanation (and Declaration): Before Abraham was, I am (v. 58).

The confrontation between Jesus and some Jewish listeners begins with Jesus' statement, "If ye continue in my word, then are ye my disciples indeed; and ye shall know the truth, and the truth shall make you free" (John 8:31–32). Jesus' invitation to discipleship, one found throughout John's writings, is misunderstood by some of the Jewish listeners, who respond with a rebuttal and a question, "We be Abraham's seed, and were never in bondage to any man: how sayest thou, Ye shall be made free"? (vv. 33–34). Their appeal to their lineage from Abraham was a response to Jesus' invitation to be "my disciples." For them, their genealogical lineage prevented any discipleship to Jesus and saved them from any true bondage because of the great promises Abraham received for his descendants. Yet their question allowed Jesus the opportunity to explain the true meaning of the freedom he was discussing: "Whosoever committeth sin is the servant of sin. And the servant abideth not in the house for ever: but the Son abideth ever. If the Son therefore shall make you free, ye shall be free indeed" (vv. 34b–36). The reference to "the Son" and "the servant" in these verses seems to have a double allusion. The primary allusion is to Jesus as the Son (and therefore the Redeemer, because he frees from bondage), and sin or Satan as the servant. The second allusion, continuing with the Abraham motif, may be to Isaac and Ishmael. The servant (Ishmael) has no permanent inheritance in his Master's house, but the covenant son (Isaac) will inherit all.

President Spencer W. Kimball taught that "only he who obeys law is free. Serfdom comes to him who defies law. 'The truth shall make you free' (John 8:32) was another of the incontrovertible truths authored by the Master. He truly is free who is master of situations, habits, passions, urges, and desires. If one must yield to appetite or passion and follow its demands, he is truly the servant of a dictator."[7] In commenting on John 8:32, President Ezra Taft Benson taught, "In these words the Master pointed out that the fundamental characteristic of truth is freedom. Every principle of truth, properly applied, will free man from doubts, fears, suspicions, prejudices, and those qualities which make for misunderstanding, pride, lust, and selfishness. Every principle of truth in its own domain can free man to achieve the greatest good, the most majestic nobility of which he is capable."[8] Elder Neal A. Maxwell stated, "Knowing the truth about those things that really matter frees us from our inhibiting and finite

perspective in the same way that turning the light on in an otherwise darkened room can keep us from stubbing toes and breaking
furniture."[9]

Continuing in the confrontation, Jesus affirmed the Jews' lineage
from Abraham and then proceeded with the direct accusation and
declaration: "But ye seek to kill me, because my word hath no place
in you. I speak that which I have seen with my Father: and ye do that
which ye have seen with your father" (vv. 37b–38). Within Jesus'
statement are two themes that run throughout the writings of John:
the efforts by various Jews to kill Jesus,[10] and Jesus' fulfillment of his
mission as the agent of God. The word or message that Jesus was trying to share was a reflection of what he had seen with the Father—
just as they were attempting to do what they had heard from their
(real) father. The Jews' rejoinder was another effort to distance themselves from Jesus and *his* father by asserting, "Abraham is our father"
(v. 39a). Jesus then taught an important lesson, "If ye were Abraham's
children, ye would do the works of Abraham. But now ye seek to kill
me, a man that hath told you the truth, which I have heard of God:
this did not Abraham" (vv. 39b–40). Jesus portrayed Abraham as a
righteous example, and in this case the specific characteristic of
Abraham that should have been emulated was his acceptance and
hospitality toward the messengers of God. If they truly were
Abraham's children and following his example, they would recognize
and accept the message of truth given by Jesus, the one sent from
God, as Abraham accepted the three messengers of God, as recorded
in Genesis 18 (see a similar admonition of hospitality for messengers
in Hebrews 13:2 and D&C 84:90–91).

Jesus' next statement, though short, implied more. "Ye do the
deeds of your father" (v. 41a). The father of these Jews, with whom
their true spiritual allegiance lay, was revealed later in this confrontation as the father of lies, the devil. The Jews countered with
a denial and an echo of the Shema (Deuteronomy 6:4), "We be
not born of fornication; we have one Father, even God" (v. 41b).
The first part of their response may have been a jab at Jesus based on
false rumors concerning Jesus' illegitimate birth,[11] or it may have
been a desire to shore up their status as covenant children of God.
Their denial of having been born of fornication followed in the same
mode of thought as the common Old Testament description of

unfaithfulness as fornication or adultery (Hosea 2:4).[12] Instead, they emphasized that God, as always, was their covenant father (Exodus 4:22; Deuteronomy 14:1–2; 32:6; Isaiah 64:8; Malachi 2:10). The irony was that though they may have been physically descended from one father, they actually did the works of another and were therefore illegitimate. In response, Jesus again described his special relationship to God as one sent from him: "If God were your Father, ye would love me: for I proceeded forth and came from God; neither came I of myself, but he sent me" (v. 42).

These words closely parallel another confrontation in John, in which Jesus stated, "But I know you, that ye have not the love of God in you. I am come in my Father's name, and ye receive me not" (5:42–43). The argument here was grounded on the notion that the identity of the son is based on the character of the father and that the son should act like the father. Therefore, the hatred and rejection some of the Jews showed toward Jesus demonstrated that they were not spiritually God's children because it was God, the Father, who had sent him.

Jesus continued his declarations by boldly accusing them of spiritual negligence and giving a small discourse on the devil, in which we learn he is a murderer from the beginning, a liar, and the father of lying: "Why do ye not understand my speech? even because ye cannot hear [*bear*, JST] my word. Ye are of your father the devil, and the lusts of your father ye will do. He was a murderer from the beginning, and abode not in the truth, because there is no truth in him. When he speaketh a lie, he speaketh of his own: for he is a liar, and the father of it. And because I tell you the truth, ye believe me not. Which of you convinceth me of sin?[13] And if I say the truth, why do ye not believe me? He that is of God heareth [*receiveth*, JST] God's words: ye therefore hear [*receive*, JST] them not, because ye are not of God" (John 8:43–47).

Jesus' strong condemnation of these listeners was on account of their desire to kill him and their denial of this desire. Because destroying Jesus and God's plan is Satan's goal, the Jewish detractors were doing the work of Satan in seeking to kill Jesus. Their denial of murderous intentions revealed that they were children of the devil, liars as he was from the beginning.

The Jews' somewhat curious retort, "Say we not well that thou art a Samaritan, and hast a devil" (v. 48), was probably in response to Jesus' challenge, "Which of you convinceth me of sin?" (v. 46a). The sins of which they accused him were being a Samaritan and having a devil. "The epithet 'Samaritan' was inspired by hate, and by its application they meant to disown Him as a Jew."[14] It could be simple name calling or a charge of heterodoxy, because the Samaritans refused to recognize the Jews as the exclusive children of Abraham. Their charge of Jesus having a devil is found in other places in the Gospel of John (see 7:20; 10:20); throughout the Synoptic Gospels Jesus' power is said to have come through the prince of the devils (Matthew 9:34; Mark 3:22; Luke 11:15). Or the two charges of being a Samaritan and having a devil could be linked. "The story of Simon Magus in Acts viii 14–24 indicates that possession of a spirit and magical powers were greatly esteemed in Samaria, an attitude that is echoed in later traditions about Simon and Dositheus."[15] Regardless of the true meaning behind their charges, Jesus denied their accusation and reaffirmed his subservient status to his father, "I have not a devil; but I honour my Father, and ye do dishonour me. And I seek not mine own glory: there is one that seeketh and judgeth" (vv. 49–50).

Jesus next proclaimed, "If a man keep my saying, he shall never see death" (v. 51). While once again Jesus was teaching of freedom from spiritual death and bondage, the Jews misunderstood Jesus' words and applied them to physical death. Consequently they proudly continued in their condemnation of Jesus: "Now we know that thou hast a devil. Abraham is dead, and the prophets; and thou sayest, If a man keep my saying, he shall never taste of death. Art thou greater than our father Abraham, which is dead?" (vv. 52–53a). The Jews thought that if such great men as the patriarchs and prophets could not avoid death, anyone who claimed such power must be superhuman or have a devil misleading them. So they tauntingly asked Jesus to consider the implications of his words, "Whom makest thou thyself [to be]"? (v. 53b).

Jesus answered in a touching description of his relationship to the Father, "If I honour myself, my honour is nothing: it is my Father that honoureth me; of whom ye say, that he is your God: Yet ye have not known him; but I know him: and if I should say, I know him not, I shall be a liar like unto you: but I know him, and keep his saying"

(vv. 54–55). Jesus' response exemplified his humility and was a disclaimer of all self-aggrandizement: he was not directly claiming a greater status for himself but testifying that his honor, or power, was given him from the Father. His words echoed an earlier conflict wherein "the Jews sought the more to kill him, because he not only had broken the sabbath, but said also that God was his Father, making himself equal with God. Then answered Jesus and said unto them, Verily, verily, I say unto you, The Son can do nothing of himself, but what he seeth the Father do: for what things soever he doeth, these also doeth the Son likewise" (John 5:18–19). Within the Gospel of John, Jesus continually emphasized his role as his Father's agent in fulfilling his mission on the earth.

Continuing with a description of his true identity, Jesus boldly declared, "Your father Abraham rejoiced to see my day: and he saw it, and was glad" (John 8:56).[16] The Jews again mistook Jesus' words literally and responded, "Thou art not yet fifty years old, and hast thou seen Abraham?" (v. 57).[17] Now reaching the climax in the confrontation, Jesus forcefully revealed his divine nature: "I say unto you, Before Abraham *was*, I *am*" (v. 58: emphasis added). "This was an unequivocal and unambiguous declaration of our Lord's eternal Godship. By the awful title I AM He had made Himself known to Moses and thereafter was so known in Israel. . . . It is the equivalent of 'Yahveh,' or 'Jahveh,' now rendered 'Jehovah,' and signifies 'The Self-existent One,' 'The Eternal,' 'The First and the Last.'"[18] I AM "is an emphatic form of speech and one that would not normally be employed in ordinary speaking. Thus to use it was recognizably to adopt the divine style."[19] "Before the great patriarch, who lived centuries before, Jesus' existence went on. . . . A mode of being that has a definite beginning is contrasted with one that is eternal."[20]

In other words, Jesus was identifying himself as Jehovah, the God of the Old Testament, just as he had to Moses centuries earlier: "Thus shalt thou say unto the children of Israel, I AM hath sent me unto you" (Exodus 3:14). Jesus' identification as Jehovah was obviously not lost upon the angry Jewish listeners, who immediately took up stones to cast at him as punishment for blasphemy.[21] Their nonverbal response proved that Jesus spoke the truth: they did have murderous intentions like their father! Jesus eluded them, however, and the confrontation ended with his divine proclamation ringing in their ears.

THEMES OF DISCIPLESHIP

Throughout Jesus' ministry, many disciples followed him to learn of his teachings. As Jesus began interacting with the Jewish listeners on the occasion described in John 8, he attempted, through the motif of Abraham, to teach them the true meaning of discipleship. Jesus taught that there was a difference between being Abraham's seed and being Abraham's children (spiritual descendants). Jesus affirmed the Jews' genealogical claim to their great forefather, but distinguished this physical line from a spiritual, covenant adoption or discipleship:

"According to the terms of the covenant which God made with Abraham, all of the literal seed of that great prophet are entitled to receive the gospel, the priesthood, and all of the ordinances of salvation and exaltation. (Abraham 2:9–11; D&C 86:8–11.) When any of those descendants do receive all of these things, 'They become the sons of Moses and of Aaron and the seed of Abraham, and the church and kingdom, and the elect of God.' (D&C 84:34.) They are then *children of the covenant,* that is, they are inheritors of the fulness of the blessings appertaining to the new and everlasting covenant which is the gospel. 'Ye are the children of the covenant' (3 Ne. 20:24–27), our Lord told the Nephites among whom he ministered, a distinction which the faithful saints of this dispensation also enjoy. Rebellious descendants of Abraham are not his children in the special sense that is intended by the designation children of the covenant. (John 8:33–59.)"[22]

"The house of Israel in a spiritual and eternal perspective will finally include all who are the true followers of Jesus Christ. Although those of the direct blood lineage of the house of Israel are genealogically the sheep of God's fold, they must fulfill all the spiritual conditions of discipleship."[23] Some of the Jews challenging Jesus had a sense of automatic divine protection because of their lineage but had lost the sense of responsibility that came with being a son of Abraham.[24] Jesus stressed a spiritual bond to Abraham through emulating his good works just as we can become spiritually reborn as children of Christ through following his example. We can also learn from this important lesson that obedience is far more important than lineage—we must beware of pride that we may fall into as descendants of pioneer stock or of prominent Church leaders. *"Each generation must establish its own righteousness.* It is not enough for us to be the seed of a great man—we must rise to greatness in our own right."[25] The righteous and faithful examples of our forefathers and foremothers can provide great strength, but in the end we have no claim on the blessings and glory they received unless we emulate their laudatory examples.

Among John's writings related to discipleship, the Greek verb *menai* ("to abide, continue"), connoting loyalty and affiliation, seems to be a key word in describing discipleship to Jesus. Remaining or continuing faithful is the primary duty of a believer, and it entails coming to know the truth. Jesus invited his listeners to continue or abide in his word and thus become his disciples and know the truth (see John 8:31–32). As mentioned above, some of the listeners refused this invitation because, as Jesus explained, they could not hear his word (see 8:43). "The hearing [of the word], and with it belief and understanding, doesn't come about because Jesus' word falls on closed ears. The disbelief is already no longer simple factual 'not-believing,' but an unbelief of such a kind that has closed itself off. Already from a 'not wanting' to hear developed a 'not able' to hear, an incapability of giving a hearing to the message of Jesus. Unbelief became an attitude of life in self-enclosure, a hardening or stubbornness."[26] The word *menai* was also used when explaining the opposite of discipleship: the slave of sin shall not abide (*menei*) in the house forever, only the Son (see v. 35).

In looking at other uses of the term *menai* in John's writings, we see that in some cases it is the word that should be abiding in us (so that we may continue or abide in the Son and the Father) (see John 5:38; 1 John 2:14, 24). In other instances, we are directly invited to abide in Jesus. That concept is especially poignant in Jesus' discourse on the vine:

"Abide in me, and I in you. As the branch cannot bear fruit of itself, except it abide in the vine; no more can ye, except ye abide in me. I am the vine, ye are the branches: He that abideth in me, and I in him, the same bringeth forth much fruit: for without me ye can do nothing. . . . If ye abide in me, and my words abide in you, ye shall ask what ye will, and it shall be done unto you. . . . So shall ye be my disciples" (John 15:4–8).

Other Johannine scriptures point out that we must abide in Jesus to be prepared for his return (see 1 John 2:28); and if we say we abide in him, we ought to walk even as he walked and not sin (see 1 John 2:6; 3:6, 24). If we sin, we are told that we do not abide in the doctrine of Christ and do not have God (see 2 John 9). In a conference address, Elder Sam K. Shimabukuro stated, "The greatest of all achievements that we can attain in our long and challenging journey through immortality is when our claim to discipleship of the Lord Jesus Christ reaches the stage where we can say, with all honesty, His ways are our ways and His thoughts our thoughts."[27]

TRUTH VERSUS LIES

Throughout John's writings, much of his thought follows a dualistic view: good versus evil, or light versus darkness. Within the Gospel of John, lying is equated with darkness, part of Satan's dominion that is opposed to the truth and light of God (see John 3:20). On the one side we have Jesus Christ, who is the truth (see John 14:6); on the other side is the devil, the liar par excellence. On which side will our discipleship and allegiance lie? Although Jesus' condemnation of his Jewish listeners as children of the devil seems harsh, it underscores the division between good and evil. According to Jesus' words and John's writings, we are either on God's side or we are against it (see also Romans 6:13, 15–16).

The contrast between truth and lies becomes apparent in this confrontation in which Jesus is challenging the listening Jews' status as faithful, covenant people. Jesus invited his listeners to abide in his word so they might know the truth and be set free (see John 8:31–32). What was the truth that Jesus described that would set them free? As evidenced by a parallel verse in which it is the Son who sets free (see v. 36), the truth that would set free was Jesus himself. Jesus as the truth was reinforced by Jesus in the Gospel of John when he proclaimed, "I am the way, *the truth,* and the life" (14:6; emphasis added). Man's knowledge of this truth, of Jesus, implies obedience to him; the freedom achieved through truth, through Jesus, is thus contrasted with the slavery of sin.[28] Stephen R. Covey has written, "As a person begins to see more as the Lord sees, to acquire more of the 'mind of Christ' (1 Cor. 2:16), that individual is empowered to become independent of all other influences and to rise above childhood, genetic, and environmental tendencies."[29] We are never

immune to sin, so John's warnings of spiritual bondage, and the revelation of the true source of freedom from such bondage, are just as
vital for us in our day.

Further on in the confrontation, Jesus taught that Satan is the
antithesis of truth: he "abode not in the truth, because there is no
truth in him. When he speaketh a lie, he speaketh of his own: for he
is a liar, and the father of it" (John 8:44). Verse 45 demonstrates "the
radical opposition that exists between the sons of the father of lying
and the truth. We might expect to have vs. 45 say that even *though*
Jesus told the truth, they did not believe him; but John actually says
that they did not believe *because* he told the truth. In [John] iii 20 we
heard that the children of darkness hate the light; here the children
of lying hate the truth."[30] Because of the listeners' rejection of the
truth, they belonged to the devil and attempted to carry out his murderous works (see John 8:44–47).

Later writings of John continue to emphasize the dualism of truth
versus lies or perversion (see 1 John 1:6, 10; 2:4; 4:20; 5:10).[31] First
John 2:22 asks, "Who is a liar but he that denieth that Jesus is the
Christ? He is antichrist, that denieth the Father and the Son." First
John 4:1–6 teaches that the spirit of truth and the spirit of error are
found in men. First John 3:8–10 echoes the relationship of sin to the
devil: "He that continueth in sin is of the devil; for the devil sinneth
from the beginning. For this purpose the Son of God was manifested,
that he might destroy the works of the devil." The Joseph Smith
Translation rendering of this passage is this: "Whosoever is born of
God doth not continue in sin; for the Spirit of God remaineth in
him; and he cannot continue in sin, because he is born of God, having received that holy Spirit of promise" (JST 1 John 3:9). We continue from the King James Version: "In this the children of God are
manifest, and the children of the devil: whosoever doeth not righteousness is not of God, neither he that loveth not his brother"
(1 John 3:10).

By looking at these passages together with John 8, we see that
Satan has lied and sinned from the beginning, and we recognize that
if we continue to sin or lie, we are his children or disciples. Yet, the
Son of God was manifested to destroy the works of the devil.

Eternal Life through Jesus

Near the end of the confrontation with the Jewish listeners, Jesus promised that whoever kept his saying would not see death (see John 8:51).[32] This assurance of eternal life, free from spiritual death and bondage, is very much like that of John 5:24: "He that heareth my word, and believeth on him that sent me, hath everlasting life, and shall not come into condemnation; but is passed from death unto life." The promise of eternal life is for all those who abide in the word of Jesus (see 1 John 2:25) and is thus the gift for proper discipleship. The Joseph Smith Translation rendering of John 3:16, 36, states a similar idea: "For God so loved the world, that he gave his Only Begotten Son, that whosoever believeth on him should not perish; but have everlasting life. . . . And he who believeth on the Son hath everlasting life; and shall receive of his fulness." Joseph Smith taught: "For if He [Jesus Christ] has risen from the dead the bands of the temporal death are broken that the grave has no victory. If then, the grave has no victory, those who keep the sayings of Jesus and obey His teachings have not only a promise of a resurrection from the dead, but an assurance of being admitted into His glorious kingdom."[33]

John also explicitly taught that Jesus is the source of life. In the Prologue to his Gospel, he stated: "In him [the Word, or Jesus] was life; and the life was the light of men" (John 1:4). The beginning of the First Epistle of John reads: "[JST: Brethren, this is the testimony which we give of] that which was from the beginning, which we have heard, which we have seen with our eyes, which we have looked upon, and our hands have handled, of the Word of life; (For the life was manifested, and we have seen it, and bear witness, and shew unto you that eternal life, which was with the Father, and was manifested unto us)" (1 John 1:1–2). Later the epistle states: "And this is the record, that God hath given to us eternal life, and this life is in his Son. He that hath the Son hath life; and he that hath not the Son of God hath not life" (1 John 5:11–12).

In the Gospel of John, Jesus declared to Martha, as he was preparing to raise Lazarus from the dead, "I am the resurrection, and the life: he that believeth in me, though he were dead, yet shall he live" (11:25). In talking to a multitude he had miraculously fed the day before, Jesus proclaimed, "He that believeth on me hath everlasting life. I am that bread of life" (6:47–48). Continuing, he taught, "I am the living bread which came down from heaven: if any man eat of this bread, he shall live for ever: and the bread that I will give is my flesh, which I will give for the life of the world" (6:51). And in yet another oft-repeated proclamation, Jesus announced, "I am the way, the truth, and *the life*" (14:6; emphasis added). Thus we see from John's writings that Jesus and his word are not only the sources of eternal life but elements of the very power of life itself on this earth.

JESUS AS GOD'S AGENT

The passages in John 8 clearly delineate Jesus' role as God's agent and provide an example of perfect, obedient, and humble discipleship to the Father. Jesus' humility is beautifully reinforced as he reiterated his commission as one sent from God, similar to many of his words throughout the writings of John, especially in the great intercessory prayer recorded in John 17. By combining various phrases from John's writings that deal with the relationship of Jesus to God, we see a close yet subservient relationship. The Father loves the Son and has given all things to him (see John 3:35). Jesus stated, "My meat is to do the will of him that sent me, and to finish his work" (John 4:34; see also 6:38–40). In a longer excursus, Jesus explained that the Son cannot do anything of himself but what he sees the Father do: for whatever the Father does, the Son does likewise (see John 5:19). This principle applies to his work (see 5:17), raising the dead (see 5:21), and giving judgment (see 5:27, 30). The Father bears witness of the Son (see 5:37; 1 John 5:10). Jesus' doctrine is not his own but is from him that sent him (see John 7:16–17; 12:49–50). Jesus told some unbelievers, and later his apostles, that had they come to know him, they would have known the Father (see John 8:19; 14:7). In a different aspect of knowledge, as the Father knows the Son, even so does the Son know the Father (see John 10:15). The Father loves the Son because he lays down his life to take it up again (see 10:17). Jesus loves the Father, and thus does whatsoever the Father commands (see John 14:31). Jesus' works are in his Father's name (see John 9:4; 10:25). The Father and Son are one (see John 10:30, 37–38; 14:11) yet the Father is greater (see John 14:28). Whoever believes on Jesus believes on him that sent him (see John

12:44; 13:20). Jesus came into the world from the Father and left it to return to the Father (see John 16:28).

Another beautiful illustration of Jesus' humble status before the Father is recorded throughout the account of Jesus' visitation to the Americas in 3 Nephi in the Book of Mormon. Jesus was fulfilling his Father's will in all things (see 3 Nephi 11:11). Jesus and the Father are one (see 11:27, 36; 28:10). Jesus' doctrine was given unto him by the Father (see 11:32). Jesus taught or went only what or where the Father commanded (see 15:15–19; 16:3, 10, 16; 18:14, 27; 20:10, 14; 21:11; 26:2). Jesus fervently prayed to the Father in the presence of his disciples (see 17:15–18; 19:20–23, 27–29). Jesus was sent by the Father to be lifted up on the cross (see 27:13–14). We thus see many parallels between the Book of Mormon account in 3 Nephi and John 8 in the great meekness and discipleship Jesus showed toward his Father. Elder Neal A. Maxwell taught: "Meekness ranks low on the mortal scale of things, yet high on God's: 'For none is acceptable before God, save the meek and lowly in heart.' (Moroni 7:44.) The rigorous requirements of Christian discipleship are clearly unattainable without meekness. In fact, meekness is needed in order to be spiritually successful, whether in matters of the intellect, in the management of power, in the dissolution of personal pride, or in coping with the challenges of daily life. Jesus, the carpenter—who, with Joseph, 'undoubtedly had experience making yokes'—gave us that marvelous metaphor: 'Take my yoke upon you, and learn of me; for I am meek and lowly in heart.' (Matthew 11:29.) The yoke of obedience to Him is far better than servitude to sin, but the demands are real."[34]

Jesus is the perfect example of humility and obedience before our Heavenly Father. As one sent from the Father, he taught and fulfilled his Father's will in all things; yet, notwithstanding his subservient role, he is the great "I am" (John 8:58).

CONCLUSION

The confrontation scene we have examined is one of several in John's writings that clearly demonstrate that John recorded conflicts in these formats to teach important doctrines. By using a rhetorical pattern in which Jesus was able to address the listeners' misunderstandings, many important issues for the early Christian community were clarified. A close reading of this one episode shows that John emphasized key themes related to discipleship that can be found throughout his other writings. And by restating some of Jesus' central declarations in this confrontation, we can gain a better sense of Jesus' humble, yet forceful, invitation to discipleship: If you abide in my word, you are truly my disciples; and you will know me, and I will set you free. I tell you what I have seen with my Father for I have not come on my own; rather, he sent me. The one who belongs to God receives God's word; and if you keep my saying, you shall never see death. If I glorify myself, my glory amounts to nothing. The one who glorifies me is the Father. I know him and I keep his word, for I am Jehovah.

Who is truly a disciple of Jesus and how does one become a disciple? At the root of the matter is the issue of being an authentic member of God's covenant community. Jesus' dialogue in this confrontation is embedded with several dualistic contrasts that illuminate the separation of the sons of God from the sons of the devil and true disciples from false ones. Abraham is presented as the paradigm of true discipleship by first, welcoming God's messengers, second, hearing their message, and third, entering into covenants with God. In a similar manner, Jesus invited his listeners to, first, accept him as a messenger sent by God; second, hear his message; and third, keep his word. In addition, Jesus provided the perfect example of humble and obedient discipleship before the Father in fulfilling all that was asked of him.

Jesus' invitation to discipleship is still relevant today as we should welcome latter-day messengers of God (namely our prophets and Church leaders), hear their message, and enter into covenants to follow the gospel. Obedience is the most important aspect of our discipleship or covenant relationship and far outweighs any lineage relationship we might have. Jesus promised that his word, received from the Father, would bring eternal life and freedom from spiritual bondage. In other words, his word would counteract Satan's efforts to fill humanity with sin and spiritual death. We must therefore abide in Jesus and his word, remaining faithful disciples, so that we might have freedom from the slavery of sin, for he both is and has the truth that will set us free. Indeed, John 14:6 seems to embody those great elements of Jesus: "I am the way, the truth, and the life: no man cometh unto the Father, but by me." If we are to be covenant children and disciples of our Heavenly Father, worthy of eternal life, we must abide in Jesus, for he is the way, the truth, and the life. If we become faithful disciples, we can then, like diamonds, "reflect and magnify the light that comes through"[35] us from the light of the world, Jesus Christ.

NOTES

1. Neal A. Maxwell, *Wherefore, Ye Must Press Forward* (Salt Lake City: Deseret Book, 1977), 125.

2. This passage in John 8 is cited throughout the discussion by verse number only.

3. Bruce R. McConkie, *Doctrinal New Testament Commentary,* 3 vols. (Salt Lake City: Bookcraft, 1965–73), 1:457.

4. R. C. H. Lenski, *The Interpretation of St. John's Gospel* (Minneapolis: Augsburg Publishing House, 1961), 627–28.

5. Leon Morris, *New International Commentary on the New Testament: The Gospel According to John,* rev. ed. (Grand Rapids, Mich.: Eerdmans, 1995), 404.

6. This pattern is based on Jerome H. Neyrey's model in "Jesus the Judge: Forensic Process in John 8, 21–59," *Biblica* (1987), 68:509–42, esp. 521.

7. Spencer W. Kimball, *Teachings of Spencer W. Kimball,* ed. Edward L. Kimball (Salt Lake City: Bookcraft, 1982), 153.

8. Ezra Taft Benson, *Teachings of Ezra Taft Benson* (Salt Lake City: Bookcraft, 1988), 118.

9. Neal A. Maxwell, *Behold, I Say unto You, I Cannot Say the Smallest Part Which I Feel* (Salt Lake City: Deseret Book, 1973), 6.

10. The notion that many Jews were trying to kill Jesus is found throughout the Gospel of John: 5:16, 18; 7:19, 25, 32; 10:31–33, 39; 11:53, 57.

11. "There is an early witness to Jewish attacks on the legitimacy of Jesus' birth in Origen *Against Celsus* I 28 (GCS 2:79); and the *Acts of Pilate* II 3, has the Jews charging Jesus: 'You were born of fornication.'" Raymond E. Brown, *The Anchor Bible: The Gospel According to John (i-xii),* ed. W. F. Albright and David Noel Freedman, 44 vols. (Garden City, N. Y.: Doubleday, 1966), 29:357.

12. James Raymond Lord, "Abraham: A Study in Ancient Jewish and Christian Interpretation" (Ph.D. diss., Duke University, 1968), 269.

13. Jesus' question, "Which of you **convinceth** me of sin," uses the Greek verb *elegcho,* which carries the idea of showing someone his fault or error or proving guilty. Therefore Jesus is asking, "Can any of you prove me guilty of sin?" His question may refer to the episode with the

adulterous woman earlier in the chapter (vv. 7–9). Although the scribes and Pharisees felt unqualified to stone the adulteress, there was no suggestion that Jesus was disqualified.

14. James E. Talmage, *Jesus the Christ*, 3d ed. (Salt Lake City: Deseret Book, 1916), 382. This name may have arisen because of Jesus' earlier stay among the Samaritans where many Samaritans believed on his word (see John 4:39–42).

15. Brown, *Gospel According to John*, 29:358.

16. In reference to this verse, Joseph Smith taught, "Because the ancients offered sacrifice it did not hinder their hearing the Gospel; but served, as we said before, to open their eyes, and enable them to look forward to the time of the coming of the Savior, and rejoice in His redemption." Richard C. Galbraith, introduction to Joseph Smith, *Teachings of the Prophet Joseph Smith*, sel. Joseph Fielding Smith (Salt Lake City: Deseret Book, 1976), 60.

17. And they mistook his words even against their own rabbinical traditions which allowed for Abraham to have seen the day of the Messiah; therefore they were 'kicking against the pricks.' "Though much of this [rabbinical tradition] seems fanciful to us, it shows that among the Jews the idea that Abraham looked forward to the day of the Messiah and rejoiced in it was not strange." Morris, *Gospel According to John*, 418.

18. Talmage, *Jesus the Christ*, 382–83. There is an important distinction between the two Greek "to be" verbs in verse 58: *ginesthai* is used for mortals, and *einai* is the divine use in the form "I AM." (Compare with John's prologue [1:1–14]: the Word *was* (*einai*), but through him all things *came into being* (*ginesthai*)). In the [Old Testament] the same distinction is found in the address to Yahweh in Psalm 90:2: "Before the mountains *came into being* . . . from age to age you *are*." Brown, *Gospel According to John*, 29:360.

19. Morris, *Gospel According to John*, 420.

20. Morris, *Gospel According to John*, 419.

21. According to their interpretation, they were following the command in Leviticus 24:16 to stone to death anyone who blasphemes the name of the Lord.

22. Bruce R. McConkie, *Mormon Doctrine*, 2d ed. (Salt Lake City: Bookcraft, 1966), 126.

23. V. Ben Bloxham, "Law of Adoption," in Daniel H. Ludlow, ed., *Encyclopedia of Mormonism*, 4 vols. (New York: Macmillan, 1992), 2:810.

24. The tension between being Abraham's true covenant son or simply his seed is prevalent in Paul's writings as well: Romans 9:6–8 and Galatians 4:22–31. There is also a denial of blessings based simply on genealogy by John the Baptist: Matthew 3:9.

25. Kimball, *Teachings of Spencer W. Kimball*, 172.

26. Translated from Josef Blank, *Krisis. Untersuchungen zur johanneis-chen Christologie und Eschatologie* (Freiburg im Breisgau: Lambertus-Verlag, 1964), 238.

27. Sam K. Shimabukuro, *Ensign,* May 1992, 85.

28. Deliverance from sin by truth is not found in the Old Testament, but at Qumran the notion that truth destroys sin is found. "And then God will purge by His truth all the deeds of men . . . and will sprinkle on him a spirit of truth like water that cleanses from every lying abomination (1QS iv 20–21)." Brown, *The Gospel According to John,* 29:355.

29. Stephen R. Covey, "Discipleship," in Ludlow, *Encyclopedia of Mormonism,* 1:385.

30. Brown, *Gospel According to John,* 29:365.

31. "A similar dualism is well known at Qumran where the spirit of truth is opposed to the spirit of perversion. These are not only two great angelic leaders locked in battle (1QS iii 19) but also two ways of life in which men walk (1QS iv 2 ff.)." Brown, *Gospel According to John,* 29:365.

32. Keeping Jesus' word or commandment is another common Johannine theme (see John 14:21, 23–24; 17:6; 1 John 2:5; Revelation 1:3; 3:8; 22:7, 9).

33. Smith, *Teachings of the Prophet Joseph Smith,* 62.

34. Neal A. Maxwell, *Meek and Lowly* (Salt Lake City: Deseret Book, 1987), ix.

35. Maxwell, *Wherefore, Ye Must Press Forward,* 125.

CHAPTER EIGHT

LIGHT, LIFE, AND LOVE IN THE EPISTLES OF JOHN

VICTOR L. LUDLOW

John's Gospel witness complemented the synoptic Gospels of Matthew, Mark, and Luke; it strengthened the faith of the early Christians as he gave his own powerful, personal testimony of the life and mission of the Son of God. As John continued to serve and lead the early Christian community, he recognized that the Saints needed further help and direction in living their struggling faith. To meet these needs, he wrote letters to the Church members. Probably written around A.D. 90–95, some sixty years after the crucifixion and resurrection of Christ and thirty years after the martyrdom of Peter, these inspiring epistles are among the last recorded writings of the New Testament. John's epistles were written to strengthen the Saints' commitment to the gospel as he admonished them to serve God in loving faith and obedience.

The three epistles of John currently in existence range in length reflecting the size of their intended audience. The first and largest epistle is a commentary that builds on important themes of the Gospel of John, and it seems to have been prepared for wide and general distribution among the early Saints. The second epistle is quite brief and was written to a Christian congregation to counter the influence of false teachers in the area. The third epistle is also short and was directed to a few specific people as John recognized some

Victor L. Ludlow is a professor of ancient scripture and coordinator of Near Eastern Studies at Brigham Young University.

problems they were having with a local dictatorial leader. Addressed to the believers, these epistles of the presiding apostle not only countered the secessionist[1] and gnostic[2] heresies spreading in Asia Minor but also encouraged the early Saints as he amplified Christ's teachings of light, life, and love. In essence, John promoted their fellowship with God and each other through the bonds of love.

1 JOHN

In the first epistle, John taught the fellowship and eternal life found in the light and love of Christ (1:2–7; 2:25; 4:7–21; 5:11, 13, 20). Of particular value to all Christians, this important epistle includes John's instruction about how they should build upon their own witness or testimony. First John can be divided into seven segments, with words of testimony and counsel alternating with lists describing key attributes of the true Saints of Christ. Each of these seven segments will be discussed in turn.[3]

1. Prologue and introductory witness
2. Five tests of Christian fellowship
3. Words of commendation and warning
4. Five recognizable attributes of the children of God
5. Words of admonition and counsel
6. Five qualities of God's love
7. Epilogue: the testimonies of eternal life

Prologue and introductory witness of the Son of God (1 John 1:1–4). This introduction is very similar to the first chapter in John's Gospel.[4] The bold claim to eyewitness testimony of the life and mission of the Son of God harmonizes with the fact that John was Jesus' disciple from the earliest days of his public ministry. He remained as the sole living, original apostle. John taught that eternal life is manifested in Jesus Christ. This life, which God lives, is available only to those who respond faithfully to Jesus Christ.[5] He then taught how to develop fellowship with Christ.

Five tests of Christian fellowship for the disciples of the God of light (1 John 1:5–2:11). Contrasting light and sin, John gives five ways to recognize Christ's followers. His disciples are those who walk in the light (1:5–7), confess their sins (1:8–10), repent of their sins (JST 2:1–2), keep the commandments (2:3–6), and love each other (2:7–11).[6] Latter-day Saints should note how these five steps compare with the first principles and ordinances of the gospel today, including the injunctions to "love one another" and "endure to the end." These steps beautifully and accurately highlight the conversion experience of any Saint who has "seen the light" and entered into the path of Christian discipleship.

Fellowship Test 1: Walking in the Light (1 John 1:5–7). How does one "walk in the light"? Light, in the gospel context, means truth, moral goodness, and holiness. Some people who think they are enlightened are walking in darkness because their light comes only from secular knowledge while they are in spiritual darkness. The witnessing of the Holy Spirit and the building of faith brings that valuable spiritual light into one's life. Christ is true light, and one's faith in him and continued fellowship with him requires walking in his light (compare John 8:12 with 1 John 1:5–7).

John provides various criteria by which people can measure themselves—whereby they can know whether or not they are walking in the light. Mainly, they will first recognize and then avoid or leave the darkness of sin. The word *sin* is a key term used by John in this epistle, occurring twenty-seven times in the Greek of these five chapters. John especially talks about the darkness of sin, recognizing sin, and removing sin. Christ's followers must first leave the darkness of sin and come toward the light of Christ.

Fellowship Test 2: Confessing Sins (1 John 1:8–10). For those who have come into the light or faith of Christ, their next step will be to recognize and confess their sins. A critical measurement of Christian discipleship is one's attitude toward sin. A person must first face his or her sins and then admit or confess them. One is then ready to move toward receiving forgiveness.

Fellowship Test 3: Repenting of Sins (1 John 2:1–2). A person's fellowship with Christ requires continual repentance and renewal of his or her covenants. Through this process of repentance, the blood of Jesus Christ cleanses one from sin. Nothing else will do; only the infinite atonement of Christ and obedience to his commandments will cleanse a person in body and spirit.

The Joseph Smith Translation clears up some confusion in the first verse of this passage. As it reads in the King James Version, "if any man sin, we have an advocate with the Father, Jesus Christ," it sounds like anyone who sins has Christ immediately as an advocate, as though Jesus might be accepting the behavior. The Joseph Smith Translation indicates that it is for the sinner *who repents* that Jesus becomes an advocate.[7]

This understanding also helps clarify verse 2. As the "propitiation" (one who becomes favorably inclined or willing to make atonement) for sin, Jesus' atoning sacrifice satisfies the demands of the laws of justice for all those sins for which people have repented. The implication is that unrepentant sinners will, of course, still have to suffer for their own sins.

Fellowship Test 4: Obedience to the Commandments (1 John 2:3–6). "Keep the Commandments" is the title of a favorite Primary song sung by Latter-day Saint children throughout the world. It resulted from some counsel given by President Spencer W. Kimball shortly after he became president of The Church of Jesus Christ of Latter-day Saints in December 1973. When news reporters asked him what his first words of counsel were for Church members, he responded, "Keep the commandments." Once one has come into fellowship with Christ, obedience keeps that person in the fold. If one is going to apostatize, the first step is almost always disobedience to some commandment, followed by rationalization and justification.

John stressed the importance of a correct knowledge of God in 1 John 2. The special knowledge of the true nature of God, by which "we do know that we know him," as promised by John in verse 3, is reserved for the faithful Saints of Christ. Forty-two times in this epistle he used one of two Greek verbs, both of which are usually translated in English as "know." One of these verbs is related to the name of the Gnostics, the heretical sect which claimed to have a "special knowledge" (*gnosis*) of God. John wanted to reveal openly where and how true Christians acquire a correct knowledge of God— by obedience to his divine commandments. As they know and obey the commandments, they demonstrate their identity with Christ.

Fellowship Test 5: Communal Love (1 John 2:7–11). An abundance of love also distinguishes true followers of the loving Master. Outsiders observing true Christian Saints must recognize that these people love and serve each other. These outsiders may not accept Christian doctrines or want to become part of the Christian community, but they should be able to see and feel the love which the Saints have for each other.

In summary, the five tests of fellowship highlight a path of righteousness that true Christians must follow as they come out of spiritual darkness into the light of Christ's gospel, recognize and then repent of their sins, learn to be obedient to God's commandments and prophets, and develop love for each other. One who meets these five criteria is on the path toward God.

Words of commendation and warning (1 John 2:12–27). The authoritative tone of verses 12–27 of 1 John 2 is what one would expect from a senior, seasoned apostle. Also, the description of heretics as antichrists and liars is consistent with this "[son] of thunder" (Mark 3:17). For John, God's children have verified their anointing when they recognize and conquer the influence of the evil one. Two passages which contrast between the good and the evil are a short didactic poem and John's warning of the antichrist.

The didactic poem in verses 12–14 is intended to provide moral instruction:

"I write unto you, *little children,* because your sins are forgiven you for his name's sake.

"I write unto you, *fathers,* because ye have known him that is from the beginning. I write unto you, *young men,* because ye have overcome the wicked one. I write unto you, *little children,* because ye have known the Father.

"I have written unto you, *fathers,* because ye have known him that is from the beginning. I have written unto you, *young men,* because ye are strong, and the word of God abideth in you, and ye have overcome the wicked one" (emphasis added).

In two synonymous sets, John addressed the children (vv. 12, 13c), the fathers (vv. 13a, 14a), and the young men (vv. 13b, 14b). He emphasized their faith and spiritual strength as they have come to know the Father and the Son, and their triumph over the evil one as they have turned away from their sins. They have gained spiritual strength in word and deed, in belief and behavior, and in faith and action.

Some commentators[8] have suggested that the three terms "children," "young men," and "fathers" refer to levels of spiritual maturity. The "children" first come to know about God our Heavenly Father and to seek for forgiveness. The "young men" learn to overcome evil (self-control) and become stronger in their gospel knowledge and moral behavior. The "fathers" are those who know "him who is from the beginning" (Christ), as they believe and live as true followers of Christ and become heirs to share eternal life with him (compare John 3:16 and 17:3). Whatever their spiritual age, one should remember that knowing the Father and Christ along with overcoming the evil one and seeking for forgiveness is a continual process of this earth life.

Starting in verse 18, John talked about a constant enemy of Christ. He apparently assumed that his readers already knew that a great enemy of the Lord and his Saints would arise before Christ's return in millennial glory. This antichrist would be a person of extreme pride and ambition (see Isaiah 14:4–23), a "man of sin" (2 Thessalonians 2:3), and "the beast" (Revelation 13:1–10). Note, however, that John also mentioned that there will also be many other "antichrists." They are not the terrible antichrist of the last days but like unto him. Although there is only one Christ, his prophets, apostles, and disciples are like him in many ways. Likewise, these antichrists will share many characteristics of the great antichrist, who is the devil himself (see Bible Dictionary, "Antichrist," 609).[9] John gave the reader some ways to recognize these antichrists: they deny God the Father (1 John 2:22); they deny that Jesus is the Christ (v. 22; 4:3; 2 John 1:7); they lack spiritual companionship from the Father (through the Holy Ghost; 1 John 2:23); they are liars and deceivers (v. 22; 2 John 1:7); and they are often apostate Christians who leave the Church but continue to fight against it (1 John 2:19).

Five recognizable attributes of the children of God (1 John 2:28–3:24). A second measurement of Christ's disciples will be to see if they are doing deeds of righteousness. God is righteous, and their fellowship with him depends upon doing righteous deeds. After they have developed the five internal attitudes described in 1 John 1:5 through 2:11, their external actions will be demonstrated with trust in the Lord, godlike behavior, righteousness, charity, and faithful obedience.

God's children will be recognized by righteous conduct—the standard found in the divine nature of Christ. Specifically, they will share five attributes: confidence (faith) in Christ (2:28–29), being like him (3:1–3), doing right (3:4–10), loving one another (3:11–18), and having confidence in God, obtained through keeping the commandments with a clear conscience (3:19–24). If true Saints have followed the five steps in the earlier list of fellowship tests, the fruits of their spiritual labors will be recognized. As these two lists are compared, although some elements are in somewhat different order, the parallels between them are obvious, with a particular emphasis upon faith, love, and obedience.

In verses 6, 8, and 9 of John 3, there is a small but significant change in the Joseph Smith Translation. Scholars are perplexed with these verses because it seems that John is restricting heaven, or the highest gifts of spirituality, to those of absolute, sinless perfection—a level lived only by Jesus himself. The text of the Joseph Smith Translation, however, reinforces the belief that there is still hope for the sinner to enjoy great spiritual rewards, if he or she repents! But those who continue to sin and refuse to repent will not enjoy the spiritual gifts that Heavenly Father has prepared for the repentant.

There is also a subtle change in the Joseph Smith Translation text of 1 John 3:18. One's love for God and others can be detected in the words of one's tongue but not in them only. One also shows his or her love in noble thoughts and good works because external behavior often reflects inner convictions. As a comparison, James 2:14–17 and Alma 12:14 teach the importance of good works as a complement to thoughts and words.

Words of admonition and counsel (1 John 4:1–6). The importance of a discerning spirit, and especially of knowing truth, life, light and love in contrast to lies, death, darkness, and hate, is a constant theme in John's writings. In this segment, John addressed his "children" and emphasized that a witness or messenger who testifies that "Jesus Christ is come in the flesh" is of God and anything else is of an antichrist. He also gave counsel on how to recognize the difference between that which is heard in the world and that which is heard of God. Those who know God can discern between "the spirit of truth, and the spirit of error."[10] These verses echo John's words to his children about the antichrists and discernment in 2:12–27.

Five qualities of God's love (1 John 4:7–5:5). God is love. The third measurement of Christ's disciples is found in the multiple layers of love that they experience. Their internal attitudes and external actions will be rewarded with blessings of a loving relationship with God. The latter part of this epistle is dominated by the affirmation that "God is love," as the earlier part is by "God is light."[11] Part of one's purpose on earth is to know God. John first emphasized love (4:7, 12) and also belief (4:16; 5:1, 5) as the means to know God, the path to life eternal (John 17:3).

The word *love* is used as a noun or verb thirty-four times in just these twenty verses. True love involves not just a person and his or her Heavenly Father but also God's Son, the Holy Spirit, and others. There are at least five characteristics of love highlighted in these sublime verses: God, through his Son, is the source of love (7–12); love depends upon faith received through the Spirit (13–16); love brings confidence and dispels fear (17–18); love of God is manifest in one's love for others (19–21); and, the ultimate reward of love is to keep God's commandments so all can share his victory through his Son (5:1–5). Here again there are obvious comparisons with items in the earlier two lists.

In essence, all three lists emphasize one's faith in Christ and the importance of acting upon one's convictions in keeping God's commandments and loving one another. Faith, obedience, and charity seem to be the cardinal principles of Christian discipleship that John expected of the Saints in his time. Love is the primary theme in these verses, with a strong secondary emphasis upon keeping the commandments. One important purpose of life on this earth is to learn to develop genuine love. And one obvious way to recognize a person's love for God is to observe whether the person obeys God. And, a person will obey God more readily as his or her faith is strengthened. God is love, and an individual's fellowship with Him depends upon his or her loving as God loves (see also 2:7–11; 3:11–18).[12]

Epilogue: The testimonies of eternal life (1 John 5:6–21). John named three elements involved in physical birth—water, blood, and spirit—all of which testify of Christ. Likewise, the spiritual birth of a child of God requires both the water of baptism, a cleansing from the blood and sins of one's natural life by the blood of Christ, and also the spirit of confirmation, a purging which prepares a soul to dwell in holy places. In addition, John reviewed the testifying nature of all three members of the Godhead, and he highlighted the eternal rewards of strengthening a person's testimony of the Son. He concluded with a strong admonition to overcome sin and follow Christ (5:6–11).

Verses 6–8 in this segment present some interesting doctrines and challenges to readers and scholars. Indeed, verses 7 and 8 are sometimes called "John's Comma" because these passages are not found in all of the earliest manuscripts. Nevertheless, some clarification of the roles of blood, water, and spirit in this earth life was revealed by the Lord to Adam in ancient days. One finds some helpful complements and antecedents to John's teachings in the words of Moses: "That by reason of transgression cometh the fall, which fall bringeth death, and inasmuch as ye were born into the world by water, and blood, and the spirit, which I have made, and so became of dust a living soul, even so ye must be born again into the kingdom of heaven, of water, and of the Spirit, and be cleansed by blood, even the blood of mine Only Begotten; that ye might be sanctified from all sin, and enjoy the words of eternal life in this world, and eternal life in the world to come, even immortal glory; for by the water ye keep the commandment; by the Spirit ye are justified, and by the blood ye are sanctified" (Moses 6:59–60).

The full harmony of natural and spiritual elements is necessary for human exaltation. Christ's atonement provides for one's exaltation. Obedience to the first principles and ordinances of the gospel brings the Atonement into a person's life.

Verses 12 through 21 highlight some promises and responsibilities given to those who have come unto Christ. The person who walks in the light can know he has eternal life (v. 13) and that his prayers are heard (vv. 14–15). Being a faithful Saint involves, according to John, correct beliefs and behavior. And if one truly loves others, one will not only serve them but will also help them avoid sin (v. 16). Also, one born of God does not live in sin, or more correctly, does not continue in sin (JST v. 18). Such disciples can know their true relationship to the Savior and Heavenly Father as they see their lifestyle and behavior in sharp contrast to the wicked patterns of the world. Ultimately, they will come to know Jesus Christ and to enjoy the eternal life he has promised (v. 20).

This epistle begins and ends with the theme of eternal life. Also, compare 4:20 with 1 John 1:2 where Jesus is called "the life" because he frees people from both physical and spiritual death. This passage echoes John's words from his gospel account in John 11:25 and 14:6. In addition, John reminds his readers in this epistle that Christ is the ultimate source and administrator of eternal life (5:11). The path to this eternal life is followed in loving faith and obedience.

In the upper room, John had heard the Savior say, "Love one another; as I have loved you, . . . love one another" (John 13:34; cf. 15:12). Those words continued to ring in the beloved apostle's ears. He could never forget them. So John kept saying over and over again, "My little children, love one another." This was his lifelong message. The Saints are to build upon light (their attitudes and beliefs) and life (their acts of obedience) as they love one another with that quality of love which is demonstrated by the Savior and Heavenly Father. That is John's central message in the first epistle: through faith and obedience, learn to love as God and Christ love us.

2 JOHN AND 3 JOHN

Both 2 and 3 John are brief and relatively insignificant compared to the other books of the New Testament. John's second epistle was written to at least one Christian community to counter the influence of false teachers. The early Saints were urged to use discernment in supporting traveling evangelists, or missionaries, who moved throughout Asia Minor. Some of them were true representatives of the apostles, bishops and other Church leaders, but others came from apostate groups or were independent agents or charlatans who were trying to win over followers for their particular philosophies. If the Saints were not careful, they might unintentionally house some of these apostate emissaries and thus contribute to the propagation of their heresies. This letter was written to a congregation of Saints emphasizing truth and love and warning them against false teachers. After extending greetings and expressing his gratitude, John exhorted the Saints to be obedient (vv. 5–6), warned against antichrists (vv. 7–9), and gave instruction in dealing with false teachers (vv. 10–11).

John's third epistle addressed specific people and recognized problems they were having with a local dictatorial leader. John first commended Gaius, a concerned member of the congregation, for the support and hospitality he had shown John's messengers, particularly Demetrius. John then chastised Diotrephes, the abusive leader, for his arrogance, inhospitality, slanderings, and authoritarian practices.[13] This letter involves four people: Gaius, Diotrephes, Demetrius, and the apostle. Again there is emphasis on truth and love (vv. 1, 3–4, 6,

8, 12). Because Gaius was living by the truth, he received warm praise from John. Diotrephes, on the other hand, because of his false pride and inhospitality, grieved the beloved apostle.

In summary, John delivered these three general epistles with powerful words and apostolic authority. He not only exposed some false teachings and teachers of his time but also gave perceptive instructions for future readers to discern between truth and error. Like those Saints John originally addressed, most people today struggle with the conflict between Christian teachings and the philosophies of the world. John's counsel helps separate light from darkness in learning from one's own behavior and beliefs whether one does indeed emulate the true and living and loving Son of God. John also provided the reader with spiritual measuring rods on how to know and follow the source and path toward eternal life. If love, along with obedience and faith, characterizes a person's attitudes and actions, then he or she is truly following the admonitions of John, the beloved apostle of the Lord Jesus Christ.[14]

NOTES

1. Various groups or congregations of people, usually following a charismatic leader, who separated from mainstream apostolic Christianity, resulting in a number of splinter or apostate churches.

2. A class of rationalists in early Christian church history who combined Christian doctrine with Greek and Oriental philosophies, with an emphasis on mysteries, secret knowledge, and hidden lore, resulting in a heretical, mystical, philosophical religion.

3. The following entries in the Bible Dictionary provide helpful insights into this epistle of John: "Antichrist" (609); "Confession" (649); "Epistles" (666–67); "General Epistles" (678); "John, Epistles of" (715); and "Paraclete" (741–42).

4. Compare 1 John 1:1 with similar phrases found in John 1:1, 14; and 1 John 1:4 with John 16:24. Also note the amplified introduction to 1 John in the Joseph Smith Translation given in footnote 1*a*.

5. See also 1:7 and compare with 2:1–2 and 4:10.

6. While emphasizing the attributes of love in this epistle, John contrasts it with the nature of sin. The Greek word for "sin" is found twenty-seven times in 1 John; the word *love* in its various forms is used forty-three times. In the English King James Version, *love* is found forty-six times (*love,* thirty-three times; *loved,* four times; *loveth,* nine times).

7. Or *paraclete;* see Bible Dictionary, 741–42. Compare John 14:16; 15:26; 16:13.

8. *The Interpreter's Bible* (New York: Abingdon Press, 1957), 12:235–37.

9. John says much about the devil and his characteristics in this short letter. Read 1 John 2:13–14; 3:8, 10, 12; 4:3; 5:18–19; and John 8:44 to learn more about him.

10. A careful review of other scriptures listed in the Topical Guide entry "Discernment, Spiritual" (103) provides helpful insights into the process of learning or knowing good from evil.

11. All six references to "light" in 1 John are in the first twenty verses; all but two of the forty-six references to "love" are in the succeeding verses, especially in this segment. The fifteen references to "life" are spread more evenly throughout 1 John.

12. Another important Joseph Smith Translation addition is in footnote 12*a* of chapter 4. It is not that absolutely no one has or ever will see God but only those who believe in God will have this privilege. The text of the Joseph Smith Translation provides a better complement to 1 John 3:6, which also talks about those who see God. The believer who turns away from sin will have an opportunity to see God. In other words, faith and purity become important prerequisites to seeing God.

13. Indeed, this Diotrephes may have been an early representative of the authoritarian bishop-teacher who was emerging in some Christian communities of what Ignatius of Antioch called "the Church Catholic." Raymond E. Brown, *The Gospel of St. John and the Johannine Epistles* (Collegeville, Minn.: Liturgical Press, 1982), 104.

14. If faith is considered as the first "principle" of the gospel, and obedience is the first "law" of the gospel, then love must be the first and foremost "practice" of the true Saints of Christ as they follow the examples of the Father and the Son. The apostle John built upon the basic foundation of these first principles, laws, and practices as he wrote these epistles.

CHAPTER NINE

WOMEN IN THE WRITINGS OF JOHN

ROBERT E. LUND

John's Gospel testifies that Christ invites all to come unto him: male and female. In a day when women were generally treated as inferior, Jesus showed great love and respect toward women. Perhaps it was John's own belief in the divine heritage of women that motivated him to include several unique accounts of women in his Gospel, when other Gospel writers did not. John testified of Christ's esteem for women and portrayed Jesus ennobling them. The women included in John's Gospel responded to the profound respect Jesus showed for them by exercising greater faith in him. Because of their faith in Jesus, these women were honored as eyewitnesses to some of Christ's greatest miracles. John also indicated that in some instances women exerted the faith necessary to generate the miracles. Through these experiences, John taught that women played an active role in miracles and in the ministry of Christ and that the gospel is for all people, both male and female. Because of the faith of these women, John was able to further testify of Jesus' divine nature.

The six women we see most clearly in the Gospel of John were Mary, the mother of Jesus (see John 2:1–11; 19:25–27); the Samaritan woman at the well (see John 4:4–30, 39–42); the woman taken in adultery (see John 8:1–11); Martha (see John 11:1–46; 12:1–8); Mary, Martha's sister (see John 11:1–46; 12:1–8); and Mary Magdalene (see John 20:1–18). Although the life experiences of these women ranged widely from the sacred to the profane, they were all uplifted after

Robert E. Lund is a seminary principal in Farmington, Utah.

conversing with the Son of God. In each instance, John was able to capture the spiritual strength of the woman interacting with Jesus.

MARY'S FAITH PRECEDED THE FIRST PUBLIC MIRACLE

John's Gospel records that while in his final hours on the cross, Jesus transferred his mother's care to John. From the cross Jesus saw both his mother and John standing together and instructed Mary, "Woman, behold thy son!" (John 19:26). Then Jesus charged John, "Behold thy mother!" (John 19:27). The meaning of Jesus' words were clear to both because "from that hour [John] took her unto his own home" (John 19:27). Why was John selected as the apostle to care for Mary? Perhaps it was because of John's esteem for women. Whatever the reason, it must have been considered a great honor by John to be selected as the guardian and protector of Mary, the mother of the Son of God.

John introduces the reader to Mary early in his Gospel. Because he had been entrusted to care for Mary, presumably until she died, it is likely that the two had many conversations about Jesus and his ministry (see John 19:26–27).[1] Mary's companionship with John probably influenced his writings. Perhaps that is why John is the only Gospel writer to record the first public miracle at the wedding in Cana. Certainly, John knew the great spiritual strength of Mary and her lifetime of faithfulness.[2] By including Mary at the beginning of his Gospel, John emphasized the important and active role that women played in the ministry of Jesus. Perhaps John also felt it was important to honor his adopted mother, whom he had come to admire while caring for her. Regardless, John began his Gospel with a tribute to Mary's faith.

John assumes the reader is aware that Mary's position at the wedding in Cana must have been one of responsibility.[3] Mary's domestic responsibility is shown by her concern about the lack of wine and by how she commanded the servants in a tone of authority.[4] John is quick to point out that when Mary lacked the resources needed to resolve the problem, her first avenue of relief was to turn to Jesus and request his help. John also assumes the reader knows that Mary had great faith in Jesus and his divine capabilities. When the guests "wanted wine, ~~the mother of Jesus saith~~ his mother said unto him, They have no wine" (JST John 2:3; throughout this paper the Joseph

Smith Translation is quoted by highlighting in **bold** the text Joseph Smith added and striking out the parts he deleted). This scripture suggests that when Mary looked to Jesus for help, she was respectfully *expecting* a miracle.[5] John understood that the pattern for miracles was simple and consistent: first the faith of a righteous person is exercised, and then the miracle is performed.[6] Because of Mary's faith in the Son of God, the first public miracle followed this same pattern, and Mary's request was granted by the hand of God.

The Joseph Smith Translation reveals Jesus' deep honor for his mother. John records, "Woman, what ~~have I to do with thee~~ **wilt thou have me do for thee? that will I do; for** mine hour is not yet come" (JST John 2:4). The title *woman* may sound harsh and disrespectful to us, but I believe its use conveys the opposite meaning.[7] One scholar explains that the "address 'woman' was so respectful that it might be, and was, addressed to the queenliest."[8] Another scholar explains that "'Woman,' or, rather 'Lady,' is in Greek a title of respect, used even in addressing queens."[9] It was as though Jesus had said, "My lady, whatsoever you ask of me in faith, I will grant it unto you." Jesus completely honored his mother.

After Jesus responded affirmatively, John chronicles Mary's great faith as she directs the servants, "Whatsoever he saith unto you, **see that ye** do it" (JST John 2:5). Her words were clear and unwavering: "Do it!" Do what? Mary's inspiring command to the servants could be rephrased something like this: "My son Jesus is going to tell you to do something, and whatever it is, just follow his instructions, and we will all be blessed."[10]

Mary taught a beautiful lesson as John's Gospel outlined her simple pattern for resolving problems: when in need, consult Jesus. Mary believed that Jesus had power over the elements and that they would obey him at his command. John used this miracle to teach both the power of a woman's faith and to reveal Jesus' true identity as the Creator. This first miracle also teaches that Jesus was interested in the routine pressures that women had to face when hosting a wedding. Jesus honored his mother by helping her with the task at hand.

It is understandable that Jesus would ennoble his mother, who had borne him and cared for him, as well as lived a life of faith and complete virtue. The contrast of Mary's example with that of the Samaritan woman, whom John introduces next, illustrates Christ's respect toward all women, even those outside one's family or nationality or religion.

JESUS SHOWED RESPECT FOR A WOMAN FROM SAMARIA

The most offensive people for most Jews were Samaritans. "To the orthodox Jew of the time a Samaritan was more unclean than a Gentile of any other nationality."[11] Yet, unlike the Jews of his day, Jesus respected even Samaritan women, as John's record shows. The Gospel writers, including John, did not give any historical background to explain why the Jews and the Samaritans hated each other. But the magnitude of the Savior's respect for the Samaritan woman may be more fully understood if we briefly review that rivalry.

Seven centuries earlier the Assyrians scattered the ten tribes of Israel and repopulated the land with colonists from other lands conquered by Assyria. These colonists began to mix with the Jews who remained. The mixed race was therefore part Jew and part Gentile. When the Jews returned, they considered the Samaritans more Gentile than Israelite and treated them as such. During the reconstruction of the temple in Jerusalem, the Samaritans were anxious to help with the construction and be recognized as Israelites. The Samaritans said, "Let us build with you: for we seek your God, as ye do" (Ezra 4:2). The Jews rejected the Samaritans' offer, however, and refused to let them help rebuild the temple (see Ezra 4:3–4). In frustration and anger, the rejected Samaritans built their own temple on Mount Gerizim to rival the temple in Jerusalem. From that time forward acts of hostility were traded between the two groups. Faithful Jews traveling from Galilee to Jerusalem to attend ceremonial feasts at the temple were often harassed or attacked by the Samaritans; the Jews retaliated by attacking Samaritan villages; thus a lasting feud was created.[12] Moreover, during Jesus' youth, Samaritans defiled the temple in Jerusalem by scattering human bones in it during Passover.[13] This act caused the worship in the temple to stop until the temple could be purified or rededicated. Because of these offenses, Jews considered Samaritans lower than the Gentiles. To call someone a Samaritan was an epithet on par with accusing the person of being possessed by a devil (see John 8:48). For some Jews, even the act of talking with a Samaritan made one unclean. Yet Jesus declared that his ministry included the house of Israel (see Matthew 15:24), and he disregarded the practice of his countrymen who added miles to their journey by going through Perea to avoid the Samaritans.[14] It seems that Jesus felt there was enough blood of Israel flowing in the veins of Samaritans to place them under the promises made to Abraham.[15] In addition, Samaritans believed that the Messiah would come and teach them all things (see John 4:25).[16]

The account of the experience of Jesus with the Samaritan woman at the well in John's Gospel begins by describing the physical conditions of Jesus at midday and concludes with a description of the spiritual conditions of the lives Jesus had touched that day. After traveling in the heat of the day, Jesus was tired, thirsty, and hungry (see John 4:6). Yet no matter how strong a desire Jesus had to rest and drink, he had a greater desire to declare his divinity to a Samaritan woman at the well. The conversion of the Samaritan woman happened gradually. Through the Spirit, the conversation led to conversion. She first addressed Jesus as "Jew," then "Sir," then "prophet," and finally as "the Christ" (see John 4:9–29). Her increasingly more respectful choice of titles indicates that her soul was uplifted and her heart softened as she spoke with Jesus. The Samaritan woman in turn desired to testify to the Samaritans in her village that Jesus was the Messiah.

John emphasizes Jesus' respect for the Samaritan woman throughout the discussion. Because it was apparent to the Samaritan woman that Jesus was a Jew, the woman might have unwittingly ignored the Messiah. Jesus therefore opened the conversation by addressing her with the ennobling term "woman," or "lady." This was the same term he used when he addressed his mother. Jesus simply requested a drink and used the image and symbolism of the nearby water to teach the woman. The woman was surprised that a Jew would speak to her, considering the rivalry between their nationalities. **"Wherefore he being alone, the woman of Samaria said** unto him, How is it that thou, being a Jew, askest drink of me, ~~which~~ **who** am a woman of Samaria?" (JST John 4:11).

Jesus' gentle voice, the dignity with which he addressed her, and his sincerity began to have an influence. She set aside their national differences and called Jesus "Sir" instead of "Jew." Jesus responded that if she knew who he was, she would have asked him for "living water" (John 4:10). Puzzled, the woman said, "Sir, thou hast nothing to draw with, and the well is deep: from whence then hast thou that living water?" (John 4:11). After Jesus explained that his water was everlasting, she mistakenly requested Jesus' water so that she would not have the rigorous chore of going to the well every day. The Samaritan woman was still in darkness, not comprehending the spiritual light of Christ's message. This is an example of what John had recorded earlier when he testified that Jesus was the "light [that] shineth in darkness; and the darkness comprehended it not" (John 1:5). Perceiving, however, that her heart was willing to repent and believe, Jesus decided to reveal to her facts about her personal life that a stranger would not know. He inquired about her husband, knowing that she had had five husbands and was now living with a man to whom she was not married. The woman denied being married, saying, "I have no husband" (John 4:17). Jesus then revealed her past life and present sinful relationship. Although she must have felt embarrassed, to her credit the woman continued to talk with Jesus, and the light began to dawn in her heart. She admitted, "Sir, I perceive that thou art a prophet" (John 4:19).

Her sins already revealed, with nothing left to hide and being compelled to be humble, the woman was receptive as Jesus then taught her how to gain salvation: "Woman, believe me" (John 4:21). Jesus reminded her that the Jews, not the Samaritans, had the truth and could minister salvation. She responded, "I know that Messias cometh, ~~which~~ **who** is called Christ, when he is come, he will tell us all things" (JST John 4:27). It was as though she were saying, "She could not believe this unknown Jew; if only the Messiah would come, if only he were here, all problems would be solved!"[17] Jesus then testified, "I ~~that~~ **who** speak unto thee am ~~he~~ **the Messias**" (JST John 4:28). These powerful words sank deep into the heart of the woman. Because of the patience and respect Jesus had shown this woman, her faith in him had taken root, and she desired to testify of Christ. She left her waterpot and went to the city proclaiming, "Come, see a man, ~~which~~ **who** told me all things that ~~ever I did~~ **I have ever done**: is not this the Christ?" (JST John 4:31). Her influence and persuasion would have created readiness to learn within the potential converts in Sychar. Indeed, many in the city were converted by the testimony of the woman, and they asked that Jesus "would tarry with them: and he abode there two days" (John 4:40).[18] John illustrated how this woman was an instrument in the hands of God. Her faith and missionary zeal helped soften the hearts of the people of Sychar.

John leaves the reader of this episode with several lessons about Jesus and his regard for women. John shows that Jesus is aware and concerned about women and knows the details of their lives. Through this experience John teaches that the gospel is for everyone, male and female, even adulterous women of rival nationalities. This message seems to have taken hold among the faithful Saints of John's day because Philip later served a mission to Samaria (see Acts 8:4–25). According to the culture of the day, Jesus could not have chosen to declare his divinity to a person lower in station than a sinful Samaritan woman. By featuring this type of person, especially in contrast to Mary, John showed that Jesus respects all women, regardless of their race or background. John's Gospel emphasizes this point by teaching about Christ's compassion for the woman caught in adultery.

JESUS SHOWED COMPASSION FOR THE WOMAN CAUGHT IN ADULTERY

The only reason that the scribes and Pharisees took to Jesus the woman caught in adultery was to trap him (see John 8:3–6).[19] The evil men challenged Jesus: "Now Moses in the law commanded us, that such should be stoned: but what sayest thou?" (John 8:5). The Pharisees hoped that no matter how Jesus responded to their question, they would be victorious in slandering him. If Jesus disagreed with Moses and "advocated anything less than death by stoning, he would be accused of perverting the law, and of advocating disrespect of and departure from the hallowed practices of the past."[20] On the other hand, if Jesus advocated stoning the woman, then the Pharisees believed it would anger the people, because most people felt the punishment was too harsh for the crime. Not only did the Pharisees hope it would anger the crowd but they "wished to embroil [Jesus] with the Roman authorities, who would not allow a death-sentence to be executed without their permission."[21]

John's Gospel contrasts the ruthless treatment of the woman by the Pharisees with the gentle respect and love of Jesus. Perhaps in an attempt to get the Pharisees to realize (and perhaps retract) their heartless treatment of the woman,[22] Jesus "stooped down, and with his finger wrote on the ground, as though he heard them not" (John 8:6). The act of "writing on the ground was a symbolical action well known in antiquity, signifying unwillingness to deal with the matter in hand."[23] Yet, unwilling to allow Jesus to gracefully decline getting involved, and blind to their own hardness, the scribes and Pharisees continued to pester him and embarrass the woman. Finally, out of compassion for the woman, Jesus "lifted up himself, and said unto them, He that is without sin among you, let him first cast a stone at her. And again he stooped down, and wrote on the ground" (John 8:7–8). Standing exposed and self-condemned, the accusers one by one shamefully filed out, leaving only the adulterous woman to face Jesus.

To her credit, the woman stayed at the side of Christ, instead of fleeing with the other sinners. It takes courage to confess one's sins. The woman must have felt lifted and strengthened by the dignity with which Jesus treated her. Perhaps that caused her to stay and stand ready to accept her judgment from Christ. "When Jesus had ~~lifted~~ **raised** up himself, and saw none ~~but the woman~~ **of her accusers, and the woman standing**, he said unto her, Woman, where are those thine accusers? hath no man condemned thee? She said, No man, Lord. And Jesus said unto her, Neither do I condemn thee: go, and sin no more. **And the woman glorified God from that hour, and believed on his name**" (JST John 8:10–11). After Jesus had spoken with the adulterous woman, she showed humility, faith, and dedication. She was willing to forsake her sins and follow Christ. She started her repentance process and began walking on the "strait and narrow path" (2 Nephi 31:19).

Again John's Gospel testifies that Jesus treated women, regardless of their serious sins, with respect and dignity. Christ's treatment of women caused them to believe in their individual worth, and then they in turn began to have greater faith in him, as John illustrates by the example of the woman taken in adultery. John's Gospel shows that Jesus lifted all women to higher spiritual plateaus regardless of their original spiritual level. Christ lifted the adulterous woman from the path of sin to the path of righteousness. This woman's life contrasted starkly with the lives of the two righteous sisters from Bethany. John next shows that the Master tested and purified the faith of Mary and Martha so that they could have a more sure witness of the divinity of Jesus Christ.

JESUS PURIFIED THE FAITH OF MARY AND MARTHA

John quickly alerts the reader to the love that Jesus felt for this family in Bethany. Mary, Martha, and Lazarus were siblings, and all were close friends to the Master. Jesus had taught the two sisters earlier when Mary had sat at the feet of Jesus, anxious to be taught the gospel (see Luke 10:38–42). Mary and Martha knew of the many miracles that Jesus had performed. They had likely heard of the widow's son at Nain who was brought to life (see Luke 7:11–18) and of Jairus's daughter being raised from the dead (see Mark 5:35–43). Lazarus was near death, and these sisters knew that Jesus could heal their brother. John explains that Martha was compassionately caring for her deathly sick brother and Mary was assisting. John's Gospel indicates that both sisters had faith that Jesus could heal their brother and thus they sent for the Master saying, "Lord, behold, he whom thou lovest is sick" (John 11:3; see also vv. 21, 32).

John records that Jesus waited rather than responding immediately to the request from Martha and Mary. Jesus deliberately delayed to increase their faith in him and teach that he was "the resurrection, and the life" (John 11:25). Therefore, Jesus stayed in Perea two more days (see John 11:6).[24] By the time Jesus arrived in Bethany, John notes that Lazarus has been buried for four days (see John 11:17, 39). By now his body had begun to rot and decay. Martha and Mary's hope that their brother would live was being tested. Yet Martha boldly rose to the occasion and expressed her faith, "Lord, if thou hadst been here, my brother had not died. But I know, that even now, whatsoever thou wilt ask of God, God will give it thee" (John 11:21–22). "The full import of these words, spoken by the power of the Holy Ghost, may not, as we shall soon see, have dawned fully upon this faithful and sweet sister, but she was in tune with the Spirit, and her faith enabled her to speak them, and glorious is her name for so doing."[25] Jesus reassured her, "Thy brother shall rise again" (John 11:23). Jesus' words caused Martha to share her testimony of the resurrection at the last day (see John 11:24), at which point Jesus testified to Martha of his divine Sonship: "I am the resurrection, and the life: he that believeth in me, though he were dead, yet shall he live: and whosoever liveth and believeth in me shall never die" (John 11:25–26). Jesus then inquired if she believed: "Believest thou this?" (John 11:26). Martha's response showed her increased faith in Jesus, "Yea, Lord: I believe that thou art the Christ, the Son of God, which should come into the world" (John 11:27).

Martha quietly notified Mary that Jesus had come. Mary now sought comfort from Jesus. "As soon as ~~she~~ **Mary** heard that **Jesus was come**, she arose quickly, and came unto him" (JST John 11:29). She fell at his feet, saying, "Lord, if thou hadst been here, my brother had not died" (John 11:32). Her words, identical to those of her sister, indicated that she too had faith that Jesus would have healed her brother. Yet both sisters still lacked full understanding of the great miracle that was about to take place.

John's Gospel records the tenderness of Jesus toward the sisters' plight with brief eloquence: "Jesus wept" (John 11:35). Christ continued to refine the faith of the sisters when he walked toward the cave where Lazarus was buried (see John 11:38). "Each step was taken with deliberation, to test and purify the faith of those who believed."[26] Jesus then directed that the stone be removed, and Martha observed that Lazarus would stink (see John 11:39). Reassuring her, Jesus responded, "Said I not unto thee, that, if thou wouldest believe, thou shouldest see the glory of God?" (John 11:40). Her faith was now strengthened and united with her sister's and Jesus' to help raise her brother from the dead.[27] Christ then thanked the Father for hearing his prayer, and he granted the desire of the sisters, according to their faith in him (see John 11:41–43), by commanding, "Lazarus, come forth" (John 11:43).[28] Then Jesus reverently commanded, "Loose him, and let him go" (John 11:44). Mary and Martha rejoiced that their brother had rejoined them.

Think of the effect this miracle had on Martha and Mary. Even though their faith had preceded the miracle of their brother's being raised from the dead, they were now more prepared to believe in the miraculous resurrection of Jesus. Because their brother had just been healed and restored to life, Mary and Martha, possibly more than any other mortals, were prepared to believe and accept the death and resurrection of Jesus. John further shows this acceptance with Mary's anointing of Jesus' feet (see JST John 12:7).

Mary knew that Christ was near the conclusion of his mortal

ministry and would soon be buried. Thus Mary paid her final tribute to Jesus. "Then took Mary a pound of ointment of spikenard, very costly, and anointed the feet of Jesus, and wiped his feet with her hair: and the house was filled with the odour of the ointment" (John 12:3). In this episode, John contrasts the pure motives of a woman with the corrupt motives of one who professed to be a disciple of Christ as he reveals the love and devotion of Mary toward Jesus, along with the contempt of Judas toward the Master. While Mary honored Jesus with her final gift, Judas wanted to dishonor him and whined, "Why was not this ointment sold for three hundred pence, and given to the poor? This he said, not that he cared for the poor; but because he was a thief, and had the bag, and bare what was put therein" (John 12:5–6).

Jesus defended Mary's token of love and devotion by stating, "Let her alone: ~~against the day of my burying hath she kept this~~ **for she hath preserved this ointment until now, that she might anoint me in token of my burial**" (JST John 12:7). John shows the reader that by defending Mary, Christ ennobled women and valued their righteous service. Mary's act showed that her faith had been purified and that she had accepted the death of Jesus. John used this simple story to testify that at least one faithful Saint, a woman, understood that Jesus must die and be resurrected to bring to pass eternal life. John's Gospel continues to highlight the faithful women surrounding the resurrection of Jesus by recording the first mortal to see the resurrected Lord: Mary Magdalene.

Mary Magdalene Was Chosen as a Witness of the Resurrected Christ

"No female name plays a more prominent part in the gospel accounts than that of the convert from Magdala, save only the Blessed Virgin herself."[29] Mary Magdalene stood near the cross and was close by while the body of Jesus was prepared for burial (see John 19:25; Matthew 27:61; Mark 15:47). "How much there is incident to the death, burial, and resurrection of our Lord which ennobles and exalts faithful women. . . . And so it is not strange that we find a woman, Mary of Magdala, chosen and singled out from all the disciples, even including the apostles, to be the first mortal to see and bow in the presence of a resurrected being."[30]

John is the only Gospel author who identifies the first person to see the resurrected Savior. Perhaps John wants the reader to know that women are just as valiant and capable as men of receiving great spiritual manifestations. John records, "The first day of the week cometh Mary Magdalene early, when it was yet dark, unto the sepulchre, and seeth the stone taken away from the sepulchre, **and two angels sitting thereon**" (JST John 20:1). Shocked that the stone was taken away and not recognizing the two individuals as angels, Mary ran to obtain help and to alert the apostles that Jesus' body was missing. She found Peter and John who ran to the sepulcher and found only the burial clothes (see John 20:2–7). Upon entering the sepulcher, John *believed* (John 20:8; emphasis added). Then the two apostles left, leaving Mary alone. Mary was weeping: the thought of not knowing what had happened to the body of Jesus overwhelmed her (see John 20:9–11). The angels, sitting at the head and feet of where Jesus had lain, inquired why she was weeping. Mary replied, "Because they have taken away my Lord, and I know not where they have laid him" (John 20:13). Through her tears she looked back and saw Jesus but did not recognize yet who was speaking to her. Mary told the questioner that she was willing to carry the body of Jesus elsewhere if need be (see John 20:14–15). "Jesus saith unto her, Mary" (John 20:16). "The recognition was instantaneous. Her river of tears became a sea of joy. It is He; he has risen; he lives; I love him as of old."[31] She turned toward Jesus and cried, "Rabboni; which is to say, Master" (John 20:16–17).[32] After speaking with Jesus, Mary was asked to go and testify to the apostles that he was alive.

John tells the reader that Mary was the first to share her witness of the resurrection with the apostles. "Mary Magdalene came and told the disciples that she had seen the Lord, and that he had spoken these things unto her" (John 20:18). Although the initial reaction of the disciples was skeptical,[33] Mary's words must have had some effect. Later, the disciples were gathered to discuss the events of the day, perhaps pondering the testimony of Mary, when Jesus "stood in the midst, and saith unto them, Peace be unto you" (John 20:19). This experience highlights Jesus' regard for women because Mary Magdalene was the first mortal ever to see the resurrected Lord and was commissioned to bear witness of him.

THE WOMEN IN THE GOSPEL OF JOHN TESTIFIED OF CHRIST

The common theme among these six women was that Jesus treated all of them with kindness and dignity. All were treated as daughters of Heavenly Father having infinite worth. In faithfulness, these women ranged from sinners to Saints. Perhaps that is why John chose their experiences—so that all could relate with at least one of these six women in their efforts to come unto Christ. The experiences these women had with Jesus strengthened and edified them. John points out that each woman was blessed for her faith and testimony in Jesus Christ, the Son of God. The Gospel of John also teaches that women receive powerful miracles and manifestations. Most significantly, the testimony of these women continues to strengthen testimonies and bless the lives of faithful women and men today.

NOTES

1. Customarily the oldest son was responsible for taking care of his widowed mother and unmarried sisters when the patriarch died. Joseph, the husband of Mary and the guardian of Jesus, was not mentioned in the account of the wedding at Cana; hence, many scholars believe him to have died sometime after Jesus' twelfth year but before his thirtieth year. To what extent Jesus had been caring for his mother during the preceding three years is unknown.

2. John must have known how valiant Mary had been throughout her life. Further, Mary's mission to raise the Son of God was foreordained in the councils before the world was. Mary is the greatest among women, for she had the honor of bearing and rearing the Son of God so that the Father might be glorified. Who could have a greater calling than mothering the Son of God? Mary is certainly "one of the noblest and greatest of all the spirit offspring of the Father" and the most honored woman in all scripture. Bruce R. McConkie, *Mormon Doctrine*, 2d ed. (Salt Lake City: Bookcraft, 1979), 471.

3. "Mary seemed to be the hostess at the marriage party, the one in charge, the one responsible for the entertainment of the guests. . . . Considering the customs of the day, it is a virtual certainty that one of Mary's children was being married." Bruce R. McConkie, *Doctrinal New Testament Commentary*, 3 vols. (Salt Lake City: Bookcraft, 1965–73), 1:135.

4. McConkie, *Commentary*, 1:135.

5. The way in which Mary told Jesus of "the insufficiency of wine probably suggested an intimation that He use His more than human power, and by such means supply the need." James E. Talmage, *Jesus the Christ* (Salt Lake City: Deseret Book, 1962), 145.

6. Moroni taught, "And neither at any time hath any wrought miracles until after their faith; wherefore they first believed in the Son of God" (Ether 12:18).

7. Talmage, *Jesus the Christ,* 144.

8. Frederic W. Farrar, *The Life of Christ* (Portland: Fountain Publications, 1964), 144.

9. J. R. Dummelow, ed., *Commentary on the Holy Bible* (New York: Macmillan, 1974), 778.

10. Jesus commanded the servants to fill the six water pots with water (see John 2:6–7), which were generally used for washing hands. The obedient servants filled the six stone pots to the brim. Each of the six pots contained two to three firkins, a firkin being about nine gallons. "Thus each of the six waterpots contained between twelve and eighteen gallons of water, with the result that Jesus then created some one hundred and fifty gallons of wine" (McConkie, *Commentary,* 1:136). The quality of the wine created by Jesus was obviously better than the wine previously served. The governor of the feast declared, "Every man at the beginning doth set forth good wine; and when men have well drunk, then that which is worse: but thou hast kept the good wine until now" (John 2:10).

11. Talmage, *Jesus the Christ,* 172.

12. Bruce R. McConkie, *The Mortal Messiah,* 4 vols. (Salt Lake City: Deseret Book, 1980–81), 1:494.

13. Talmage, *Jesus the Christ,* 184.

14. The story of the Samaritan woman began before Jesus met her at the well. Jesus "**said unto his disciples, I** must needs go through Samaria" (JST John 4:6). The wording of this passage in the Joseph Smith Translation suggests purpose in traveling through Samaria, not merely a geographic shortcut from Judea to Galilee. One purpose might have been for safety, for at the beginning of the chapter, John warns that the Pharisees were seeking "**diligently some means that they might put him to death**" (JST John 4:2). Perhaps another purpose was that Jesus knew that the Samaritans of Sychar were ready to hear the gospel and a certain woman was ready to receive him as the Messiah.

15. Jehovah promised Abraham that his seed would have the gospel (see Abraham 2:8–11). Now Jehovah personally preached the gospel in Samaria, fulfilling his promise to Abraham. Jesus had great missionary success in Sychar.

16. The Samaritans had their own version of the Pentateuch. Samaritans rejected the prophetical writings of the Old Testament since they were not treated with sufficient deference. "They boasted, however, of being Israelites, and with some degree of justification, for there was probably a considerable Jewish element in the population. Their worship, originally a compromise with heathenism, was now purely Jewish.

They kept the sabbath, and the Jewish feasts, and observed circumcision and other traditional ordinances" (Dummelow, *Commentary,* 781). Many Samaritans were expecting a Messiah that would establish a spiritual kingdom.

17. McConkie, *Mortal Messiah,* 1:501.

18. "The field [was] white already to harvest" (D&C 4:4). Jesus' success as a missionary was borne out by the people, who testified, "Now we believe, not because of thy saying: for we have heard him **for** ourselves, and know that this is indeed the Christ, the ~~Saviour~~ **Savior** of the world" (JST John 4:44). She was warned, and in turn warned her neighbors with her testimony that Jesus was the promised Messiah (see D&C 88:81). Later the disciples returned to Samaria on another successful mission to bestow the gift of the Holy Ghost (see Acts 8:4–25).

19. The sin of adultery was punishable by death under the law of Moses. "If a man be found lying with a woman married to an husband, then they shall both of them die, both the man that lay with the woman, and the woman: so shalt thou put away evil from Israel" (Deuteronomy 22:22; see also Leviticus 20:10; Exodus 20:14). Before stoning the accused, two witnesses were required to testify and then witnesses were required to throw the first stone. "At the mouth of two witnesses, . . . shall he that is worthy of death be put to death; . . . The hands of the witnesses shall be first upon him to put him to death, and afterward the hands of all the people" (Deuteronomy 17:6–7; see also 13:9). The custom of stoning by death had long ceased, however. "Not even the Scribes and Pharisees . . . had any genuine horror of an impurity from the sin of adultery with which their own lives were often stained" (Farrar, *Life of Christ,* 409). Even if the Jews had wished to continue the custom of stoning for adultery, they would have needed permission from the Romans for capital punishment. Such permission would likely have been impossible to obtain because Roman law, which took precedent in capital cases, did not punish adultery by death.

20. McConkie, *Commentary,* 1:451.

21. Dummelow, *Commentary,* 788.

22. The scribes and Pharisees had no business to accuse the woman. That was the right of the husband, and they had no legal or moral right to accuse the woman (see Dummelow, *Commentary,* 788). One scholar points out the utter cruelty of the scribes and Pharisees toward the woman: "And, therefore, to subject her to the superfluous horror of this odious publicity—to drag her, fresh from the agony of detection, into the sacred precincts of the Temple—to subject this unveiled, dishevelled, terror-stricken woman to the cold and sensual curiosity of a malignant mob—to make her, with total disregard to her own sufferings, the mere passive instrument of their hatred against Jesus; . . . in order to gratify a calculating malice—showed on their parts a cold, hard cynicism, a

graceless, pitiless, barbarous brutality of heart and conscience" (Farrar, *Life of Christ,* 409–10).

23. Dummelow, *Commentary,* 788–89.

24. Why did Jesus allow Lazarus to die? Because "Lazarus was foreordained to die; it was part of the eternal plan" (McConkie, *Mortal Messiah,* 3:271). Lazarus needed to die and be brought back to life so that Jesus' close friends and disciples could see a foreshadowing of his own death and resurrection.

25. McConkie, *Mortal Messiah,* 3:275.

26. McConkie, *Mortal Messiah,* 3:278.

27. McConkie, *Mortal Messiah,* 3:279.

28. Commenting on the greatness of the miracle performed, Farrar said: "Those words thrilled once more through that region of impenetrable darkness which separates us from the world to come; and scarcely were they spoken when, like a spectre, from the rocky tomb issued a figure, swathed indeed in its white ghastly cerements—with the napkin round the head which had upheld the jaw that four days previously had dropped in death, bound hand and foot and face, but not livid, not horrible—the figure of a youth with healthy blood of a restored life flowing through his veins; of life restored—so tradition tells us—for thirty more long years to life, and light, and love" (*Life of Christ,* 481).

29. McConkie, *Mortal Messiah,* 4:262.

30. McConkie, *Commentary,* 1:843.

31. McConkie, *Mortal Messiah,* 4:263.

32. "Jesus saith unto her, ~~Touch~~ Hold me not; for I am not yet ascended to my Father" (JST John 20:17). There are two explanations why Jesus said to Mary, "Touch me not," or "Hold me not." The first is by Elder James E. Talmage, who said that Jesus now had a "divine dignity that forbade close personal familiarity. To Mary Magdalene Christ had said: 'Touch me not; for I am not yet ascended to my Father.' If the second clause was spoken in explanation of the first, we have to infer that no human hand was to be permitted to touch the Lord's resurrected and immortalized body until after He had presented Himself to the Father" (*Jesus the Christ,* 682). Later, other women held Jesus by the feet in worshipful reverence, giving the implication that Christ had ascended to the Father before going to them (see Matthew 28:9). The second explanation is by Elder Bruce R. McConkie, who suggests that various "translations from the Greek render the passage as 'Do not cling to me' or 'Do not hold me.' Some give the meaning as 'Do not cling to me any longer,' or 'Do not hold me any longer.' Some speak of ceasing to hold him or cling to him" (*Mortal Messiah,* 4:264).

33. Mary's testimony "seemed to them as idle tales, and they believed them not" (Luke 24:11).

CHAPTER TEN

"GIVE UNTO ME POWER OVER DEATH"

DAVID B. MARSH

While translating the New Testament in April 1829, Joseph Smith and Oliver Cowdery encountered John 21:22. During a discussion of its meaning, "a difference of opinion [arose] between [them] about the account of John the Apostle . . . as to whether he died or continued to live."[1] Since we do not have a record of their specific deliberations, we can only imagine its substance and wonder which opinion was held by each. They "mutually agreed to settle their 'difference of opinion' by the Urim and Thummim"[2] and received what we now know as Doctrine and Covenants 7. Joseph Smith and Oliver Cowdery were not the first, however, to consider the condition, state, and reason for translated beings. Eighteen hundred years previous to their latter-day discussion, Mormon also wondered about the mortality or immortality of the three Nephite disciples who had received the same blessing as John (see 3 Nephi 28:17). Mormon "inquired of the Lord" and received revelation concerning the matter (see 3 Nephi 28:36–40). Because of the diligent searching and inquiry of these prophets, we have inspiring information regarding the nature of and purpose for translated beings in the Lord's great and eternal plan for the salvation of his children. This revealed knowledge helps us to better understand what John the Beloved was, and is, doing as a translated being.

Accounts of translated beings are found in all five books that compose the standard works. The existence of such beings and the

David B. Marsh is the Church Educational System coordinator in Visalia, California.

doctrine they are founded upon can be an inspiring testimony to the mercy of our Heavenly Father in his plan to help us know him and return to his presence. Once we understand the reason for their miraculous condition and power, we begin to realize just how vital they are to the fulfillment of the plan of salvation and the "everlasting covenant" that was made between members of the Godhead "before the organization of this earth."[3] Studying the doctrine of translated beings as found in the scriptures and the teachings of latter-day prophets and, in particular, John's calling as a translated being will help us gain a greater appreciation for the extended life and service of John the Beloved.

THE DOCTRINE OF TRANSLATED BEINGS

At least five principles taught in the scriptures and by the prophets of this last dispensation reveal to us the doctrine of translated beings. Translated beings exist by virtue of the Melchizedek Priesthood, have been given future missions, have power over death, have the convincing power of God, and can conceal their identity.

By virtue of the Melchizedek Priesthood. Speaking of the powers and the keys of the Melchizedek Priesthood, the Prophet Joseph Smith declared: "Now the doctrine of translation is a power which belongs to this Priesthood. There are many things which belong to the powers of the Priesthood and the keys thereof, that have been kept hid from before the foundation of the world; they are hid from the wise and prudent to be revealed in the last times."[4]

The keys and authority that allow the power of translation to operate among the children of God reside within the Melchizedek Priesthood. It should not be supposed that every Melchizedek Priesthood holder has these keys conferred upon him. Keys are not universally distributed among the body of priesthood holders. Additionally, this does not imply that only men can be translated. It simply means that when a person—man or woman—is translated, it is performed within the stewardship of the keys and authority of the Melchizedek Priesthood. Moreover, though there are no specific scriptural accounts of women being translated, there is nothing in the scriptures that would cause us to believe that the Lord did not include the women of Enoch's city when they were "taken up into heaven" (Moses 7:21).

Moses further explained that coupled with the power of the priesthood there must be a requisite faith: "Now Melchizedek was a man of faith, who wrought righteousness; and when a child he feared God, and stopped the mouths of lions, and quenched the violence of fire.

"And thus, having been approved of God, he was ordained an high priest after the order of the covenant which God made with Enoch,

"It being after the order of the Son of God; which order came, not by man, nor the will of man; neither by father nor mother; neither by beginning of days nor end of years; but of God. . . .

"For God having sworn unto Enoch and unto his seed with an oath by himself; that every one being ordained after this order and calling should have power, by faith, to break mountains, to divide the seas, to dry up waters, to turn them out of their course;

"To put at defiance the armies of nations, to divide the earth, to break every band, to stand in the presence of God; to do all things according to his will, according to his command, subdue principalities and powers; and this by the will of the Son of God which was from before the foundation of the world.

"And men having this faith, coming up unto this order of God, were translated and taken up into heaven" (JST Genesis 14:27–28, 30–32).

Yoked with the order of the priesthood, faith is essential for a person to be "translated and taken up into heaven." This faith, no doubt, would include worthiness, discipleship, gospel knowledge, obedience, and submission to the will of the Father and the Son, to name a few important principles. Additionally, "by the virtue of [his] blood," the Savior has "pleaded before the Father for them" (D&C 38:4), and hence, they will be cleansed and eventually received into the celestial kingdom (see D&C 76:66–69). Without the Atonement, no thing and no one could reenter the presence of our Heavenly Father (see Mosiah 3:17; 4:7; 16; Alma 5:21; 21:9; 22:13–14; D&C 45:3–5).

Translated beings are an integral part of God's organization and are governed and regulated by the keys and authority embraced by the Melchizedek Priesthood. Furthermore, they are intended for future missions that contribute to fulfilling the great plan of salvation.

Designed for future missions. Joseph Smith succinctly taught that "translated bodies are designed for future missions."[5] This being the case, we might seek to identify the future missions of those translated beings that are mentioned in the scriptures, namely, Enoch and his city, Moses, Elijah, the three Nephites, and John the Beloved. Others mentioned in the scriptures, such as Alma (see Alma 45:19), will not be treated here because of a lack of information at this time regarding their future mission.

Enoch and His City. According to Joseph Smith, Enoch was "appointed . . . a ministry unto terrestrial bodies" and was "reserved also unto the presidency of a dispensation."[6] Jude, after Enoch appeared unto him,[7] prophesied of this dispensation, stating: "Behold, the Lord cometh with ten thousands of his saints, To execute judgment upon all, and to convince all that are ungodly among them of all their ungodly deeds which they have ungodly committed, and of all their hard speeches which ungodly sinners have spoken against him" (Jude 1:14–15).

Enoch and his city of Saints were reserved "until a day of righteousness shall come" (D&C 45:12). They will help to usher in that day by receiving power to convince the ungodly of their ungodly ways. The Lord showed Enoch that day when he and his city would be called upon to continue the preparation of a people who would also be called Zion, the New Jerusalem:

"And righteousness and truth will I cause to sweep the earth as with a flood, to gather out mine elect from the four quarters of the earth, unto a place which I shall prepare, an Holy City . . . and it shall be called Zion, a New Jerusalem.

"And the Lord said unto Enoch: Then shalt thou and all thy city meet them there, and we will receive them into our bosom, and they shall see us; and we will fall upon their necks, and they shall fall upon our necks, and we will kiss each other;

"And there shall be mine abode, and it shall be Zion, which shall come forth out of all the creations which I have made; and for the space of a thousand years the earth shall rest" (Moses 7:62–64).

From these scriptures and prophetic declarations it seems reasonable to conclude that much of Enoch's mission, dispensation, and ministry will be among terrestrial beings during the millennial or paradisiacal period of the earth's existence. The Prophet Joseph's reference to Enoch's dispensational presidency may allude either to his being a president of those in his translated city, or to a presidency in which he will serve during the Millennium, or both.

Moses. Moses' future mission dealt with at least two impending dispensations, one at the meridian of time, during the Savior's mortal ministry, and the other at the opening of the dispensation of the fulness of times, during which all things "shall be revealed" (D&C 121:31). Although the testimony of Matthew does not indicate specifically what Moses did with Peter, James, John, and Jesus (see Matthew 17:1–3), we know that the Lord had promised them "the keys of the kingdom of heaven" and the attending powers (Matthew 16:19). We also know that when Moses appeared to Joseph Smith and Oliver Cowdery in the Kirtland Temple, he committed to them "the keys of the gathering of Israel from the four parts of the earth, and the leading of the ten tribes from the land of the north" (D&C 110:11). It is reasonable to conclude that during his biblical visit, Moses was authorized to commit those same keys to the leadership of that early Church. Of this visit Elder Bruce R. McConkie taught: "Then it was, on the snowy mountain heights, after the Father had spoken from the cloud, that Moses and Elijah, both taken to heaven without tasting death, had come in their corporeal bodies to a temple not made with hands, and given for that day and time their keys and powers to Peter, James, and John."[8]

Elijah. Elijah was one of the more prominent prophets during Old Testament times who "held the sealing power of the Melchizedek Priesthood."[9] He accompanied Moses to the Mount in Jerusalem and to the Kirtland Temple on 3 April 1836 to confer this authority and power.

The Three Nephites. These Nephite disciples were neither reserved for a particular dispensation nor responsible for committing specific keys to future Church leaders. Rather, the scope of their calling spans centuries of time and includes all the inhabitants of the earth. Just as Enoch was reserved to minister among terrestrial beings, so these translated Nephites were to minister among telestial beings—those who were and are still living on the earth. They were charged to minister among the Gentiles, the Jews, the scattered tribes of Israel, and "unto all nations, kindreds, tongues and people" (3 Nephi 28:29). They can "show themselves unto whatsoever man it seemeth them good" and "great and marvelous works shall be wrought by them, before the great and coming day when all people must surely stand before the judgment-seat of Christ" (3 Nephi 28:30–31). They also ministered unto both Mormon and Moroni (see 3 Nephi 28:26; Mormon 8:11). While their works are many and varied, as well as great and marvelous, the essential purpose of their mission is to bring souls unto Christ (see 3 Nephi 28:29).

John the Beloved. The work that John would do is identical to that of the three Nephites. Also similar are the length of time and the breadth of their missions, for the Lord told John: "Verily, verily, I say unto thee, because thou desirest this thou shalt tarry until I come in my glory, and shalt prophesy before nations, kindreds, tongues and people" (D&C 7:3).

When the resurrected Savior appeared to his disciples at the sea of Tiberias (see John 21:1) and asked John what he desired, John answered, saying, "Lord, give unto me power over death, that I may live and bring souls unto thee" (D&C 7:2). To an inquiry from Peter in the same discussion, the Lord confirmed John's desire, declaring, "For he desired of me that he might bring souls unto me" (D&C 7:4).

Bringing people to Christ is a foundational principle which undergirds all that we do in the Church, and it appears particularly pertinent to the purpose for John's translation. As a trusted friend of Christ and as one of the special witnesses of the Savior, John occupies a singular position to testify to the world of both the reality and the divinity of the Son of God. The design and focus of John's testimony, as contained in the Bible, is to convince us that Jesus of Nazareth is indeed the Christ. Every story, event, and discourse recorded by John seems geared toward persuading us to believe in the Only Begotten and to come unto him for salvation. Near the end of his record, John himself declares: "These are written, that ye might believe that Jesus is the Christ, the Son of God; and that believing ye might have life through his name" (John 20:31).

His testimony of the Lord is clear and undiluted, focused and persuasive. His knowledge and witness extend from the premortal power of "the Word" (John 1:14) through the mortal messiahship of the "Light" (John 8:12), to the postmortal preeminence of the "Resurrection" (John 11:25). The record of his testimony is laced with a conviction of the divinity of the Son of the living God. By reading from John's early accounts of those who proclaim, "We have found the Messias" (John 1:41), to the final declarations of the Good Shepherd himself, inviting all to "Follow thou me" (John 21:22), the earnest seeker of truth will likewise proclaim, "we know that his [John's] testimony is true" (John 21:24).

Should there be a search for one who could be called on to testify boldly, yet meekly, of the sacred life and mission of the Lord; one who would wear out his mortal life and then continue to labor through the miracle of a divine extension of the call, to "bring souls unto [Christ]" (D&C 7:4), John would no doubt top the list. His visions of the future recorded in the book of Revelation qualify him to understand their fulfillment and to stand as a witness of the prophecies of all the prophets concerning the last days and the second coming of the Lord.

During his great vision regarding the last days, John received a "little book" from an angel (Revelation 10:2). After digesting the book, John was commissioned by the angel to "prophesy again before many peoples, and nations, and tongues, and kings" (Revelation 10:11). The word *again* implies a future mission for John. This implication is confirmed in latter-day revelation, which teaches that John would participate in the restoration of all things by fulfilling "a mission, and an ordinance, . . . to gather the tribes of Israel" (D&C 77:14). John Whitmer, as Church historian, recorded that during a conference held on June 3 through 6 of 1831, "the Spirit of the Lord fell upon Joseph in an unusual manner, and he prophesied that John the Revelator was then among the Ten Tribes of Israel who had been led away by Shalmaneser, King of Assyria, to prepare them for their return from their long dispersion, to again possess the land of their fathers."[10]

Joseph Smith would surely have known about John's mission to the ten tribes because he is the head of the final dispensation, the one to whom the Lord has "committed the keys of my kingdom, and a dispensation of the gospel for the last times; and for the fulness of times, in the which I will gather together in one all things, both which are in heaven, and which are on earth" (D&C 27:13; see also 81:1–2; 113:6).

The Lord, in his economy, does not give keys, and hence authority and responsibility, to one person only to have another person accomplish the work, without notifying the one who received the keys to direct the work. It is a matter of order and respect—both cardinal qualities of the Lord. Consequently, because John's mission involved work among the latter-day tribes of Israel, he would have submitted himself and his missionary efforts to the authority of the living prophet, seer, and revelator, who holds all the keys of "the gathering of Israel from the four parts of the earth, and the leading of the ten tribes from the land of the north" (D&C 110:11).

Some may wonder why the Lord would have need to translate a person to fulfill a future mission—why not send an angel from the spirit world to accomplish the work rather than have someone continue living for so many years before doing the work? It may have something to do with the perfect order God has established concerning spiritual and heavenly worlds and beings. The Prophet Joseph taught, "The organization of the spiritual and heavenly worlds, and of spiritual and heavenly beings, was agreeable to the most perfect order and harmony: their limits and bounds were fixed irrevocably, and voluntarily subscribed to in their heavenly estate by themselves, and were by our first parents subscribed to upon the earth."[11]

In God's "most perfect order" he desires that translated or embodied spirits minister unto embodied spirits, while disembodied spirits minister unto disembodied spirits.[12] Consequently, if a mission must be accomplished among mortals, or embodied spirits, the heavenly order requires that an embodied spirit, with authority, not a disembodied spirit from the spirit world, perform the mission. Nevertheless, it is evident that when we are allowed to read the heavenly history that chronicles John's mission, we will be astonished by the number and the influence of all his works. No doubt we will exclaim, if only within ourselves, that he accomplished many great and marvelous works among the children of men. To do "more, or a greater work yet among men than what he has before done" (D&C 7:5), John, and all other translated beings, would need to receive power over death.

Power over death. Of all the principles encompassed in the doctrine of translation, the principle of power over death seems to be the one that has caused the most misunderstanding and inquiry. The general Church membership seems to have misunderstood, and then prophets have inquired of the Lord for enlightenment. In John's day, the Lord's statement that John would "tarry till I come" (John 21:22) was apparently misunderstood among the membership generally, for the record reveals that the "saying" went "abroad among the brethren" (John 21:23). In these latter days, it led to a difference of opinion between Joseph Smith and Oliver Cowdery.[13] Revelation was necessary in former days to shed light on this principle. We, too, have been blessed to receive, through modern-day prophets, revelation to help us understand this miraculous power over death.

John's record attempts a clarification of the Savior's declaration: "Yet Jesus said not unto him, He shall not die; but, If I will that he tarry till I come" (John 21:23), implying that John would eventually experience something similar to death when the Savior came again. Similarly, Jesus told the three Nephite disciples on the American continent that they would "never taste of death" (3 Nephi 28:7). Like the members of the early Christian church, we could mistakenly surmise from this phrase that the Lord meant they would never die; however, the subsequent verses seem to explain more clearly what the Savior intended:

"And ye shall never endure the pains of death; but when I shall come in my glory ye shall be changed in the twinkling of an eye from mortality to immortality; and then shall ye be blessed in the kingdom of my Father.

"And again, ye shall not have pain while ye shall dwell in the flesh, neither sorrow save it be for the sins of the world" (3 Nephi 28:8–9).

This explanation conforms to John's record that Jesus did not say translated beings would not die. Mormon, uncertain regarding the bodily condition of the Nephite disciples, inquired of the Lord and received the following revelation:

"And now behold, as I spake concerning those whom the Lord hath chosen, yea, even three who were caught up into the heavens, that I knew not whether they were cleansed from mortality to immortality—

"But behold, since I wrote, I have inquired of the Lord, and he hath made it manifest unto me that there must needs be a change wrought upon their bodies, or else it needs be that they must taste of death;

"Therefore, that they might not taste of death there was a change wrought upon their bodies, that they might not suffer pain nor sorrow save it were for the sins of the world.

"Now this change was not equal to that which shall take place at the last day; but there was a change wrought upon them, insomuch that Satan could have no power over them, that he could not tempt them; and they were sanctified in the flesh, that they were holy, and that the powers of the earth could not hold them.

"And in this state they were to remain until the judgment day of Christ; and at that day they were to receive a greater change, and to be received into the kingdom of the Father to go no more out, but to dwell with God eternally in the heavens" (3 Nephi 28:36–40).

These verses provide an abundance of knowledge regarding the principle of power over death. From them we learn that translated beings have a change wrought upon their bodies; do not suffer physical pain or sorrow but do suffer by witnessing the sins of the world; are not buffeted by the temptations of Satan—he has no power over them; are sanctified in the flesh and made holy; are not held by the powers of the earth; will remain in this translated state until Judgment Day, when they will receive a greater change, or resurrection, and be received in the celestial kingdom to dwell with God eternally. Confirming the principle of a "greater change," Joseph Smith taught that translated beings "as yet have not entered into so great a fullness as those who are resurrected from the dead. . . .

" . . . This distinction is made between the doctrine of the actual resurrection and translation: translation obtains deliverance from the tortures and sufferings of the body, but their existence will prolong as to the labors and toils of the ministry, before they can enter into so great a rest and glory."[14] Additionally, the Prophet Joseph taught that translated bodies must undergo "a change equivalent to death."[15]

Other prophets of the Restoration have provided us with revealed knowledge and confirmation of Joseph's words. President Wilford Woodruff further enlightened our understanding of the universal nature of death and translated beings: "We acknowledge that through Adam all have died, that death through the fall must pass upon the whole human family, also upon the beasts of the field, the fishes of the sea and the fowls of the air and all the works of God, as far as this earth is concerned. It is a law that is unchangeable and irrevocable. It is true a few have been translated, and there will be living upon the earth thousands and millions of people when the Messiah comes in power and great glory to reward every man according to the deeds done in the body, who will be changed in the twinkling of an eye, from mortality to immortality. Nevertheless, they must pass through the ordeal of death."[16]

In an article in the *Deseret Weekly News*, President Joseph F. Smith taught: "There is not a soul that has escaped death, except those upon whom God has passed, by the power of his Spirit, that they should live in the flesh until the second coming of the Son of Man; but they will eventually have to pass through the ordeal called death; it may be in the twinkling of an eye, and without pain or suffering; but they will pass through the change, because it is an irrevocable edict of the Almighty. 'In the day that thou eatest thereof thou shalt surely die.' This was the edict of the Almighty and it pertains to Adam—that is, all the human race; for Adam is many, and it means you and me and every soul that lives and that bears the image of the Father. We shall all die."[17]

Likewise, President Joseph Fielding Smith explained: "Translated beings are still mortal and will have to pass through the experience of death, or the separation of the spirit and the body, although this will be instantaneous."[18]

Hence, while translated beings do experience a change in their bodies so that the effects of the Fall, the powers of mortality, and the seduction of Satan are suspended, they will eventually undergo a quick (in the twinkling of an eye) and painless equivalent of death.

The convincing power of God. Because translated beings can neither be detoured nor distracted by the afflictions of the flesh, and because they cannot be corrupted personally by the temptations of Satan, it would follow that their righteousness would invite an augmented ability and power to persuade, even to convincing people of the truth. This being the case, it is no wonder that these incorruptible emissaries will "bring . . . unto Jesus many souls" from "all the scattered tribes of Israel" (3 Nephi 28:29). This occurs as a result of "the convincing power of God which is in them" (3 Nephi 28:29). Because of being "sanctified in the flesh, that they [are] holy" (3 Nephi 28:39), and because they have obtained the word and the spirit of God through their desire and diligence, they receive what modern revelation calls "the power of God unto the convincing of men" (D&C 11:21; see also Jude 1:14–15). John surely met these qualifications. We learn in the Doctrine and Covenants about his desire to bring many souls unto Christ (see D&C 7:1, 3–5, 8). Additionally, from his own testimony contained in the New Testament, we are assured that he obtained the "word" and the Spirit of the Lord (D&C 11:21).

We can only imagine, for now, the "many" who have been convinced of the Lord their Redeemer through the translated instrumentality of John the Beloved. Some may have been ministered to by John or other translated beings but may not have recognized them as such because translated beings have the miraculous ability to conceal their identity.

Concealing their identity. Mormon saw the Three Nephites and they ministered to him, but translated beings will not always be recognized by those to whom they have ministered. Mormon declared, "And behold they will be among the Gentiles, and the Gentiles shall know them not. They will also be among the Jews, and the Jews shall know them not" (3 Nephi 28:27–28).

The privilege to recognize translated beings seems to be the result of their petition rather than ours. Mormon explains, "And they are as the angels of God, and if they shall pray unto the Father in the name of Jesus they can show themselves unto whatsoever man it seemeth them good" (3 Nephi 28:30).

Whether they minister to us or not, and whether we recognize them or not, we know that "great and marvelous works shall be wrought by them, before the great and coming day when all people must surely stand before the judgment-seat of Christ" (3 Nephi 28:31).

CONCLUSION

John's life as an apostle of Jesus Christ and as a beloved friend to the Savior could only be superseded by doing "more, or a greater work yet among men than what he has before done" (D&C 7:5). The Lord graciously bestowed on this special servant a blessing according to his desires (see D&C 7:8). He became as "flaming fire and a ministering angel" to "minister for those who shall be heirs of salvation who dwell on the earth" (D&C 7:6). Even during those times when the Church has not been officially organized among mortals, the

Lord in his mercy and wisdom provided translated beings, including John, who, by the power and authority of the Melchizedek Priesthood, could "hold Satan in check."[19]

Who can calculate the influence and effect John the Beloved has had during the centuries of the Apostasy as well as throughout the history and development of the Restoration in these last days? Indeed, as a translated being, he has done a greater work among men than he did during his mortal life in Jerusalem (see D&C 7:5). It is possible that many of our ancestors who belonged to the scattered tribes of Israel have been brought to the Savior through John's divinely conferred convincing power. Furthermore, we can only imagine the service he will render in our day and through the Millennium. Unfettered and unaffected by death or disease and aided by an increased ability to preach and persuade, John the Beloved will no doubt accomplish great things in building up the kingdom of God in this last dispensation. Though his identity may be concealed as he works among us, we can suppose that in a future day he will be known for what he is—a "flaming fire and a ministering angel" (D&C 7:6). We should be grateful for the providential providing of translated beings, such as John the Beloved, and the power granted unto them to bring souls unto Christ. Surely there are untold blessings that extend to our generation, and perhaps to each of us personally, from our generous Father in Heaven through the miraculous ministration of these purified beings, particularly John the Beloved.

NOTES

1. Joseph Smith, *History of The Church of Jesus Christ of Latter-day Saints,* ed. B. H. Roberts, 2d ed. rev., 7 vols. (Salt Lake City: The Church of Jesus Christ of Latter-day Saints, 1932–51), 1:35–36.

2. Smith, *History of the Church,* 1:36.

3. Joseph Smith, *Teachings of the Prophet Joseph Smith,* sel. Joseph Fielding Smith (Salt Lake City: Deseret Book, 1976), 190.

4. Smith, *Teachings of the Prophet Joseph Smith,* 70.

5. Smith, *Teachings of the Prophet Joseph Smith,* 191.

6. Smith, *Teachings of the Prophet Joseph Smith,* 170.

7. Smith, *Teachings of the Prophet Joseph Smith,* 170.

8. Bruce R. McConkie, *Ensign,* May 1983, 22.

9. Bible Dictionary, "Elijah," 664.

10. Smith, *History of the Church,* 1:176.

11. Smith, *Teachings of the Prophet Joseph Smith*, 325.

12. Smith, *Teachings of the Prophet Joseph Smith*, 191.

13. Smith, *History of the Church*, 1:35–36.

14. Smith, *Teachings of the Prophet Joseph Smith*, 170–71.

15. Smith, *Teachings of the Prophet Joseph Smith*, 191.

16. Wilford Woodruff, *Discourses of Wilford Woodruff*, sel. G. Homer Durham (Salt Lake City: Bookcraft, 1990), 244.

17. Joseph F. Smith, *Gospel Doctrine* (Salt Lake City: Deseret Book, 1986), 32.

18. Joseph Fielding Smith, *Doctrines of Salvation*, comp. Bruce R. McConkie, 3 vols. (Salt Lake City: Bookcraft, 1954–56), 2:300.

19. Harold B. Lee, *Teachings of Harold B. Lee*, sel. Clyde J. Williams (Salt Lake City: Bookcraft, 1996), 486.

CHAPTER ELEVEN

THE IMPROBABILITY OF THE NEW COMMANDMENT

HAROLD L. MILLER JR.

The culminating supper of Jesus' mortal ministry was both a coming full circle and the occasion of looking forward and giving new directives. Those assembled in the large upper room were the same men with whom Christ had begun his ministry. Now they were with him in its conclusion. In the quiet of a few hours, the Master set in motion critical events leading to his death by crucifixion and the transition to a new regime of Church administration in his absence. Most important was his vivid indication that the apostles were to carry on in a manner resembling his own.

The remarkable story of the Last Supper in the Gospel According to St. John is a sublime setting in context of the duties to be assumed by the surviving apostles. The work was to be performed with continued divine attention from the Father, the resurrected Son, and the Holy Ghost. The prayer by which Jesus ended the solemn gathering underscored the keenness of his interest in the brethren who would carry on after him. He expected that their ministry would be typified by the same qualities he had demonstrated. Chief among them was love—his theme for their last hours together, a theme sounded in the first verse of John 13: "Having loved his own which were in the world, he loved them unto the end."

Their meal gave way to Jesus' invocation of symbols by which

Harold L. Miller Jr. is a professor of psychology at Brigham Young University.

they could properly remember him in the future. In doing so he revisited a sermon from an early period in his ministry that had proven to be a crossroads of sort (see John 6). At that time he had spoken of eating his flesh and drinking his blood—strange references that had confused his hearers and caused many to reject him. Now, at this late point in his ministry, he clarified the connection between his imminent sacrifice—the breaking of his body (see 1 Corinthians 11:24) and the shedding of his blood (see Luke 22:20)—and its consequences for salvation. He and the apostles raised bread and wine to their lips and, in those gestures, instituted a new ordinance. They established a new communion that adumbrated what Jesus was soon to do. The apostles' subsequent adoption of the ritual would remind them and others of that final occasion with him. It would also evidence the inescapability of common (communal) dependence on him for salvation.

Jesus' institution of the sacrament was followed by a further demonstration (see John 13:4–17) that set the tone for the remainder of his time with the apostles. He took water and a towel and proceeded to wash each man's feet. This, too, was new to their experience and, like the sacrament, brought something new to their awareness. Jesus explained that what he had just done was meant as a precedent: "For I have given you an example, that ye should do as I have done to you" (v. 15). The point was not so much the novelty of what he had involved them in (his breaking the bread and pouring the wine, his bending to wash their feet) so much as his encouragement that they do likewise. More than ever before, he meant for them to act in his similitude. How better to remember him than to perpetuate his practices?

Following this instructive gesture, Jesus gave a pair of directives, one to Judas Iscariot and the other to Peter. Between them, in understated fashion, John inserts mention of Jesus issuing a new commandment: "A new commandment I give unto you, That ye love one another; as I have loved you, that ye also love one another" (John 13:34). On an occasion marked by newness, the introduction of a new commandment may have had particular moment, especially since it seemed to capture the essence of the earlier demonstrations of the sacrament and the washing of feet.

Much of what John reports in chapters 14 through 17 can be

considered an elaboration of the new commandment. For example, John 15:12 repeats the commandment, with the following verse pointing again to the ultimate expression of Jesus' love: "Greater love hath no man than this, that a man lay down his life for his friends." The final words of his intercessory prayer (see John 17:26) extend the frame of reference to the Father: "And I have declared unto them thy name, and will declare it: that the love wherewith thou hast loved me may be in them, and I in them." These words suggest that the love Jesus enjoined in the new commandment was characteristic not only of him but also of the Father. It is a love that is thoroughgoing between Father and Son.

The apostles who would now carry on in Jesus' absence were nevertheless to carry on in like manner. Just as Jesus had faithfully evidenced the Father's love throughout his ministry, so they would henceforth show their Master's love in their own ministry. After all, they had known him best. They had been closest to his work. Who better to replicate his ways? He would be in them in the sense that their ways of loving would be unmistakably his own as well as of the Father. Such love was of a piece: the test of oneness.

The primacy of love in these chapters in John establishes a motif for the apostolic ministry described in the remainder of the New Testament. Indeed, the Gospel of John and the books that follow dominate the New Testament references to *love* that appear in the Topical Guide. Clearly, the new commandment signaled a move of great significance and consequence. It anticipated the realities of Church governance and expansion that would ensue in a time when Jesus would no longer be available in the same way as during his three-year ministry.

It is difficult to know how the apostles understood the new commandment when they first heard it. Jesus had actively presaged his death and resurrection and had orchestrated the chain of events that would lead to them. Yet the questions and conversation that directly followed his announcement of the new commandment, as we have them from John, suggest that the full implications of what he was about to do had not yet dawned on the apostles. The questions posed by Peter (see John 13:36) and by Thomas (see 14:5) and the request by Philip (see 14:8) convey a limited comprehension. So used were they to taking their lead from him that there was an understandable supposition on their part that he would always be there. They may have assumed that his death would be quickly reversed by his resurrection (however he might accomplish it) and that he would continue at their head—in short, business as usual.

It also seems reasonable to suppose that though the new commandment was arresting, it was also orienting. It may have caught the apostles off guard at the same time it was establishing their new agenda. In any event, it likely struck them as improbable. In other words, coming as it did on the heels of the twin institution of new ordinances with the injunction "Do likewise," they may well have wondered whether such a thing could ever be possible.

The improbability is founded on the Savior's qualifying phrase in John 13:34. It is one thing to say, "Love one another"; that much was hardly novel. Jesus had previously summarized the Mosaic code as two commandments. The first commandment—to love God devoutly—had ample precedent in Mosaic scripture and tradition (see, for example, Deuteronomy 6:5; 10:12; 11:1). The second—to love others unselfishly—was also part of that tradition (see Leviticus 19:18; Matthew 22:37–40; Mark 12:30–33). Indeed, the apostles might wonder why it would even need to be stated.

No doubt they would have readily affirmed Jesus' injunction to love. Of course they should love each other, especially if they were to assume and succeed in the leadership roles the Master intended for them. Love lubricates the harmonies and efficiencies essential for the form of corporate leadership they would soon engage in. What comes after the injunction is, however, monumental, if not staggering, in its implications: "As I have loved you, that ye also love one another." What look would have been on their faces when they first heard this? What might they have said in response? Perhaps there was only a profound silence.

Jesus properly referred to his commandment as *new*. His timing in doing so was altogether appropriate. Their three years' acquaintance with him had placed the apostles in a well-informed position. The same commandment would have been out of place at the commencement of his ministry and incompletely specified at any other point except its end. Now, in the waning hours, he could utter the new commandment on the basis of all that had transpired between them. It was genuinely new because at no previous point could it have been as meaningful as now. Never before had Jesus undertaken a ministry. Never before had the world seen him in the flesh. Never before had he come down from heaven in this way, moving among people and moving them with his gospel and his works within it. For this reason, his final commandment to the apostles before his death was necessarily *new*. And decidedly improbable.

What would it mean to love as Jesus had? Could such love ever be considered duplicable except by those similarly divine? To the apostles, Jesus must have seemed One of a kind, unique in all the universe. Their regular association with him over the years had equipped them with a healthy respect for what he was capable of. Now and then it must have seemed dazzling, even overwhelming. From the outset of their separate calls to join him, however inauspicious their prior occupations, they had been his select companions, along for an incomparable ride—the parade of miracles, the take-your-breath-away teachings, the endless ironies, the bounteous personal favors.

In many ways they shadowed him. He was undeniably in the lead, setting the pace, prescribing the itinerary. They were advance men, sideline players, witnesses to a life that could not be out-guessed. Their role was, first, simply to keep up, to hold on, to sustain, and second, to witness and absorb, to follow the lead, to play their parts in synchrony in order for his death to be eventually accomplished. Theirs was a proper attitude of deference.

Once he had officially declared his ministry, Jesus set about ministering in ways that called attention to his gifts. He healed lifelong disabilities and terminal illnesses, cast out devils, tempered and transformed the elements, and spoke his gospel to audiences that followed him, growing in size. Once the apostles had been commissioned, they set about in similar fashion, charged to heal, to cast out, and also to baptize. They performed dutifully, though their exploits and notoriety were never what his were. The Gospels are largely silent about their achievements during Jesus' ministry.

Nor is much said in the Gospels about Jesus' direct instrumentality in the personal and family lives of the apostles. There is reference to his intervention in behalf of Peter's mother-in-law (see Luke 4:38–39). While similar acts of benevolence might be supposed in the others' cases, the official record of his interactions with them takes the form of their being eye- and ear-witnesses to the skeins of match-less incidents from which his ministry was woven. Therein was their privilege: to be there when he worked his miracles and spoke his singularly informed words. Sometimes the occasions were open to the public and became the media events of the day. At other, more private times, they were the sole audience—what he said was meant just for them.

Their penumbral position was never without dignity. Jesus clearly valued their companionship and was gracious in his acknowledgment of their role in the promotion of his gospel. The ministry was punctuated by moments of high drama—aboard ship or on mountains or outside a cave in which a dead man was interred, for example—where the apostles were exposed to demonstrations of an unearthly sort that must have left them changed. The steady march of the ministry sounded their transformation. They were the ones whose seats were always on the front row where the light and the feeling were best.

Yet all that Jesus had shared with them before that final supper would soon be dwarfed by the infinite dimensions of his atoning act. Indeed, everything was building in his carefully scripted crescendo toward the pinnacle of love. He had saved the best for last, even though it lay beyond their comprehension. The apostles were people who knew, as clearly as anyone could, that they had been loved. What he had given them in the too-brief season of their togetherness was love that, by definition, knows no equal. Now, in his wonderfully paradoxical way, he was commanding them to replicate it.

To love each other as he had loved them? How could it be possible? Where would one begin? How to assume his ways with authenticity? Not only to strike the same poses, to say the same words, but to achieve the same effects? There was only one Jesus. There would not be another. How could one possibly presume to keep the new commandment? No one loves as he does. Small wonder that after his resurrection, at least some of them returned to fishing (see John 21:1–3).

He was waiting for them when they did, just as he had when first he called them (compare John 21:1–6 with Luke 5:1–11). On that occasion, too, he had advised them about the placement of their nets. This time he waited with fresh-broiled fish and bread. And, feeding them, he drove home the metaphor: You have received your last meal from me. There must be no more dalliance. As I have fed you, now you must commence to feed yourselves and others in my absence. Feed them. Feed them. Feed them.

The kickoff of the apostles' ministry came on the Day of Pentecost, when the Holy Ghost joined them in fiery and unforgettable fashion. The outpouring supplied important emboldening, and from the incident the apostles came away with new words, new notions, and new powers. The Pentecostal initiation was also a watershed. They would not ever again be the same. From that day onward they were irreversibly caught up in the reality of their own, new-founded ministry.

As that ministry took shape and gathered momentum, the apostles worked in ways that were increasingly reminiscent of the Master, thereby honoring the new commandment. An early instance came at the Gate Beautiful (see Acts 3). Peter and John arrived there, intent upon entering the temple. A lame beggar solicited them. He sought a handout and probably expected one, especially when Peter asked him to look directly at them. Instead, Peter, in eloquent and commanding voice, gave the beggar more than he expected—much more. With words that referenced Jesus and extending a helping hand, Peter lifted the man from lameness. The remedy was so potent that the man not only walked but leapt (see v. 8).

The ensuing chapters of the Acts of the Apostles offer numerous incidents in which contexts and the apostolic responses within them suggested strong continuity with Jesus' ministry. The apostles confronted and bested political authorities, discerned hidden thoughts, healed the sick, rebuked evil spirits, evaded conspiratorial plots, raised the dead, and preached with particular persuasion. They anchored the fledgling Church impressively, being the instruments of "many signs and wonders" (Acts 5:12; see also v. 16). These achievements were more than dramatic facsimiles of precedents performed by Jesus. They were powerful evidence of the principle that lay at the heart of the new commandment.

Perhaps no incident makes the point so strongly as that recorded in Acts 10. At issue was the evangelical mission of the Church. To that point it had focused exclusively on Jews and converts to Judaism—a policy that was in place during Jesus' ministry. The central figure in the chapter is a Roman official, Cornelius, who, with his family, is God-fearing and charitably disposed. As the result of a vision, Cornelius understands that he is to invite Peter, who is residing in a nearby city, into his home.

In a tandem vision of his own, Peter, who is soon to have lunch, sees a large assortment of animals from which to choose a meal. Peter is urged to do so ("kill, and eat") but recoils because the animals are those proscribed by his Jewish tradition. He avers that he has never eaten anything unclean. In turn, he is assured that, in effect, God has removed the ban on the animals he has seen. The scenario is presented three times. (Recall the resurrected Jesus' thrice-repeated injunction to Peter on the seashore.) Nevertheless, Peter remains unsure of its meaning.

When Cornelius' emissaries arrive, Peter is prompted to accept their invitation and subsequently accompanies them to meet Cornelius. In response to Peter's question about the reasons for the invitation, Cornelius rehearses his own vision and states the interest of those assembled in hearing what God will say to them through Peter.

At this point, the pattern of parallels becomes clear, and Peter utters his classic statement of God's fairness, acknowledging that Cornelius and his house are eligible for baptism in the same way that Jewish converts would be. To underscore the aptness of his conclusion, the Holy Ghost is convincingly present, and attendant gifts are displayed in a manner like that on the Day of Pentecost by those at whose invitation Peter had come. Their baptism followed.

The boldness with which Peter acted stemmed from his discerning the intent of the resurrected Jesus as it was reflected in the outpouring of the Holy Ghost. In his apostolic commission, Peter now understood in a fresh light the Master's injunction to feed his sheep. When he later reported his experience to Church leaders in Jerusalem (see Acts 11:1–18), he emphasized that what he had sensed in Cornelius' home was no different from that on the day of Pentecost: "As I began to speak, the Holy Ghost fell on them, as on us at the beginning. . . . God gave them the like gift as he did unto us" (vv. 15, 17). The conclusion was unanimous—"God also to the Gentiles granted repentance unto life" (v. 18). Whereas Jesus had offered the gospel exclusively to the Jews, it was now extended, through the apostles, to all. No longer would they work in a restricted range. The world with all its peoples was to be their field. The course of Christianity was forever changed.

Such consequential decision making, framed by stunning spiritual phenomena, is consistent with the view that as the apostles made their way into the larger world in order to stimulate the growth of the Church, their ministry increasingly resembled that of Jesus. They assumed his manner. Their actions in his name took on heroic dimensions. They became larger than life, celebrated for their prowess in confounding naysayers and undoing the forces arrayed against them—in slipping the constraints of perceived reality to deliver divinely supplied balm to the needy and oppressed. They, too, were miracle workers in the mold of the Master and ultimately, in similar ignominy, martyrs for his cause.

Their remarkable success may be seen as proper keeping of the new commandment. As Jesus had loved them, so they had come to love one another and the Church. In other words, in much the way that the powers and realities of heaven had accompanied the Master and defined his ministry, so a distinct sense of the heaven-sent suffused the ministry of the apostles. There was no necessary discontinuity, no conspicuous lapse as his ministry gave way to theirs. Jesus had inaugurated the work of heaven on earth. He had shown the Father's love. In a real sense, the apostles assured its continuance. In doing so, they kept the new commandment.

The analysis of love in the First Epistle General of John is resonant with this view and, in its own way, installs the new commandment anew. In the first chapter John celebrates the forgiveness of sin that Jesus made possible. In the next chapter, John first notes that forgiveness of sin is now available to the whole world, and then he states that keeping the commandments of Jesus is essentially "to walk, even as he walked" (1 John 2:6). At this point he makes an intriguing turn, one with a familiar ring to it. He introduces a "new commandment" (v. 7) while acknowledging that it was of old ordained of God; and "is true in him, and in you" (v. 8). What follows is summarized as God's commandment: "That we should believe on the name of his Son Jesus Christ, and love one another, as he gave us commandment" (v. 23) or, alternatively, "That he who loveth God loveth his brother also" (1 John 4:21).

At several points, John enjoins his readers to brotherly love as consistent with loving that God who had sent Jesus. According to John, such love is free of fear and conducive to confidence. It exists as a possibility because God initiated it: God loved us first (see 1 John 4:10, 19). His love was expressed in his Son, Jesus, whose ministry allowed the pent-up displays of heavenly powers and persuasions to be once more available to human experience. Nor were they ever more transcendently on display than in the form of Jesus, the "propitiation for our sins" (v. 10).

John's logic continues: "If God so loved us, we ought also to love one another. . . . If we love one another, God dwelleth in us, and his love is perfected in us" (1 John 4:11–12). He then testifies: "And we have known and believed the love that God hath to us. God is love; and he that dwelleth in love dwelleth in God, and God in him" (v. 16). Finally, in words that are haunting for their echoes of the new commandment uttered by Jesus, John states: "Herein is our love made perfect, that we may have boldness in the day of judgment: because as he is, so are we in this world" (v. 17). What counts for confidence in the final reckoning is evidenced in one's approximation to what Jesus is.

What is remarkable in John's epistle is its extension of the new commandment, analogous to Peter's revolutionary extension of the gospel of salvation to the non-Jewish world. Originally the new commandment was meant for the apostles, because they would soon formally bear the responsibility to carry forth Jesus' ministry in their own. What John teaches is that the new commandment itself has been extended to all. In other words, anyone who is a faithful follower of Christ can know the love of the Father and the Son, can exhibit similar love for others in ways reminiscent of Jesus, and, in the process, can somehow gain the likeness of the Son.

John's lesson about love provides a window on his apostolic role and suggests a pattern by which the Father's will can be universally known. The apostles knew Jesus intimately and were the hearers of words he sometimes spoke in private only to them. Some of what they learned in this way they later understood as meant for everyone. Their privilege as Jesus' intimates, as direct receivers of his light, implied a duty to enlighten others in turn. The new commandment passed from him to them to the membership of the Church. It was not a commandment for a few. Moreover, their transmission of Jesus' gospel was to be accomplished with high fidelity. In sharing what had been imparted to them, their manner was to be strongly evocative of his own.

In summary, with his ministry accomplished, Jesus extended a new commandment to his successors: to love as he had. Yet the very majesty of who he was and what he had wrought made this commission daunting. Who, after all, was enough like him to be capable of loving as he had? With the help of heaven, notably in the potent accompaniment of the Holy Ghost, the apostles proceeded in ways that were, for all intents and purposes, a similitude of what they had witnessed during their apprenticeship with Jesus. By so doing, they effectively obeyed the new commandment given to them as his ministry concluded. In their own ministry, heaven attended them as it had him. Their expressions of love became tantamount to his, as unlikely as that might have seemed when first they assumed the apostolic commission and as improbable as it might have struck them when the new commandment was first announced.

The logic of John's first epistle points to a practical consequence of the new commandment—perhaps to its actual intent. It seems to be the case that those who come to love as Jesus loves, in fact, become like he is. John talks of reunion, of the time when Jesus will come again (see 1 John 4:2). While it is not clear to John what form the sons of God will ultimately take, one thing is clear: Jesus will be seen as he is by those who are like him. Theirs will be the eyes, the ears, the hearts adequate for recognition. Why? Because, as John explains, they love as he loves. In other words, they love in a manner that allows heaven to show itself on earth. The love of the Father, extended through his Son, is, in turn, extended through them.

According to John, those who love as Jesus loves ultimately are graced with what may be called a confident likeness. They are, in Peter's felicitous phrase, "partakers of the divine nature" (2 Peter 1:4). This much may certainly be assumed of the apostles. But can it be assumed of those who are not apostles?

Jesus' new commandment has become the lyrics of a widely sung hymn. Its remarkable implication, consistent with John's epistle, is that the new commandment is meant for all. Apparently Jesus' goodness is sufficiently encompassing that what was first meant for the apostles can be extended universally. He is no respecter of persons, just as Peter discerned.

Presumably, therefore, any person is capable of mediating heaven's work—the will of the Father done on earth. Though the effective sphere of that mediation may not approach the dimensions of the apostles' and certainly not of Jesus', there is the possibility that it may be sufficient to allow for experience in common. Thus each person who has qualified by the criteria that John's epistle specifies can come to know what it means, in ultimate terms, to love as Jesus loves. In that knowledge is formed the acquaintance by which his likeness is achieved. Each person can become like Jesus is. That hope is the message of John and the essence of the new commandment.

CHAPTER TWELVE

THE MINISTRY OF THE HOLY GHOST

ROBERT L. MILLET

John the Beloved has delivered to us in his Gospel, Epistles, and Apocalypse an apostolic witness, a penetrating testimony of his Lord and Savior. John identified himself as "the one that Jesus loved," and that love of the Lord permeates his writings. Indeed, there is a spirit that broods over the works of the beloved disciple, a spirit that attests to their essential truthfulness and especially to the reality of their central character, Jesus the Christ. John was a witness of the risen Lord, one who saw and heard and touched (see 1 John 1:1). He knew by the physical senses, and he knew by an inward sense—a sense more real and powerful than anything earthly—that the Word, the supreme Messenger of Salvation, had come and dwelt among men in the flesh (see John 1:1; D&C 93:8).

One could profitably devote a lifetime to the study of John's writings and, with each reading, come away refreshed, renewed, and infused with light and truth and added understanding. There is much that might be said, but I have chosen to focus on the work of the Holy Ghost as set forth in the Gospel and the Epistles of John. Although the Holy Ghost is a vital figure in each of the other Gospels and writings of the New Testament, the fourth Gospel is often called the "spiritual Gospel." The central themes of the Gospel of John, many of which attest to the work of the Holy Ghost, carry over consistently into his epistles.

Robert L. Millet is dean of Religious Education at Brigham Young University.

THE LIGHT OF Christ

The four Gospels are particularly straightforward in setting forth the true nature of God and the various labors of the members of the Godhead. Indeed, one has to become involved in a stretching series of doctrinal maneuvers to derive the concept of Trinity or of a triune God in the New Testament. The simplest reading of the text reveals the supremacy of God the Eternal Father, the divine Sonship of Jesus of Nazareth, and the mission of the Holy Ghost to make known the persons and will of the Father and the Son.

But Latter-day Saints are not limited by what is in the text of the New Testament. Through modern revelation we can perceive and appreciate precious truths that have been lost to the rest of the religious world—insights that bring clarity and conviction to the study of the Bible. The Prophet Joseph Smith explained, "I have always declared God to be a distinct personage, Jesus Christ a separate and distinct personage from God the Father, and that the Holy Ghost was a distinct personage and a Spirit; and these three constitute three distinct personages and three Gods."[1] The "marvelous flood of light" which we know as the Restoration first establishes the essential truthfulness of the Bible (see 1 Nephi 13:39–40; Mormon 7:9; D&C 20:11) and then makes known the mysteries of God—those revealed doctrines associated with the nature and kind of Beings we worship.

John wrote, "This then is the message which we have heard of [Christ], and declare unto you, that God is light, and in him is no darkness at all" (1 John 1:5). We do not travel far in our study of the Gospel of John before we read that Jesus Christ is "the true Light, which lighteth every man that cometh into the world" (John 1:9). Because Jehovah was the foreordained Redeemer and Savior of worlds (see D&C 76:22–24; Moses 1:32–35), the Lamb slain from the foundation of the world (see Revelation 5:6; 13:8; Moses 7:47), the Father's plan became his by adoption; the gospel of God (see Romans 1:1–3) thus became known as the gospel of Jesus Christ. Because Elohim has invested his Beloved Son with his own attributes and powers (see Mosiah 15:3; D&C 93:4), and because the "Father of lights" (James 1:17) has ordained that Christ is to be the Light of lights and the Light of the world, those powers of life and light that we know as the power of God have come to be known as the Light of Christ or the Spirit of Jesus Christ.

Though there is but passing reference to the Light of Christ in the New Testament, the scriptures of the Restoration abound in detail, assisting us immeasurably to understand how and in what manner the Light of Christ lights every man and woman born into mortality. We come to know, first of all, that that light is a manifestation of the glory of God, a divine influence that fills the immensity of space, and the means whereby God, a corporeal being who can be in only one place at one time, is omnipresent. Elder Charles W. Penrose declared that "this spirit which pervades all things, which is the light and life of all things, by which our heavenly Father operates, by which He is omnipotent, never had a beginning and never will have an end. It is the light of truth; it is the spirit of intelligence."[2]

The Light of Christ has both natural and redemptive functions. Elder Parley P. Pratt explained: "It is, in its less refined existence, the physical light that reflects from the sun, moon, and stars, and other substances, and, by reflection on the eye, makes visible the truths of the outward world. It is also in its higher degrees the intellectual light of our inward and spiritual organs, by which we reason, discern, judge, compare, comprehend, and remember the subjects within our reach. Its inspiration constitutes instinct in animal life, reason in man, and vision in the prophets, and is continually flowing from the Godhead throughout all his creations."[3] The Holy Ghost, who is a male personage of spirit, and thus, like the Father, can be in only one place at a time, draws upon the Light of Christ to communicate sacred truths and to dispense spiritual gifts to a myriad of beings separated in time and space (see Moroni 10:17).[4]

The same power that makes it possible for us to see with our physical eyes also makes it possible for us to see with our spiritual eyes (see D&C 88:6–13). Discernment, the innate capacity to distinguish good from evil and the relevant from the irrelevant, also comes through this Spirit of Jesus Christ (see Moroni 7:12–19). Further, those who are true to this Spirit within them—which includes their conscience and thus the canons of right and wrong and decency in society—will be led, either in this life or the next, to the higher light of the Holy Ghost that comes through the gospel covenant (see D&C 84:44–53).

Elder Bruce R. McConkie wrote: "The light of Christ (also called the Spirit of Christ and the Spirit of the Lord) is a light, a power, and an influence that proceeds forth from the presence of God to fill the immensity of space. . . . It is the agency of God's power and the law by which all things are governed. It is also the agency used by the Holy Ghost to manifest truth and dispense spiritual gifts to many people at one and the same time. For instance, it is as though the Holy Ghost, who is a personage of spirit, was broadcasting all truth throughout the whole universe all the time, using the light of Christ as the agency by which the message is delivered. But only those who attune their souls to the Holy Spirit receive the available revelation. It is in this way that the person of the Holy Ghost makes his influence felt in the heart of every righteous person at one and the same time."[5]

THE FATHER, SON, AND HOLY GHOST

By inheritance as well as by perfect obedience, Jesus Christ was entitled to a fulness of the Spirit. Jesus spoke often of his divine inheritance. "Therefore doth my Father love me," John recorded, "because I lay down my life, that I might take it again. No man taketh it from me, but I lay it down of myself. I have power to lay it down, and I have power to take it again. This commandment have I received of my Father" (John 10:17–18). Herein is the fundamental truth to be believed if we are to accept the divine Sonship of Christ. Jesus was the son of Mary, a mortal woman, and from her he inherited mortality, including the capacity to die. Jesus was also the Son of God, an immortal resurrected being, and from him he inherited the capacity to rise up from the dead in resurrected immortality. In discoursing on the redemption of the Messiah, Lehi stressed how vital it is to make these truths known "unto the inhabitants of the earth, that they may know that there is no flesh that can dwell in the presence of God, save it be through the merits, and mercy, and grace of the Holy Messiah, *who layeth down his life according to the flesh, and taketh it again by the power of the Spirit,* that he may bring to pass the resurrection of the dead, being the first that should rise" (2 Nephi 2:8; emphasis added). The Savior thus had "power given unto him from the Father" (Helaman 5:11; Mormon 7:5) to do what he was sent to earth to do.

Though the fulness of the glory of the Father would not be Christ's until after the resurrection (see Matthew 28:18;

D&C 93:16–17),[6] Jesus lived and moved and had his being in the Spirit of God, "for God giveth him not the Spirit by measure, for he dwelleth in him, even the fulness" (JST John 3:34). It was this fulness that enabled and empowered the lowly Nazarene to resist evil, dismiss Satan from his life, and enjoy constant communion with the Father. "Where is the man that is free from vanity?" Joseph Smith asked. "None ever were perfect but Jesus; and why was He perfect? Because He was the Son of God, and had the fullness of the Spirit, and greater power than any man."[7] In speaking of becoming perfect in this life, Elder Bruce R. McConkie observed: "We have to become perfect to be saved in the celestial kingdom. But nobody becomes perfect in this life. Only the Lord Jesus attained that state, and he had an advantage that none of us has. He was the Son of God, and he came into this life with a spiritual capacity and a talent and an inheritance that exceeded beyond all comprehension what any of the rest of us was born with."[8]

Latter-day Saints teach, and the New Testament affirms, that the Beloved Son was subordinate to his Father in mortality. Jesus came to carry out the will of the Father (see John 4:34). He explained, "I seek not mine own will, but the will of the Father which hath sent me" (John 5:30; compare 6:38–40). In addition, the scriptures attest that Elohim had power, knowledge, glory, and dominion that Jesus did not have at the time. Truly, "the Son can do nothing of himself, but what he seeth the Father do" (John 5:19). Even what the Son spoke was what the Father desired to be spoken. "For I have not spoken of myself; but the Father which sent me, he gave me a commandment, what I should say, and what I should speak. And I know that his commandment is life everlasting: whatsoever I speak therefore, even as the Father said unto me, so I speak" (John 12:49–50). How much more plainly could the Lord speak concerning his subordinate position than when he said, "If ye loved me, ye would rejoice, because I said, I go unto the Father: for my Father is greater than I"? (John 14:28).

On the other hand, the Father and the Son enjoyed much more than what we might call closeness; theirs was a divine, indwelling relationship: because he kept the law of God, Jesus was in the Father, and the Father was in Jesus (see John 14:10, 20; 17:21; 1 John 3:24). Though they were two separate and distinct beings, they were one—

infinitely more one than separate. Their transcendent unity epitomizes what unity ought to exist between God and all of his children. That is to say, we are under commission to seek the Spirit of God, to strive to be one with the Gods, to be, as the Prophet Joseph explained, "agreed as one,"[9] to have, as Paul wrote, "the mind of Christ" (1 Corinthians 2:16). "Hereby know we that we dwell in him, and he in us, because he hath given us of his Spirit" (1 John 4:13). We thus gain the mind of Christ as Christ gained the mind of the Father—through the power of the Spirit.

The Holy Ghost, as the third member of the Godhead, is the minister of the Father and the Son. The Godhead does not consist, as some suppose, of a supreme Being who operates with the assistance of his two counselors, the Son and the Holy Ghost. Rather, Christ sends the Comforter (see John 15:26; 16:7). That Comforter is not an independent Being in the sense of speaking his own mind and delivering a completely original message. Jesus taught: "When he, the Spirit of truth, is come, he will guide you into all truth: for he shall not speak of himself; but whatsoever he shall hear [presumably, from the Father and/or the Son], that shall he speak: and he will shew you things to come. He shall glorify me: for he shall receive of mine, and shall shew it unto you" (John 16:13–14). The three separate members of the Godhead are one—they bear the same witness and teach the same truths (see 1 John 5:7).

For reasons that are not completely clear in the New Testament, the full powers and gifts of the Holy Ghost were not given in the Old World meridian Church until the Day of Pentecost. "He that believeth on me," Jesus stated, "as the scripture hath said, out of his belly shall flow rivers of living water. (But this spake he of the Spirit, which they that believe on him should receive; for the Holy Ghost was promised unto them who believe, after that Jesus was glorified" (JST John 7:38–39). While the Bridegroom was present with his disciples in the flesh, he was their Comforter, their Revelator, their Testator. He was their Life and Light, their source of power and might. "Hence, as long as Jesus was with the disciples in person, there was not the full need for them to have the constant companionship of the Spirit that there would be after Jesus left."[10] But because of the vital role that the Spirit would play thereafter in the growth, development, and expansion of the early Christian Church,

Jesus said, "It is expedient for you that I go away: for if I go not away, the Comforter will not come unto you; but if I depart, I will send him unto you" (John 16:7).

Though Jesus loved those among whom he ministered—indeed, the love of the Father and the Son underlies the work of redemption (see John 3:16–17; 1 Nephi 11:22, 25; D&C 34:1–3)—he was neither controlled by men's views nor deterred by their ridicule, taunts, or rejection. "I receive not honor from men" (John 5:41), the Master said simply. His sense of worth, like that of every other man and woman, derived not from the fickle plaudits of myopic mortals but from the approbation of heaven. "He that sent me is with me: the Father hath not left me alone; for I do always those things that please him" (John 8:29). That constant closeness is what empowered the Savior to act in quiet confidence and assurance in behalf of his Father. A knowledge of such consummate intimacy also highlights the profound sense of loss, the awful alienation which the Son of Man experienced when, in the garden and on the cross, he trod the winepress alone, "even the winepress of the fierceness of the wrath of Almighty God" (D&C 76:107).

Jesus explained to the woman at the well at Samaria: "Ye [the Samaritans] worship ye know not what: we [the Jews] know what we worship: for salvation is of the Jews." The true God had been revealed through the prophets of Israel, and salvation comes only to those who worship that divine Being. The Master continued: "But the hour cometh, and now is, when the true worshippers shall worship the Father in spirit and in truth: for the Father seeketh such to worship him. God is a Spirit: and they that worship him must worship him in spirit and in truth" (John 4:22–24). As you know, these verses, particularly the reference to God's being a spirit, have been used often against the Latter-day Saints by those offended with our doctrine of the corporeality of the Father. An alteration in the Prophet Joseph Smith's inspired translation of the Bible suggests a problem with this verse, whether textual tampering has taken place or meaning and clarity have simply been lost through the years. In the Joseph Smith Translation we find that "true worshippers shall worship the Father in spirit and in truth; for the Father seeketh such to worship him. For unto such hath God promised his Spirit. And they who worship him, must worship in spirit and in truth" (JST John 4:25–26).

But even if we were not blessed with this prophetic insight, we could discern that the present rendering of the verse and the typical interpretation are incorrect. "There is a sense," Elder McConkie has written, "in which it might be said, without impropriety, that God is a Spirit. He is most assuredly not a spirit in the sense in which the [Christian] creeds speak. . . . But when it is remembered that a spirit is a personage, an entity, a living personality whose body is made of more pure and refined substance than the temporal bodies of men; and when it is remembered that such spirits live in preexistence, come to earth to gain temporary physical bodies, are separated from those bodies by the natural death, with the assurance that eventually body and spirit will be inseparably connected again in resurrected immortality; and when it is remembered, further, that God himself is an exalted, perfected, glorified, resurrected Man; then it might truly be said that God is a spirit. He is a Spirit Personage, a Personage with a body of flesh and bones. (D&C 130:22.) He is a Spirit in the same sense that all men are spirits [see D&C 93:33], and in the sense that all men eventually will have resurrected or spiritual bodies as contrasted with their present natural or mortal bodies."[11]

Rather than "God is a Spirit," a better reading from the Greek is "God is spirit" (New King James Version; New International Version; New Revised English Bible; New Revised Standard Version). Raymond E. Brown has written concerning this verse: "God gives the Spirit. (We find three great equations in the Fourth Gospel and First John: 'God is spirit'; 'God is light'; 'God is love.' These are not definitions of God's essence, but refer to God's relation to people. He gives them the Spirit; he loves them; he gives them his Son, their light.) And the Spirit enables them to worship the Father."[12]

THE NEW BIRTH

John records that there came to Jesus by night a man named Nicodemus, a "ruler of the Jews," presumably a member of the Sanhedrin, a man who was "a master in Israel," meaning a master teacher or acknowledged scholar among the Jews. He and others had been impressed with the miracles of Jesus. He said: "Rabbi, we know that thou art a teacher come from God: for no man can do these miracles that thou doest, except God be with him." It was as if Jesus desired to do two things: to point out to Nicodemus that more was required of him than a verbal recognition of Jesus as a miracle worker; and to anticipate the question that must have lurked in the shadows of Nicodemus's mind but went unasked: "What must I do to inherit eternal life?" Jesus answered, "Except a man be born again, he cannot see the kingdom of God" (John 3:1–3).

This was no new idea, no novel conception revealed for the first time, for the doctrine of rebirth was as old as the world. God spoke to Adam and Eve: "I give unto you a commandment, to teach these things freely unto your children, saying: That by reason of transgression cometh the fall, which fall bringeth death, and inasmuch as ye were born into the world by water, and blood, and the spirit, which I have made, and so became of dust a living soul, even so *ye must be born again into the kingdom of heaven, of water, and of the Spirit,* and be cleansed by blood, even the blood of mine Only Begotten; that ye might be sanctified from all sin, and enjoy the words of eternal life in this world, and eternal life in the world to come, even immortal glory" (Moses 6:58–59; emphasis added).

Jeremiah had spoken of a time when the Lord would again propose a covenant to his covenant people, when he would "put [his] law in their inward parts, and write it in their hearts" (Jeremiah 31:31–34) and when Jehovah would truly be their God and Israel would be his people. Likewise, the Lord had spoken through Ezekiel: "Then will I sprinkle clean water upon you, and ye shall be clean: from all your filthiness, and from all your idols, will I cleanse you. A new heart also will I give you, and a new spirit will I put within you: and I will take away the stony heart out of your flesh, and I will give you an heart of flesh" (Ezekiel 36:25–26). Even in the book of Jubilees, an apocryphal work, the concept of a new birth was to be found: "But after this they will return to me in all uprighteousness and with all of their heart and soul. And I shall cut off the foreskin of their heart and the foreskin of the heart of their descendants. And I shall create for them a holy spirit, and I shall purify them so that they will not turn away from following me from that day and forever. And their souls will cleave to me and to all my commandments. And they will do my commandments. And I shall be a father to them, and they will be sons to me" (Jubilees 1:23–25).

Nicodemus either did not understand what Jesus was teaching or he sought to prolong an otherwise interesting discussion, for he asked, "How can a man be born when he is old? can he enter the second time into his mother's womb, and be born?" (John 3:4). According to President Marion G. Romney, Nicodemus "did not know who Jesus was. All he could see in the Son of God was a great teacher. This was all he could be expected to see, however, because he based his knowledge of who Jesus was upon what he had seen and heard of the Master's miracles. . . . Although Nicodemus was wise in the things of the world, he could not understand this simple statement of truth."[13]

Jesus continued, "Except a man be born of water and of the Spirit, he cannot enter into the kingdom of God" (John 3:5). The Christian world is largely divided over this matter of the new birth. A large segment of Christianity today believes that being born again consists of having a personal spiritual experience with Jesus. Another large segment of Christianity believes that being born again consists of receiving the sacraments (ordinances) of the church. And where are the Latter-day Saints? Where do we stand on this vital issue? Is it enough to receive the revelation that God lives, that Jesus is the Christ? Is it sufficient to receive the proper ordinances? The Prophet Joseph Smith stated simply but powerfully that "being born again, comes by the Spirit of God through ordinances."[14] Brother Joseph explained on another occasion that it is one thing to see the kingdom of God and another to enter into that kingdom. One must have "a change of heart" to see the kingdom; that is, he or she must be awakened spiritually to recognize the truth, recognize that the Church of Jesus Christ is the custodian of the truth and of the required ordinances, and recognize that the fulness of salvation is to be had through acceptance of those principles and ordinances. Further, the Prophet taught, a person must "subscribe the articles of adoption"—the first principles and ordinances of the gospel—to enter into the kingdom.[15] True conversion includes acting upon the revealed witness and submitting to those divine statutes that make it possible for us to be born again and thereby adopted into the family of the Lord Jesus Christ.

Daniel Tyler heard the Prophet Joseph explain that the birth spoken of in John 3:3—the birth to see—"was not the gift of the Holy Ghost, which was promised after baptism, but was a portion of the Spirit, which attended the preaching of the gospel by the elders of the Church. The people wondered why they had not previously understood the plain declarations of scripture, as explained by the elder, as they had read them hundreds of times. When they read the Bible [now] it was a new book to them. This was being born again to see the kingdom of God. They were not in it, but could see it from the outside, which they could not do until the Spirit of the Lord took the veil from their eyes. It was a change of heart, but not of state; they were converted, but were yet in their sins. Although Cornelius [Acts 10] had seen an holy angel, and on the preaching of Peter the Holy Ghost was poured out upon him and his household, they were only born again to see the kingdom of God. Had they not been baptized afterwards they would not have been saved."[16]

Although the new birth is made possible through the atoning blood of our Lord and Savior, the Holy Ghost is vital in bringing about change. The Holy Ghost is a revelator, a comforter, a teacher, a sanctifier, a sealer. Elder Parley P. Pratt wrote that the Spirit "quickens all the intellectual faculties, increases, enlarges, expands, and purifies all the natural passions and affections, and adapts them, by the gift of wisdom, to their lawful use. It inspires, develops, cultivates, and matures all the fine-toned sympathies, joys, tastes, kindred feelings, and affections of our nature. It inspires virtue, kindness, goodness, tenderness, gentleness, and charity. It develops beauty of person, form, and features. It tends to health, vigor, animation, and social feeling. It invigorates all the faculties of the physical and intellectual man. It strengthens and gives tone to the nerves. In short, it is, as it were, marrow to the bone, joy to the heart, light to the eyes, music to the ears, and life to the whole being."[17]

There are some things that cannot be taught by mortals, some lessons that can only be learned through close association with God and his Spirit. Of Christ's young manhood the holy word attests: "And he served under his father, and he spake not as other men, neither could he be taught; for he needed not that any man should teach him" (JST Matthew 3:25). It was certainly not the case that young Jesus was resistant to instruction or that he did not in fact learn a great deal from his parents and teachers; rather, there were eternal verities that could be learned only by entering the realm of divine experience. And so it is with us. The anointing or unction of the Holy Ghost that comes through the birth of the Spirit places us in a position to acquire new feelings, new insights, new perspectives that no mortal instructor could ever convey to us (see 1 John 2:20, 27). Those who are born of the Spirit begin to embody the "fruit of the Spirit," the patience, longsuffering, gentleness, kindness, meekness, joy, and pure love of Christ that characterize the true sons and daughters of the Lord Jesus Christ (see Galatians 5:22–25; see also Moroni 7:47–48). Truly, "We know that we have passed from death unto life, because we love the brethren" (1 John 3:14). "Beloved, let us love one another," John wrote, "for love is of God; and every one that loveth is born of God, and knoweth God" (1 John 4:7).

"Whosoever is born of God," John the Beloved declared, "doth not commit sin; for his [Christ's] seed remaineth in him: and he cannot sin, because he is born of God" (1 John 3:9; see also v. 6; 1 John 5:18). This is a troublesome passage to me, perhaps because I have had the privilege of associating with wonderful people in my life— holy people, men and women of faith who have given their all to God and his work—but they are not perfect, at least they are not perfect in the sense that we generally think about the term: they are not free from sin. To some degree at least, I have been born of the Spirit, have tasted of the sweet fruits of rebirth, have had my mind and heart expanded by the powers of the Holy Ghost, have had my witness of this work deepened and solidified. But I painfully and honestly admit that I am not free from sin. There is nothing I desire more than to be free from sin, nothing I long for more than to be holy before God, but I am not there yet.

The Prophet Joseph altered this verse as follows: "Whosoever is born of God *doth not continue in sin; for the Spirit of God remaineth in him; and he cannot continue in sin, because he is born of God,* having received that holy Spirit of promise" (JST 1 John 3:9; emphasis added). One who has walked in the light comes to treasure the light. Should he or she step into the darkness momentarily, he or she is repulsed by the darkness and yearns to return as soon as possible to the light. "The new birth results in new behavior. Sin and the child of God are incompatible. They may occasionally meet; they cannot live together in harmony."[18] That is, those who have been born of the Spirit learn to repent quickly, to confess and forsake their misdeeds, and to move on. Obviously serious sins require more time, but many of our transgressions may be faced head on and dispensed with in no time at all. Thus the Prophet Joseph Smith prayed in the Kirtland Temple: "And when thy people transgress, any of them, they may speedily repent and return unto thee, and find favor in thy sight, and be restored to the blessings which thou hast ordained to be poured out upon those who shall reverence thee in thy house" (D&C 109:21).

Our challenge is to learn to abide in Christ. Jesus taught in the fifteenth chapter of John that he is the vine and we are the branches. We tend to get ourselves in trouble when we see ourselves as the producers of fruit. We are at best the bearers of fruit. In that sense, may I suggest that we do all we can do by way of living a good life but remember that it is not difficult to live the Christian life. It is impossible! At least it is impossible by ourselves. It is only as the Lord assists us in that endeavor that we are able to bring to pass great things. An Evangelical minister noted: "If you do not learn to abide in Christ, you will never have a marriage characterized by love, joy, and peace. You will never have the self-control necessary to consistently overcome temptation. And you will always be an emotional hostage of your circumstances. Why? Because apart from abiding in Christ, you can do nothing. . . .

"Jesus makes a clear delineation between the vine and the branch. The two are not the same. *He* is the vine; *we* are the branches. The two are joined but not one. The common denominator in nature is the sap. The sap is the life of the vine and its branches. Cut off the flow of the sap to the branch, and it slowly withers and dies. As the branch draws its life from the vine, so we draw life from Christ. *To abide in Christ is to draw upon His life.*"[19]

THE PROMISE OF ETERNAL LIFE

At the Last Supper the Savior delivered some of the most profound teachings of his ministry concerning the work of the Holy Ghost in leading souls to salvation. Jesus had been with his disciples for three years, had taught them, empowered them, and prepared them for what was to come. He had been their Tutor, their Comforter. "If ye love me," he taught his chosen followers, "keep my commandments. And I will pray the Father, and *he shall give you another Comforter,* that he may abide with you forever; even the Spirit of truth; whom the world cannot receive, because it seeth him not, neither knoweth him: but ye know him; for he dwelleth with you, and shall be in you" (John 14:15–17; emphasis added). The word *another* literally means "another of the same kind," that is, "someone like Jesus Himself who will take His place and do His work."[20] The Greek word translated in the King James Version as Comforter is *paraclete*, "one called to stand along side of." Other meanings include "a friend, especially a legal friend."[21] The word refers to "a counselor who supports a defendant at a trial. The Spirit, then, will be the great defender of the disciples."[22] Other translations render the passage as "another Helper" (New King James Version), "another Counselor" (New International Version), and even "another Advocate" (New Revised Standard Version; see also Revised English Bible). Although ultimately Christ is our Advocate with the Father (see D&C 45:3–5), the Savior has sent his Spirit to convict us of sin, convince us of the truth, and direct us toward righteousness (see John 16:8–11). The *paraclete* was "any person who helped someone in trouble with the law. The Spirit will always stand by Christ's people."[23] The Holy Ghost, "one called alongside to help," would be that member of the Godhead who "encourages and exhorts" the Saints.[24]

This other Helper or Advocate, the Holy Ghost, is called the First Comforter. He is the First Comforter in the sense that his sacred influence is preparatory, fundamental, and foundational to all spiritual growth; by means of the powers of the Spirit, men and women gain the witness of the divinity of Jesus Christ and come to know the things of eternity (see 1 Corinthians 12:3). One cannot enjoy the blessings of the Second Comforter without having first received and cultivated the gifts of the First Comforter. The Savior later added: "These things have I spoken unto you, being yet present with you. But the Comforter, which is the Holy Ghost, whom the Father will send in my name, he shall teach you all things, and bring all things to your remembrance, whatsoever I have said unto you" (John 14:25–26). In the opening verses of the majestic revelation we know as the Olive Leaf (D&C 88), Jesus informed the early Saints that "the alms of your prayers have come up into the ears of the Lord of Sabaoth, and are recorded in the book of the names of the sanctified, even them of the celestial world. Wherefore, I now send upon you another Comforter, even upon you my friends, that it may abide in your hearts, even the Holy Spirit of promise; which other Comforter is the same that I promised unto my disciples, as is recorded in the testimony of John" (D&C 88:2–3).

The Holy Spirit of Promise is, of course, the Holy Ghost: the Holy Spirit promised the Saints.[25] The Lord continued, "This Comforter is the promise which I give unto you of eternal life, even the glory of the celestial kingdom" (D&C 88:4). It is by that Holy Spirit of Promise that the Saints of the Most High receive what the apostle Paul called the "earnest of our inheritance" (Ephesians 1:13–14; compare 2 Corinthians 1:21–22; 5:5), by which they come to know that their lives are in order, that they are on course and in covenant, that they are "in Christ" and thus in line for eternal life. It is through that Holy Spirit of Promise that the people of God receive their reward, "even peace in this world, and eternal life in the world to come" (D&C 59:23). Elder Marion G. Romney observed that "the fulness of eternal life is not attainable in mortality, but the peace which is its harbinger and which comes as a result of making one's calling and election sure is attainable in this life."[26] That peace, unlike anything the world has to offer (see John 14:27), a peace that "passeth all understanding" (Philippians 4:7), comes through the Spirit.

The Savior said earlier concerning the Comforter: "He shall teach you all things, and bring all things to your remembrance, whatsoever I have said unto you" (John 14:26). In a sermon delivered in 1839, the Prophet Joseph Smith paraphrased the Lord as follows: The Holy Ghost "shall bring all things to remembrance, whatsoever things I have said unto you. He shall teach you until ye come to me and my Father."[27] This statement implies that the Holy Ghost is given to the Saints to mature them, motivate them, empower and prepare them to eventually come into the presence of God. Perhaps that is what is intended in the Prophet Joseph's words in the dedicatory prayer of the Kirtland Temple: "And do thou grant, Holy Father, that all those who shall worship in this house may be taught words of wisdom out of the best books, and that they may seek learning even by study, and also by faith, as thou hast said; and that they may grow up in thee, and receive a fulness of the Holy Ghost" (D&C 109:14–15).

Thus the Lord said to his disciples at the Last Supper: "I will not leave you comfortless"—or, more literally, "I will not leave you orphans"—"I will come to you" (John 14:18). To be orphaned is to be left alone, comfortless, without the Spirit, without familial ties that foster warmth and security. Jesus continued: "He that hath my commandments, and keepeth them, he it is that loveth me: and he that loveth me shall be loved of my Father, and I will love him, and will manifest myself to him. . . . If a man love me, he will keep my words: and my Father will love him, and we will come unto him, and make our abode with him" (John 14:21, 23). The Prophet Joseph Smith explained that after we have been baptized and receive the gift of the Holy Ghost, which is the First Comforter, after we continue to hunger and thirst after righteousness and covenant to remain true and faithful no matter what is required of us, we will eventually make our calling and election sure. That is, we will receive the assurance of eternal life. The Prophet went on to say that if we then continue faithful—for continual striving and an additional measure of faith is required—we may qualify for the highest of revelations in this life: the privilege of seeing the face of the Lord.[28] This unspeakable blessing, the scriptures attest, comes to us according to the Lord's timetable, for he knows best our capacity to bear sacred things: "Therefore, sanctify yourselves that your minds become single to God, and the days will come that you shall see him; for he will unveil his face unto you, and it shall be in his own time, and in his own way, and according to his own will" (D&C 88:68).

Elder Bruce R. McConkie wrote: "It is the privilege of all those who have made their calling and election sure to see God; to talk with him face to face; to commune with him on a personal basis from time to time. These are the ones upon whom the Lord sends the Second Comforter. Their inheritance of exaltation and eternal life is assured, and so it becomes with them here and now in this life as it will be with all exalted beings in the life to come. They become the friends of God and converse with him on a friendly basis as one man speaks to another. . . .

"There are, of course, those whose callings and election have been made sure who have never exercised the faith nor exhibited the righteousness which would enable them to commune with the Lord on the promised basis. There are even those who neither believe nor know that it is possible to see the Lord in this day, and they therefore are without the personal incentive that would urge them onward in the pursuit of this consummation so devoutly desired by those with spiritual insight."[29]

Truly, those who are "in Christ" become "new creatures" of the Holy Ghost (2 Corinthians 5:17). It is by the power of the Spirit that we come to know the Lord. "And this is life eternal," the Master explained just before leaving the upper room for Gethsemane, "that they might know thee the only true God, and Jesus Christ, whom thou hast sent" (John 17:3). John testified: "We know that we are of God, and the whole world lieth in wickedness. And we know that the Son of God is come, and hath given us an understanding, that we may know him that is true, and we are in him that is true, even in his Son Jesus Christ. This is the true God, and eternal life" (1 John 5:19–20). Modern revelation expands that truth: "Verily, verily, I say unto you, except ye abide my law ye cannot attain to this glory. For strait is the gate, and narrow the way that leadeth unto the exaltation and continuation of the lives, and few there be that find it, because ye receive me not in the world neither do ye know me. But if ye receive me in the world, then shall ye know me, and shall receive your exaltation; that where I am ye shall be also. This is eternal lives—to know the only wise and true God, and Jesus Christ, whom he hath sent. I am he. Receive ye, therefore, my law" (D&C 132:21–24). Or, as the Prophet Joseph Smith paraphrased the Savior: "Make your calling and election sure. Go on from grace to grace until you obtain a promise from God for yourselves that you shall have eternal life. This is eternal life—to know God and his Son Jesus Christ. It is to be sealed up unto eternal life and obtain a promise for our posterity."[30]

CONCLUSION

Joseph Smith, the Prophet of the Restoration, explained that "everlasting covenant was made between three personages before the organization of this earth, and relates to their dispensation of things to men on the earth; these personages, according to Abraham's record, are called God the first, the Creator; God the second, the Redeemer; and God the third, the witness or Testator."[31] Clearly we owe everything to our Heavenly Father, who created us. In addition, our everlasting gratitude must always be offered to our Lord and Savior, who was sent to earth on a search-and-rescue mission to retrieve the wandering sheep and to redeem us from death and hell and endless torment. Had there been no atonement, no amount of labor on our part could ever, worlds without end, compensate for the loss. Truly, as Jesus proclaimed at the Last Supper, without him we can do nothing (see John 15:1–5). And finally, one of the priceless blessings extended to the Saints is the gift of the Holy Ghost, a sacred endowment of power, a supernal privilege of enjoying companionship with a member of the Eternal Godhead. Thanks be to God that that Spirit, about which the world knows precious little (see John 14:17), is sent to quicken, inspire, teach, testify, reprove, sanctify, comfort, and seal.

We cannot, simply cannot, face the challenges of life and triumph over the flesh without divine assistance. And so we worship, we pray, we labor, and we trust in the merits and mercy of the Holy Messiah. And we rejoice in the reality that the Holy Ghost is given to prepare us for association with God and holy beings hereafter. "Man's natural powers are unequal to this task," Elder B. H. Roberts pointed out, "so, I believe, all will testify who have made the experiment. Mankind stand in some need of a strength superior to any they possess of themselves, to accomplish this work of rendering pure our fallen nature. Such strength, such power, such a sanctifying grace is conferred on man in being born of the Spirit—in receiving the Holy Ghost. Such, in the main, is its office, its work."[32]

NOTES

1. Joseph Smith, *Teachings of the Prophet Joseph Smith,* sel. Joseph Fielding Smith (Salt Lake City: Deseret Book, 1976), 370.

2. *Journal of Discourses,* 26 vols. (Liverpool: F. D. Richards & Sons, 1851–86), 26:23.

3. Parley P. Pratt, *Key to the Science of Theology,* Classics in Mormon Literature series (Salt Lake City: Deseret Book, 1978), 25.

4. Joseph Fielding Smith, *Doctrines of Salvation,* comp. Bruce R. McConkie, 3 vols. (Salt Lake City: Bookcraft, 1954–56), 1:54; see also Bruce R. McConkie, *A New Witness for the Articles of Faith* (Salt Lake City: Deseret Book, 1985), 258.

5. McConkie, *New Witness for the Articles of Faith,* 70.

6. Smith, *Doctrines of Salvation,* 2:269; Bruce R. McConkie, *Mormon Doctrine,* 2d ed. (Salt Lake City: Bookcraft, 1966), 333.

7. Smith, *Teachings of the Prophet Joseph Smith,* 187–88.

8. Bruce R. McConkie, "Jesus Christ and Him Crucified," *Speeches of the Year, 1976* (Provo: Brigham Young University, 1976), 399.

9. Smith, *Teachings of the Prophet Joseph Smith,* 372.

10. Bruce R. McConkie, *Doctrinal New Testament Commentary,* 3 vols. (Salt Lake City: Bookcraft, 1965–73), 1:753.

11. McConkie, *Doctrinal New Testament Commentary* 1:153.

12. Raymond E. Brown, *The Gospel and Epistles of John: A Concise Commentary* (Collegeville, Minn.: Liturgical Press, 1988), 37; see also *The Gospel According to John,* 2 vols., volumes 29 and 29A in the Anchor Bible Series (New York: Doubleday, 1966), 1:172; F. F. Bruce, *The Gospel of John* (Grand Rapids, Mich.: Eerdmans, 1983), 110–11.

13. Marion G. Romney, Conference Report, October 1981, 18–19.

14. Smith, *Teachings of the Prophet Joseph Smith,* 162.

15. Smith, *Teachings of the Prophet Joseph Smith,* 328.

16. "Recollections of the Prophet Joseph Smith," *Juvenile Instructor* 27 (February 1892): 93–94.

17. Pratt, *Key to the Science of Theology,* 61.

18. *Authentic Christianity from the Writings of John Stott,* ed. Timothy Dudley-Smith (Downers Grove, Ill.: InterVarsity Press, 1995), 207.

19. Charles Stanley, *The Wonderful, Spirit-Filled Life* (Nashville: Thomas Nelson, 1992), 64; emphasis added.

20. *The MacArthur Study Bible,* ed. John MacArthur (Nashville: Word, 1997), 1614.

21. Leon Morris, *The Gospel According to John* (Grand Rapids, Mich.: Eerdmans, 1971), 649.

22. Brown, *Gospel and Epistles of John,* 76.

23. *The New International Version Study Bible,* ed. Kenneth Barker (Grand Rapids, Mich.: Zondervan, 1985), 1625.

24. *MacArthur Study Bible,* 1614.

25. Smith, *Doctrines of Salvation,* 1:55.

26. Marion G. Romney, Conference Report, October 1965, 20.

27. *The Words of Joseph Smith,* eds. Andrew F. Ehat and Lyndon W. Cook (Provo: Brigham Young University Religious Studies Center, 1980), 14–15; punctuation standardized.

28. Smith, *Teachings of the Prophet Joseph Smith,* 150–51.

29. Bruce R. McConkie, *The Promised Messiah: The First Coming of Christ* (Salt Lake City: Deseret Book, 1978), 584, 586.

30. *Words of Joseph Smith,* 334; spelling and punctuation standardized.

31. Smith, *Teachings of the Prophet Joseph Smith,* 190.

32. B. H. Roberts, *The Gospel: An Exposition of Its First Principles and Man's Relationship to Deity* (Salt Lake City: Deseret Book, 1966), 170.

CHAPTER THIRTEEN

JOHN'S TESTIMONY AND TEACHINGS ON TRUTH

LLOYD D. NEWELL

The apostle John bears a unique and powerful witness of the doctrine and significance of the truth found in Christ. Other Gospel authors speak of "truth" in only a few brief passages: Matthew mentions truth three times; for instance, he writes, "Master, we know that thou art true, and teachest the way of God in truth" (Matthew 22:16); Mark refers to truth three times as well, for example, "Master, thou hast said the truth" (Mark 12:32); and Luke's five passages of truth are recorded more as a figure of speech, such as, "Of a truth I say unto you" (Luke 12:44). The Gospel and the Epistles of John, however, contain two score references to "the truth," as it is taught by and revealed in Christ. Indeed, John the Beloved's testimony and teachings of Christ, written more particularly to the Saints who have already embraced the truth, focus on the meaning of truth and instruct us in the vital questions of our time: what truth is, what truth does, and how we gain truth.

WHAT IS TRUTH?

Shortly before his agony in Gethsemane and his death on the cross, Jesus was tried and condemned by the Sanhedrin and then brought before the Roman governor Pilate to be examined. John's Gospel records that Christ responded only with silence to the Jews and later to Herod, but he chose to answer Pilate's questions. When asked if he were a king, the Savior replied, "Thou sayest that I am a

---

Lloyd D. Newell is an instructor of Church history and doctrine at Brigham Young University.

king." And then he continued by revealing his mission and ministry: "To this end was I born, and for this cause came I into the world, that I should bear witness unto the truth. Every one that is of the truth heareth my voice." Pilate then asked the question of the ages, "What is truth?" (John 18:37–38). Of this event and question, Elder James E. Talmage wrote: "It was clear to [Pilate] that this wonderful Man, with His exalted views of a kingdom not of this world, and an empire of truth in which He was to reign, was no political insurrectionist; and that to consider Him a menace to Roman institutions would be absurd. Those last words—about truth—were of all the most puzzling; Pilate was restive, and perhaps a little frightened under their import. 'What is truth?' he rather exclaimed in apprehension than inquired in expectation of an answer, as he started to leave the hall. To the Jews without he announced officially the acquittal of the Prisoner. 'I find in him no fault at all' was the verdict."[1]

It is supremely ironic that standing before Pilate was the embodiment of truth, the meaning of truth, the message of truth, and yet Pilate, who was blind to the truth or uninterested in it, asked what truth is. Earlier in his Gospel, John wrote, "Jesus saith unto him, I am the way, the truth, and the life: no man cometh unto the Father, but by me" (John 14:6). Christ is not just *a* way, *a* truth, and *a* life but *the* way, *the* truth, and *the* life. He is the sum and substance, the essence of eternal truth. So Pilate's two questions, "Are you a king?" and "What is truth?" provoke essentially the same response. Both are answered in Christ: yes, he is the king of heaven and earth, and yes, he is the truth.

Pilate's question of two thousand years ago still resounds today. "What is truth?" To this query we find three answers clearly and powerfully outlined in the teachings and life of Christ.

TRUTH AS KNOWLEDGE

We have no record of the Lord's response to Pilate's question about truth, but in May of 1833 the Lord revealed to Joseph Smith a clear definition of truth: "And truth is knowledge of things as they are, and as they were, and as they are to come" (D&C 93:24). The Book of Mormon prophet Jacob similarly defines truth and uses the adverb *really* for emphasis: "The Spirit speaketh the truth and lieth not. Wherefore, it speaketh of things as they really are, and of things as they really will be" (Jacob 4:13). In other words, the Spirit "speaketh the truth," which is "things as they really are, and of things as they really will be."

Later in Doctrine and Covenants 93, the Lord gives us a definition of what truth is not: "And whatsoever is more or less than this"—the knowledge of things past, present, and future—"is the spirit of that wicked one who was a liar from the beginning" (v. 25). In this sense, knowledge-truth is more than simply knowing facts or possessing an in-depth understanding of something. Knowledge-truth is *really* knowing. Any truth that does not stand the test of time, that is not consistent with revealed truth, that does not fit in with a knowledge of things past, present, and future, is of the "wicked one."

Satan would have us hold on to certain truths and ignore others. He would have us believe that one truth is as important as another. But eternal perspective (knowledge of things as they really are, were, and are to come) insists upon a hierarchy of truth. Plain and simply, some truths matter more than others. Although it is important to have knowledge and comprehension of facts, although it is critical to gain all the learning and intelligence we can, only certain truths are saving. Elder Neal A. Maxwell has written: "We constantly need to distinguish between the truths which are useful and those which are crucial, and between truths which are important and those which are eternal. The restored gospel gives us this special sense of proportion."[2]

The life and teachings of Christ demonstrate the difference between useful truths and crucial truths. Because Christ knows all things (past, present, and future), he knows so much more than facts alone; he possesses so much more than a body of knowledge; he embodies so much more than just correct information. He not only has a fulness of cognition-truth but he is also a perfect embodiment of behavior-truth: he not only knows truth but is truth.

CHRIST AS TRUTH

Among the definitions of truth, none is more important, none more crucial to Christians, than Christ as Truth. Just before Pilate sentenced Christ to be crucified, he made a feeble effort to exonerate Him. Though lacking the courage to release him, Pilate affirmed that he found no fault in Jesus (see John 19:4) and presented him (having already been mocked, scourged, and smitten) to the assembled chief priests, scribes, and elders of the people, saying, "Behold the man!" He could have just as appropriately exclaimed, "Behold the Truth!" Undeterred, those desiring his blood cried out, "Crucify him, crucify him" (John 19:5–6). In essence, they demanded, "Kill the Truth. Crucify the Truth." But despite their nefarious efforts, neither they nor anyone else could destroy the immortal and eternal Truth.

The scriptures repeatedly use truth, Christ, and light as synonyms. Christ is the Spirit of Truth; he is the Truth; he is the Light of Truth. The apostle John testified that he is the light of the world, and if we follow him, we will not walk in darkness "but shall have the light of life" (John 8:12). Christ is the Truth. In him is found no deception, no untruth. He knows all truth, lives all truth, and is all truth. Therefore, as we embrace truth, we come unto him.

The light of Christ and the Holy Ghost lead us to the truth found in Christ. The Lord revealed in Doctrine and Covenants section 88 that the Light of Christ, or "the light of truth . . . shineth, . . . enlighteneth your eyes, . . . [and] quickeneth your understandings; . . . is in all things, which giveth life to all things, . . . [and] is the law by which all things are governed" (vv. 6, 11, 13). On another occasion, the Lord, referring to the light of Christ, told Joseph Smith that "the word of the Lord is truth, and whatsoever is truth is light, and whatsoever is light is Spirit, even the Spirit of Jesus Christ. And the Spirit giveth light to every man that cometh into the world; and the Spirit enlighteneth every man through the world, that hearkeneth to the voice of the Spirit" (D&C 84:45–46). Giving heed to the light of Christ, "hearken[ing] to the voice of the Spirit," will bring truth into our lives.

John taught that the Holy Ghost further manifests the truth: "It is the Spirit that beareth witness, because the Spirit is truth. For there are three that bear record in heaven, the Father, the Word, and the Holy Ghost: and these three are one" (1 John 5:6–7). The Spirit, the Holy Ghost, is truth and brings us to the truth found in Christ—and in the Father. The apostle Paul made this connection clear: "No man can say that Jesus is the Lord, but by the Holy Ghost" (1 Corinthians 12:3). The reality of the fulness of truth is found only in Christ, comes only by Christ (see Moses 6:52; John 1:17) and is accessed through the Holy Ghost as we come unto Christ.

LIVED TRUTH

Truth, as found in Christ, is so much more than knowing or even telling the truth, being honest, or refraining from fudging on facts: it is living the truth in a deeper and more comprehensive sense. Indeed, "truth is found in living the type of life exemplified by Jesus Christ."[3] As Professor Terry Warner pointed out in his entry on truth in the *Encyclopedia of Mormonism*, "For Latter-day Saints . . . truth is not primarily a matter of the correctness of ideas or statements. . . . They most often use the word 'truth' to signify an entire way of life— specifically, the way of life exemplified, prescribed, and guided by Jesus Christ." He went on, "Central to the original idea of being true was 'steadfast . . . adherence to a commander or friend, to a principle or cause, . . . faithful, loyal, constant, trusty,' 'honest, honourable, upright, virtuous, . . . free from deceit, sincere'. . . . And among the main original senses of 'truth' was 'troth'—a pledge or covenant of faithfulness made uprightly and without deceit. . . . It is in the spirit of these ancient etymologies that Latter-day Saints believe that to walk in truth is to keep one's commitments to follow Christ's way uprightly."[4]

Living truthfully means we must know truth and have the courage to act upon it. Moroni promised us that "by the power of the Holy Ghost ye may know the truth of all things" (Moroni 10:5). Later the Lord revealed to Joseph Smith that "he that keepeth his commandments receiveth truth and light, until he is glorified in truth and knoweth all things" (D&C 93:28). Knowing becomes linked with keeping the commandments, which is linked to receiving more light and truth, which increases our knowing and helps us live truthfully. Just the cognitive portion, unattached to the doing and living and being part, is destined to fail. The process of knowing truth and living truthfully can have a synergistic, geometric effect on the spiritual development of the individual. Faithfully walking in truth and steadfastly living the truth brings to us more of the light of truth, deepens our resolve to follow and become more like the Savior, and makes unwavering our commitment to the gospel. Living the truth becomes an entire way of life, and in fact, the key to eternal life.

"Understood in this way, disobedience and unfaithfulness are rejections of the light of truth. Satan 'was a liar from the beginning' (D&C 93:25) and seeks always to 'turn . . . hearts away from the truth' (D&C 78:10), partly by enticing people to become liars and deceivers themselves (D&C 10:25)."⁵ We deceive ourselves if we walk untruthfully, and we suffer eternally to the extent that we reject the truth as found in Christ. The apostle John explained that the reason "men love darkness rather than light" was "because their deeds [are] evil. For every one that doeth evil hateth the light, neither cometh to the light, lest his deeds should be reproved" (John 3:19–20). Those who are "strangers to the truth" may actually prefer, even seek, darkness rather than light, falsity rather than veracity, and self-deception rather than the clarity of revelation.

Salvation is found not just in learning and knowing truth but in living truth. It is found not in an intellectual, cognitive, and detached approach to the study of truth but in submission and surrender: in humbly striving to emulate all the qualities of truth found in the Savior. The fact is, we may know many things and yet not know the Truth, never embracing "the way, the truth, and the life." There is a big difference between knowing truth and knowing *the* Truth. Likewise, there is a big difference between knowing and living truth. In April conference 1916, President Joseph F. Smith said: "The devil knows the Father much better than we. Lucifer, the son of the morning, knows Jesus Christ, the Son of God, much better than we; but in him it is not and will not redound to eternal life; for knowing, he yet rebels; knowing, he is yet disobedient; he will not receive the truth; he will not abide in the truth; hence he is perdition, and there is no salvation for him."⁶ John again wrote of truth, "He that saith, I know him, and keepeth not his commandments, is a liar, and the truth is not in him" (1 John 2:4). Knowing and doing can be two very different things altogether. Living truthfully requires that we not only seek after but also respond to the Spirit of truth, that we strive to live up to the best within us, and that we humbly repent of our sins and conduct our lives without hypocrisy. In other words, living truthfully means coming unto Christ and emulating his life.

Without the life and teachings of the Savior as our model for living truthfully (see 3 Nephi 12:48; 27:27), without the scriptures and living prophets as teachers of truth (see D&C 21:4–6), without personal revelatory power that brings us to truth and empowers us to live truthfully (see 1 Corinthians 2:11; Revelation 19:10), we would be left to grope and wander in the dark. We might get lost if we blindly pursue a single truth—or even a single set of truths, failing to subordinate that truth to the whole of truth that centers in Christ. The apostle John encouraged us to love the truth that leads us to God: "He who loveth truth, cometh to the light, that his deeds may be made manifest. And he who obeyeth the truth, the works which he doeth they are of God" (JST, John 3:21–22). Without light, not only would we never find truth or be able to discern between truths that are important and those that are eternal, we could never live truthfully, or do the works which "are of God." Only as we embrace eternal truths—as we obey those truths, and live them—do we receive more light and truth. Elder Dallin H. Oaks has written that "Learning the mysteries of God and attaining to what the apostle Paul called 'the measure of the stature of the fulness of Christ' (Eph. 4:13) requires far more than learning a specified body of facts. It requires us *to learn* certain facts, *to practice* what we have learned, and, as a result, *to become* what we, as children of God, are destined to become."[7] Living the truth as found in Christ is what enables us *to be* men and women of Christ.

WHAT TRUTH DOES

Accepting the truth found in Christ can change our lives and set us on the path to eternal life. Indeed, the path to exaltation is paved with redeeming truth. John taught us that the truth found in Christ would bring freedom, protection, sanctification, and peace.

Truth makes us free. John wrote, "And ye shall know the truth, and the truth shall make you free" (John 8:32). It is not cognitive truth, knowledge, or facts that make us free. We become free from death and sin only through the truth of the infinite atonement of Jesus Christ. Truth, here, could be another name for Christ. It is the truth of and in Christ that makes us free. Elder Bruce R. McConkie wrote of this passage in John: "Free from the damning power of false doctrine; free from the bondage of appetite and lust; free from the shackles of sin; free from every evil and corrupt influence and from every restraining and curtailing power; free to go on to the unlimited freedom enjoyed in its fulness only by exalted beings."[8] Only the truth found in the Son of God makes us completely free. John's record continues with the words of Christ: "If the Son therefore shall make you free, ye shall be free indeed" (John 8:36). And in our dispensation, the Lord revealed, "I, the Lord God, make you free, therefore ye are free indeed; and the law also maketh you free" (D&C 98:8). The truth found in Christ and the truth found in the law make us free. The law and the truth of the Lord lead us to the same thing. Abiding by the law of the Lord (the commandments, the gospel, the ordinances), and the truth of the Lord (his life, example, atonement, and resurrection), are what make us truly free.

The Savior was teaching the Jews of his time and all of us today that it matters not, in the eternal scheme of things, if you see yourself as the chosen seed; it matters not how much knowledge, skill, or ability you may have. What matters is that only Christ, his law, and his truth make us free. The Savior said, in effect: "Only those who believe in me as the Son of God shall abide in the household of faithful Abraham in the eternal worlds. If you forsake sin, and believe in the Son, he shall make you free from spiritual bondage, and only the free shall be Abraham's seed hereafter."[9] Endowed with agency and obedient to God's law we have the capacity to become truly free. It is ironic that real freedom—everlasting liberty—comes through submission and surrender to the truth—both cognitive and behavioral, inner and outward, as found in the law and as embodied and exemplified in the truth of the Savior.

Christ taught and exemplified the truth that there is no lasting freedom outside of him, just as there is no salvation outside of his truth (see Mosiah 3:17). Information, science, and technology do not make us free. They are useful and valuable and may give us more free time, but they do not make us free. Laws, regulations, and behavioral proscriptions alone do not make us free. Certainly, it's more than political independence or even living in a free country that makes us free. Freedom, *true freedom,* is found in Christ, in a covenant relationship with him. We become free; we become "alive in Christ" (2 Nephi 25:25). He frees us from the fetters of sin and the burden of sorrows, as we come unto him. Our freedom is dependent on our understanding and living of his truth and accepting his infinite gift.

If we live falsely or make choices based on falsehood, those choices and their consequences are bound by the untruths that influenced them—until we come unto him.

Perhaps the best way to illustrate this larger understanding of how the truth found in Christ can make us free is to look at a very basic example of truth telling. Every child has encountered the soul-wrenching question of whether or not to tell the truth when he or she has done wrong. Remaining quiet or lying about the situation brings a temporary freedom from punishment, but telling the truth—even at the expense of punishment or short-term loss of freedom—enacts a process of restitution that promises long-term freedom from guilt and other entangling lies.

On a larger scale, when we ignore or cover some truths in order to follow after more enticing half-truths, the rush of freedom we initially feel can deteriorate into addiction, imprisonment, or a complete loss of freedom. We become bound by fears: the fear of being found out, the fear of addictive craving of partial truth, the fear of having to change and repent. On the other hand, explained President Gordon B. Hinckley, "We have nothing to fear when we walk by the light of eternal truth. But we had better be discerning. Sophistry has a way of masking itself as truth. Half truths are used to mislead under the representation that they are whole truths. Innuendo is often used by enemies of this work as representing truth. Theories and hypotheses are often set forth as if they were confirmed truth, . . . when as a matter of fact such procedure may be the very essence of falsehood."[10]

Only the truth found in Christ can free us from this world. The world will present us with shadows of truth and fleeting moments of freedom, but true and lasting freedom is found only in Christ. Only his perfect life, his fulness of truth, can unlock the shackles of sin and death and ultimately, eternally, make us free. To be free is to have truth, and to live truthfully is to emulate the Savior's life. He who was the embodiment of truth is also the embodiment of freedom because he lived truthfully.

Prophets, as truth tellers, continue to speak clearly about the power of truth to make us free. President Joseph F. Smith told the Saints that "if we would build up ourselves, or ever become worthy to inherit the kingdom of God, we will do so on the principle of eternal truth. The truth is what will make us free; free from error, prejudice, selfishness, ignorance, contention, the power of the adversary of our souls, free from the power of death and hell; free to inherit the fulness of the everlasting gospel; free to have joy in our hearts for all things good and for the welfare of mankind; free to forgive those who err because of lack of judgment and understanding."[11] Elder Ezra Taft Benson similarly declared, "It is the truth that endures. It is truth that makes men courageous. It is the truth that makes men and nations free—and keeps them free."[12] And more recently, President Hinckley said, "[God] has established His church, which carries the name of His divine Son, as the conservator and teacher of truth, that truth which will make and keep us free."[13]

Truth keeps us from evil. Everlasting truth protects us against the "mighty winds" of the adversary (Helaman 5:12), the temptations of the flesh, and the errors of uncertainty. Truth keeps us from evil, or darkness, by giving us more and more light. "That which is of God is light; and he that receiveth light, and continueth in God, receiveth more light; and that light groweth brighter and brighter until the perfect day" (D&C 50:24). The light and truth of Christ are inextricable. Where there is light, always there is truth. The devil knows many facts, he has knowledge and possesses great cognitive-truth, but all of that knowledge of truth does not bless him with light or redound to salvation for him. All the "truth" in the world does him no good or changes him not in the slightest degree. He has knowledge, but no light; he has no light because he embraces none of the changing, exalting truth found in Christ. But because the adversary is a liar, he may use the truth to deceive and beguile. In John's record of a stinging rebuke the Savior gives to the Jews, he affirms that truth is not found in Satan: "Ye are of your father the devil, and the lusts of your father ye will do. He was a murderer from the beginning, and abode not in the truth, because *there is no truth in him.* When he speaketh a lie, he speaketh of his own: for *he is a liar, and the father of it*" (John 8:44; emphasis added). "Satan neither originates nor sponsors truth. He may use truth interlarded with error for his own destructive purposes, but in the long perspective his purpose is to blot out the light and enshroud the world in darkness."[14]

Jesus, on the other hand, embodies all light and all truth. In his first epistle, John warned us, "If we say that we have fellowship with [Christ], and walk in darkness, we lie, and do not the truth" (1 John 1:6). In the same epistle, he warned of arrogance and the perils of self-righteousness, "If we say that we have no sin, we deceive ourselves, and the truth is not in us" (1 John 1:8). Thinking one possesses the light of truth while being in reality a stranger to truth may be the greatest self-deception of all because it blocks out the illumination of the real Spirit of truth. The Prophet Joseph Smith said that "nothing is a greater injury to the children of men than to be under the influence of a false spirit when they think they have the Spirit of God."[15] A false spirit is one that takes us away from or confuses our reception of the Spirit of truth. As such, it would be difficult, if not impossible, for the Spirit of God to touch a heart consumed by darkness, self-righteousness, and arrogance.

Truth sanctifies. "There would be no strife, no anger, nothing of the spirit of unforgiveness, unchastity and injustice, in the hearts of the children of men, if we loved the truth and obeyed it as it was taught by the Son of Man" wrote President Joseph F. Smith.[16] The power of truth found in Christ transforms lives. John recorded the great intercessory prayer wherein Christ foreshadowed his atonement as he taught of truth: "Sanctify them through thy truth: thy word is truth. . . . And for their sakes I sanctify myself, that they also might be sanctified through the truth" (John 17:17, 19). Sanctification—becoming holy, pure, and without sin—is possible only through Christ, the Truth. And truth is only fully realized as we become sanctified. Being sanctified and cleansed, having the film and façade of this world removed from our eyes, enables us to see things not as we are but as they really are. Eventually, through sincerely coming unto Christ, the Truth, we not only *see* truth but *are* truth.

Truth brings peace. Finally, receiving and living truth brings peace. Elder Howard W. Hunter taught that "two eternal truths must be accepted by all if we are to find peace in this world and eternal life in the world to come. (1) That Jesus is the Christ, the very eternal son of our Heavenly Father, who came to earth for the express purpose of redeeming mankind from sin and the grave, and that he lives to bring us back to the presence of the Father. (2) That Joseph Smith was his prophet, raised up in this latter-day to restore the truth which had been lost to mankind because of transgression. If all men would *accept and live* these two fundamental truths, peace would be brought to the world."[17]

And to those who repent, *For the Strength of Youth* promises: "You will feel and experience the power of the Spirit of the Lord, you will come to know the truth, and you will gain confidence in yourself and the Lord. The Savior taught, 'The truth shall make you free' (John 8:32). As you grow in that truth and freedom, you will experience the peace of the Lord Jesus Christ, a peace that brings great strength."[18]

HOW WE GAIN TRUTH

Those who emulate the Lord through sincere obedience to the commandments receive further light and truth and come to know of the glory of God (see D&C 93:28, 36). Because "light and truth forsake that evil one" (D&C 93:37), they lose every desire to be supported by the strength of the world; indeed the enticements of the world hold no appeal. So what can we do to learn of truth and live it more fully?

The Spirit of truth, the Holy Ghost, brings us to the knowledge of truth and can strengthen and comfort us in our moments of weakness or despair. The Savior taught, as recorded in John, "Howbeit when he, the Spirit of truth, is come, he will guide you into all truth: for he shall not speak of himself; but whatsoever he shall hear, that shall he speak: and he will shew you things to come" (John 16:13). The Spirit of truth, even the Holy Ghost—the other Comforter— reveals the truth of Christ. To gain truth and live truthfully we must "hearken to the voice of the Spirit" and give heed to the still, small voice that gives guidance, encouragement, and peace.

In 1831 the Lord told the Prophet Joseph: "Verily I say unto you, he that is ordained of me and sent forth to preach the word of truth by the Comforter, in the Spirit of truth, doth he preach it by the Spirit of truth or some other way? And if it be by some other way it is not of God. And again, he that receiveth the word of truth, doth he receive it by the Spirit of truth or some other way? If it be some other way it is not of God" (D&C 50:17–20). The Spirit of truth reveals the truth found in Christ, just as living truthfully is possible only by that same Spirit. Our human efforts to overcome will falter; our sincere strivings will fall short if we rely solely upon our own capacities. Christ, our Exemplar, shows us the way. President Joseph F. Smith said: "There is nothing mysterious and unaccountable in the dealings of God with his children if we can only see and understand by the spirit of truth. Jesus has given us in this life the example, the type of that which exists in greater perfection, in a purer, higher and more glorious excellence where he dwells himself. The gospel teaches us to do here just what we would be required to do in the heavens, with God and the angels, if we would listen to its teachings, and obey it, and put it into practice. There would be no covetousness in the hearts of the children of men, if they possessed the Spirit of Jesus Christ, and understood the precepts of the gospel as he taught and admonished all men to observe them."[19]

To gain truth we must believe in God (see John 3:16; Ether 3:25–26) and keep the commandments (see D&C 93:28). Brigham Young said that "it requires the whole man, the whole life to be devoted to improvement in order to come to knowledge of the truth as it is in Jesus Christ. Herein is the fulness of perfection. It was couched in the character of our Savior."[20] When Christ entreats us to "learn of Him," it is a summons to learn and live his truth—wholly.

Elder Ezra Taft Benson gave us further counsel: "Continue to grow mentally—to grow in wisdom—to grow in truth. Desire it! Pray for it! Study it! Practice it! Do all this, and you will find truth; it cannot be denied you. Having found it, never forget its source, remembering always that 'glory of God is intelligence, or, in other words, light and truth' (D&C 93:36)."[21] *Desire, pray, study, practice*—these all imply *being* true in our thoughts, intents, and actions.

We gain more truth by sharing the truth. Like the parable of the talents, we will be added upon to the extent that we draw closer to Christ, live truthfully, and do for others. As President Brigham Young said: "A man who wishes to receive light and knowledge, to increase in the faith of the Holy Gospel, and to grow in the knowledge of the truth as it is in Jesus Christ, will find that when he imparts knowledge to others he will also grow and increase. Be not miserly in your feelings, but get knowledge and understanding by freely imparting it to others, and be not like a man who selfishly hoards his gold; for that man will not thus increase upon the mount, but will become contracted in his views and feelings. So the man who will not impart freely of the knowledge he has received, will become so contracted in his mind that he cannot receive truth when it is presented to him. Wherever you see an opportunity to do good, do it, for that is the way to increase and grow in the knowledge of the truth."[22]

CONCLUSION

The Lord commands us "to bring up [our] children in light and truth," even while he warns that the "wicked one cometh and taketh away light and truth, through disobedience, from the children of men, and because of the tradition of their fathers" (D&C 93:39–40). Disobeying the Spirit of truth and following false traditions, even sincere false traditions, will lead us away from the truth of Christ. All of which gives new meaning to John's fatherly expression, "I have no greater joy than to hear that my children walk in truth" (3 John 1:4). What greater parental hope could be uttered than to know that one's children have sought after, found, and embraced the truth; that they are living truthfully, and they are being true to the truth!

The apostle John's writings, along with other inspired words, bear strong testimony and present vital doctrinal insight into the truth as taught by and embodied in Christ. Those writings help us to make important connections in understanding what truth is, what truth does, and how we gain truth. The meaning and message of the truth as found in and lived by Christ serve as a model for us of what it is to live truthfully. Elder Heber J. Grant summarized well the inherent transforming power in truth and what it means to live truth: "Truth is the rock foundation of every great character. It is loyalty to the right as we see it; it is courageous living of our lives in harmony with our ideals; it is always—power. Truth ever defies full definition. Like electricity it can only be explained by noting its manifestation. It is the compass of the soul, the guardian of conscience, the final touchstone of right. Truth is the revelation of the ideal; but it is also an inspiration to realize that ideal, a constant impulse to live it."[23]

NOTES

1. James E. Talmage, *Jesus the Christ* (Salt Lake City: Deseret Book, 1976), 634–35.

2. Neal A. Maxwell, *On Becoming a Disciple-Scholar,* ed. Henry B. Eyring (Salt Lake City: Bookcraft, 1995), 6.

3. Terry Warner, "Truth," in *Jesus Christ and His Gospel: Selections from the Encyclopedia of Mormonism,* ed. Daniel H. Ludlow (Salt Lake City: Deseret Book, 1994), 463.

4. Warner, "Truth," 464.

5. Warner, "Truth," 465.

6. Joseph F. Smith, *Gospel Doctrine* (Salt Lake City: Deseret Book, 1986), 371.

7. Dallin H. Oaks, *The Lord's Way* (Salt Lake City: Deseret Book, 1991), 42.

8. Bruce R. McConkie, *Doctrinal New Testament Commentary,* 3 vols. (Salt Lake City: Bookcraft, 1965–73), 1:456–57.

9. McConkie, *Doctrinal New Testament Commentary,* 1:457.

10. Gordon B. Hinckley, "God Hath Not Given Us the Spirit of Fear," *Ensign,* October 1984, 4.

11. Smith, *Gospel Doctrine,* 214.

12. Ezra Taft Benson, *Teachings of Ezra Taft Benson* (Salt Lake City: Bookcraft, 1988), 119.

13. Gordon B. Hinckley, *Speeches of the Year, 1995–96* (Provo: Brigham Young University, 1996), 52.

14. McConkie, *Doctrinal New Testament Commentary,* 1:461.

15. Joseph Smith, *Teachings of the Prophet Joseph Smith,* sel. Joseph Fielding Smith (Salt Lake City: Deseret Book, 1976), 205.

16. Smith, *Gospel Doctrine,* 213–14.

17. Howard W. Hunter, *Teachings of Howard W. Hunter,* ed. Clyde J. Williams (Salt Lake City: Bookcraft, 1997), 172–73; emphasis added.

18. *For the Strength of Youth* [pamphlet] (The Church of Jesus Christ of Latter-day Saints, 1990), 18.

19. Smith, *Gospel Doctrine,* 213.

20. Brigham Young, *Discourses of Brigham Young,* sel. John A. Widtsoe (Salt Lake City: Deseret Book, 1978), 11.

21. Benson, *Teachings of Ezra Taft Benson,* 120.

22. Young, *Discourses of Brigham Young,* 335.

23. Heber J. Grant, Conference Report, April 1909, 114.

CHAPTER FOURTEEN

THE GOSPEL OF GRACE IN THE WRITINGS OF JOHN

BLAKE T. OSTLER

The Gospel and the Epistles of John use very specialized words to express the interplay of God's grace and human response. Because John never employs Paul's terminology of justifying grace through faith, the importance of grace in John's writings is often overlooked or simply misunderstood. John focuses on the process of movement from grace to grace and activity that leads to eternal life through grace. The purpose of John's Gospel is to reveal the Only Begotten Son, who is "full of grace and truth" (John 1:14). John's message is expressed in terms pregnant with meaning and loaded with theological importance. Cloaked within the layers of meaning of the key terms in the writings attributed to John is the doctrine of grace, which lies at the heart of the Gospel and the Epistles of John. There, at the core of these multiple layers, we find a dynamic gospel of growth from one grace to another, from seeing to believing, from believing to obedient perseverance, from obedience to love, from love to knowledge, from knowledge to unity in Christ, and from union to deification and eternal life.

CHRIST AS THE GIFT

The starting point to understanding John's use of the term *grace* is the simple statement that "of his fulness have all we received, and grace for grace" (John 1:16). Such grace is not an abstract theological principle in the writings of John; rather, it denotes an active and

Blake T. Ostler is an attorney in Salt Lake City, Utah.

dynamic interpersonal relationship between God and his children. John records the Savior's doctrine that "no man can come to me, except the Father which hath sent me draw him" (John 6:44). The Greek verb used here and translated as "to draw," *elko,* could also be translated to mean that the Father "pursues us," "woos us," "seeks to win us over" or "influences us" to come to accept his gift.[1] The Father's gift is the very life and light of Christ, given to us unmerited and frankly undeserved: "In him was life; and the life was the light of men" (John 1:4). Like the light of the sun, which radiates its warmth on all persons regardless of their station in life or how good they are, Christ has given life and light to all persons. His life is actually in us. Just as the light of the sun is the ultimate source of all biological life on earth, so the light of Christ is the source of our lives both physically and spiritually. As Christ revealed to the Samaritan woman, "If thou knewest the gift of God, and who it is that saith to thee, Give me to drink; thou wouldest have asked of him, and he would have given thee living water" (John 4:10). Christ's life is the gift offered to us by God in unconditional love.

John teaches that Christ's life enters into us when we enter into a loving relationship with Christ. Moreover, this loving relationship is offered to us without any prior conditions. He has already given his life for us regardless of our merit. He has accepted us without any conditions to his love and before any act or decision on our part. As John wrote, "We love him, because he first loved us" (1 John 4:19). The life of Christ is a grace, a gift given to us by the Father out of his love for us: "For God so loved the world, that he gave his Only Begotten Son, that whosoever believeth in him should not perish, but have everlasting life" (John 3:16). The focal point to understanding John's view of grace is the recognition that not only has the Father given his Son but also Christ has offered himself, his very life, as a gift to us. There is nothing we must do, indeed nothing we could ever do, that would merit this gift. Indeed, if we tried to earn this gift by our good works, we would forever fall short of meriting the value of Christ's life given for us. In the end we would show only that we have misunderstood that Christ offered himself to us and for us out of love that knows no bounds and imposes no prior conditions.

For John, Christ's gift is not merely a past event that occurred while Christ was on earth as a mortal but is also a gift that continues to give life and light in the here and now. The fact that Christ himself is the gift given to us is expressed in many ways in the Gospel of John. Christ declared to those who followed him that just as God had given manna to the Hebrews during the Exodus, so the Father had given his Only Begotten Son (see John 6:31–33). Then Christ revealed: "I am the bread of life: he that cometh to me shall never hunger" (John 6:35). The same metaphor is expanded and intensified later in the same discourse: "I am the living bread which came down from heaven: if any man eat of this bread, he shall live forever: and the bread that I will give is my flesh, which I will give for the life of the world" (John 6:51). In this passage, Christ uses a very significant term: *life*. The Greek word translated "life," *zoe,* occurs 36 times in the Gospel of John and another 13 times in the Epistles. John 20:31 tells us that the chief purpose for which the Gospel was written is "that believing ye might have life through his name." *Zoe* always means spiritual life as opposed to biological life in John's writings. Just as food is the source of our biological life (the Greek word for biological life is *psyche*), so Christ has given himself, his very life, or *zoe,* to become the vital principle of our lives. He is to become a part of us—the spiritual power that moves us in the here and now—just as the food we eat is made a part of us and gives us energy to carry on life's activities.[2]

The Greek verb *didonai,* "to give," is used throughout the Gospel of John to refer to the gracious gifts of the gospel, such as living water "given" by Christ to the Samaritan woman (John 4:10), the bread of life that Jesus "gave" to the multitude (John 6:31), God's word and commandments "given" by Jesus to his disciples (see John 13:34). And again I emphasize, Christ himself is the unmerited gift offered out of sheer love without any prior conditions. Christ *is* the living water, he *is* the bread of life, he *is* the Word of God given as a sheer grace and unmerited gift to save us.[3]

THE GIFT OF SIGHT

God's wooing of us begins by giving us eyes to see the power of God shown in the mighty miracles or "signs" performed by Christ. As Christ stated to the nobleman whose son was near death, "Except ye see signs and wonders, ye will not believe" (John 4:48); however, signs and wonders influence only those who have eyes "to see." John uses five verbs that are all translated in English "to see" (Greek, *blepin, theasthai, theorein, idein* or *eidon,* and *horan*). The verb "to see" occurs in one of these forms 147 times in the Gospel of John and another 16 times in the Epistles, almost always with the double meaning not only of seeing with mortal eyes but also of seeing the eternal meaning with eyes of faith.[4] As Christ told his disciples: "[It] is the will of him that sent me, that every one which seeth the Son, and believeth on him, may have everlasting life" (John 6:40). Thus, when Christ first met his disciples, his simple invitation was, "Come and see. They came and saw where he dwelt, and abode with him that day" (John 1:39). When the first disciples tried to persuade others to follow Christ, their invitation was the same. When the first two disciples told Nathaniel that Jesus was the long-awaited Messiah, he gave this skeptical reply, "Can there any good thing come out of Nazareth?" The simple response of the two disciples was, "Come and see" (John 1:46). It is only with this inner spiritual sight that true faith can develop. As the Baptist testified, "And I saw, and bare record that this is the Son of God" (John 1:34). Both those who did not believe and those who would become Christ's disciples saw the same person when "seeing" Christ, but they did not use the same eyes. The disciples received a gift of spiritual sight: whereas those who were in darkness—rejecting God's gift of light—saw only a man, those who were illuminated by spiritual light "to see" had eyes of faith to recognize Christ as the Son of God.[5]

FAITHFUL BELIEF

Although there are no conditions to God's love for us, we must accept the gift he has so graciously offered if we hope to have eternal life. "A man can receive nothing, except it be given him from heaven" (John 3:27). We can't receive unless God gives; however, we must receive the gift of God through believing. Believing is much more than just an intellectual acknowledgment that Jesus is the Christ. The Greek verb "to believe" (*pisteuein*) occurs in one form or another in the Gospel of John 98 times and in the Epistles another 9 times. This verb always means faithfulness as a dynamic act of acceptance that is manifested in behavior. The verb form of "to believe" is the same root in Greek as the word for "faith" (*pisits*); however, the noun for "faith," *pistis,* never occurs in either the Gospel or the

Epistles of John. John's preference for verbs shows his emphasis upon the active and dynamic nature of faithful belief. Such believing means faithfulness to God in the same way that a husband is faithful to his wife. The meaning is one of interpersonal commitment manifested in one's entire life and activity rather than merely an acceptance of cognitive content. "He that believeth on the Son hath everlasting life [Greek, *zoe aionios*]: and he that believeth not the Son shall not see life; but the wrath of God abideth on him" (John 3:36). Those who do not believe in this sense are condemned because "light is come into the world, and men loved darkness rather than light, because their deeds were evil" (John 3:19). John's record uses a verb form "to do the truth," which is awkward in English, but it expresses well the meaning of the active and interpersonal sense of "faithful believing": "He that doeth truth cometh to the light" (John 3:21). One does the truth by being faithful to the loving relationship which saves us. As Raymond Brown commented:

"Thus, *pisteuein ies* ['belief in'] may be defined in terms of an active commitment to a person and, in particular, to Jesus. It involves much more than trust in Jesus or confidence in him; it is an acceptance of Jesus and of what he claims to be and a dedication of one's life to him. The commitment is not emotional but involves a willingness to respond to God's demands as they are presented in and by Jesus (see 1 John 3:23). This is why there is no conflict in John between the primacy of faith and the importance of good works. To have faith in Jesus whom God sent is the work demanded by God (see John 6:29), for to have faith implies that one will abide in the word and commands of Jesus (John 8:31; 1 John 5:10)."[6]

ABIDING IN GRACE

By coming "to see" that Christ is the gift from the Father and accepting him through our faithful belief, we enter into a relationship with God the Father and his Only Begotten Son. John taught, however, that once in this relationship we must be careful not to compromise it by acts that are unfaithful or harmful to the relationship. We "abide" in this relationship of love by keeping the commandments: "As the Father hath loved me, so have I loved you: continue ye in my love. If ye keep my commandments, ye shall abide in my love; even as I have kept my Father's commandments, and abide in his love" (John 15:9–10). The verb "to abide" (Greek, *menein*) is used in one form or another 40 times in the Gospel of John and another 27 times in the Epistles; however, the English translation "to abide" used in the King James Version (although the best English translation) is not adequate to express the intensity of the verb *menein,* which means to endure and actually live an entire life devoted to Christ. This word can be translated variously as "to stay, to remain, to continue, to dwell, to lodge, to sojourn, to last, to endure, to be permanent, to persevere, to be constant, to be stead-fast, to abide, to be in close and settled union, or to indwell."[7] The verb *menein* has the double meaning of physically dwelling with Christ and also of complete unity with or "dwelling in" Christ: "And he that keepeth his commandments dwelleth in him, and he in him. And hereby we know that he abideth in us, by the Spirit which he hath given us" (1 John 3:24).

Yet the choice to translate this verb *menein* as "to abide" is a good one in English because it shows the connection with another English word, *abode* (Greek, *monen*), or a place of dwelling. For example, Jesus told his disciples, "If a man love me, he will keep my words: and my Father will love him, and we will come unto him, and make our abode with him" (John 14:23). Similarly, when the disciples were invited to come and "see" Jesus, they "came and saw where [Jesus] dwelt, and abode with him that day" (John 1:39). The Greek word for *abode* is the noun form of the verb *menein.* John teaches that in heaven there are many abodes or mansions (Greek, *monai*), and Jesus has prepared one for us to come and dwell with him (see John 14:2).[8] If we keep God's commandments, then Christ dwells in us and makes his abode with us.[9]

John's concept of commandments is rooted deeply in the Old Testament covenant.[10] By keeping the commandments, we show our active faithfulness to the New Covenant, or our "covenant love."[11] This covenant is also a grace, a gift from God (see John 1:16–17). There are no conditions to entering the covenant relationship graciously offered by God the Father through his Only Begotten Son. One is prepared for this relationship by repentance and baptism as signs of the covenant to keep his commandments (see John 3:3–7). But there are conditions to remaining or abiding in the covenant relationship. Once in the relationship, we abide in the covenant by keeping the commandments.

Moreover, it is important to keep in mind that the commandments we must keep really boil down to just two: to believe in Christ and to love one another. "And this is his commandment, That we should believe on the name of his Son Jesus Christ, and love one another, as he gave us commandment" (1 John 3:23; see also John 15:12). Thus, we should not think of the commandments of God as a long laundry list of things we must do to merit eternal life. All of the commandments, such as refraining from stealing, refraining from lying, and so forth, are all contained implicitly in the command to love one another (see Matthew 22:36–40). The commandments illustrate ways that we are to act that demonstrate love for God and for each other. If we believe in Christ truly, then we have this love. If we have this love, then we keep his commandments because they are written on our hearts.

The love demanded by Christ in the writings of John is distinctive. The writings of John use three words that are all translated as "to love" or "beloved": Greek, *agapan, agape, philein*. The word *love* occurs in one of these forms 56 times in the Gospel of John and another 52 times in the Epistles. Moreover, John prefers the active verb form of love, *agapan* (67 times), to the passive noun, *agape* (28 times). This preference indicates that love is a dynamic activity manifested in one's entire life rather than merely a verbal assent or passing commitment. This form of love is the spontaneous, unmerited, creative love given by the Father to Christ and by Christ to his disciples. It is a divine form of love that transforms both its source and its recipient into divine beings. It is unconditional. It is gracious. It is a gift. It involves the entire heart, might, mind, and strength. It is an intimate sharing of life so meaningful and deep that one's life is actually "in" that of the beloved and the beloved "in" the life of the lover.[12]

The purpose of the three Epistles of John, in particular, is to encourage the Saints to abide in Christ by loving faithfulness. John pleads with the Saints: "Let that therefore abide in you, which ye have heard from the beginning. If that which ye have heard from the beginning shall remain in you, ye also shall continue in the Son, and in the Father" (1 John 2:24). The Saints had received an anointing, which strengthened their endurance in Christ: "But the anointing which ye have received of him abideth in you . . . and even as it hath taught you, ye shall abide in him" (1 John 2:27). By this anointing (Greek, *chrism*) the Saints became anointed ones, or messiahs. The Greek root for "anoint" is *christos,* translated from the Hebrew *messiah* or "anointed one." If we keep the commandments by loving one another, God dwells "in" us and we are made over in God's very image. His life becomes our life. As he is anointed, so are we. We become one in a very real sense with the Father and his Only Begotten Son.

KNOWING GOD

By abiding in God's grace by keeping his commandments, we also come "to know" God. The verb "to know" (either in its form *eidenai* or *ginoskein*) appears 141 times in the Gospel of John and another 42 times in the Epistles of John. This form of knowledge, however, is not the impersonal "knowledge about" facts; rather, it always expresses a profound interpersonal relationship. The record attributed to John invariably speaks of personal knowledge of God: "And hereby we do know that we know him, if we keep his commandments. He that saith, I know him, and keepeth not his commandments, is a liar, and the truth is not in him. But whoso keepeth his word, in him verily is the love of God perfected: hereby know we that we are in him" (1 John 2:3–5). This passage is hard to translate into English because the Greek language distinguishes types of "knowing" that English does not. English does not have separate words for "knowledge" which distinguish between "interpersonally knowing a person," and "knowing about facts." However, this distinction exists in most languages, including Greek (*ginosko* and *episteme*) and Latin (*conoscere* and *sapere*). It is important to keep this distinction in mind in John, because knowing God personally rather than merely knowing about God as an academic exercise is crucial to salvation and exaltation. To know (*ginoskein*) the only true God and Jesus Christ whom he has sent, is life eternal (see John 17:3). By knowing God, we begin to live the very kind of divine life that the Father and the Son live—that is, eternal life. To know God means to understand God in a profoundly personal sense because we begin to live the very kind of life that God enjoys, or eternal life.[13]

LOVING UNION

By keeping God's commandment to love him and each other, and thus coming to know the only true God and his Son, we are invited to become "one" "in" the Father and the Son as they are one in each other. We are invited to share the divine life. Christ prayed that his disciples would "be one, as we are" (John 17:11, 22). Moreover, Christ prayed that the Holy Ghost would come also to dwell "in" the disciples: "Even the Spirit of truth; whom the world cannot receive, because it seeth him not, neither knoweth him: but ye know him; for he dwelleth with you, and shall be in you" (John 14:17). The culmination of John's view of grace is deification of humans in the sense that we have been invited into a loving reunion to be one in the Father, Son, and Holy Ghost. By becoming one, Christ "gives" us the same glory that he had with the Father before the world was.[14] By becoming united as one in the Father, Son, and Holy Ghost, we have "eternal life" and participate in the very kind of existence that God enjoys.[15]

This indwelling oneness is not merely the type of unity enjoyed by members of the same football team who have the common purpose of winning a game. The unity spoken of in John's writings is much more intense and profound. The Father and the Son are said to be "in" each other and are one (John 14:10). The unity is so profound that the Father, Son, and Holy Ghost have the same mind in the sense that what one wills, all will as one (see John 6:38). What one knows, all know as one. What one does, all do as one (see John 10:25). The divine persons exist in a unity that includes loving and intimate knowledge of another who is also in one's self.

It is stunning but true: John teaches that we, mere mortals, can become one in the same sense. Referring to his disciples, Christ prayed to the Father: "That they all may be one; as thou, Father, art in me, and I in thee, that they also may be one in us. . . . And the glory which thou gavest me I have given them; that they may be one, even as we are one: I in them, and thou in me, that they may be made perfect in one" (John 17:21–23). This incredibly intimate sense of unity leads to perfection of our knowledge of God. We come to know God in the sense that we become just as God is. Thus, just as a son becomes what his father is, so we become sons [and daughters] of God by intimate knowledge. The First Epistle of John expresses this reality in these words: "Behold, what manner of love the Father hath bestowed upon us, that we should be called the sons of God: therefore the world knoweth us not, because it knew him not. Beloved, now are we the sons of God, and it doth not yet appear what we shall be: but we know that, when he shall appear, we shall be like him; for we shall see him as he is. And every man that hath this hope in him purifieth himself, even as he is pure" (1 John 3:1–3).

The culmination of God's grace received through living faith is thus to be like God. All of the elements of John's view of grace come together here. We come to know God. Such knowledge gives us sight to see God as he truly is. We are recognized as God's children who grow to resemble their parent. We become pure or sanctified, just as our Father is pure and sanctified. We become as God is through grace. Thus, although we forever remain distinct individuals, we become one "in" the Father, Son and Holy Ghost (see John 17:21).

Conclusion

In summary, there are no conditions to enter into the saving covenant relationship with God. The gift of his Son, Jesus Christ, is offered freely as a sheer grace. He already loves us without any prior conditions. God bestows the grace of spiritual sight upon us and we are thereby led to believe in Christ. Such belief is an active and loving commitment to keep the commandments. There are thus conditions to abiding in the saving relationship: the condition of keeping the commandments. By keeping the commandments, we come to know the Father and the Son. Such knowledge brings us into union "in" them. Such union glorifies us and makes us pure as they are pure. The culmination of grace in John's writings is deification of Christ's true disciples and complete unity with the Godhead.

Notes

1. Joseph Henry Thayer, *A Greek-English Lexicon of the New Testament* (Grand Rapids, Mich.: Zondervan, 1979), 204–5.

2. J. Blank, "Ich bin das Lebensbrot," *Bibel und Leben* 7 (1966), 255–70.

3. See P. Borgen, *"Bread from Heaven,"* SNTS Supp. 10 (Leiden: Brill, 1965), 154–58.

4. See R. T. Fortna, *The Gospel of Signs* (London: Cambridge University Press, 1970); A. Vanhoye, "Notre foi, oeuvre divine, d'apres

le quatrieme evangile," *Nouvelle Revue Theologique* 86 (1964), 337–54; and G. L. Phillips, "Faith and Vision in the Fourth Gospel," in Floyd L. Cross, ed., *Studies in the Fourth Gospel* (London: Mowbray, 1957), 83–96.

5. G. R. Osborne, "Soteriology in the Gospel of John," in Clark H. Pinnock, ed., *The Grace of God, The Will of Man: A Case for Arminianism* (Grand Rapids, Mich.: Zondervan, 1989), 245–46.

6. Raymond E. Brown, *The Anchor Bible Commentary on the Gospel of John,* 2 vols. (Garden City, N. Y.: Doubleday, 1966), 1:513.

7. See Thayer, *Greek-English Lexicon,* s.v., *menein.*

8. See R. Gundry, "In my Father's House are many *Monai* (John 14:2)," *Zeitschrift fur Neutestamentliche Wissenschaft* 58 (1967), 68–72.

9. See G. Pecorara, *"De verbo 'manere' apud Joannem," Divus Thomas* 40 (1937), 159–71.

10. R. Brown, *John,* 1:505.

11. E. Schillebeeckx, *Christ: The Experience of Jesus as Lord,* John Bowden, trans. (New York: The Crossroad Publishing Co., 1983), 312–21, originally published under the title *Gerechitigheid en liefde: Genade en bevrijding* by Uitgeverij H. Nelissen, Bloemendaal, 1977.

12. C. Spicq, "La charite est amour manifeste," *Revue Biblique* 65 (1958), 358–70.

13. See I. de la Potterie, *"Oida* et *ginosko,* les deux modes de la con-naisance dans le quatrieme evangile," *Biblica* 40 (1959), 795–825; J. Gaffney, "Believing and Knowing in the Fourth Gospel," *Theological Studies* 26 (1965), 215–41.

14. P. Van Boxtel, "Die praexistente *Doxa* Jesu im Johannese-vangelium," *Bijdragon. Tidjdscrift voor Filosofie en Theologie* 34 (1973), 268–81.

15. See A. Feuillet, "La participation actuelle a la vie divine d'apres le quatrieme evangile," *Studia Evangelica* (Berlin: Akademie-Verlag, 1965), 1:295–308.

CHAPTER FIFTEEN

The Lands of the Gospel of John

CRAIG J. OSTLER

The Gospel of John is unique among the four Gospels in the choice of events that were recorded. Indeed, Robert J. Matthews, former dean of Religious Education at Brigham Young University, determined that 92 percent of the Gospel of John is material not found in any of the other three Gospels.[1] Part of this uniqueness is the often-overlooked contribution to our knowledge of the lands where the Savior's ministry took place. John is the only writer who named such locations as Bethabara, Cana, Jacob's well, the Pool of Bethesda, the garden in Gethsemane,[2] and the garden tomb near the place of crucifixion. These particular sites hold a place in the hearts of Bible students because they are the lands where Jesus walked during his mortal ministry. In addition to these sites, several locations are mentioned by all four of the Gospel writers. Our knowledge of these important locations is enhanced by John's unique narrative of the events that took place in such areas as Capernaum, Bethany, and Jerusalem.[3]

By no means are we as Latter-day Saints to venerate historic places. Such veneration was part of the Great Apostasy in the meridian-day Church of Jesus Christ. As President J. Reuben Clark Jr. explained: "Historical sites or places noted in our history are not to be worshipped or clothed with sanctity. It is interesting to visit them. On such occasions we may be moved emotionally or spiritually, but this comes, not from the place, but from our inner selves stirred thereto

Craig J. Ostler is an assistant professor of Church history and doctrine at Brigham Young University.

by the thoughts and spiritual reflections our visit has engendered."[4] With this spirit of reflection we will examine several places mentioned by John.

BETHABARA BEYOND JORDAN

John was a participating witness to the events recorded in his Gospel, beginning with the ministry of John the Baptist. John referred to the Baptist's early ministry, indicating, "These things were done in Bethabara beyond Jordan, where John was baptizing" (John 1:28). The other three synoptic Gospel writers are not as specific in their designation of the area where John taught and baptized. They simply indicate that John taught in the area of the Jordan River, convenient for the ordinance of baptism by immersion. The importance of Bethabara is rooted in the sacred events that took place there. It was there that John the Baptist bore witness to his listeners that he was preparing the way for the Messiah, who soon was to walk among them. "Looking upon Jesus as he walked" at Bethabara, John heard the Baptist testify, "Behold the Lamb of God!" (John 1:36). It was there that Jesus came to John and requested baptism at his hands that he might "fulfil all righteousness" (Matthew 3:15). It was there that the Holy Ghost descended as a dove upon the Savior, and John received the sign that had been given of the promised Messiah (see John 1:32–34). Luke clarified that "the Holy Ghost descended in a bodily shape" (Luke 3:22). The only other recorded vision of the Holy Ghost in bodily shape is Nephi's interview with the Spirit of the Lord as he appeared to him "in the form of a man" (1 Nephi 11:11).[5] Most important of all of the events that are recorded to have taken place at Bethabara is that following the baptism of the Savior: God the Father spoke from heaven testifying that Jesus of Nazareth is His Son, in whom he is well pleased. Bethabara is one of a privileged few locations known on earth where God the Father has spoken to mortals. Only on the Mount of Transfiguration, and later in the precincts of the temple during the Savior's last week in mortality, is it recorded in the Bible that the voice of the Father spoke from the heavens.[6] Further, it was at Bethabara that all three members of the Godhead were manifest: the Father speaking from heaven, the Son fulfilling all righteousness in being baptized, and the Holy Ghost descending upon the Savior in bodily form.

The actual location of the New Testament Bethabara has not been identified with certainty. In fact, many modern translations of the Bible take the view that the site of the Baptist's ministry was in a location called Bethany.[7] This Bethany, however, should not be confused with the Bethany of Judea, the home of Mary, Martha, and Lazarus. It would have been a Bethany near the Jordan River. The Book of Mormon employs the word *Bethabara* for the location where, according to Lehi's prophecy, John the Baptist would preach and baptize (see 1 Nephi 10:9). This reference indicates that Lehi may have been familiar with the area known to him as Bethabara. It is possible that the designation of Bethabara also had some significance in Old Testament times.

The meaning of the word *Bethabara* is "ford, crossing" where a stream may be crossed.[8] Berrett and Ogden suggest that Bethabara may be near a "natural fording place today called Allenby Bridge, or King Hussein Bridge."[9] For centuries Christian pilgrims have resorted to the Jordan River near the Hajlah ford for baptisms and bathing. Viewing the slow and quiet waters of the Jordan River at this location provides the visitor with a sense of peace through nature's hallowed setting. The tremendous events recorded by John and the other Gospel writers to have taken place at Bethabara are couched in an understanding of the stillness of the wilderness.

AENON NEAR TO SALIM

John received the witness borne by the Baptist that Jesus of Nazareth was the awaited Messiah of Israel. The need to prepare people to receive the Messiah through faith, repentance, and baptism by immersion continued. This work moved forward by the hands of the Master's disciples, who taught and baptized throughout Judea. Indeed, Jesus and his disciples baptized more individuals than did John the Baptist (see John 3:22; 4:1–3). Joseph Smith clarified that Jesus himself did baptize but "not so many as his disciples; for he suffered them for an example, preferring one another" (JST John 4:3–4). This was a time of a growing discipleship that believed in and followed the Master. John the Baptist continued to bear his witness of Jesus Christ and to baptize those who came to him. Apparently, the Baptist thought it needful to move to a new location, possibly to escape the growing scrutiny of the Jewish leaders.[10] The apostle John records that John the Baptist sought out another site that could meet the needs of the ordinance of baptism by immersion. The Baptist moved to "Aenon near to Salim, because there was much water there" (John 3:23). It was at Aenon that John the Baptist referred to himself as merely the friend of the Bridegroom, who, he testified, was Jesus of Nazareth.

The reference to Aenon as a place of much water seems to refer to an area near the Jordan River identified by the early Christian leader Eusebius as the Aenon of the New Testament. The word means "double springs," and Tell Sheikh Selim has several springs that would fit John's description;[11] however, this site cannot be identified with certainty. If Aenon is located near the area identified by Eusebius, then it is possible to shed light on John's description of the area as one where there was much water. This general area, near present-day Beth She'an, has several pools of water surrounded by luxuriant plant growth and is a popular recreation area. These conditions would indicate that John was no longer baptizing in the Jordan River but had resorted to pools of water in which his listeners were immersed for the ordinance of baptism.

CANA OF GALILEE

Cana is a small village in the area of Galilee. As with Bethabara and Aenon, John is the only Gospel writer to mention Cana. Two events of note are recorded by John to have taken place there. Both of these references are to miracles at the word of the Lord. The first of these two miracles is the changing of water into wine at a wedding feast. John refers to it as the "beginning of miracles [that] did Jesus in Cana of Galilee, and manifested forth his glory; and his disciples believed on him" (John 2:11). We do not know the relationship of the Savior to either the bridegroom or the bride, yet Jesus was called upon to rescue them from the embarrassment of running short of wine for those who attended the wedding celebration. Jesus instructed that the servants fill six stone pots with water, which miraculously poured out wine at the wedding. John, who likely was one of the Master's disciples present at the wedding feast, testified to the Lord's power over the elements. This event is unique in the miracles of Christ in that, unlike the later multiplying of loaves and fishes, this miracle involves a change in the nature of the substance.

Further, Jesus illustrated, by changing the water to wine, that not only does he have power over elements such that water may become wine but also that his power transcends time—in the aging process of the wine.[12]

Later in the Savior's ministry, while he was again passing through Cana, he was met by "a certain nobleman, whose son was sick at Capernaum" (John 4:46). The man pleaded with the Lord to accompany him to his home, where his son lay. Jesus chose to show forth his power once again. Without leaving Cana he told the nobleman to return home, and he would find his son made whole. When the nobleman returned to Capernaum, he met his servants, who confirmed that the son had recovered at the very hour Jesus had spoken the words, "Thy son liveth" (John 4:53).

The small village of Cana is known today because John recorded the events that took place there as part of his witness that Jesus of Nazareth is the Son of God. Yet, like the location of Bethabara and Aenon, the exact location of Cana is uncertain. A modern village claiming to be the Cana of Galilee referred to in John's Gospel is Cana (Kafr Kanna), which lies four miles northeast of Nazareth. Three churches in this town claim ties to the events of the Cana of New Testament times. The visitor to modern Cana will see stone waterpots and stone basins connected with the "six waterpots of stone" (John 2:6) mentioned in John's account. In addition, the Greek Orthodox church in modern Cana has a red dome, reminding the visitor of the red-colored wine that was a result of the Savior's power at the wedding. It is more likely, however, that the site of the biblical Cana is some five miles north of modern Cana. This archaeological site that lies across the Beit Netofa Valley overlooking a marshy plain is more in line with the meaning of Cana as a "place of reeds," for reeds are still plentiful in the area.[13]

Capernaum: "His Own City"

John recorded that after the Lord's miracle of changing water to wine at Cana, "he went down to Capernaum, he, and his mother, and his brethren, and his disciples: and they continued there not many days" (John 2:12). Capernaum's significance is attested to by Matthew, who stated that Jesus "dwelt in Capernaum" (Matthew 4:13) and referred to Capernaum as "his own city" (Matthew 9:1).

John is notably silent compared to the other Gospel writers regarding the events that took place in Capernaum; however, the one discourse that he does record is of greatest importance: the Savior's sermon given in the synagogue at Capernaum (see John 6:59) in which he declared "I am the bread of life" (John 6:35). Greater perspective is gained from this discourse and the place of Capernaum with a review of the events recorded by Matthew, Mark, and Luke. Before the Savior's declaration that he was "the living bread which came down from heaven" (John 6:51), Jesus had been a familiar figure in Capernaum, for Peter and others of Jesus' disciples lived there, and Jesus visited there often. President David O. McKay explained:

"Peter at this time was a married man, and was perhaps the father of a little boy. He had moved from his old home in Bethsaida, and lived with his wife's mother, or she with him, in Capernaum. With him were also Andrew and their two faithful companions and friends, James and John, the sons of Zebedee.

"Peter's home became the most distinguished home in all Capernaum, and later one of the most memorable spots in all the world. Here, undoubtedly, Jesus stayed whenever He was at Capernaum! Indeed after Jesus had been so ruthlessly rejected by His own townsmen in Nazareth, He made Capernaum His 'own city'; and it is supposed that much of the time, the honor fell upon Peter to entertain in his home the Savior of the world."[14]

While in Capernaum the Savior had become well-known through teaching astonishing doctrine in the synagogue on the Sabbath (see Luke 4:31–32). On one occasion he was confronted by a man with an unclean spirit who pleaded with the Savior to let him alone, as he knew He was "the Holy One of God" (Luke 4:34). Those present in the synagogue that day were amazed as the unclean spirit left the man at Jesus' command.

From the biblical record available to us today, it appears that the city of Capernaum was the site of more healings by the mortal Messiah than any other city on the earth. A listing of the miracles of God among men is necessary to fix the place of Capernaum in the Savior's ministry. It was in Capernaum that Peter's mother-in-law was healed of a burning fever, a centurion's servant was healed, a palsied man took up his bed and walked, and "all they that had any sick with divers diseases brought them unto him; and he laid his hands on every one of them, and healed them. And devils also came out of many" (Luke 4:40–41). On a return visit to Capernaum the Lord was thronged by multitudes of people, including a woman with an issue of blood who touched the hem of his garment and was healed (see Matthew 9:20–22; Luke 8:40, 43–48). The twelve-year-old daughter of Jairus, ruler of the synagogue in Capernaum, was raised from the dead as she lay on her bed in the home of her parents. When he departed the home of Jairus, two blind men followed him and were healed at the Master's touch, as was a man who was dumb (see Matthew 9:27–33). Applying Edersheim's words regarding one night of healing to all the manifestations of Christ's power in Capernaum, "never, surely, was He more truly the Christ . . . than when . . . He went through that suffering throng, laying His hands in the blessing of healing on every one of them, and casting out many devils."[15]

It was in the city of Capernaum, scene of so many of the Lord's compassionate healings, that John recorded the Savior's rejection by many of his disciples. Just previous to this rejection the Master had fed five thousand with "five barley loaves, and two small fishes" (John 6:9–13). Men who had witnessed the miracle proclaimed that Jesus was "of a truth that prophet that should come into the world" (John 6:14). He had escaped the intentions of the multitude to make him a king by departing in the darkness of night, walking upon the waters of the Sea of Galilee (see John 6:15–19). In the synagogue at Capernaum where he taught on the Sabbath among those with whom he was familiar, he openly declared that he was sent from heaven by the Father to do the Father's will. He explained, "And this is the Father's will which hath sent me, . . . that every one which seeth the Son, and believeth on him, may have everlasting life: and I will raise him up at the last day" (John 6:39–40). And it was also in this synagogue built by the centurion whose servant Jesus had healed (see Luke 7:1–10), the same synagogue over which Jairus was the ruler, where, John recorded, Christ's sermon was too demanding for his listener's hearts to receive. Christ declared that he was living bread and would give his flesh "for the life of the world" (John 6:51). John explained, "Many therefore of his disciples, when they had heard this, said, This is an hard saying; who can hear it?" (John 6:60). Capernaum was the place that "from that time many of his disciples went back, and walked no more with him" (John 6:66). In contrast, it was also at Capernaum that in response to Jesus' asking the Twelve if they also would go away, Peter responded, "Lord, to whom shall we go? thou hast the words of eternal life. And we believe and are sure that thou art that Christ, the Son of the living God" (John 6:68–69).

Unlike Bethabara, Aenon, and Cana, it is quite certain where the New Testament city of Capernaum was located. On the north shores of the Sea of Galilee lie the ruins of Tell Hum, identified as Capernaum.[16] Among the ruins has been found one of the best-preserved synagogues in the Holy Land. This synagogue dates to the fourth to fifth century—much too late to be the synagogue in the Gospels—however, beneath this synagogue is the foundation of another, which dates to the time of the New Testament and may have been the synagogue built for the Jews by the Roman centurion. Also, the home of Peter has been identified by archaeologists, based on the assumption that early Christians accurately marked New Testament sites. This home was built earlier during the Hellenistic period and must have been occupied later by Peter and his family when they moved there. The foundation of this multiroomed dwelling is of stone—black basalt being common to the area. Archaeological finds indicate that during the second half of the fifth century, the home identified as Peter's home was razed and an octagonal church was built over the site to mark the spot of the original home.[17] It stands apart from the other excavated homes by the plaster that was applied to the walls of one of the rooms. It is likely this room received such special attention because it is where meetings of the young church of Christ were held.

JACOB'S WELL IN SAMARIA

John alone recorded the conversation that the Savior had with a woman of Samaria in which he spoke of the "living water" that he has to give. The conversation took place as Jesus sat on Jacob's Well, possibly meaning on a rock or covering over the well opening. Christ and his disciples were traveling from Judea into Galilee. John describes their route as going through Samaria by a city called Sychar (see John 4:3–5). He further described the area as being "near to the parcel of ground that Jacob gave to his son Joseph" (John 3:5). The book of Genesis relates a purchase of a field that Jacob bought in

Shechem, the area inhabited by the Samaritans in New Testament times (see Genesis 33:18–20). Only John's account, however, mentions that Jacob had a well there. This well figures in the account because Jesus was wearied from his journey and remained at the well to rest while his disciples went into the city to buy food. While he was resting a Samaritan woman came to Jacob's Well to draw water and the Savior asked her to give him water to drink. Apparently, to draw water, each individual needed a jar and a rope to drop the jar into the well and to draw the jar up again. When the Savior offered the woman "living water" that he could give to her, she replied, "Sir, thou has nothing to draw with, and the well is deep" (John 4:11). Following the demonstration of the Savior's spiritual insight into the woman's past (having had five husbands and living at the time with a man who was not her husband), the woman recognized Jesus as a prophet.

Jacob's Well was near Mount Gerizim. The woman declared, "Our fathers worshipped in this mountain" (John 4:20), but the Jews say men ought to worship in Jerusalem. She may have spoken in the hope that this prophet sitting on the well before her could clear up the question of who was correct. She was disappointed with his answer that salvation was of the Jews and that the Samaritans did not even know what they worshipped. She retorted that when the "Messiah cometh, . . . he will tell us all things" (John 4:25). John recorded that while resting at Jacob's Well in Samaria, Jesus identified himself as the Messiah to this Samaritan woman in the simple words, "I that speak unto thee am he" (John 4:26). Her heart was penetrated with the truth of his testimony, and she testified to others in the nearby city of Sychar that she had found the Christ.

The site that has been identified as Jacob's Well is near Shechem, or Nablus. Some archaeologists have declared that this site is "the most authentic of all the Holy Places in Palestine."[18] This assertion stems not only from the fact that the well is more than one hundred feet deep, as reflected in the Samaritan woman's words, but also that "all traditions—Jewish, Samaritan, Christian, and Muslim—support it."[19] The well that is recognized as that in John's New Testament account is housed in a Greek Orthodox church that has remained unfinished for nearly a century. In the partially finished church or chapel the caretaker still offers visitors to the site a drink of water from the well, a reminder of the "living water" Jesus offered the Samaritan woman nearly two millennia ago.

The city of Sychar has not been as positively identified. Two nearby locations have adherents that declare that their site is the original referred to in John's writings. They both lie near Mount Gerizim which, along with its companion, Mount Ebal, figured in the reading of the law to the children of Israel anciently, as recorded in Joshua 8:32–35. There is still a community of several hundred Samaritans living in nearby Shechem, or Nablus. They have remained a separate people from the Christian and Moslem Arabs who dominate this area of Palestine. They marry within their own group and celebrate the Passover upon Mount Gerizim each year.

BETHANY

Elder Bruce R. McConkie wrote: "Lazarus lived in the town of Bethany some two miles east of Jerusalem, but hidden from the Holy City by a spur of the mount of Olives. There also dwelt in this Judean village of blessed memory the beloved sisters Mary and Martha, in whose family circle the Lord Jesus so often found surcease from toil and rest from his labors. They and their brother Lazarus were three of the most intimate friends Jesus had on earth."[20]

We do not know from today's record the particular circumstances of the relationship of the Lord and this family. We are told by John that when Lazarus took ill, his sisters sent to Jesus, "saying, Lord, behold, he whom thou lovest is sick" (John 11:3). The town of Bethany is a symbol of the Savior's power over death. As is well known to readers of the Bible, by the time the Son of God arrived in Bethany, Lazarus had died and his body had lain in the tomb for four days (see John 11:17). John recorded that when Jesus was taken by Mary and Martha to the tomb, "Jesus wept" (John 11:35). The tomb "was a cave, and a stone lay upon it" (John 11:38). Jesus commanded them to take the stone away, and at the mouth of the tomb-cave the Savior "cried with a loud voice, Lazarus, come forth" (John 11:43). Elder McConkie shared his feelings about this event: "Though Jesus spoke often of his own resurrection and the resurrection of all men, in my judgment the most persuasive and convincing witness, both of his divine Sonship and of the reality of the resurrection, that ever came from mortal lips, his or any others, were the words he spoke at the tomb of Lazarus."[21]

Thus, John alone recorded the event, and Bethany was the site of the Lord's singular utterance. Moreover, it was in Bethany that "he that was dead came forth, bound hand and foot with graveclothes: and his face was bound about with a napkin" (John 11:44). There is a site dating to A.D. 333 that is reputed to be the very tomb from which Lazarus was called forth.[22] It is in the town of Bethany, approximately two miles east of Jerusalem. The visitor enters the room housing the underground chamber directly from the street by descending a steep, narrow staircase into a room identified as the "tomb of Lazarus." This designation of locale is consistent with Brown's observation that "vertical shaft tombs were more common for private burial than horizontal cave tombs."[23]

John also exclusively recorded in his Gospel testimony that the home of Mary and Martha in Bethany was the location of a supper during the last week of the Savior's life in which Mary "anointed the feet of Jesus, and wiped his feet with her hair" (John 12:3). The occasion of the supper found Lazarus sitting at the table and testifying by his very presence of the power of the Master to raise the dead from the tomb. Bethany was, while Lazarus continued to reside there, a place of living witness to the Lord's power over death. John wrote that "the chief priests consulted that they might put Lazarus also to death; because that by reason of him many of the Jews went away, and believed on Jesus" (John 12:10–11). Thus, upon the roads of Bethany and within the home of Mary and Martha, many had their hearts awakened to the reality that Jesus is the Christ as they saw, listened to and perhaps spoke to Lazarus, his sisters, and the townspeople. It was also from Bethany, the city of the irrefutable living witness, that Jesus entered the city of Jerusalem in triumph, riding upon a colt of an ass, and met by those people who had "heard that he had done this miracle" (John 12:18).

JERUSALEM

Most of John's writings have the city of Jerusalem as their setting, in stark contrast to the other Gospel authors, who are virtually silent concerning the Savior's ministry in Jerusalem before the week of the atoning sacrifice.[24] Over half of John's testimony concerning the

Savior's ministry before his last week in mortality took place in Jerusalem. Indeed, immediately following the changing of water to wine at Cana, John alone recorded the visit of the Savior to Jerusalem for the Passover feast. The other references to the Savior's ministry in Jerusalem that are related by John have Jewish feasts as their focus. There are several locations in Jerusalem to which John referred.

THE POOLS OF BETHESDA AND SILOAM

John's writings indicate that two pools in Jerusalem were sites of the healing power of Jesus Christ. Each healing took place while Jesus attended a Jewish feast; however, John does not specifically name the feast to which the Lord "went up to Jerusalem" (John 5:1) and passed by the Pool of Bethesda. John identified that "there is at Jerusalem by the sheep market a pool, which is called in the Hebrew tongue Bethesda, having five porches" (John 5:2). John described the scene at the pool of Bethesda as one in which "a great multitude of impotent folk, of blind, halt, [and] withered" lay waiting for the moving of the water (John 5:3). There was a superstitious belief that an angel would touch the water and the first individual into the pool following the "troubling of the water . . . was made whole of whatsoever disease he had" (John 5:4). While walking on the porches that surrounded the pool, Jesus came upon a man who had been infirm for thirty-eight years. He had compassion on the man and commanded him to take up his bed and walk. Immediately rising to his feet, the man was healed of his malady.

The Pool of Bethesda has been identified today by archaeologists as very likely being near the present-day Crusader Church of St. Anne north of the temple area. Excavations revealed a pool with five porticoes over which several successive structures had been built throughout the centuries that have passed since the time Jesus healed the infirm man. These excavations show that the pool was actually twin pools, 165 to 220 feet wide by 315 feet long, with four colonnaded sides divided by a central fifth portico. Stairways in the corners descend into the pools.[25] It is rather difficult for the modern visitor to envision the setting of this healing as the pool area has only been partially excavated and is now located about sixty feet beneath the present ground level. The structure above the water in the pool is what remains of a Crusader chapel built over the ruins of a

Byzantine church.[26] The successive scenes of destruction of Jerusalem over the centuries left the city in heaps of rubble. The city has been rebuilt a number of times upon the ruins of previous societies that inhabited Jerusalem.

The second pool mentioned in John's writings is the Pool of Siloam. There is no indication that the Savior himself ever went to this location. He did, however, send a blind man to wash in the pool. After the Savior taught at the Feast of Tabernacles (see John 7–8), he came upon "a man which was blind from his birth" (John 9:1).[27] The blind man was sent to the pool after Jesus "spat on the ground, and made clay of the spittle, and he anointed the eyes of the blind man with the clay" (John 9:6). The Savior gave him the simple instructions to wash in the Pool of Siloam. In what we could call "blind obedience," the man felt his way to the pool "and washed, and came seeing" (John 9:7).

The Pool of Siloam is identified with a tunnel built in King Hezekiah's reign. This tunnel, southeast of the walled portion of present-day Jerusalem, runs between the Kidron and the Tyropoen Valleys. Water from the Spring of Gihon is conducted by means of the tunnel-canal to the Pool of Siloam. As the visitor leaves Hezekiah's Tunnel in the Tyropoen Valley, he or she passes by a small pool of water enclosed by stone walls and ascends a more modern staircase to ground level. It is believed that this is a remnant of the Pool of Siloam to which the blind man was sent by the Savior to wash.

The Temple

On several occasions John mentioned the temple built by Herod as the site of Jesus Christ's ministry. The Savior did not enter the actual building enclosing the Holy Place, which housed the sacred furniture of the temple, nor did he enter into the Holy of Holies. According to Mosaic law, only Levitical priests entered the Holy Place, and even the high priest entered the Holy of Holies on but one day each year, the Day of Atonement.[28] Jesus' ministry primarily took place in the outer precincts or courtyard of the temple. Surrounding the outer courtyard was a portico. The Jewish historian Josephus recorded that the colonnades of the portico "were all double, the supporting pillars were 37½ feet high, cut from single blocks of the whitest marble, and the ceiling was panelled with cedar. The natural magnificence of it all, the perfect polish, the accurate joining, afforded a remarkable spectacle, without any superficial ornament either painted or carved."[29]

It is possible that from one or more of the colonnaded sides of the courtyard Jesus drove out those "that sold oxen and sheep and doves, and the changers of money" (John 2:14). It would have been in a similar area of the portico where earlier, as a twelve-year-old boy, he was "sitting in the midst of the doctors, and they were hearing him, and asking him questions" (JST Luke 2:46). After the healing of the man at the pool of Bethesda, Jesus spoke to him again while he walked in the temple precincts. During each visit to Jerusalem of which we have record, the Savior sought to go to the mount upon which the temple and its attendant portico and courtyard were located. During the last week of his mortal life, the Savior again cast the moneychangers from the temple and was repeatedly challenged by the chief priests as he taught the people in the temple precincts.

John alone recorded the Savior's earlier visits to Jerusalem for the Feast of Tabernacles and the Feast of Dedication. During the Feast of Tabernacles "Jesus went up into the temple, and taught" (John 7:14). Alarmed that "many of the people believed on him, . . . the Pharisees and the chief priests sent officers to take him" (John 7:31–32). Such a desperate attempt only led to the officers of the temple returning to bear testimony of Jesus' teachings and a refusal to arrest him. John recorded that the next day "early in the morning he came again into the temple, and all the people came unto him; and he sat down, and taught them" (John 8:2). The Temple Mount was the place to which the woman taken in adultery was brought to the Master as he taught. It was there that he challenged the scribes and Pharisees to cast the first stone if they were without sin. Referring to the incident with the adulterous woman and the Savior's teachings that morning concerning his Messiahship as the light of the world, John wrote, "These words spake Jesus in the treasury, as he taught in the temple" (John 8:20).

The temple building itself was separated from the outer courtyard by an inner wall, which surrounded and enclosed the temple proper from activities of the courtyard, which even the Gentiles were permitted to observe. The gate leading to the inner temple courtyard opened to an area nearly two hundred feet square, called the Court of the Women. Entry into this court was restricted to Israelites. In each of the four corners of the court was a chamber with the entire court surrounded by porticoes. The treasury was located in the center of the north portico. Elder James E. Talmage explained that "within that space were thirteen chests, each provided with a trumpet-shaped receptacle; and into these the people dropped their contributions for the several purposes indicated by inscriptions on the boxes."[30] It was from this temple treasury that the chief priests took the money they paid to Judas for his betrayal of the Savior. In addition, "in this court stood giant lampstands (menorot), seventy-five feet in height, giving light to the Temple Mount and to much of the City."[31] Thus, John identified the Savior's choice of a perfect setting, the treasury of the temple beneath the giant menorah, where he declared "I am the light of the world" (John 8:12).

John indicated that during the Feast of Dedication Jesus walked in the colonnaded area on the east side of the courtyard known as Solomon's Porch "in recognition of a tradition that the porch covered and included a portion of the original wall belonging to the Temple of Solomon."[32] While there the Jews gathered "round about him, and said unto him, How long dost thou make us to doubt? If thou be the Christ, tell us plainly" (John 10:24). At Solomon's Porch, near his father's house, Jesus answered the Jews, indicating that he worked in his father's name and that he and his father are one. He declared openly to the Jews that he is God and the Son of God. For that plain testimony, in the area of Solomon's Porch, the Jews took up stones to put him to death for blasphemy.

It is quite certain where the temple precincts of the New Testament were located. In the eastern area of the city of Old Jerusalem is the Holy Mount, called by the Moslems, who own and administer that area, Haram esh-Sharif, "the Noble Sanctuary." The Holy Mount is one of the most prominent features of the city of Old Jerusalem. The Roman armies destroyed the temple in A.D. 70 as the Savior foretold his disciples. All that remains today of King Herod's temple is the Western Wall below the Holy Mount. In honor of the sacred events and the holy houses of God that stood on the mount, the Moslems built two important structures: El Aqsa Mosque and the Dome of the Rock. The magnificent Dome of the Rock was completed in A.D. 691 soon after the city of Jerusalem came under Moslem control.[33]

THE BROOK CEDRON AND GARDEN IN GETHSEMANE

John is notably silent concerning the Savior's ministry on the temple grounds during his last week in mortality. The other Gospel writers give attention in their records to the Savior's teaching on the Temple Mount and identify locations around Jerusalem at which the Savior taught and ate the Passover meal, but John records little identifying information for his reader. It is very likely that the Savior's instructions recorded by John to love one another as he had loved them, his promise of the Comforter, and the great intercessory prayer were given while in the "upper room" (Luke 22:12) where the Savior and his disciples ate the Passover meal.[34] John is also silent concerning the atoning events of which he was an eyewitness at Gethsemane. He did record that the disciples went "over the brook Cedron, where was a garden" (John 18:1). Further, John indicated that "Jesus ofttimes resorted thither with his disciples" (John 18:2). The brook Cedron is actually a brook of the Kidron Valley that separates the city of Jerusalem and the Mount of Olives.[35] The Savior chose a garden on the slopes of this mount for the site of the atoning sacrifice for which he was foreordained to come into the world. As Elder Bruce R. McConkie wrote: "In reality the pain and suffering, the triumph and grandeur, of the atonement took place primarily in Gethsemane. It was there Jesus took upon himself the sins of the world on conditions of repentance. It was there he suffered beyond human power to endure. It was there he sweat great drops of blood from every pore. It was there his anguish was so great he fain would have let the bitter cup pass. It was there he made the final choice to follow the will of the Father. It was there that an angel from heaven came to strengthen him in his greatest trial . . . in which he descended below all things as he prepared himself to rise above them all."[36]

It was also to Gethsemane that Judas came by night with "a band of men and officers from the chief priests and Pharisees, . . . with lanterns and torches and weapons" that they might arrest the Savior (John 18:3).

Today it is simple to visually identify the Mount of Olives. The visitor looking east of the Old City of Jerusalem sees the mount running the length of the view. But the location of the garden referred to by John is not quite as easy to ascertain. "The name Gethsemane derives from Hebrew and Aramaic words for 'oil press.'"[37] As a result, it is supposed that the garden included an orchard of olive trees and a press to obtain oil from the olive fruit. Today each of four sites has advocates claiming it to be the location of the original Gethsemane of the Gospels. Olive trees, some of great age, cover the hillside, but none of the trees in the olive orchards were there during the events recorded in the Bible, for the Roman army under Titus cut down the trees on the Mount of Olives in the siege of Jerusalem in A.D. 70.[38] Still, somewhere on the Mount of Olives, took place the most important event in all history—the atoning sacrifice of the Son of God, the Savior of the world.

TRIALS BEFORE ANNAS, CAIAPHAS, AND PILATE

John, along with the other three Gospel writers, recorded that from Gethsemane Jesus was taken to "the palace of the high priest" (John 18:15). Caiaphas was the high priest at the time of the Savior's illegal trial before the Jewish Sanhedrin. Jesus was first taken within the palace to Caiaphas' father-in-law and the earlier high priest, Annas. He was questioned concerning his doctrine, struck on the face, and sent bound to Caiaphas. The courtyard of this palace was also the site of Peter's denials, in which he refused to acknowledge his relationship with the Lord.

It is not certain where the palace was located. Two sites southwest of the Old City of Jerusalem, outside the wall, claim to be the biblical location. One is located on the summit of today's Mount Zion within the area owned by the Armenian Church; the other is "down the slope a hundred yards on what are now the grounds of St. Peter in Gallicantu."[39]

John recorded that from the interrogation at the palace of the high priest, "then led they Jesus from Caiaphas unto the hall of judgment" (John 18:28). This hall was the site of Jesus' trial before Pilate. John referred to this hall as "the Pavement, but in the Hebrew, Gabbatha" (John 19:13). Mark called this same hall the Praetorium (see Mark 15:16), "a Latin term for the palace with its hearing room to which the Roman governor came to transact public business."[40]

John wrote of a raised seat upon which Pilate sat as the judgment seat (see John 19:13). Here the Son of God stood before an earthly governor for judgment! Elder James E. Talmage described the scene that was enacted in the hall of judgment: "Pilate was surprised at the submissive yet majestic demeanor of Jesus; there was certainly much that was kingly about the Man; never before had such a One stood before him. . . . That some of the disciples, and among them almost certainly John, also went in, is apparent from the detailed accounts of the proceedings preserved in the fourth Gospel. Anyone was at liberty to enter, for publicity was an actual and a widely proclaimed feature of Roman trials."[41]

In this hall of judgment Jesus was sentenced to die by crucifixion. The echoes of the persuading voices of the chief priests may still be heard as "they cried out, saying, Crucify him, crucify him" (John 19:6).

Two locations are possibilities as the site of the hall of judgment. Pilate may have been at either King Herod's palace or at the Antonia Fortress during the Passover celebration. Excavations at both sites have yielded stone pavements like those of which John wrote in his description. The more popular of the two to visit is the ancient site of the Antonia Fortress, north of the Temple Mount beneath the modern Sisters of Zion Convent. Indications are, however, that the more likely site was that of King Herod's Palace in the western part of the upper city in the Armenian quarter.[42] "Without additional evidence, it is impossible to conclusively determine which of the two sites might be the location of Jesus' presentation before Pilate."[43]

GOLGOTHA

John, along with Matthew and Mark, identified the place of the Savior's crucifixion as Golgotha. John wrote, "And he bearing his cross went forth into a place called the place of a skull, which is called in the Hebrew Golgotha: where they crucified him, and two other with him, on either side one, and Jesus in the midst" (John 19:17–18). The Joseph Smith Translation of this same passage indicates that it was a place of burial. Golgotha is the one place in all of creation that the Son of God was nailed to a cross. The horror of crucifixion and the pains of suffering for sin combined together on this site of godly sacrifice. No pen can write the feelings that are associated with Golgotha. It is the focus of Christian reflection, for on Golgotha Jesus Christ suffered the pains of sin and death for all humankind. Elder Bruce R. McConkie explained regarding the Savior's cry from the cross, "My God, my God, why hast thou forsaken me?" (Matthew 27:46): "It seems, that in addition to the fearful suffering incident to crucifixion, the agony of Gethsemane had recurred, intensified beyond human power to endure."[44] The last words uttered in mortality from the lips of the Messiah were at Golgotha. He said, "Father, it is finished, thy will is done" (JST Matthew 27:54). Or, in the words of Luke, "Father, into thy hands I commend my spirit" (Luke 23:46). Following which, John recorded, "he bowed his head, and gave up the ghost" (John 19:30).

John wrote that after the Savior gave up his life on the cross at Golgotha, the soldiers came to break the legs of the three men that had been crucified that day. "But when they came to Jesus, and saw that he was dead already, they brake not his legs: but one of the soldiers with a spear pierced his side, and forthwith came there out blood and water" (John 19:33–34). Later, Joseph of Arimathaea and Nicodemus came to Golgotha and took the body of Jesus from the cross to prepare it for burial and to lay it in a tomb.

Where was Golgotha? John wrote "the place where Jesus was crucified was nigh to the city" (John 19:20). Therefore, it is assumed with considerable confidence that Golgotha was located outside of the city wall. Christian tradition dating to more than three hundred years after the event places Golgotha at the site of the Church of the Holy Sepulchre, which is located within the present walls of Jerusalem. That does not prevent this site from being authentic, however, for this location may have been outside the city wall in the Savior's time.[45] Another possible site is that of Gordon's Calvary, north of Damascus Gate. This site has become the destination of many Christian pilgrims within the last century. The artistic focus of Gordon's Calvary is the face of a hill pockmarked by little caves that give the viewer the impression of a skull. Whether the Golgotha of the crucifixion was at either of these two locations is not certain.

A Garden and a New Sepulchre

After the removal of the Savior's body from the cross, Joseph of Arimathaea and Nicodemus hurriedly prepared it for burial. John indicated that "then took they the body of Jesus, and wound it in linen clothes with the spices, as the manner of the Jews is to bury" (John 19:40). John further described the burial site: "Now in the place where he was crucified there was a garden; and in the garden a new sepulchre, wherein was never man yet laid. There laid they Jesus" (John 19:41–42). This sepulchre, in and of itself, would be associated with sacred reverence because it is where the Son of God was entombed. Yet the true significance of the sepulchre is due to its association with the fact that the Savior's body did not remain there for more than three days and three nights. It was at the mouth of this sepulchre that the stone was taken away, "and two angels sitting thereon" (JST John 20:1) were seen by Mary Magdalene in the early morning hours of the greatest day to dawn in the history of the earth. It was from this sepulchre that the resurrected Lord broke the bands of death. John himself was one of the first witnesses to see the empty tomb. He and Peter went running to the tomb at the bidding of Mary Magdalene. John arriving first at the sepulchre, "stooping down, and looking in, saw the linen clothes lying; yet went he not in" (John 20:5). After Peter arrived and entered the sepulchre, he observed the linen grave clothes and "the napkin, that was about his head, not lying with the linen clothes, but wrapped together in a place by itself" (John 20:7).

The garden in which the sepulchre was located is also a focal point of the gospel of Jesus Christ. It was in this garden that the resurrected Lord first appeared to Mary Magdalene. What setting could be more beautiful than a garden with a sepulchre whose stone has been rolled away for the first appearance of the resurrected Son of God? Even today, the Christian heart breaks forth in song as the scene at the garden tomb is contemplated.

All that is true of the location of Golgotha is true of the sepulchre and the garden. When we can be certain of the location of one, we will be nearer to knowing the location of the others. Of the Church of the Holy Sepulchre and Gordon's Calvary, the latter has a modern setting near a sepulchre within a garden. It is, however, the newer garden tomb that has stirred the hearts of latter-day prophets. In 1988, Elder Howard W. Hunter said, "I've stood in front of the garden tomb and imagined that glorious day of resurrection when the

Savior emerged from the tomb alive, resurrected, immortal. In that contemplation my heart has swelled with joy."[46]

Previously, Presidents Harold B. Lee and Spencer W. Kimball had expressed their feelings regarding visits to the garden tomb. President Lee stated, "Something seemed to impress us as we stood there that this was the holiest place of all, and we fancied we could have witnessed the dramatic scene that took place there."[47] President Kimball added, "I feel quite sure that this is the spot where His body was laid. It gives me such a sacred feeling just to be here."[48]

SEA OF TIBERIAS

The shores of the Sea of Tiberias, also called Galilee, are the place last-named in the Gospel of John. It was there that the resurrected Savior appeared to seven of his disciples. In mortality Jesus had calmed a storm—the winds and the waves obeyed his command—while in a boat upon the Sea of Galilee. On another occasion the Lord had walked upon the water of the Sea of Galilee to reach the boat in which his disciples were traveling. After the resurrection, in the morning hours following a night of fishing in which the seven disciples had caught nothing, "Jesus stood on the shore" (John 21:4). When Peter recognized the Master, he jumped into the lake and swam to meet Jesus on shore. There, on the shores of the Sea of Galilee, the seven disciples feasted upon fish with the risen Lord. After the dinner, Peter was questioned by the Master concerning his love for his Lord and was charged to feed the Savior's sheep.

The shores of the Sea of Galilee were of particular importance to John. It was there that he asked the Lord to have power to tarry until Jesus returned in glory. His request was granted, and John was given power over death that he might bring souls unto Christ.[49] John gave no identifying information about where on the shores of the Sea of Galilee this commission was given; however, it was from the shores of this lake that "went this saying abroad among the brethren, that that disciple should not die" (John 21:23).

CONCLUSION

The Gospel of John is invaluable in its identification of the lands where Jesus walked during mortality. Additionally, John's unique contributions regarding the Savior's ministry not only enhance our understanding of those events that bear witness that Jesus Christ is the Son of God but also stir our hearts to new heights of appreciation for his life among men. The singular contributions John made to our knowledge of the Jerusalem of Christ's day have given Christians vivid pictures regarding the garden settings of Gethsemane and the sepulchre from which he rose triumphantly. As one reads the Bible or is privileged to walk the lands of Palestine, John's Gospel writings add color and shape to the backdrops of the Savior's teachings, miracles, atoning sacrifice, and resurrection.

NOTES

1. Robert J. Matthews, *Behold the Messiah* (Salt Lake City: Bookcraft, 1994), 27.

2. The garden location for the tomb is also mentioned in JST Mark 14:36.

3. It is possibly important to note that John, at one time, was believed to have used symbolic names that did not exist as real locations; however, as Raymond Brown stated, "Scholars have become more cautious now that some Johannine place names, once accounted to be purely symbolic, have been shown to be factual." *The Gospel According to John (I-XII)*, vol. 29 of *The Anchor Bible*, 38 vols. (New York: Doubleday, 1966), 45.

4. J. Reuben Clark Jr., *On the Way to Immortality and Eternal Life*, 2d ed. (Salt Lake City: Deseret Book, 1949), 292.

5. James E. Talmage, *Articles of Faith* (Salt Lake City: The Church of Jesus Christ of Latter-day Saints, 1968), 159–60.

6. Matthew 17:1–5; Mark 9:2–7; Luke 9:28–35; John 12:27–29.

7. See John 1:28 in the Living Bible, Today's English Version, New International Version, Phillips Modern English, Revised Standard Version, Jerusalem Bible, and New English Bible. *Eight Translation New Testament* (Wheaton, Ill.: Tyndale House Publishers, 1974), 642–43.

8. *The Interpreter's Dictionary of the Bible,* ed. George A. Buttrick, 4 vols. (New York: Abingdon Press, 1962), 1:387.

9. LaMar C. Berrett and D. Kelly Ogden, *Discovering the World of the Bible* (Provo: Grandin Book Co., 1996), 83. Tradition holds that near this, the Hajlah ford, Joshua crossed the Jordan River in leading the children of Israel into the promised land. If such is the case, it may be that Bethabara is a name used by John to tie events of the Old and New Testaments together as he also does in the opening phrase of his Gospel—"in the beginning," referring to the first words of Genesis.

10. John 1:19–28.

11. *Interpreter's Dictionary of the Bible,* 1:52; *Anchor Bible Dictionary,* ed. David Noel Freedman, 6 vols. (New York: Doubleday, 1992), 1:87.

12. Matthews, *Behold the Messiah,* 130–31.

13. Berrett and Ogden, *Discovering the World of the Bible,* 112; *Interpreter's Dictionary of the Bible,* 1:493.

14. David O. McKay, *Ancient Apostles* (Salt Lake City: Deseret News Press, 1952), 7.

15. Alfred Edersheim, *The Life and Times of Jesus the Messiah, Part One,* (Grand Rapids, Mich.: Eerdmans, 1981), 487.

16. *Interpreter's Dictionary of the Bible,* 1:533.

17. *Anchor Bible Dictionary, 1:*866–68. For a further discussion of the home identified as Peter's in Capernaum, see James F. Strange and Hershel Shanks, "Has the House Where Jesus Stayed in Capernaum Been Found?" *Biblical Archaeology Review* 8 (November/December 1982): 26–35.

18. *Anchor Bible Dictionary,* 3:608.

19. *Anchor Bible Dictionary,* 3:608.

20. Bruce R. McConkie, *The Mortal Messiah,* 4 vols. (Salt Lake City: Deseret Book, 1980), 3:270.

21. Bruce R. McConkie, *The Promised Messiah* (Salt Lake City: Deseret Book, 1978), 275–76.

22. *Anchor Bible Dictionary,* 1:703.

23. Brown, *Gospel According to John,* 426.

24. A comparison by verse count of the Gospels reveals that Matthew makes no mention of the Savior in Jerusalem before the week of the atoning sacrifice. His lone reference to Jerusalem is the Nativity account, which mentions King Herod the Great being approached by the magi. Mark makes no mention of Jesus in Jerusalem during that same time period. Luke records the presentation of the Messiah as a baby in the temple at Jerusalem and the Savior's experience in the temple as a twelve-year-old boy but mentions nothing of the Savior's ministry in Jerusalem after those events. The one exception in Luke may be the giving of the parable of the Good Samaritan and a visit to Bethany at the home of Mary and Martha, if we consider Bethany as part of the environs of Jerusalem.

25. Brown, *Gospel According to John,* 207.

26. Berrett and Ogden, *Discovering the World of the Bible,* 29–30.

27. The pool of Siloam had been the site of ritual drawing of water during the eight days of the feast.

28. Exodus 29:29–30; 30:10; Numbers 18:7; Hebrews 9:1–7.

29. Flavius Josephus, *The Jewish War,* trans. G. A. Williamson (New York: Penguin Books, 1959), 291.

30. James E. Talmage, *Jesus the Christ,* 3d ed. (Salt Lake City: Deseret Book, 1976), 561.

31. David Galbraith, D. Kelly Ogden, and Andrew Skinner, *Jerusalem, the Eternal City* (Salt Lake City: Deseret Book, 1996), 190.

32. Talmage, *Jesus the Christ,* 500.

33. Galbraith et al., *Jerusalem,* 281.

34. John 13–17.

35. Buttrick, 3:10–11.

36. Bruce R. McConkie, *Doctrinal New Testament Commentary,* 3 vols. (Salt Lake City: Bookcraft, 1965–73) 1:774–75.

37. *Anchor Bible Dictionary,* 2:997.

38. Flavius Josephus, *Complete Works,* trans. William Whiston (Grand Rapids, Mich.: Kregel Publications, 1981), 571.

39. Galbraith, et al., *Jerusalem,* 174.

40. Galbraith, et al., *Jerusalem,* 176.

41. Talmage, *Jesus the Christ,* 633–34.

42. *Anchor Bible Dictionary,* 2:862.

43. Galbraith, et al., *Jerusalem,* 176. Also see Brown, *Gospel According to John,* 845.

44. McConkie, *Mortal Messiah,* 4:226.

45. *Anchor Bible Dictionary,* 2:1071–73.

46. Howard W. Hunter, *Teachings of Howard W. Hunter,* ed. Clyde J. Williams (Salt Lake City: Bookcraft, 1997), 9.

47. Harold B. Lee, "I Walked Today Where Jesus Walked," *Ensign,* April, 1972, 6.

48. Spencer W. Kimball, *Deseret News,* 3 November 1979, Church Section, 5, as cited in Galbraith, et al., 507.

49. See John 21:20–25; D&C 7.

CHAPTER SIXTEEN

THE LOVE OF GOD

MATTHEW O. RICHARDSON

The friction between Jewish traditionalism and Hellenistic philoso-
phy became apparent among the members of the early Christian
church. Many of the Jewish Christians professed a commitment to
Jesus Christ but still felt a loyalty to Jewish law. As a result, Christ's
role as the Messiah was a difficult concept for most of them to
accept. Many of the Hellenistic Christians, on the other hand, were
influenced by an early form of Gnosticism and found it difficult to
accept the "humanity" of Jesus Christ. On both accounts, the identity and role of Christ was distorted. It was under such circumstances
that John attempted to appeal to the faithful Saints and correct the
misguided teachings of the time. It makes sense that John testified of
a corporeal (physical) resurrected Jesus (see 1 John 1–2) to counter
Gnostic claims of a "phantom" (nonphysical) Savior. Likewise,
Christ's role in our cleansing (see 1 John 1:7), advocacy with the
Father (see 1 John 2:1–3), and overcoming the world through rebirth
(see 1 John 5:4–6) testifies that Jesus Christ is the Messiah. Not to be
forgotten, however, in providing a full understanding of the identity
of Jesus Christ and the gospel is love. Love, as taught in John's writings, provides necessary insight for understanding the Savior, Jesus
Christ.

WHAT IS LOVE

I do not believe it is coincidence that love becomes one of the pre-
dominant themes[1] of the disciple "whom Jesus loved" (John 13:23;
20:2; 21:7; 21:20), or "John the Beloved." It is likely that because

Matthew O. Richardson is an assistant professor of Church history and
doctrine at Brigham Young University.

John felt he was beloved, he approached this topic in a simple yet deeply profound manner. To gain this comprehensive insight, however, we must consider all of John's writings rather than concentrating on a single verse, chapter, or book. Biblical scholars often use repeated textual analysis as a way of discovering meaning from religious texts. The process requires returning again and again to the text. That is especially helpful when studying a concept as broad as love. John's writings not only become clearer when compared with his other texts but reveal fascinating relationships as well. By returning to John's texts, we find that he unfolds the meaning of love and how it relates with the gospel of Jesus Christ.

"That Your Joy May Be Full"

In an attempt to dispel the pervading philosophies of the time, John's writings reflect his desire that we obtain not a portion of truth but a fulness thereof. This is made clear as John writes, "And these things write we unto you, that your joy may be full" (1 John 1:4). *Full,* in this context, is used to translate the Greek word *pleroo,* meaning "replete, or finished." In some interpretations, *pleroo* is described as a "filler" that rounds out imperfections, or dents, or makes something complete. Because it was John's desire to provide a means whereby our joy may be made complete or full, his approach to love is not a doctrinal decoration but a load-bearing beam.

John approaches love in its fullest sense, and those who study his writings must be willing to consider that the scriptural essence of love might be something different from what they are either used to hearing or have come to expect. If one approaches John's text with a casual, self-satisfied attitude, only varying portions of the fulness can be realized. That is not to say that we are incapable of loving or that the love John describes is beyond our grasp but merely that John's message of love is profoundly simple. It is not wrought with distractions or pomp of its own. Therein lies the danger. With such a clean doctrine, we are tempted to spruce it up a bit, add our own agendas, become satisfied with a status quo vision, or allow the views of the world to define our doctrine. When properly understood, the love described in John's works provides direction for all mankind.

For God Is Love

John invites us to "love one another" (John 13:34; 13:35; 15:12; 1 John 3:11; 3:23; 4:11). Most of us have accepted this invitation at one time or another in our lives and have loved someone (or at least some*thing*). But John's notion of what love is, however, does not mesh with traditional concepts. The fulness of love, according to John, is considerably narrow in comparison to the world's concept of love. "Love one another," John wrote, "for love is of God" (1 John 4:7). John continued: "[He] that dwelleth in love dwelleth in God, and God in him" (1 John 4:16). John connects the fulness of love not with casual emotions, affection, or even passion but with God. To ensure that he was not misunderstood, John taught in the simplest of terms that "God is love" (1 John 4:8, 16). If one desires true love, one must understand God.

Some may become nervous using God as the standard and definition of love. They may think such a standard is too restrictive or unrealistic. Some may feel that if God defines love, then romance will be replaced with benevolence and brotherly love. But when we understand John's teaching of love correctly, romantic love, brotherly love, and benevolence can be appropriate under God's divine guidance.[2] God's definition of love will, however, exclude feelings, actions, and motives that are contrary to his law. That filters out the misconceptions of love, leaving only a "pure" love. To those who feel that "God is love" is an unrealistic standard, I offer Elder Henry B. Eyring's advice: "And you need not fear that using God as your standard will overwhelm you. On the contrary—God asks only that we approach him humbly, as a child."[3] As we raise our standards to meet those of our God, we not only begin to act like him but become more like him as well.

We Loved Him, Because He First Loved Us

Another important consideration in understanding the meaning of love is John's statement that "herein is love, not that we loved God, but that he loved us" (1 John 4:10). Although love is intended eventually to become a reciprocal relationship, we must understand that the love of God is not contingent upon our love for him. It begins with God, not with us. John explained that "we love him, because he first loved us" (1 John 4:19). Rather than considering these statements as a reason for us to love God, we can see that John's point is that love begins with God. Thus, his love is what allows us to love, not only him, but everything.

"HE THAT DWELLETH IN LOVE DWELLETH IN GOD"

John makes it clear that "he that dwelleth in love dwelleth in God, and God in him" (1 John 4:16). Because the love of God is the genesis of our ability to truly love, if we remove God, for any reason, we forfeit our ability to practice love in its fullest sense. For example, John taught that "if any man love the world, the love of the Father is not in him" (1 John 2:15). This is not to say that if one indulges in worldliness God will no longer love him. C. S. Lewis emphasized that "the great thing to remember is that, though our feelings come and go, His (God's) love for us does not. It is not wearied by our sins, or our indifference."[4]

Although God will always love us, John emphasized that our love of the world limits the degree to which God's Spirit is manifest in our life. How we embrace the world, whether with unabashed acceptance or with flirtatious encounters with its subtleties, creates a boundary between us and God. James, author of the Epistle of James, queried, "Know ye not that the friendship of the world is enmity with God?" He concluded, "Whosoever therefore will be a friend of the world is the enemy of God" (James 4:4). When we entertain that which removes God from our lives, it is not his love for us that decreases but the presence of his Spirit that diminishes (see D&C 121:37). Although God still loves us, our understanding and ability to truly love is forfeited because of the loss of his Spirit. Where God is not, love in its fulness cannot be.

This forfeiture is not restricted to wicked acts alone but can include using the world to define gospel principles. President Gordon B. Hinckley spoke of those who allow the world to define love. He said, "Their expression may sound genuine, but their coin is counterfeit. Too often the love of which they speak is at best only hollow mummery."[5] In similar tone, Elder Marvin J. Ashton warned, "Too often expediency, infatuation, stimulation, persuasion, or lust are mistaken for love. How hollow, how empty if our love is no deeper than the arousal of momentary feeling or the expression in words of what is no more lasting than the time it takes to speak them."[6] Far too many of us have fallen for love's counterfeits. When we have a skewed understanding of what love really is, we are left in a frenzy to constantly feed an ever-fading emotion or we become frustrated, discouraged, disillusioned, or even cynical.

President Hinckley taught that "love is like the Polar Star. In a changing world, it is a constant. It is of the very essence of the gospel. It is the security of the home. It is the safeguard of community life. It is a beacon of hope in a world of distress."[7] When seeking this type of love, we must understand that the night sky is filled with love's counterfeits, each fawning for our attention as if it were the sure guiding light. Like every star, these counterfeits can provide some measure of illumination and guidance, but there is only one star that provides the constant answer for an ever-changing world. That guiding love, as John so aptly describes, is free from the world's dilutions and wickedness and is inseparably connected with God and Jesus Christ.

THE LOVE OF GOD

With the connection between love and God established, we can turn our focus to John's teachings about the "love of God." When discussing God's (the Father's) love for us, John provides critical commentary: "For God so loved the world, that he gave his only begotten Son" (John 3:16). Here John links God's love for the world with Jesus Christ. Later, John writes, "In this was manifested the love of God toward us, because that God sent his only begotten Son into the world, that we might live through him" (1 John 4:9). According to John, the love of God manifest to us is Jesus Christ.

An earlier witness of this concept is found in the Book of Mormon. Young Nephi saw a tree "and the beauty thereof was far beyond, yea, exceeding of all beauty; and the whiteness thereof did exceed the whiteness of the driven snow" (1 Nephi 11:8). When Nephi asked for an interpretation of what the tree is, rather than giving an immediate answer, a vision of the birth of Jesus Christ was opened to him (see 1 Nephi 11:13–20). As the vision closed, the angel proclaimed, "Behold the Lamb of God, yea, even the Son of the Eternal Father!" (1 Nephi 11:21). The angel then asked Nephi, "Knowest thou the meaning of the tree which thy father saw?" (1 Nephi 11:21). The angel seems to have been checking to see if

Nephi grasped the relationship between the vision of the Savior and his inquiry concerning the interpretation of the tree. Immediately, Nephi astutely answered, "Yea, it (the tree) is the love of God, which sheddeth itself abroad in the hearts of the children of men; wherefore, it is the most desirable above all things" (1 Nephi 11:22). Both Nephi and John testified that Jesus Christ is the love of God manifest to us.

THE FATHER GAVE ALL THINGS TO THE SON

Although Christ emphasized "my Father is greater than I" (John 14:28), he did not diminish his authoritative role in manifesting the Father's love. John recorded Christ's words as "Father, I will that they also, whom thou hast given me, be with me where I am; that they may behold my glory, which thou hast given me: for thou lovedst me before the foundation of the world" (John 17:24). Christ's glory was given to him by God because of the Father's love. John further testified that "the Father loveth the Son, and hath given all things into his hand" (John 3:35). It was through God's love that Christ became the chosen and authoritative manifestation of the Father. John said of Christ's ministry that "the Father loveth the Son, and sheweth him all things that himself doeth: and he will shew him greater works than these, that ye may marvel" (John 5:20). Christ, commissioned of the Father, manifests the fulness of the Father to all mankind. Thus, Christ is a mediator or a propitiator (see 1 John 4:10). Though a mediator and a propitiator are similar, Richard D. Draper, associate professor of ancient scripture at Brigham Young University, explains that propitiation goes beyond mediation by uniting two parties in friendship.[8] It is Christ, therefore, who makes it possible for us to receive the fulness of God's love. John emphasized this relationship as he taught, "I am the way, the truth, and the life: no man cometh unto the Father, but by me" (John 14:6).

BORN OF GOD

If we expect to obtain the fulness of God's love, we must receive it through the propitiation of Christ. John reminds us that "love is of God; and every one that loveth is born of God, and knoweth God" (1 John 4:7). To receive and exercise God's love requires us to be "born of God." To some, being born of God is a receiving the

realization that God is our spiritual father and we are his spiritual offspring. To others, being born of God involves recognizing that Christ
is their Savior. It is clear that being "born of God," as spoken of by
John, is more than coming to a realization that our beginnings were
with God the Father or a proclamation that Christ is our Savior.

As Jesus taught Nicodemus, he emphasized that one must be
"born again" to see the kingdom of God (John 3:3). Joseph Smith
further clarified that "we must have a change of heart to see the kingdom of God."[9] John later emphasized that our ability to love ("everyone that loveth") is born of God. It is true that our ability to love
stems from God, but how is the love of God born in us? We may also
ponder, How does love relate to changing our hearts and becoming
born again? Elder Bruce R. McConkie wrote: "To be born does not
mean to come into existence out of nothing, but rather to begin a
new type of existence, to live again in a changed situation. Birth is
the continuation of life under different circumstances."[10] John wrote
that "whosoever believeth that Jesus is the Christ is born of God"
(1 John 5:1). If we truly believe in Christ, we must begin a renova-
tion. We can no longer remain the same person we once were. Those
who embrace the gospel of Christ become new creatures, born into
new situations, new circumstances, new expectations, a new way to
approach daily experiences, and a new way to love. When we believe
in Christ, we begin a new existence, a life with Christ and of Christ.
Those who were once unable to love in the past can be transformed
and find a love born in them. This type of transformation is accomplished only through Christ.

CALLED THE SONS OF GOD

It is interesting that John linked the love of God with not only a
symbolic rebirth but a metaphorical adoption as well. John taught
that the love of God necessarily leads to both a rebirth and an adoption. "Behold, what manner of love that Father hath bestowed upon
us," John wrote, "that we should be called the sons of God" (1 John
3:1). This verse possesses a flavor of wonderment that God's love is
so grand that mere men can be called the sons of God. To some it
may seem odd that John wrote of this event with wonder. John
understood that we were created by God, thus becoming, as God's

creations, his "sons and daughters." But John stated that God's love was bestowed upon us so that we *should* be called sons of God.

Other prophets testify of this relationship between love, rebirth, and becoming the children of God. The prophet Moroni was emphatic about obtaining the love of God and thus becoming sons of God. He pleaded with those who would hear his message to "pray unto the Father with all the energy of heart, that ye may be filled with this love [the love of Christ, or charity], which he hath bestowed upon all who are true followers of his Son, Jesus Christ; that ye may become the sons of God" (Moroni 7:48).

Another prophet, King Benjamin, addressed the importance of understanding this adoptive process. He explained that "because of the covenant which ye have made ye shall be called the children of Christ, his sons, and his daughters, for behold, this day he hath spiritually begotten you; for ye say that your hearts are changed through faith on his name; therefore, ye are born of him and have become his sons and his daughters. And under this head ye are made free, and there is no other head whereby ye can be made free" (Mosiah 5:7–8). Benjamin testified that this adoption was made possible because of the covenant we made with God.

This adoptive process is an essential part of the rebirth taught by John. Again we return to Christ's discourse to Nicodemus. After teaching of the necessity of the rebirth of heart, Christ told Nicodemus, "Verily, verily, I say unto thee, Except a man be born of water and of the Spirit, he cannot enter into the kingdom of God" (John 3:5). He summarized, "Marvel not that I said unto thee, Ye must be born again" (John 3:7). Joseph Smith, when referring to these passages, taught that we must "subscribe the articles of adoption to enter therein."[11] John taught that the process of being born again requires more than acknowledging Christ and his mission. It requires even more than a change of heart. It also requires subscribing to the articles of adoption—making covenants. Elder Bruce R. McConkie stated that the sons and daughters of Jesus Christ "take upon them his name in the waters of baptism and certify anew each time they partake of the sacrament that they have so done; or, more accurately, in the waters of baptism power is given them to become the sons of Christ, which eventuates when they are in fact born of the Spirit and become new creatures of the Holy Ghost."[12] Because the love of God is manifest through Christ, we can only know God through Christ. We can only experience the fulness of God's love by entering into a covenant relationship with Jesus Christ. By maintaining our covenanted status, we are born of God and thus become the sons and daughters of Christ.

Whether discussing rebirth or becoming children of God, Christ is always at the center of the discussion. John testified that we have received Christ and exercised the power given us by him to become his (Christ's) sons (see John 1:12). Elder McConkie further clarified the connection between rebirth/adoption and Jesus Christ when he explained: "Those accountable mortals who then believe and obey the gospel are born again; they are born of the Spirit; they become alive to the things of righteousness or of the Spirit. They become members of another family, have new brothers and sisters, and a new Father. They are the sons and daughters of Jesus Christ."[13]

Although this adoption is necessary, it is not a culminating event but a part of a continual process of change. That is apparent in John's writing: "Beloved, now are we the sons of God, and it doth not yet appear what we shall be: but we know that, when he shall appear, we shall be like him; for we shall see him as he is" (1 John 3:2). The process of receiving God's love, rebirth, and becoming the children of Christ is not a one-time event but a gradual experience. In this process, we shall, as John described, become like Christ (see 1 John 3:2).

"IF YE LOVE ME, KEEP MY COMMANDMENTS"

As sons and daughters of Christ, we have covenanted to keep his commandments. Jesus taught, "If ye love me, keep my commandments" (John 14:15). This implies that we will keep the commandments because we love Christ (see 1 John 5:2–3; 2 John 1:6). Though this is true, an additional aspect of obedience is presented in John's writings. Christ taught that "he that hath my commandments, and keepth them, he it is that loveth me: and he that loveth me shall be loved of my Father, and I will love him, and will manifest myself to him" (John 14:21). When we keep the commandments, we find that Christ manifests himself to us.

This simple concept presents an interesting situation. Many of those who keep the commandments do so because they already possess a love of Christ. They, according to the prophetic blessing, will have a manifestation of Christ. But consider these verses applied in other circumstances. What of those who have not yet come to love Christ? Are they to be obedient to God's commandments as well?

C. S. Lewis felt that some people worry because they are unsure if they love God. He said concerning these people: "They are told they ought to love God. They cannot find any such feelings in themselves. What are they to do? . . . Act as if you did. Do not sit trying to manufacture feelings. Ask yourself, 'If I were sure that I loved God, what would I do?' When you have found the answer, go and do it."[14] Lewis further observed: "As soon as we do this we find one of the great secrets. When you are behaving as if you loved someone, you will presently come to love him."[15] John taught that "if any man will do his [God's] will, he shall know of the doctrine, whether it be of God, or whether I speak of myself" (John 7:17). Not only will the obedient know the divine source of the doctrine but they will grow in love toward the Master as well. Thus the cycle of love and obedience begins anew, ever deepening with each act of obedience and receipt of divine manifestation.

Our obedience maintains our covenant relationship with Christ, which facilitates the manifestation of God's love. We can feel the fulness of the Father only when our covenants with Christ are in effect. As we become more proficient in maintaining our covenant of keeping the commandments, not only do we draw ever closer to the Savior but he becomes a constant fixture in our lives. Christ taught, "If a man love me, he will keep my words: and my Father will love him, and we will come unto him, and make our abode with him" (John 14:23).

LOVE ONE ANOTHER

John reminded the disciples of Christ that mere familiarity with the Savior's message was not sufficient to obtain the full love of God. "My little children," John counseled, "let us not love in word, neither in tongue; but in deed" (1 John 3:18). Elder Howard W. Hunter taught: "Merely saying, accepting, believing are not enough. They are incomplete until that which they imply is translated into the dynamic action of daily living."[16] A disciple of Christ, therefore, is one who not only receives Christ's law, but one who seeks to follow the given counsel (see D&C 41:5). In the same manner, we find that a disciple of Christ is not only one who receives God's love and loves God, but one who seeks to love others. Christ commanded "that he who loveth God love his brother also" (1 John 4:21). This commandment was at the heart of Christ's ministry from the beginning (see 1 John 3:11; John 15:17).

Loving others is regarded as the badge of Christianity. Christ taught that "by their fruits ye shall know them" (Matthew 7:20). The discerning fruit of discipleship was determined by whether the followers of Christ loved others. "By this shall all men know ye are my disciples," Christ taught, "if ye have love one to another" (John 13:35).

"Love One Another, As I Have Loved You"

Although we have covenanted to love others, it is not enough to merely go through the motions in hopes of checking off one more requirement of discipleship. It is true that Christ admonished us to "love one another." But his commandment was not merely to learn to love others, but to "love one another; *as* I have loved you, that ye also love one another" (John 13:34; emphasis added; see also John 15:12; 1 John 3:23). This pattern was familiar to Christ for he taught that "as the Father hath loved me, so have I loved you: continue ye in my love" (John 15:9). No wonder John, who was self-described as "the disciple whom Jesus loved" wrote so much concerning loving others. Since John received Christ's love, he was in a position to love others and he understood that he must continue in that love by loving others as Christ loved him. Elder C. Max Caldwell said, "Jesus' love was inseparably connected to and resulted from his life of serving, sacrificing, and giving in behalf of others. We cannot develop Christ-like love except by practicing the process prescribed by the Master."[17]

"Greater Love Hath No Man"

As we consider the depth of the love that is God's to give, it is really quite amazing to think that it has been made available to us. The pinnacle of our understanding of the love of God is centered not only upon Christ, but also upon his sacrifice (see 1 John 4:9). John taught that we "perceive . . . the love of God, because he laid down his life for us," (1 John 3:16) and that the love of God is manifested toward us, *because* God sent his only begotten Son into the world so "that we might live through him" (1 John 4:9). Paul taught that "if any man live in Christ, he is a new creature; old things are passed away; behold, all things are become new" (JST 2 Corinthians 5:17). The Savior's mission—his sacrifice—in some miraculous way, not only changes how we live and love but also changes us. "The Atonement in some way," wrote Bruce C. Hafen, "apparently through the Holy Ghost, makes possible the infusion of spiritual endowments that actually change and purify our nature, moving us toward that state of holiness or completeness we call eternal life or Godlike life. At that ultimate stage we will exhibit divine characteristics not just because we think we should but because that is the way we are."[18] It is through this change that we can find everlasting life. John reminded us that "God so loved the world, that he gave his only begotten Son, that whosoever believeth on him should not perish; but have everlasting life" (JST John 3:16). Jesus Christ, the love of God, provides hope of salvation. No wonder John exults, "There is no fear in love; but perfect love casteth out fear: because fear hath torment. He that feareth is not made perfect in love" (1 John 4:18).

"THE FULNESS"

"What manner of love the Father hath bestowed upon us?" (1 John 3:1). The writings of John clearly teach of a fulness of love: not a counterfeit love, nor a portion of love, but a fulness thereof. John taught that the full measure of love is founded in God. It is from God that all love springs forth. He taught that Jesus Christ is, in reality, the love of God, and thus we can feel of the fulness of God's love as we enter into a covenant and become born of Christ. We reciprocate God's love by keeping the commandments and loving others. It is because of the ultimate sacrifice, the fulfilling of the mission of Christ, that we are able to become new creatures and thereby love others as Christ loved us. John taught that the only way to find the love that will guide and direct our lives for peace, dispose of fear, and bring us to a fulness of joy, is to be filled with pure love—even Jesus Christ.

NOTES

1. Bruce R. McConkie, *Doctrinal New Testament Commentary,* 3 vols. (Salt Lake City: Bookcraft, 1965–73), 3:371.

2. Dr. Richard D. Draper, associate professor of ancient scripture at Brigham Young University, concludes that all of the forms of love (*agape, philos,* and *eros*), when used appropriately, are necessary in achieving the highest or noblest love. Richard D. Draper, "Love and Joy," unpublished manuscript.

3. Henry B. Eyring, *To Draw Closer to God* (Salt Lake City: Deseret Book, 1997), 68.

4. C. S. Lewis, *Mere Christianity* (New York: Macmillan, 1952), 102–3.

5. Gordon B. Hinckley, Conference Report, April 1969, 61.

6. Marvin J. Ashton, *Ensign,* November 1975, 108.

7. Gordon B. Hinckley, *Ensign,* May 1989, 66.

8. Draper, "Love and Joy" (January 16, 1998, *n.p.*).

9. Joseph Smith, *Teachings of the Prophet Joseph Smith,* sel. Joseph Fielding Smith (Salt Lake City: Deseret Book, 1976), 328.

10. McConkie, *Doctrinal New Testament Commentary,* 2:471.

11. Smith, *Teachings of the Prophet Joseph Smith,* 328.

12. McConkie, *Doctrinal New Testament Commentary,* 2:471–72.

13. McConkie, *Doctrinal New Testament Commentary,* 2:471.

14. C. S. Lewis, *Mere Christianity,* 102.

15. Lewis, *Mere Christianity,* 101.

16. Howard W. Hunter, Conference Report, October 1967, 116.

17. C. Max Caldwell, Conference Report, October 1992, 40.

18. Bruce C. Hafen, *The Broken Heart* (Salt Lake City: Deseret Book, 1989), 18.

CHAPTER SEVENTEEN

JOHN AND THE FEAST OF TABERNACLES

BRUCE K. SATTERFIELD

One of several themes woven through the Gospel of John is that Christ is the fulfillment of ancient Israel's sacred times such as the Sabbath or the Feast of Passover. For John, these sacred times, which were an important part of New Testament period Judaism, were types and shadows of Christ and his role as savior and redeemer of the world. This theme is a central aspect of John 7 through 9. In these chapters, John records the Savior's activities during the Feast of Tabernacles, or, in Hebrew, *Sukkoth.*

The Feast of Tabernacles was one of the three feasts the Lord commanded that all males should annually attend (see Exodus 23:17; 34:23) and what Josephus calls the "most holy and most eminent" of the three feasts of the Hebrews.[1] Understanding how Christ was the fulfillment of this most important feast is intimately connected with the feast itself; but as is often the case in scripture, John assumes the reader is already aware of the activities associated with the Feast of Tabernacles and gives no details of the feast. John tells only of the movements and sayings of Christ in connection with the feast. But in order to understand what the Savior said in John 7 through 9, "one must have an intimate knowledge of the celebration of the Tabernacles."[2] The following discussion provides that "intimate knowledge" of the Feast of Tabernacles to reveal how that sacred time was meant to be a type and shadow of the Savior. The feast will be examined through both biblical and rabbinical sources. It will then

Bruce K. Satterfield is a member of the Religious Education faculty at Ricks College.

be possible to examine John 7 through 9 in light of this background, noting the effect of Jesus' sayings upon his listeners.

THE THREE FEASTS OF THE JEWS

Two important sources aid our understanding of how the Feast of Tabernacles was practiced during the Second Temple period: biblical and rabbinical or Jewish writings. Biblical legislation regarding the feast is found in the five books of Moses (see Exodus 23:14–17; 34:22, 23; Leviticus 23:33–44; Numbers 29:12–40; Deuteronomy 16:13–17), and in Nehemiah (8:13–18). Added to the biblical legislation are various descriptions of the Feast of Tabernacles found in rabbinical writings. These are important to consider because by the time of Christ, several additional developments had become part of the activities associated with the feast. Familiarity with these developments is essential to understanding John 7 through 9. Our only sources for these additional activities are the rabbinical writings, chief among them being the legislation in the Mishnah and Talmud.[3] Though these regulations were codified years after the destruction of the Second Temple and present an idealized picture of the customs associated with the Feast of Tabernacles, much of what the rabbis have said still seems to be applicable.

After the children of Israel were freed from Egyptian bondage and led by Moses to Mount Sinai, the Lord had Moses prepare Israel to enter into a covenant with him in order to make of them "a peculiar treasure unto [the Lord] above all people" (Exodus 19:5). The initial covenant Israel entered into included this command: "Three times thou shalt keep a feast unto me in the year. . . . Three times in the year all thy males shall appear before the Lord God" (Exodus 23:14, 17). The three feasts became known as the Feast of Passover, the Feast of Weeks (often called the Feast of Pentecost), and the Feast of Tabernacles.

The central activities of the feasts were in the temple. This is apparent from the injunction that all "males shall appear before the Lord God." Though no word for temple or sanctuary is used in this command, the phrase "before the Lord" does refer to a temple or sanctuary. Menahem Haran states: "In general, any cultic activity to which the biblical text applies the formula 'before the Lord' can be considered an indication of the existence of a temple at the site, since this expression stems from the basic conception of the temple as a divine dwelling-place and actually belongs to the temple's technical terminology."[4]

That these feasts were to be held at a temple can be seen in the name given to the first sanctuary of the Israelites. What is called in the King James Version "the tabernacle" is in Hebrew named *ohel mo'ed,* meaning "tent of meeting" or "tent of feasts." Of this, Roland de Vaux wrote: "Against [the] background of daily, weekly and monthly worship, the great annual feasts stood out in relief. The general word for a 'feast' is *mo'ed:* the term means a fixed place or a fixed time—a rendezvous—and the desert Tent was called '*ohel mo'ed* or 'The Tent of Meeting.' Thus the word came to mean a meeting or an assembly, and finally an assembly or meeting to celebrate a feast."[5] Though the Lord commanded that all males should come to the temple during these three feasts, it appears that, at least during the Second Temple period, often the whole family participated in the worship associated with the feasts (see Luke 2:41–50).

In light of how modern temples are used, it seems clear that these feasts were intended to be teaching experiences in which Israel would be reminded of past events and taught of future events. Further, this would be a time to renew covenants made with God. The Feast of Passover reminded Israel of their exodus from Egyptian bondage and the triumph of God over idolatry (see Exodus 12:12). It also was to remind them of the future coming of the Messiah, who would free them from spiritual bondage. The Feast of Weeks, or Pentecost, reminded Israel of the law God gave to Israel at Mount Sinai in the third month after their exodus from Egypt.[6] It also foreshadowed the giving of the higher law at a future time.[7] The Feast of Tabernacles recalled Israel's wandering in the wilderness for forty years and their eventual arrival in the promised land—Israel's permanent home. It also anticipated the future coming of the Messiah.

THE FEAST OF TABERNACLES

Length of the feast. From Leviticus (23:33–44), we learn that the Feast of Tabernacles was to be held for seven days. The first day was to be a holy convocation; the Hebrew *mikra kodesh* means "a holy summons." "It stresses the summons to an assembly where Israel, in a state of special holiness, is called to fulfil its sacred functions. Holy convocations were central aspects of each of the three great Feasts and the Day of Atonement. They were days of rest, like the sabbath, and in later times were known as sabbaths."[8] An additional holy convocation was to be called after the seven days were complete, making the feast a total of eight days.[9] The eighth day was referred to as the "great day of the feast" (John 7:37).

Dwelling in booths. We are told in Leviticus that the Israelites were to build booths, or small huts, outside their houses. During the seven days of the feast they were to live in the booths so that their "generations may know that I made the children of Israel to dwell in booths, when I brought them out of the land of Egypt" (Leviticus 23:43). It is from these booths (Hebrew, *Sukkoth*) that the Feast of Tabernacles receives its name. These booths were to remind Israel that their forefathers lived in tents during the wilderness journey and did so until they came into the promised land where they dwelt in permanent houses. Living in booths may have also reminded Israel that mortality is not the final and permanent resting place for mankind. Just as Israel was brought to a promised land for a permanent home, God's children will be brought into their final resting place only during the millennial reign of the Messiah.

The booths were generally of modest size, at least three walls and roof, and had to be outside. They could be placed in a courtyard or on the roof of a house.[10] In Nehemiah 8:16, we are told that when the Feast of Tabernacles was reinstituted after the return of the Jews from Babylonian exile, the Jews set up their booths in a number of different places: "every one upon the roof of his house, and in their courts, and in the courts of the house of God, and in the street of the water gate, and in the street of the gate of Ephraim." Rabbinical writings tell us that those traveling some distances were exempt from living in booths if they so desired (see Talmud Sukkah 26a).

Water-drawing ceremony. The order of events of an average day during the Feast of Tabernacles is revealed, albeit incompletely, in these words of Rabbi Joshua ben Hanania in the Talmud regarding the Feast of Tabernacles: "The first hour was occupied with the daily morning sacrifice; from there we proceeded to prayers; from there we proceeded to the additional sacrifice, then the prayers to the additional sacrifice, then to the House of Study, then the eating and drinking, then the afternoon prayer, then the daily evening sacrifice, and after that the Rejoicing at the place of the Water-Drawing all night" (Talmud Sukkah 53a).

A usual day began with the normal daily morning burnt offering; however, during the Feast of Tabernacles a rite was added to the daily burnt offering, called the water-drawing ceremony. During the preparation of the burnt offering,[11] a procession of priests, with the accompaniment of singing and flute playing, wended their way from the temple down to the Pool of Siloam, where a priest filled a golden flask with water while a choir repeated Isaiah 12:3: "With joy shall ye draw water out of the wells of salvation" (see Mishnah Sukkah 4:9; 5:1; Talmud Sukkah 48b). The Pool of Siloam was a collecting pool for the Spring Gihon, the principal water supply for Jerusalem. The Jews referred to water from springs or streams that was fit for drinking as "living water." Living water was considered the most superior form of water for ritual purification.[12]

The priests returned to the temple via the Water Gate, a gate on the south side of the wall immediately surrounding the temple within the Court of the Gentiles.[13] When they arrived at the Water Gate, a blast was made on a *shofar,* or ram's horn. The *shofar* was a signaling instrument used to announce such major events as the beginning of the Sabbath, new moons, and the death of a notable person, as well as to warn of approaching danger. In this case, the *shofar* announced the beginning of the Feast of Tabernacles, which began with the water-drawing ceremony.

When the procession of priests and Levites returned from the pool of Siloam, they were met by pilgrims who had come to the temple mount. Each pilgrim brought a *lulab,* which consisted of a tree branch in one hand and a citron in the other (see Mishnah 3:1–7). The *lulab* was to be waved while the morning sacrifice was being offered with the special water libation. The waving of the *lulab* was a biblical injunction: "And ye shall take you on the first day the boughs of goodly trees, branches of palm trees, and the boughs of thick trees, and willows of the brook; and ye shall rejoice before the Lord your God seven days" (Leviticus 23:40).

Upon the blasting of the *shofar,* the group moved toward the altar of sacrifice located in the Court of the Priests that immediately surrounded the temple. The priest carrying the golden flask filled with water ascended the altar and prepared to pour the libation on the morning burnt offering. While doing this, the procession that had followed the priest circled the altar.

It appears that pilgrims were often allowed to join in with the priests who were circling the altar, though how many participated is not stated.[14] George W. MacRae suggests that this procession was of priests alone,[15] but an incident mentioned in the Mishnah may suggest otherwise. Mishnah Sukkah 4:9 tells us that after the water was poured into the silver bowl, it was said to the officiating priest: "Raise thy hand!" The reason for saying this was that "on one occasion [a Sadducean priest] poured . . . over his feet" the water (for the Sadducees did not hold to this tradition). This action so outraged the pilgrims that "all the people pelted him with their citrons." This event suggests that if the pilgrims were not in the procession itself, they were at least close enough to be able to pelt the priest. The only logical place would be the Court of the Priests itself or perhaps the Court of the Israelites, though the latter seems less likely because of its size.[16]

Whether walking around the altar or observing the procession, the following was said by the pilgrims while waving[17] their *lulabs:* "We beseech Thee, O Eternal, save us, we pray" (Mishnah Sukkah 3:9; see also 4:5). The priest who had charge of pouring the water then offered the water libation with a wine libation in two silver bowls on the southwest corner of the altar.

The water-drawing ceremony proceeded in this manner every day of the feast except on the seventh day, when the priests (and perhaps the pilgrims) circled the altar seven times instead of just once (see Mishnah Sukkah 4:5). The circumambulation of the altar seven times ended the water-drawing ritual. It was not performed on the eighth day (see Mishnah Sukkah 4:1, 5),[18] though it appears that a prayer for rain was given on the eighth day (see Talmud Taanith 2a-3a).

Additional sacrifices. The chronicle outlined by Rabbi Joshua ben Hanania indicates that after the water-drawing ceremony there was an "additional sacrifice." According to Numbers 29:12–40, in addition to the daily morning and evening burnt offering required by the law of Moses,[19] there were additional sacrifices to be made during the Feast of Tabernacles. On the first day of the feast there were to be offered thirteen young bullocks, two rams, fourteen lambs of the first year, and one kid for a sin offering. On the second day of the feast, there were to be offered the same offerings except instead of thirteen young bullocks, only twelve were to be offered. On the third day the offerings were again the same with the exception of the bullocks: eleven were offered. This declination of bullocks continued until the seventh day when seven bullocks were offered (the other sacrifices remaining the same). On the eighth day, one bullock was offered with one ram, seven lambs and one kid for a sin offering. The account concludes with this injunction: "These things ye shall do unto the Lord in your set feasts, beside your vows, and your freewill offerings, for your burnt offerings, and for your meat offerings, and for your drink offerings and for your peace offerings."

Upon the conclusion of the "additional sacrifice," the pilgrims would have an opportunity to present their individual offerings, such as expressing personal devotion to God (through the burnt offering), or the cleansing of severe impurities (through the sin offering). This was a time of great rejoicing and singing including the singing of the complete Hallel or Psalms 113 to 118 (see Mishnah Sukkah 4:8).[20] When the personal offerings were completed, the afternoon burnt offering was performed.[21]

The lighting ceremony. Normally, upon the conclusion of the afternoon burnt offering, probably around sunset, the gates of the Temple were closed.[22] On the first day of the Feast of Tabernacles, however, the gates were left open so that all might participate in the final rite of the day: the lighting ceremony. This occasion proved to be a most joyous and festive observance. From the Mishnah (Sukkah 5:2–3) we are told that "at the close of the first Holyday" the priests would descend from the Court of the Israelites to the Court of the Women.[23] In the court four huge candelabra were placed, each "with four golden bowls at their tops and four ladders to each one." Each candelabra was fifty cubits in height. Wicks made "from the worn-out drawers and girdles of the priests" were placed in each bowl and lit. It is said that "there was no courtyard in Jerusalem that was not lit up with the light" which came from these candelabras.

The rest of the night was spent in joyous activities in the Court of the Women. Mishnah Sukkah 5:4 says: "Pious men and men of good deeds used to dance before them (the candelabra) with burning torches in their hands and sang before them songs and praises. And the Levites on harps, and on lyres, and with cymbals, and with trumpets and with other instruments of music without number upon the fifteen steps leading down from the court of the Israelites to the Court of the Women, corresponding to *The Fifteen Songs of Ascent in the Psalms* [Psalms 120–34]; upon them the Levites used to stand with musical instruments and sing hymns."

The festivities surrounding the illumination rite concluded the festival day. It is not clear whether or not the illumination rite was performed every night or whether the lights simply remained lit during the whole feast.

The messianic nature of the feast. Both the water-drawing ceremony and the lighting of the candelabra were aspects of the feast not found in biblical legislation.[24] Nevertheless, they had apparently become part of the ceremonies of the feast to portray the future messianic age. That is evident from the fact that as part of the ceremonies associated with the Feast of Tabernacles, Zechariah 14, a well-known messianic chapter of the scriptures, was read to all the people. Talmud Megillah 31a says: "On the first day of Tabernacles we read the section of the festivals in Leviticus, and for haftarah [a section from the prophetic books recited after the reading from the Pentateuch on Sabbaths and Holy-days], Behold a day cometh for the Lord (Zech. 14)."

What is the connection between Zechariah 14 and the Feast of Tabernacles? Zechariah describes the time when "the day of the Lord cometh." At a time when "all nations" have gathered against Jerusalem, the Lord will return and save his people by standing upon the Mount of Olives which shall "cleave in the midst thereof toward the east and toward the west" providing a way to escape through the valley thus created (v. 4). Having saved his people, the Lord insists that "every one that is left of all the nations which came against Jerusalem shall even go up from year to year to worship the King, the Lord of hosts, and to keep the feast of tabernacles" (v. 16). Failure to keep this command would result in the rains failing (see vv. 17–19). This is the first biblical association of rain with the festival. But as MacRae said, "the fact that it was celebrated at the end of the harvest and immediately before the autumnal rainy season, we can well imagine that the petition for rain is as old as the feast itself."[25]

With the coming of the Lord, the messianic age is inaugurated.

Zechariah points out two important aspects associated with the messianic age. The first is perpetual light. Zechariah 14:6–7, describing the day when the Lord comes, says: "And it shall come to pass in that day, that the light shall not be clear, nor dark: but it shall be one day which shall be known to the Lord, not day, nor night: but it shall come to pass, that at evening time it shall be light." The second characteristic of the messianic age is akin to rain, that of water. Zechariah says: "And it shall be in that day, that living waters shall go out from Jerusalem" (Zechariah 14:8).[26] It seems safe to assume that by the reading of Zechariah 14 during the feast the application of these messianic features to the Feast of Tabernacles was commonplace among the people.

It is evident that the two features of the messianic age described by Zechariah in chapter 14 were made an important part of the Feast of Tabernacles ceremonies. The water-drawing ceremony is the complement of the living water flowing from Jerusalem in 14:8. The lighting of the huge candelabra is the symbolic counterpart of the continuous day found in 14:6–7.

Zechariah 14 gives us further insight into the meaning of the lighting ceremony. When the Messiah comes, inaugurating the messianic age, he will be the light of all the world, not just of the Jews. This is perhaps why four candelabra were used in the lighting ceremony. Four is often a symbolic number representing geographical completeness or the four corners of the world. Thus, the lighting of the four candelabra would have symbolized that light would be given to all the world through the coming Messiah. This association would have been emphasized further by the fact that each candelabra had four bowls.[27]

JESUS AND THE FEAST OF TABERNACLES

Jesus is the living waters. John 7:14 tells us that Jesus arrived in Jerusalem midway through the Feast of Tabernacles.[28] His first few days at the temple were filled with confrontations concerning the authority of his teachings (see John 7:15–36). Then on "the last day, that great day of the feast," Jesus "stood" and issued this challenge: "If any man thirst, let him come unto me, and drink. He that believeth on me, as the scripture hath said, out of his belly shall flow rivers of living water" (John 7:37–38). John added, "But this spake he of the Spirit, which they that believe on him should receive" (John 7:39). That is, the Holy Ghost, which is given to those who come unto Christ, brings life to their souls.

The effect of this challenge is more meaningful when we understand the water-drawing ceremony of the Feast of Tabernacles. Having daily drawn water from the Pool of Siloam, then pouring it on the morning offering while shouting, "Save us Lord," the absence of the water-drawing ceremony on the eighth day would have been profound. Hence, on the day when living water was not drawn from the spring and only a prayer for rain was offered—a day that perhaps symbolized Israel's dependence upon God for water that sustains life—the Savior declared that if anyone thirsted, he should come to Him for living waters. The water he offered was not for physical but for spiritual survival. His water was the cleansing and sustaining influence of the Holy Ghost necessary for the salvation of the souls of mankind. Interestingly enough, the Jerusalem Talmud[29] states that the Jews understood the water-drawing ceremony to be symbolic of the Holy Ghost: "Why is the name of it called, The drawing out of water? Because of the pouring out of the Holy Spirit, according to what is said: 'With joy shall ye draw water out of the wells of salvation.'"[30] Thus the prayers of the priests and pilgrims attending the Feast of Tabernacles had been answered but not in the way they had expected.[31]

Jesus is the light of the world. On the day after the Savior's challenge to come to him for living water, the Savior was once again at the temple teaching. While in the Court of the Women,[32] the Savior declared to the multitude, "I am the light of the world: he that followeth me shall not walk in darkness, but shall have the light of life" (John 8:12). Could there be any doubt in the minds of his listeners as to what he was claiming? In the very place where the huge candelabras were lit giving light to "every courtyard in Jerusalem," symbolizing the continuous light given to all the world during the messianic age, Jesus proclaimed that he was that light,[33] not only the light of Jerusalem but of all the world. Jewish tradition held that God gives man light.[34] It is obvious that he was claiming to be the Messiah in their hearing.

To give credence to his claim, the Savior demonstrated his power to give light to the world through a miracle that is recorded only by John. In John 9:1–7, the story of a man born blind follows on the heals of the Feast of the Tabernacles. The story begins when Jesus "saw a man which was blind from his birth." When asked why, the Savior responded "that the works of God should be made manifest in him." Then he said, "I must work the works of him that sent me, while it is day: the night cometh, when no man can work. As long as I am in the world, I am the light of the world." Upon that "he spat on the ground, and made clay of the spittle, and he anointed the eyes of the blind man with the clay, and said unto him, Go, wash in the pool of Siloam." The man did exactly what he was told. After he had washed his eyes in the same pool that the priest had drawn water from as part of the water-drawing ceremony of the Feast of Tabernacles, he came out seeing.

Two important symbols of the Feast of Tabernacles—water and light—were present in the miracle. By spitting onto the ground, Jesus demonstrated that indeed the living waters, or the Spirit of the Holy Ghost which can give man light, does indeed come from him, for "out of his belly shall flow rivers of living water" (John 7:38). That is further emphasized by the man's washing in the waters in the pool of Siloam, which also symbolized the Holy Ghost.

Conclusion

It is undeniable that Jesus' statements during the Feast of Tabernacles are highlighted by the feast itself. The Savior chose a sacred time of the year when the Jews looked forward with great rejoicing through ritual action to the coming of the Messiah. Through the instrumentality of the feast, Jesus declared that he was the promised Messiah, the literal fulfillment of everything promised in the Feast of Tabernacles. It is clear from the hostile reactions of the Jews that they saw it this way, supposing that he was speaking blasphemy (see John 7:30, 32, 44–53; 8:59).

Notes

1. Flavius Josephus, *Antiquities of the Jews,* in *Complete Works,* trans. William Whiston (Grand Rapids, Mich.: Kregel Publications, 1981), 8.4.1. See also George W. MacRae, "The Meaning and Evolution of the Feast of Tabernacles," *Catholic Biblical Quarterly,* 22, no. 3 (1960): 251.

2. Raymond E. Brown, *The Gospel According to John,* vol. 29 of the Anchor Bible Series (Garden City, N.Y.: Doubleday, 1983), 326.

3. During the Second Temple period, many Jews, including the Pharisees, followed an oral interpretation of the written law of Moses found in Exodus through Deuteronomy. This is often referred to as the "oral law." In the New Testament, the oral law is called "the tradition of the elders" (Matthew 15:2; Mark 7:3, 5). In the second century after Christ, the oral tradition was reduced to writing and systematically organized by Rabbi Judah the Prince. It is called the Mishnah. The Mishnah is grouped into six orders, which in turn are divided into sixty-three treatises called tractates.

Over time, the rabbis held many debates concerning the Mishnah. The records and minutes of these debates were added to the Mishnah. This compilation has become known as the Talmud. Two different groups of rabbis produced a Talmud: a group in Babylon and a group in Jerusalem. The Babylonian Talmud is the most commonly used of the two. It has been translated into several languages. The Jerusalem Talmud is not often used and is only found in Hebrew. For a complete discussion of the history of the Mishnah and Talmud, see Isaac Unterman, *The Talmud: An Analytical Guide to Its History and Teachings* (New York: Bloch, 1952).

In this paper, all references to the Talmud refer to the Babylonian Talmud unless otherwise stated. Further, in this paper, I will follow MacRae's thinking who states: "We shall not be concerned with the dating of the Mishnah; there is no doubt that at least some of the precepts in it go back long before the final crystallization of the written form. It would be idle also to be deterred by the fact that many of the legal prescriptions are meaningless in view of the destruction of the Temple. As far as the feast is concerned, the Mishnah presents an idealized picture of the Temple ritual but also the necessary information for the proper observance of them elsewhere." "The Meaning and Evolution of the Feast of Tabernacles," 270–71.

4. Menahem Haran, *Temples and Temple Service in Ancient Israel* (Winona Lake, Ind.: Eisenbrauns, 1985), 26.

5. Roland de Vaux, *Ancient Israel,* 2 vols. (New York: McGraw-Hill,1965), 2:470.

6. Talmud Pesahim 68b states that the Feast of Weeks commemorated "the day on which the Torah was given." See also Talmud Meglillah 31a and the book of Jubilees 1:1; 6:17–19. This is the view not only of ancient Judaism but of modern Jewry as well. Writing of this feast, Rabbi Hayim Halevy Donin states: "Shavuot [Hebrew, 'Feast of Weeks'] commemorates the awesome event experienced by the children of Israel seven weeks after their exodus from Egypt when they camped at the foot of Mt. Sinai somewhere in the Sinai Peninsula. This event was

the Revelation, when God's will was revealed to Israel. It marked the declaration of the Ten Commandments." Hayim Halvey Donin, *To Be a Jew* (New York: Basic Books, 1972), 239.

7. It should be remembered that as a result of rebellion, the law Israel ultimately received at Mount Sinai was the law of Moses, which was only preparatory for the higher law that would be given later. The law of Moses functioned through the authority of the lesser, or Aaronic, priesthood. The higher law promised would function under the authority of the higher, or Melchizedek, priesthood. It would include the ordinances associated with that priesthood, the first of which is the laying on of hands for the gift of the Holy Ghost. The reception of the gift of the Holy Ghost was given on the Day of Pentecost (see Acts 1–2), an appropriate time to demonstrate that the higher law had been given by God to Israel.

8. J. C. Rylaarsdam, "Convocation, Holy," in *Interpreter's Dictionary of the Bible,* 4 vols. (Nashville: Abingdon, 1962), 1:678–79.

9. In the Talmud the eighth day is actually considered a separate festival (see Sukkah 48a).

10. See Talmud Shabbath 154b and Louis Ginzberg, *The Legends of the Jews,* 7 vols. (Philadephia: Jewish Publication Society of America, 1913), 4:405. Roofs were generally flat with a staircase ascending from the outside and were used for a variety of reasons.

11. The Mishnah describes the rite of the burnt offering as being performed in four parts with each part being determined by lot. The first lot was the clearing of the ashes from the Altar (Yoma 2:2; Tamid 1:4). The ashes were cleared from the Altar "at cockcrow or close to it, either before it or after it" but during "the Festivals at the first watch" for "before cockcrow time drew near the Forecourt was already filled with Israelites" (Yoma 1:8). Josephus tells us that the temple gates, which were normally kept closed until morning, were opened at midnight during festivals (*Antiquities of the Jews,* 18.2.2). The second lot determined "who should slaughter, who should toss the blood, (and) who should remove the ashes from the Inner Altar, (and) who should clear away the ashes from the Candlestick, (and) who should take up the limbs [of the burnt offering] to the Altar-slope" (Yoma 2:3; see also Tamid 3:1). The animal could not be slaughtered before dawn; therefore, the captain of the temple (*sagan ha kohanim*) said to one, "Go forth and see if the time has arrived for slaughtering." The priest went to a high point of the temple to see if the light of morning lit up the east "as far as Hebron." If so, the animal could be slaughtered (Yoma 3:1; see also Tamid 3:2–7). The third lot determined who would offer the incense upon the inner altar (see Yoma 2:4; Tamid 5:2–6:3). The fourth lot determined which priests would offer the burnt offering on the altar (see Yoma 2:5; Tamid 4:3). For detailed descriptions concerning the offering of the morning and evening burnt offerings (the

Tamid), see Shmuel Safrai, Ritual in "Temple," *Encyclopedia Judaica* (Jerusalem: Keter, 1971), 15:974–77; Shmuel Safrai, Daily whole-offerings in "The Temple," in *The Jewish People in the First Century*, 2 vols. (Philadelphia: Fortress, 1987), 2:887–90; Aaron Rothkoff, Second Temple Period in "Sacrifice," *Encyclopedia Judaica* (Jerusalem: Keter, 1971), 14:607–9; and Emil Schurer, *A History of the Jewish People in the Age of Jesus Christ*, ed. Geza Vermes, Ferges Millar, and Matthew Black, 2 vols. (Edinburg: T&T Clark, 1973), 2:299–308.

12. According to Mishnah Mikvaoth 1:1: "There are six grades among ritual baths, in ascending order of superiority." These are (1) water in cisterns, (2) water of rain drippings, (3) mikvehs, (4) wells, (5) salty water or hot water from a spring, and (6) living water (see Mikvaoth 1:1–8). Only "living water" could be used in the purification of lepers (Leviticus 14:5) and the purification necessary after defilement caused by dead corpses (Numbers 19:17).

13. The main sources for a description of the temple come from the Mishnah and Josephus. But there is discrepancy in the different accounts. According to Middoth, 1:4–5, and Josephus, *Antiquities of the Jews*, 15.11.5, there are seven gates into the Court of the Priests, including the Nicanor Gate (which does not actually open into the Court of Priests but into the Court of the Israelites). In Middoth 2:6, Shekalim 6:3, and Josephus, *Wars of the Jews* 5.5.2, eight gates are mentioned, not including the Nicanor Gate. Most scholars accept the smaller number, placing the water gate as the third gate from the west on the southern side of the Court of the Priests. This would place it close to the laver (see Shmuel Safrai and Michael Avi-Yona, "Temple," *Encyclopaedia Judaica*, 15:962–67).

14. It is Safrai's belief that the people were involved in the procession itself. Says he: "The people participated in all the rites of the Feast of Tabernacles and, with the exception of the water-libation which was performed by a priest or the high priest, their role in Temple rites and customs was equal to that of the priests. They surrounded the altar with palm-branches and with willow, which is, of course, the essence of the water-libation ceremonies. . . . All the people participated in the procession around the altar, (from which they were barred during the rest of the year) with the palm-branch." "Temple," in *Jewish People of the First Century*, 2:894–95.

15. McCrae, "Meaning and Evolution of the Feast of Tabernacles," 272.

16. This is the view of J. C. Rylaarsdam, who describes this scene in this manner: "The water was brought up in solemn fashion with the blowing of the shofar at the city gate. The pilgrims, singing the Hallel and carrying their lulabs, witnessed the circumambulation of the altar by the priestly procession and waving their lulabs, joined in the great cry: 'Save us, we beseech thee, O Lord.'" "Booths, Feast of," in

Interpreter's Dictionary of the Bible, 4 vols. (Nashville: Abingdon, 1962), 1:456.

17. Mishnah Sukkah 3:9 says: "And where do they wave?—At the beginning and end of *Give thanks unto the Eternal* and at *We beseech Thee, O Eternal, save us, we pray;* this is the view of the School of Hillel. The School of Shammai says, Also at *We beseech Thee, O Eternal, send us prosperity, we pray."*

18. In the Talmud, there is a debate about how often the water-drawing rite was done as well as when it was performed last in the feast (see Taanith 2a–3a). The Mishnah, which consists of earlier rabbinical writings, however, suggests that the last day the water-drawing ritual was performed was the seventh day (Sukkah 4:1; but see Rabbi Judah's comments in Sukkah 4:9). This agrees with biblical legislation that requires the waving of the *lulab,* a ritual performed during the pouring of the water on the altar, for seven days (see Leviticus 23:40).

19. See Exodus 29:38–42; Numbers 28:2–4.

20. See Safrai, Ritual in "Temple," *Encylopedia Judaica,* 982.

21. Mishnah Pesachim 5:1 says: "The daily burnt-offering was slaughtered at the eighth hour and a half and offered up at the ninth hour and a half." It is not clear, however, whether the time on this was strictly held during the Feast of Tabernacles.

22. See Safrai, Ritual in "Temple," in *Encylopedia Judaica,* 15:976.

23. From Talmudic sources it appears that "the place of the Water-Drawing" is in the Court of the Women. Talmud Sukkah 53a tells of the rejoicing that took place after the lighting of the huge candelabra's which Mishnah Sukkah 5:2 says took place in the Court of the Women. Yet Talmud Sukkah 53a speaks of this place as "the place of Water-Drawing." In a note on Mishnah Sukkah 5:1, Philip Backman suggests the reason for this name was that there was a "well, in the Women's Forecourt, from which the water was drawn for libation on Sukkoth" (Backman, *Mishnayoth,* 7 vols. [New York: Judaica Press, 1964], 2:341). But Raymond Brown says of this place: "In connection with the water ceremonies at the feast of Tabernacles, the Jerusalem Talmud (Sukkah 55a) says that the part of the temple precincts traversed during the procession with the water was called the 'Place of Drawing,' because from there 'they drew *the holy spirit'* (also Midrash Rabbah lxx 8 on Gen xxix 1)" (*Gospel According to John,* 329).

24. The rabbis believed that these traditions were given at Mount Sinai but only passed down orally. See John Lightfoot, *A Commentary on the New Testament from the Talmud and Hebraica,* 4 vols. (Peabody, Mass.: Hendrickson, 1979), 3:322.

25. MacRae, "Meaning and Evolution of the Feast of Tabernacles," 269. The association of the Feast of Tabernacles with rain is well known from Mishnaic times. The tractate Ta'anith, which deals with special

fasts that are called for due to continued drought, begins with the statement: "From what time should they begin to mention the *Power of Rain?* R. Eliezer says, From the first Holyday day of the Festival of Tabernacles; R. Joshua says, From the last Holyday day of the Festival of Tabernacles" (1:1).

26. Compare Psalms 46:4; 65:9; Isaiah 8:6; Jeremiah 2:13; Ezekiel 47:1–12; Joel 3:18; Revelation 22:1–2. On this, Brown comments thus: "The fountain of waters that overflows from Jerusalem . . . can be interpreted against the background of abundant rain sent by God during Tabernacles" (*Gospel According to John,* 327). Joyce Baldwin interprets this verse in this way: "The dream of an abundant water supply in Jerusalem will become fact. Instead of the spring Gihon, which supplied water that 'flowed gently' to become the Siloam brook (Isaiah 8:6), and was never really adequate for the city's needs, rivers independent of seasonal rainfall would rise in Jerusalem, to flow constantly to east and west until they reached the Dead Sea and the Mediterranean." *Haggai, Zechariah, Malachi,* vol. 24 of Old Testament Commentaries (London: Tyndale, 1972), 203.

27. Numerology is an important aspect of Jewish thought. Numbers such as three, four, and seven represented wholeness or completeness: three because the number three has a beginning, a middle, and an end; four, because there are four corners of the world; seven, because the world was created in seven days. To emphasize the completeness of something, often the number was multiplied by itself: 3 x 3, 4 x 4, or 7 x 7.

28. The reason for his late arrival seems to be on account of the pressure of his nonbelieving brothers who wished him to go to the feast simply to perform miracles. Brown sees this as a temptation faced by the Savior similar to the account in Matthew (4:1–11) and Luke (4:1–13) where the Savior is tempted to display his power by jumping from the pinnacle of the temple (see Brown, *Gospel According to John,* 308, for a complete discussion). Therefore, the Savior delays his departure to the feast so that it is clear that his reasons for being there are not to display his power.

29. See note 3.

30. Jerusalem Talmud Sukkah 55a, quoted from Morris, *Gospel According to John,* 421; see also F. F. Bruce, *The Gospel of John* (Grand Rapids, Mich.: Eerdmans, 1983), 182, 187 n.13; John Lightfoot, *A Commentary on the New Testament from the Talmud and Hebraica,* 4 vols. (Peabody, Mass.: Hendrickson, 1979), 3:322–23.

31. The theme of Christ as the living waters permeates the gospel of John wherein is recorded several incidences that occurred during the ministry of Christ that revolve around water. For example, John records the story of the Savior offering living water to the woman of Samaria who was drawing water from a well. To her, he said:

"Whosoever drinketh of this water shall thirst again: But whosoever drinketh of the water that I shall give him shall never thirst; but the water that I shall give him shall be in him a well of water springing up into everlasting life" (John 4:13–14). That Christ has the power to give this living water is demonstrated through two stories that evidence Christ's power over water: the marriage at Cana where Christ turned water turn to wine (see John 2:1–11) and the Savior's walking on water (see John 6:15–21). To dramatize the point further, John, alone, records the piercing of the Savior's side while upon the cross. In that account it is said the when the soldiers were breaking the legs of the three who were crucified, they saw that the Savior was already dead and "they brake not his legs: but one of the soldiers with a spear pierced his side, and forthwith came there out blood *and water*" (John 19:33–34; emphasis added). John's point is clear. The living waters do come from the Savior.

In view of this, the reader of John's Gospel is stunned to discover that while on the cross the Savior cried out, "I thirst" (John 19:28), a statement recorded only by John. He to whom all must go to receive "living waters" so they may "never thirst" again (John 4:14), now thirsted! This pathetic statement reveals that while on the cross, the Savior, in bearing our sins, infirmities, fears, guilt, and remorse, had "descended below all things" (D&C 88:6) and become like "the poor and needy" who "seek water, and there is none" (Isaiah 41:17). He had become like us—lost, alone, and thirsty. In this condition, the Savior gained the compassion and mercy needed to bring the living waters to those who seek it.

32. John 8:20 tells us that he was in the treasury, which is the Court of the Women.

33. J. H. Bernard sees the lighting of the candelabras as a possible background behind Jesus' saying but offers another possible reason: "But Philo's account of the Feast of Tabernacles would furnish an equally plausible explanation. He says that this feast is held at the autumnal equinox, in order that the world (*kosmos*) may be full, not only by day but also by night, of the all-beautiful light (*tou pagkalou photos*), as at this season there is no twilight (*de septen.* 24). . . . The passage of Philo shows, however, that the Feast of Tabernacles suggested the idea of *light* to some minds" (J. H. Bernard, *A Critical and Exegetical Commentary on the Gospel According to St. John,* 2 vols. The New International Critical Commentary (Edinburgh: T&T Clark, 1985), 2:291.

34. See, for example, Psalm 27:1; Isaiah 60:19. "The later Rabbis applied the thought to the Messiah: 'Light is the Name of Messiah,' they said" (Bernard, *Critical and Exegetical Commentary,* 2:292).

CHAPTER EIGHTEEN

THE WITNESS OF JOHN

BRIAN L. SMITH

From early times, scholars have found the writings of John dramatically different from the synoptic Gospels. Some conclude that John had no interest in describing the historical Jesus but wanted to emphasize the theological significance of who Jesus was. John presents his Gospel with a postresurrection perspective. It was written after he reflected and pondered on what he had witnessed. Some scholars have concluded that the Gospel of John is not of John's own writing, yet even they still concede that John's teachings are its primary source.

As Latter-day Saints, how do we know that the fourth Gospel was written by John the Beloved? Professor C. Wilfred Griggs said: "No Gospel author identifies himself by name in his work, but the uniqueness of each writer's style serves as an identification for his writings. It is generally agreed, for example, that the same person is responsible for both Luke and Acts. Likewise, even a casual reading of John, 1 John, and Revelation would show sufficient similarities in vocabulary and style to argue for common authorship. . . . One need not feel intellectually shy about an assertion that John the Beloved Apostle is the author of the fourth Gospel."[1]

Elder Neal A. Maxwell stated: "Some fear that the Gospel of John may not actually have been written by him. The Restoration makes it clear, however, that John was actually assigned by the Lord to write certain scripture, whether the Book of Revelation, or his Gospel, or those and other writings as well. . . . (1 Nephi 14:25). What John wrote was 'plain and pure, and most precious and easy to the

Brian L. Smith is director of the Portland Institute of Religion in Portland, Oregon.

understanding of all men' (1 Nephi 14:23; see also 20–27; D&C 88:141). Multiple and validating references to John's writings are in the 'other books' of scripture. However, the fullness of John's record is yet to be revealed. . . . (Ether 4:16)."[2]

As to the dating of the writing of the Gospel, one scholar wrote, "We know that the Fourth Gospel was circulating in Egypt before the middle of the second century, for the oldest fragment of New Testament material we have is a little chunk of the Gospel of John. That means, the scholars claim, that the Gospel had to have been written before the turn of the century. We may assume, too, that it was not written before 70 C.E. when the Jerusalem Temple was destroyed in the war between the Jews and the Romans. The manner in which the Temple is alluded to in the Gospel has convinced most scholars . . . that [it was written after the destruction of the temple] (see [John] 2:13–22)."[3]

THE SYNOPTIC GOSPELS AND THE GOSPEL OF JOHN

The term *synoptic* means to have a "common point of view" or to "see alike," meaning to perceive a subject in a similar fashion. Throughout history it has been a common practice for the first three Gospels to be placed in a so-called harmony because of their similarities. Some scholars, in their efforts to harmonize the four Gospels, have overlooked some distinctive contributions and messages of each Gospel.

But there have always been noticeable differences between the synoptic writers and John. One difference is the general emphasis of how the Gospel writers sought to testify and witness of the divine nature of Christ. John the apostle sought to depict Jesus as one who came to reveal the Father. He wanted to emphasize Jesus' divine nature and did not give as much attention to the historical Jesus as the other Gospel writers portrayed him. He shares with us the theological significance of why Jesus came and how we can partake of his divine nature and return to the Father. The synoptic Gospels concentrate on depicting Jesus as one who performed miracles, taught parables, and dealt with reinterpretations of the Torah. They sought to establish Jesus' divinity by showing how he fulfilled the historical prophecies found in the Old Testament.

If we were to identify which events from the four Gospels were the most similar, those would be the events of the week of the atoning sacrifice of the Savior. Some scholars believe that the Gospel of John followed this part of Mark's Gospel very closely, which has led some to believe that John's intent was to write a supplementary Gospel. Others feel that John was exposed to the oral tradition of the time and had no actual documents before him but drew from his knowledge of what he remembered along with his personal witness. That would explain some of the similarities. Yet how John wrote his Gospel is not as important as the material he recorded and the personal witness he shared with us. He wanted to leave no doubt in the reader's heart and mind that Jesus was the Son of God, in the flesh.

The fourth Gospel includes no nativity narrative or account of Christ's birth, no genealogy of Christ, no account of the angel Gabriel's announcement to Mary of the forthcoming child. The synoptic Gospels portray Jesus working mainly in Galilee and then traveling south only during the last week of his life. In the Gospel of John, Jesus travels back and forth between Galilee and Jerusalem throughout his ministry. The synoptic writers indicate that Jesus began his mission after John the Baptist was in prison; John seems to indicate that their missions overlapped (see John 3:23–4:3).

Events we find only in the Gospel of John include the miracle at Cana, the late-night conversation with Nicodemus, the encounter with the Samaritan woman at the well, and the healing of the paralytic at the Pool of Bethesda. John shows us that Jesus could even read the thoughts of others (see John 1:47; 2:25) and could miraculously escape from a crowd without being harmed (see John 7:30; 8:20). John's account of the woman caught in adultery (see John 7:53–8:11) differs in style in many of the Greek texts and is discounted by many scholars. The account is not found in the earlier, more widely accepted manuscripts of John. Nevertheless it is a moving account showing the forgiving nature of the Savior.

From the synoptic writers we get a feeling that Jesus was a rabbi-type figure who went about confronting the scribes and pharisees, clarifying the doctrines found in scripture, and commenting on such topics as the Sabbath, divorce, fasting, and the Beatitudes. In John's Gospel the controversies are not so much over the doctrines of the scriptures as over the Savior's true identity. Those who had ears to hear and eyes to see recognized him and were consistently blessed, according to John. Others who could not hear or see frequently misunderstood and misrepresented Jesus. Jesus was not afraid to teach and witness to his real identity. He was divine.

The raising of Lazarus from the dead is found only in John's Gospel. It was a public act that caught the attention of many people. To the believers Jesus was undeniably the Resurrection and the Life. To the leaders of the Jews he was someone who must be taken captive and stopped (see John 11:57).

The cleansing of the temple was a significant event during the last week of Christ's life recorded in the synoptic Gospels (see Matthew 21:12–13; Mark 11:15–19; Luke 19:45–46), but in John's Gospel it was one of Christ's first public acts at the beginning of his mission, not at the end (see John 2:13–22). Christ may have cleansed the temple twice, not just once as some scholars would have us believe.

In the Gospel of John there are no details of the suffering in Gethsemane, nor is the fleeing of the disciples at Jesus' arrest reported. John seems to emphasize Peter's denial, which is spoken of in two places, John 18:15–18 and 25–27. Peter is given a less prominent role in John's Gospel than he is given in the synoptic Gospels.

Concerning the sacrament, John gives a slightly different description of the Last Supper than that found in the synoptic Gospels. John states that the Last Supper took place on the day before Passover and at that time Jesus washed the feet of the disciples (see John 13:1–16). The synoptic Gospels first mention the Passover during the last week of the Lord's life, but in John there are three Passover occasions (see John 2:13; 6:4; 11:55). Only John shares with us the account of the washing of the disciples' feet.

The synoptic Gospels give the impression that Jesus spent much of his time in Galilee and rarely went to Jerusalem, but John says that Jesus regularly attended the Passover in Jerusalem throughout his three-year ministry. John tells us that Jesus moved freely back and forth between Galilee and Jerusalem. One might conclude from the synoptic chronology that Jesus' ministry possibly only covered one year, but the fourth Gospel readily documents that his ministry spans three years. In the synoptic Gospels Jesus' last meal occurred at the very time that the Jews were celebrating the Passover, but John's Gospel places the last meal twenty-four hours earlier. That timing indicates that Christ was crucified at the very time the arrangements for the Passover were being made by the Jews and that he was slain at the same time the Passover lambs were being slain in the temple complex and throughout Israel.

John recounts carefully Jesus' trial before Pilate. He documents Pilate's weakness and his fear of the people which eventually led to Christ's crucifixion. One could not remain neutral with Jesus. Like Pilate, each of us must decide what to do with Christ. John leaves his readers accountable for their own acceptance or rejection of Christ. Near the end of John's testimony he includes discourses on the Holy Spirit and recounts the appearances of the resurrected Christ to Mary Magdalene and the disciples, including the Lord's appearances in Galilee.

Some details noticeably lacking in John's Gospel include Jesus' actually being baptized by John (John the Baptist is described as only a witness in the text), the forty days in the wilderness and the temptations that followed (we find no example of Christ being tempted in any situation at all in John's Gospel), the Mount of Transfiguration (this omission is interesting, considering John was a special witness there), the confession of Peter that Jesus is the Christ, the parables, the casting out of evil spirits, the struggle in the Garden of Gethsemane, and the institution of the Last Supper.[4] Neither do we find in the Gospel of John any prophecies of Jerusalem's fall, and John does not prophecy of Christ's second coming. He does not stress future events in his Gospel; but in his book of Revelation, the Second Coming is covered in great detail.

DIFFERENT TERMS AMONG THE GOSPELS

Throughout John's writings are many levels of understanding. His use of symbolism and literary style give the spiritually mature reader much to ponder and learn. The Gospel as a whole does not appear to be a missionary document. It is too complicated and symbolic for the nonbeliever. John wished to nurture the members more than to convert the nonmembers. He wanted to encourage those who already had faith and to strengthen their belief in Jesus Christ.

It is interesting that John does not use the word *apostle* in his Gospel but instead uses the word *disciples*. Notable terms in John's Gospel include the "I am" sayings: "the Way," "the Truth," "the Bread of Life," "the Good Shepherd," "the Resurrection and the Life," and "the Light of the World." Other terms, such as "life," "light," "darkness," "world," "Father and Son," and "the Word" are used distinctively throughout his text. Another term frequently used by John is his reference to God as "The Father." The term "Father" is used only 64 times in the first three Gospels but 120 times in John's Gospel. Terms rarely found in John include "kingdom of God," "repent," "adultery," "Pharisees," "scribes," "apostles," and "demon." All of this shows that the Gospel of John has a different vocabulary from that of the first three Gospels.

Some of the terms describing opposites found in John include "life and death," "spirit and flesh," "truth and falsehood," "heaven and earth," "God and Satan," and "light and darkness." Opposites are found throughout all of the Gospels, but they are prominent in the Gospel of John. John taught us that there were two entirely different worlds and a person must choose between them. John used opposites to emphasize a variety of doctrines throughout his Gospel.[5]

IDENTITY AND RECOGNITION THEMES

John began his Gospel with the premortal status of Christ, explaining why Christ came to earth. He established the fact that Jesus' roots are far deeper than the stable in Bethlehem. Jesus was not born of a kingly lineage but he had always existed in an eternal world and came to earth to bear witness of the Father. John included John the Baptist's testimony along with his own witness that the Word had become flesh (had been born) and was now in their midst. The people could personally observe him and witness his glory and see that he was full of grace and truth (see John 1:14). The Greek verb used in John 1:14 is often translated "dwelt among," but it can mean something like "camped for awhile." That would suggest that Christ was here to interact intimately with those with whom he shared his daily life—like one who sat with friends around a campfire.

In the Old Testament some were allowed to be in Jehovah's presence but were not allowed to see him. They always experienced a veiled encounter, such as the pillar of fire or the glory that was witnessed at the tabernacle. John wanted other people to realize they could see and associate with Christ while he was among them. Surely they would receive him, because he was willing to give them such personal contact. In John 1:11–12 we are taught that he came to his own creation, but his own people would not accept him. Those who did accept him and continued faithful were given a promise that they could become his children (see also Mosiah 5:7; 3 Nephi 9:15–21). Everyone would be accountable for his own reaction to who Christ was. The rejection of Christ meant ultimately a rejection of God. The people's ability to recognize the Savior had been dulled because of their sins and traditions (see John 3:19; 5:39–40). Many looked "beyond the mark" (Jacob 4:14).

John the apostle shares with us in some detail the relationship between John the Baptist and Christ. John the Baptist clearly emphasized that Christ was greater than himself and was before him (see John 1:27, 30). Obviously John the Baptist was born before Jesus was, as recorded in scripture, but John was here referring to the premortal existence. John clearly witnessed that Jesus was the Messiah. This was likely an effort to help those who believed that John the Baptist was the Messiah make the transition to Christ. John the Beloved was a disciple of John the Baptist before becoming one of the Twelve Apostles. He would have witnessed this "Elias" transition unfold between one of the greatest prophets and the Messiah (see Luke 7:24–30).

PARABLES AND SERMONS

Not only is the selection of some words and topics different in John, but there is not a single parable within the Gospel. John makes comparisons and uses imagery in his writing without using parables, although he does record two allegories (the good shepherd, 10:1–16; and the vine and branches, 15:1–7). John often expands upon an incident or miracle with a doctrinal insight.

The synoptic Gospels are filled with shorter sayings and parables. In the synoptic Gospels the subject of the parables often relates to the kingdom of God. The discourses recorded in John generally deal with the identity of Christ and his relationship with the Father. For example, in John 17 we find Jesus' discourse on the unity of the Father and the Son including the individuality and separateness of the Father and the Son.

Some Bible scholars have challenged the longer synoptic discourses, such as the Sermon on the Mount, and consider them to be a collection of sayings on various themes. Latter-day Saints recognize that such comprehensive sermons were given by Christ, for we have as a second witness the sermon given by Christ when he appeared in America. (see 3 Nephi 12–14).

MIRACLES AND FAITH

Another difference between the writings of John and those of the other Gospel writers is the recorded accounts of the casting out of devils. No such incidents are recorded in the Gospel of John, but a number of examples of demon possession are referred to in the Gospel of Mark. Only in one place in John do we find any mention of demons, and that is where Jesus is accused of being possessed (see John 8:48).

John's documentation of the miraculous healings performed by Jesus are more drawn out and more impressive than those found in the synoptic Gospels. John records Jesus' healing of lengthy illnesses such as those of individuals who have been afflicted from birth. Such miracles as these and raising the dead are more impressive and less refutable by observers. The miracles John records are very impressive and irrefutable: the changing water to wine (see John 2:1–10); and the catch of fish (see John 21:1–11). The fourth Gospel records eight miracles: the changing of water to wine (2:1–11), the healing of the nobleman's son (4:46–54), the healing of the infirm man at the Pool of Bethesda (5:2–9), feeding the five thousand (6:1–15), walking on the water and calming the sea (6:16–21), healing a man who was blind from birth (9:1–7), raising Lazarus from the grave after four days (11:1–53), and the miraculous catch of fish (21:1–7).[6]

John saw Jesus' miracles as opportunities for people to witness and understand Christ's true identity. They were all performed as evidence of the authority that he possessed as the Messiah, who was expected to be identified by his signs and wonders. In addition one had to have faith in Christ to understand his miracles correctly. John frequently taught that faith in Jesus was required before one could experience miracles. Signs correctly understood required faith, but they also increased one's faith. If one followed Jesus just to get something to eat, one was missing the point. To follow him for the sake of physical benefits was not enough, and just seeing miracles would not convert.

Signs themselves became less and less important and faith and confidence in the Messiah became more and more important to John. Ultimately one should have faith without having to see everything (see John 20:29). To John the concept of seeing was more than just a visual acknowledgment. It was a form of spiritual discernment. Such seeing went beyond physical perception. Once a truth was perceived (or seen), then believers could receive an increase of faith in the Messiah. It is the same with hearing. Hearing was more than just a vibration of the eardrum (see John 6:60). If one could truly hear, one could be born again (see John 5:24). Active faith seeing and faith hearing led to real conversion and salvation. More than ninety-eight times in John's Gospel he uses the verb "to believe." To John "belief" was always an active process. One who believed always wanted to see and hear more of the gospel. It is not something that one had for the moment; it is something that one continues to do, again and again. It is not necessarily a state of being but a state of becoming. John's Gospel is best understood by those who are converted to the gospel and are active in their faith.

C. Wilfred Griggs stated: "I believe that John, however, is written to those who were already disciples of Jesus and who were to be guided into a more profound understanding of and appreciation for the redeeming mission of Jesus. . . . All spiritual teaching can lead to conversion, and John's testimony has doubtless brought many to discipleship. But the contents of the Gospel of John are not likely to be comprehended well until a person has embraced the practices and beliefs they elucidate. The Gospel of John was written to the Saints to teach them about the Savior and his mission."[7]

"I AM" AND JEHOVAH

John frequently uses the identifying phrase "I AM" in significant ways throughout his writings. In John 8:58 we find Christ teaching his true identity. While at the Temple Jesus reminded those who had gathered to listen to him and question him that before Abraham lived on the earth, Jesus was the great "I AM" of the Old Testament (see Exodus 3:14). The Jewish rulers would not stand for such declarations. They picked up stones to kill him for blasphemy. Their actions indicated that they understood very well the meaning of what Jesus declared. They utterly refused to accept him as their Messiah, saying, in effect, Although you are a man, you make yourself a god (see John 10:33). When Jesus pronounced himself as the great "I AM," he was uttering the very name of God. There was no other interpretation than that he was claiming to be the Jehovah of the Old Testament. He was the one who gave the name and had every right to use it. The encounter at the temple with the Jewish leaders was one of the most significant declarations of his divine nature, because it came from him personally. Elder Bruce R. McConkie said: "Christ is the *Great I AM,* the *I AM,* the *I AM THAT I AM,* meaning that he is the Eternal One, the one 'who is from all eternity to all eternity' (D&C 39:1), the God who is 'from everlasting to everlasting' (Ps. 90:2)."[8]

Most scholars agree that the use of the phrase "I AM" is more than a simple emphatic statement. The use and meaning of this form suggests a deeper interpretation and pronouncement. In the Jewish religion we find something like the absolute "I AM," the sacred name of God, revealed to Moses in Exodus 3:14. It is often closely translated into something like "I AM: That is Who I Am" or "tell them that the great I AM have sent you to them." It is the sacred name of God. In the Septuagint "I AM" (*ego eimi*) can be translated as "I YAHWEH" (Isaiah 41:4; 45:18; Hosea 13:4; Joel 2:27). In some passages of Isaiah the Hebrew reads "I, I am He." The Greek translation is often "I AM I AM." These passages clearly identify the one speaking as the Jehovah of the Old Testament. "YHWH" is the same as "I AM."

Three of the more significant forms of "I AM" are those with an explicit predicate, those with an implied predicate, and those without a predicate. An example of the explicit predicate form would be John 6:35, "I am the bread of life." An example of an implied predicate can be found in John 6:20, which could be rendered as "It is I." But the implied predicate form can be rendered more like "I am He."[9]

The form without a predicate form implies something special. It is obviously intended to announce the absolute "I AM" doctrine. Sayings without any predicates, either implicit or explicit (see John 8:24, 28, 58; 13:19), informed Jesus' listeners that they would die in their sins unless they believed that "I Am He." The "I AM" statements must be taken as an identification of Jesus revealing himself as the Jehovah of the Old Testament. He used the sacred name for God that had been revealed to Moses, a name that the Jewish leaders had long forbidden to be pronounced.[10]

S. Kent Brown stated: "The credentials of the resurrected Jesus included more than the physical and spiritual dimensions that his hearers experienced that day. They also included a name, the same name that Moses carried from the holy mount into the Hebrew slave camps. It was the name I AM. Please notice the words with which Jesus began his visit in the New World: 'Behold, I AM' (3 Nephi 11:10; emphasis added). Of course, the fuller statement is, 'Behold, I AM Jesus Christ.' . . . Let me observe that scholars of John's Gospel are agreed that the so-called 'I AM' sayings of Jesus, which are quoted in that Gospel, are all references to the divine name that was revealed to Moses at the burning bush. That is to say, whenever Jesus used the 'I am' clause of himself—whether to say that he was the light of the world, the resurrection and the life, or the true bread come down from heaven—he was consciously recalling the divine name and applying it to himself. He was therefore saying that one of his names is I AM and that he was the same person who had called Moses to be a prophet at the burning bush."[11] Jesus further testified of this when he stated, "Behold, I am he that gave the law, and I am he who covenanted with my people Israel"(3 Nephi 15:5).[12]

Jesus was not simply a carrier of revelation or another prophet; he was the Revealer himself, the Lord and Messiah. He was the giver of the law to the prophets and it was him of whom they testified and witnessed. He was the great "I AM—Jehovah" from the Old Testament.

AMEN, AMEN AND VERILY, VERILY

In the Gospel of John we find another example of how Jesus spoke with unusual authority. Often Jesus would begin his discourses with "verily, verily" (the Greek is *amen, amen*). In this way, he officially emphasized doctrines, oaths, and covenants. The phrase "verily, verily" used at the beginning of a statement is unique to Christ.

Prophets often spoke in the third person, "Thus saith the Lord," or "it is written." These phrases were used by the Lord's prophets to indicate that they were speaking the words of the Lord and not speaking for themselves. Jesus often spoke in the first person, "Verily, verily I say unto you." The phrase "verily, I say unto you" was very close to the prophet's expression of "thus saith the Lord," but it is stronger. Jesus spoke as one having binding authority. He had the authority to make scripture and to reinterpret it. We often find Jesus asserting his authority in contrast with what had been taught in the Old Testament. (Jesus, after all, was Jehovah, who taught the Old Testament prophets in the first place!) Many of the religious leaders of that day considered that a significant show of disrespect for the Torah. For example, in the Sermon on the Mount we find Jesus making such statements as, "You have heard that it was said . . . but I say unto you" (Matthew 5:22, 28, 32, 34, 39, 44). His authority was from heaven, not from the earthly schools, governments, or apostate leaders. He spoke with greater authority.

When Jesus used the phrase "verily, verily" at the beginning of his sayings, it had the effect of an oath. It informed his listeners that what he was about to say was binding on himself and on his hearers. He was, in effect, stating, "As God is my witness" or "I swear to God" when he began with the double "amen, amen." Some followers responded to Christ's teachings with, "Never man spake like this man" (John 7:46). To others it was disturbing and shocking. To believers it was a sign of his Messiahship.

In the Book of Mormon we find that "verily" is used almost exclusively in the same way as it is in the Bible, except in one instance: where Mormon comments about the greatness of Captain Moroni (72 B.C.). Mormon declared, "Verily, verily I say unto you, if all men had been, and were, and ever would be, like unto Moroni . . . " (Alma 48:17). Here the prophet Mormon used a very strong statement to emphasize his great respect and admiration for Moroni. Some forty-six times in 3 Nephi 9–27 we find the sayings of Jesus beginning with "verily" or "verily, verily," and this formula remains true throughout modern scripture. In the Doctrine and Covenants we can find more than three hundred examples of "verily" being used almost exclusively by the Lord. Today, as in ancient times, listeners use the phrase "amen" at the end of discourses and prayers when expressing agreement with what they have just heard.

CONCLUSION

John lived in a day when the eyewitnesses to Jesus' actual appearance on earth were dying. Increasingly the Saints had to rely on second- and third-generation witnesses. How strong would they be? Who would direct the Church? How strong and loyal were these second-generation Christians? A tidal wave of apostasy was enveloping the Church. One of the false doctrines aggressively circulated was the denial of the divinity of Christ. It became increasingly difficult to protect the Church from the Hellenistic views that fueled the Apostasy. John knew that true conversion involved an understanding of who Christ was and a commitment to his teachings. If one accepted him, one accepted the Father; if one rejected him, one rejected God the Father.

Recognizing the promptings and living worthy of the companionship of the Holy Ghost was critical. Those who had the Holy Ghost as their guide were strong in the faith. Jesus had returned to the celestial realms from whence he came. He was divine, and his origin was not of this world. John, as a true apostle, desired to share his sure witness with the Saints ancient and modern by giving his priceless testimony of Jesus Christ. Every Saint who desires to see and hear and gain a witness of Christ should study John's testimony, which we call the Gospel of John.

A latter-day apostle, Elder Bruce R. McConkie, witnessed, "The gospel of John is the account for the saints; it is pre-eminently the gospel for the Church, for those who understand the scriptures and their symbolisms and who are concerned with spiritual and eternal things."[13] One of the clearest statements in the Bible in relation to why John wrote his Gospel is from his own writings: "But these are written, that ye might believe that Jesus is the Christ, the Son of God; and that believing ye might have life through his name" (John 20:31).

NOTES

1. C. Wilfred Griggs, "The Testimony of John," in *The Gospels*, ed. Kent P. Jackson and Robert L. Millet, vol. 5 of *Studies in Scripture* Series (Salt Lake City: Deseret Book, 1986), 109–10.

2. Neal A. Maxwell, *"Not My Will, but Thine"* (Salt Lake City: Bookcraft, 1988), 44. See also Bruce R. McConkie, *Mormon Doctrine*, 2d ed. (Salt Lake City: Bookcraft, 1958), 307.

3. Robert Kysar, *John: The Maverick Gospel*, rev. ed. (Louisville: Westminster/John Knox Press, 1993), 25. "Some critics once believed that John's Gospel was composed late in the second century (when Christian authors first mention it), but tiny manuscript fragments of

John discovered in the Egyptian desert have been dated at about 125 and 150 C.E, making them the oldest surviving copy of a New Testament book. Allowing time for the Gospel to have circulated abroad as far as Egypt, the work could not have originated much later than about 100 C.E." Stephen L. Harris, *Understanding the Bible,* 1992 (London: Mayfield Publishing Company, 1992), 322. With a discovery of such documents as the Chester/Beaty fragment and other internal as well as external research, there is no compelling reason to reject him as the "beloved disciple" or the one "whom Jesus loved" (John 21:20) and the writer of the fourth Gospel.

4. Kysar, *John,* 6.

5. Griggs, "Testimony of John," 125.

6. Some scholars would not list the eighth miracle mentioned in the text above because they consider it to be an unauthorized addition added later to the Gospel.

7. Griggs, "Testimony of John," 111.

8. McConkie, *Mormon Doctrine,* 311.

9. I am indebted to Robert Kysar, *John,* 45–48; and Geoffrey W. Bromiley, *Theological Dictionary of the New Testament* (Grand Rapids, Mich.: Eerdmans, 1985), 196–200, for their discussion of the Greek grammar of the phrase "I Am." Examples of three of the more significant forms of the "I AM" sayings are (1) without a predicate: 8:24, 28, 58; 13:19; (2) with an implied predicate: 6:20; 18:5; (3) with an explicit predicate: 6:35, 51; 8:12, 18, 23; 9:5; 10:7, 9, 11, 14; 11:25; 14:6; 15:1, 5 and possibly 4:26.

10. See also James R Harris, "The 'I AM' Passages in the Gospels and in 3 Nephi," *The New Testament and the Latter-day Saints* (Orem, Ut.: Randall Book, 1987), 89–115; Joel B. Green and Scot McKnight, *Dictionary of Jesus and the Gospels* (Downers Grove, Ill.: InterVarsity Press, 1992), 354–56.

11. S. Kent Brown, "Moses and Jesus: The Old Adorns the New," *The Book of Mormon: 3 Nephi 9–30, This Is My Gospel,* ed. Monte S. Nyman and Charles D. Tate Jr. (Provo: Religious Studies Center, Brigham Young University, 1993), 98–99.

12. Other places of self-disclosure that can be found outside the Gospel of John include Jesus identifying himself during the calming of the storm with the disciples (see Mark 6:45–50); in Mark 13:6 he warns of a future age when many would come in his name saying they are the I AM. During Jesus' trial (see Mark 14:62) the priest asked if Jesus was the Christ. He answered *"Ego eimi,"* meaning he was the I AM. In Luke 24:39 the resurrected Christ identified himself (see my hands and my feet . . . it is *ego eimi*). These are all expressions that identify with the Jehovah of the Old Testament. "Matthew uses *ego* 29 times, Mark 17 times, Luke 23 times and John 134 times. Likewise *ego eimi* is used by

Matthew five times (Mt14:27; 22:32; 24:5; 26:22, 25), Mark three times (MK6:50; 13:6; 14:62) and Luke four times (LK1:19; 21:8; 22:70; 24:39), but John employs it thirty times." Green and McKnight, *Dictionary,* 354.

13. Bruce R. McConkie, *Doctrinal New Testament Commentary,* 3 vols. (Salt Lake City: Bookcraft, 1965–73), 1:65.

CHAPTER NINETEEN

REVELATION: JOHN'S MESSAGE OF COMFORT AND HOPE

GAYE STRATHEARN

We live in a world where news reports invariably highlight the negative. It is almost impossible to pick up a paper or turn on the evening news without being bombarded by reports of governmental corruption, gang violence, abuse, or the atrocities of war, just to name a few. The dichotomy between present reality and the scriptural ideal experienced by Enoch (see Moses 7:17–19), Melchizedek (see JST Genesis 14:33–34), and the Nephite-Lamanite civilization (see 4 Nephi 1–19) seems to be ever widening; yet the promise of a future Zion, a New Jerusalem, where the Saints live in paradisiacal glory (see Article of Faith 1:10), punctuates the scriptures with a recurring rhythm that reverberates in our souls. The apostle John was keenly aware of the disparity between his own present reality and future possibilities. His literary legacy gives us keys to bridging the spatial gap with the future: how to use the promise of the future to enable us to successfully negotiate the present. That message runs through all of his extant writings, particularly in the book of Revelation.

Historically, Revelation has evoked tremendous interest even though its message is couched in symbolic imagery. That imagery can be both a blessing and a curse to latter-day readers. It can be a blessing in that its imagery paints a vivid picture of the struggle

---

Gaye Strathearn is an instructor in ancient scripture at Brigham Young University and a doctoral candidate in New Testament at the Claremont Graduate University, Claremont, California.

between good and evil throughout the earth's existence. It can be a curse in that we can get so caught up with trying to decipher that imagery that we can leave ourselves with neither the time nor the energy to get beyond the symbols to appreciate Revelation's underlying, straightforward message: we are not alone in our struggles, and eventually God will vindicate his covenant people. With that end in mind I will leave aside an interpretation of the events of the seven seals, the trumpets, the plagues, and even the descriptions of the beast and the red dragon. Others have done excellent work in these areas. Instead, I will examine the ways in which Revelation gave comfort and hope to the Saints at the end of the first century who were experiencing tribulation[1] because of their religious beliefs and then to draw four specific lessons that we can use for our own inevitable encounters with tribulation. In doing so it is important to first place the author, the Church, and the book in their historical contexts.

THE APOSTLE JOHN

Throughout his life, the apostle John was keenly aware of the continuing struggle between good and evil and its effects upon the members of the Church. Jesus had warned all his followers, and particularly his apostles, of the persecutions that they would encounter. Twice the Beatitudes make explicit reference to persecution that disciples could anticipate because of their associations with the Savior (see Matthew 5:10–11). During the apostolic commission Christ specifically warned the Twelve that he was sending them out "as sheep in the midst of wolves" (Matthew 10:16) and that they would be "hated of all men for [his] name's sake" (Matthew 10:22). Although we have little definitive knowledge of John's mortal ministry, we know that he knew about religious persecution from firsthand experience and the scriptures record that he was maligned both by those within and without the Church.

Like his master before him and his successor Joseph Smith, John was at times defamed by members of the Church—people who should have known better.[2] John does not include many details in his third epistle, but apparently a man by the name of Diotrephes sought to usurp his apostolic authority. Diotrephes, like the Pharisees before him (see Matthew 23:6), loved to be on the center stage of his local church—he loved to be in charge and calling the shots. As a result, John says that he "receiveth us not" (3 John 1:9). Unfortunately the epistle does not include many specifics. We don't know, for example, whether verse 9 means that he refused to receive or acknowledge John himself or a letter that he sent to the Church but, as Raymond E. Brown notes, the "present tense of the verb (*epidechesthai*) indicates that Diotrephes' action was not a solitary incident but part of an enduring attitude."[3] We also know that he refused to allow any of the other Brethren to visit his church and that he excommunicated anyone who sought to accept them (see 3 John 1:10). His rejection of the Brethren included "prating against [them] with malicious words" (3 John 1:10). The exact nature of his verbal assaults is lost to history, but the Greek word for "prating" (*phlyareō*) indicates he was "talk[ing] nonsense (about)" or bringing "unjustified charges against" John and the other brethren.[4] This incident clearly upset the apostle.

John's tribulations, however, were much more global that those that originated within the Church. We know of at least two incidents when he was arrested for preaching the gospel. Luke records the first when John and Peter healed the lame man at the temple and then preached to the crowd (see Acts 3). The Jewish hierarchy arrested them specifically because "they taught the people, and preached through Jesus the resurrection from the dead" (Acts 4:2). John himself records the second occasion in his introduction to the book of Revelation, in which he describes his exile to the island of Patmos "for the word of God, and for the testimony of Jesus Christ" (Revelation 1:9). It was this latter experience which provided the catalyst for his great revelation. John, therefore, was no novice when it came to tribulation. Instead he wrote with a perspective that was forged from a mountain of personal experience.

In dealing with tribulation John understood some basic elements of the plan of salvation that enabled him to confront his situations. In the prologue to his Gospel we read: "In the beginning was the Word, and the Word was with God, and the Word was God. The same was in the beginning with God. All things were made by him: and without him was not anything made that was made. In him was life; and the life was the light of men. And the light shineth in darkness; and the darkness comprehended it not" (John 1:1–5).

Although these verses are often quoted for their description of the "Word," let us look now at what they tell us about the contrast between light and darkness. This contrast is a theme that runs throughout John's writings (see, for example, John 3:19; 8:12; 12:35, 46; 1 John 1:5). He uses the two metaphors as symbols for the continuing battle between Christ and Satan. The word which the King James translators rendered as "comprehended" is *katelaben,* which has a basic meaning of to "seize with hostile intent."[5] In other words, the Greek text of verse 5 reads, "And the light shines (present tense) in darkness; and the darkness did not defeat (aorist, or past tense) it." The context of this verse makes it abundantly clear that the light is a metaphor for Christ. The darkness that did not defeat the light must therefore be Satan, and the verse as a whole must refer to the war in heaven, in which Christ defeated Satan's aspirations for glory (see Moses 4:1–4; see also Abraham 3:27–28; Revelation 12:7–9).

The struggle between Christ, Satan, and their respective followers is a prominent theme in all of John's writings. He had experienced both the light that came from his intimate association with the Savior and the darkness of tribulation that came when individuals or groups chose to follow Satan. From the very beginning he wanted to assure his readers that darkness would not prevail. It could not prevail in the premortal existence and, although it would find some success here in mortality, ultimately it would also succumb to the light of Jesus Christ. The battleground may have shifted, but the result would be the same. It is this insight into the plan of salvation that undergirded John's message of comfort and hope to those enduring tribulation.

CHRISTIAN PERSECUTION IN THE FIRST CENTURY

John was not alone in experiencing tribulation because of his association with Christ. The early Church as a whole had to fight for its survival. Christ's death did not alleviate Jewish feelings of insecurity about the fledgling movement. The Sanhedrin ordered Stephen to be stoned to death because he said that he saw "the glory of God, and Jesus standing on the right hand of God" (Acts 7:55); Herod Agrippa beheaded James and arrested Peter because "it pleased the Jews" (Acts 12:3); and Paul experienced Jewish wrath more than once because of his gospel message (see Acts 14:1–7, 19; 19:8–9; 2 Corinthians

11:23–28). These incidents, however, seem to have been isolated attacks that originated from religious conflict rather than political malevolence.

Such conflict apparently led Emperor Claudius to expel from Rome all Jews, including such Jewish Christians as Aquila and Priscilla (see Acts 18:2), because of a disturbance over the teachings of Christ.[6] As far as the Roman authorities were concerned, Christianity in the forties and early fifties of the first century after Christ was still a Jewish sect. Not until the time of Nero (A.D. 54–68) do we have any record of Christians being politically persecuted as a separate entity. Tacitus records that when suspicion began to mount that Nero had set fire to Rome, the emperor adroitly deflected the public outcry onto the Christians. He describes some of the techniques Nero used in his persecution, such as covering the Christians in animal skins and having them mauled by dogs, crucifying them, and burning them alive, including using them as lighted lamps for some of his garden parties (*Annals,* 15.44).[7] It was during this time, tradition holds, that both Peter and Paul become martyrs at Nero's hands. Fortunately, Nero's successors do not seem to have continued these anti-Christian policies. By then, however, the Christians were painfully aware of how precarious their situation was and how devastating the fortunes of politics could be for them.

As Revelation opens, we find John writing to the seven churches that he is their brother, who shares with them in Jesus the tribulation and the kingdom and patient endurance (see Revelation 1:9). The obvious question that this verse raises centers on the type of tribulation that John and his associates had to patiently endure. Our earliest tradition from Irenaeus dates Revelation "towards the end of Domitian's reign" (*Against Heresies,* 5.30.3).[8] Because Domitian reigned from A.D. 81 to 96, many scholars date Revelation to about A.D. 95–96. We have very little information about Domitian's policies toward the Christians, although later sources paint a very negative picture. At the end of the second century Tertullian compared Domitian to Nero in his persecution of the Christians,[9] and by the fourth century Eusebius implied that he instigated widespread political persecution.[10] These descriptions, however, have come under some serious criticism in recent years.[11] It is probably more realistic to view the tribulations mentioned in Revelation as more sporadic events.

What we know about Domitian's reign must be gleaned from a number of sources. We do know that he actively promoted the emperor cult, in which emperors, past and present, were worshiped as deities. In his *Lives of the Caesars* Suetonius records that Domitian required that his correspondences all begin with the phrase, "Our Master and our God" (*Domitian*, 13) in reference to himself. Dio Cassius recorded that those who failed to worship the emperor-gods were charged with atheism and either put to death or deprived of their property and banished (*Roman History*, 67.14). These practices would have placed the members of such monotheistic groups as Judaism and Christianity in a very awkward position of deciding between religious conviction and political expediency and could well explain John's exile "for the word of God, and for the testimony of Jesus Christ" (Revelation 1:9).

The Christian position at the end of the first century is further highlighted by Pliny, the Roman governor of Bithynia, in the first decade of the second century. He writes to the emperor Trajan seeking advice on how to deal with Christians. In that letter he admits that he has tortured them if they refuse to renounce their Christianity. For Pliny the quintessential test of whether Christians had renounced their faith was to require them to offer sacrifice and incense before an image of the emperor (that is, participate in the emperor cult) and then to curse Christ, because "none of [these] acts, it is said, those who are really Christians can be forced into performing" (*Letters*, 10.96).[12] Although this letter was written after Domitian's reign, Pliny refers to Christians who had renounced their Christianity "as much as twenty-five years ago," which would have certainly been during the time of Domitian. It would appear that these practices contributed to the tribulation suggested in Revelation.

JOHN'S REVELATION

When John received his revelation on Patmos, three of the seven congregations in Asia had already experienced problems: Ephesus had been infiltrated by "evil" people who "[said] that they [were] apostles, and [were] not" (Revelation 2:2); a man by the name of Antipas had become a martyr in Pergamos (see Revelation 2:13); and people from the Jewish synagogue had tormented members of the Church in Philadelphia (see Revelation 3:8–9). Yet it is easy to get the impression that these incidents were but ripples in the great cosmic battle between the forces of good and evil. Later, during the description of the fifth seal—the events during their own period of time— John sees "the souls of them that were slain for the word of God, and for the testimony which they held" (Revelation 6:9), indicating that Antipas was not the only martyr. These descriptions, however, are not the focus of Revelation's message to the Saints.

As John introduced himself in the opening chapter, his message was as follows: "John to the seven churches which are in Asia: Grace be unto you, and peace, from him which is, and which was, and which is to come" (Revelation 1:4). The Lord's message, which John delivers, is primarily one of grace and peace, not of persecution and death—grace, which is made possible through the atoning sacrifice; and inner peace, which comes from a knowledge of one's relationship with God. It is through these that the Lord offers comfort and hope to his people. They should therefore be a focus in our reading of Revelation.

MESSAGE OF COMFORT

If we look at an abbreviated outline of Revelation, the Lord's message of comfort becomes readily apparent.[13]

Revelation 1:1–10. Introduction.

Revelation 1:11–20. Vision of the seven candlesticks.

Revelation 2–3. Letters to the seven churches.

Revelation 4. Vision of God's throne.

Revelation 5–18. Opening the seven seals, including vivid descriptions of Satan's power in the last days (11–18) and the restoration of the gospel (14).

Revelation 19–22. Christ's ultimate victory over Satan.

Two sections describe periods of tribulation: the letters to the seven churches and the opening of the seven seals. It is instructive to study the way these sections are introduced and the entire revelation is concluded.

Before he specifically addresses the seven churches, which will include a discussion of each of their shortcomings, the Lord gives John the vision of the seven candlesticks which, the angel informs us, represent those seven churches (see Revelation 1:20). What is significant is that in the midst of the candlesticks is "one like unto the Son of man" (Revelation 1:13; compare Daniel 7:13–14). Verse 19 clearly identifies this individual as Christ. The poignancy of this vision is that before talking about their tribulations and shortcomings, the Lord wants them to know that he is in their midst (see Revelation 1:13). While in mortality the Savior had promised that "where two or three are gathered together in my name, there am I in the midst of them" (Matthew 18:20). Now he was gone physically but not spiritually. As one scholar cogently noted, Christ is "no absentee landlord."[14] What a wonderful concept! Alma prophesied to the people of Gideon that Christ "will take upon him death, that he may loose the bands of death which bind his people; and he will take upon him their infirmities, that his bowels may be filled with mercy, according to the flesh, that he may know according to the flesh how to succor his people according to their infirmities" (Alma 7:12). Christ did not promise that we would be immune from tribulations. He wasn't immune from them, so can we really expect to be? As he told the Prophet Joseph, "The Son of Man hath descended below them all. Art thou greater than he?" (D&C 122:8). He does promise, however, that he will "be in their midst" and that he will "succor his people according to their infirmities."

Note how the visions associated with the opening of the seven seals are introduced. Once again John describes a vision of divinity. This time it is of God sitting on his throne surrounded by twenty-four elders and four beasts (see Revelation 4:2–11).[15] John's expressive language attempts, however inadequately, to capture the glory and magnificence of God. This is the throne upon which God will later sit in judgment (see Revelation 20:11–15). It is not mere coincidence that John receives this vision before viewing the opening of the seven seals and hence gaining a glimpse of the history of this world. God knows the beginning from the end, and accountability during judgment is an integral part of the plan of salvation. It is interesting, though, that the throne of judgment is surrounded by a rainbow. For the ancients, as indeed it should be for us, this symbol is rich in meaning. It harks back to the original rainbow that God placed in the sky after the Flood—a time when God's judgment came upon the earth because of its wickedness. The rainbow, however, was the symbol not of God's judgment but rather of his mercy, both to Noah and his family and the world, in promise that he would never flood the earth again (see Genesis 9:12–17).[16] In a similar manner, the Lord seeks to reassure John and his audience that although his judgments must come upon the earth and its inhabitants, the Saints can take comfort in the fact that God's great mercy will temper the demands of justice. Amulek taught that it is through Christ's atoning sacrifice that "mercy can satisfy the demands of justice, and encircles them in the arms of safety" (Alma 34:16).

It is surely not coincidence that the Lord introduces two sections on judgment with passages that remind us of his constant vigilance and God's tempering mercy. Admittedly the message is more subtle than much of the rest of the Revelation, but that should not prevent us from appreciating its pivotal importance. "He that hath an ear, let him hear what the Spirit saith unto the churches" (Revelation 2:7, 11, 17, 29; 3:6, 13, 22). Viewed in its proper perspective, this message would have provided great comfort for the struggling Saints at the end of the first century.

MESSAGE OF HOPE

The Lord's message is one not only of comfort for the present but also of hope for the future. In Revelation he offers it on two levels, each related to the other like two sides of a coin. On the cosmic level, Revelation provides hope for the Saints that Satan will be destroyed: just as Satan could not defeat Christ in the premortal existence, neither will he ultimately prevail in mortality. Revelation 19:11–20:10 graphically describes that defeat. The result will be that Satan will be bound during the Millennium and, after the Judgment, the earth will be transformed into celestial glory. It is interesting that Satan's defeat occurs only after the marriage of the Lamb. Earlier in Revelation 19 we read, "Let us be glad and rejoice, and give honour to him: for the marriage of the Lamb is come, and his wife hath made herself ready" (v. 7). What, if any, is the relationship between the marriage and Satan's defeat? The answer is an important element in understanding the Lord's message of hope for his people.

Throughout the Old and New Testaments, the bride represents Christ's covenant people (see Isaiah 54:5; Hosea 2:19–20; Matthew 25:1–13; Ephesians 5:25). Revelation 19:7 specifically reads that the bride, or the Church, "made herself ready" for this wedding. As with any wedding, there are tremendous physical preparations that need to be tended to. The Church must also make spiritual preparations to enter into that covenant relationship. If we return to the letters to the seven churches, we gain some insight into what those spiritual preparations entail. In every letter the Lord tells the churches that they must overcome Satan's machinations (see Revelation 2:7, 11, 17, 26; 3:5, 12, 21). The Greek word used throughout John's writings for "overcome" is *nikaō,* meaning "the overthrow of an opposing force" with a success that "is palpable and manifest to all eyes."[17] In other words, the Church's readiness is active. Church members cannot just sit back and wait for Christ to come and take care of everything for them. Instead, they have to be actively involved in the fight against Satan.

Nephi taught that we can achieve this state only through personal righteousness (see 1 Nephi 22:26). In his epistles John expounds further. He tells us that those who overcome are those who have been "born of God" and who believe "that Jesus is the Son of God" (1 John 5:4–5). They receive power to overcome by actively making Christ's atonement a force in their lives. Herein lies great power: the overcoming of Satan is a partnership between Christ and the Saints. The next verse in Revelation 19 reads, "And to her was granted that she should be arrayed in fine linen, bright white and clean: for the fine linen is the righteousness of the saints" (v. 8, author's translation). The dress itself is a gift from Christ, but its fabric is created from the "righteous deeds" of the Saints.[18]

Those who enter into a covenant relationship with Christ and become his bride are those who, according to Revelation 19:11–14, also join with him in the final assault on Satan: "And I saw heaven opened, and behold a white horse; and he that sat upon him was called Faithful and True, and in righteousness he doth judge and make war. His eyes were as a flame of fire, and on his head were many crowns; and he had a name written, that no man knew, but he himself. And he was clothed with a vesture dipped in blood: and his name is called The Word of God. And the armies which were in heaven followed him upon white horses, clothed in fine linen, white and clean." The armies are wearing the same clothing that Christ gives to his bride. It is through overcoming Satan on a personal level that we are prepared to assist in overthrowing him on the global and cosmic level. What a beautiful promise of hope.

On the other side of the coin, the Lord's message of hope is that as the Saints "overcome" they will receive exaltation or eternal life "which gift is the greatest of all the gifts of God" (D&C 14:7). In the letters to the seven churches this gift is delineated. The Lord promises each of the churches different elements of the exaltation process. As we examine each promise individually, we can gain a fuller appreciation of what exaltation entails and the magnitude of the message of hope that Revelation offers to the Saints.

The Lord promises the Ephesians that they will "eat of the tree of life, which is in the midst of the paradise of God" (Revelation 2:7; see also 22:1–2). We know that access to that tree was cut off after the fall of Adam and Eve because, as Alma explains to Corianton, "If Adam had put forth his hand immediately [after the Fall], and partaken of the tree of life, he would have lived forever, according to the word of God, having no space for repentance" (Alma 42:5). In other words, he would have become immortal in a fallen state. The fact that the Ephesian Saints will partake of the fruit indicates that their sins will no longer impede their access to eternal life.

The Saints in Smyrna are promised that they will not be hurt by the second death (see Revelation 2:11). The second death, John tells us, is to be "cast into the lake of fire" (Revelation 20:14), or "the lake which burneth with fire and brimstone" (Revelation 21:8). In contrast, he assures us that those upon whom "the second death hath no power" are those who become "priests of God and of Christ, and . . . reign with him" during the Millennium (Revelation 20:6). The Lord doesn't promise his Saints that they will not be hurt by the first death, meaning mortal death, but that they will not be hurt by the second death. In other words, the Lord wants his Saints to view their present tribulation from an eternal perspective. He taught the same principle to Joseph Smith in Liberty jail when he declared, "Thine afflictions shall be but a small moment; and then, if thou endure it well, God shall exalt thee on high; thou shalt triumph over all thy foes" (D&C 121:7–8).

The Saints in Pergamos are promised that they will "eat of the hidden manna, and [the Lord] will give them a white stone, and in the stone a new name written, which no man knoweth saving he that receiveth it" (Revelation 2:17). Manna was the miraculous substance by which God provided physical nourishment for the Israelites as they journeyed through the wilderness (see Exodus 16:4). Part of that manna was collected and kept in an urn in the tabernacle (see Exodus 16:32–34). It was thus hidden from the congregation at large and became "both a symbol and a promise of the true Bread of Life that was yet to be given."[19] In his sermon on the bread of life, Jesus declared, "I am the bread of life: he that cometh to me shall never hunger; and he that believeth on me shall never thirst" (John 6:35), and later, "if any man eat of this bread he shall live for ever" (John 6:51). The promise that the Saints would eat of the hidden manna means, therefore, that Christ would provide their spiritual nourishment: his atoning sacrifice would provide everything the Saints need for exaltation. Having partaken of that manna the Saints would then receive a white stone with a new name written upon it. The Prophet Joseph Smith informs us that this stone is a Urim and Thummim, which is given to those who enter the celestial kingdom so that they can know of the "things pertaining to a higher order of kingdoms" (D&C 130:10).

The prophet doesn't say much about the new name, only that it is "the key word" (D&C 130:11), but it does play a significant role in the ancient world. Receiving a new name often indicated some kind of change in status.[20] The most prominent biblical examples are Abraham, Sarah, Jacob, and Paul. Abram became Abraham when he entered into a covenant with the Lord (see Genesis 17:1–8); Sarai became Sarah when the Lord promised her that she would bear a child (see Genesis 17:15–16); Jacob became Israel when he wrestled with a holy messenger so that he could receive a blessing (see Genesis 32:24–28; 35:9–10); and Saul apparently became Paul when he became a missionary to the Gentiles (see Acts 13:9). That in Revelation the new name is known only to the individual recipient also draws upon ancient beliefs that knowledge of another's name elicited power over the individual. Hidden names served two purposes: first, they prevented evil powers from gaining control of an individual; and second, they were "a key to permit the initiate to enter into the true fold of God."[21] Here, therefore, that the Saints are given a new name which "no man knoweth" seems to indicates two things: they are no longer subject to the powers of Satan or anyone acting at his behest, and they can enter into God's presence. This must have been an especially compelling blessing to people who had experienced persecution.

The Lord promises those who "overcome" in Thyatira that they will have power over the nations through two related means. First, they will rule "with a rod of iron" (Revelation 2:27), which Nephi learned was "the word of God" (1 Nephi 11:25). Second, they will receive the morning star (see Revelation 2:28), which John later identifies as Christ himself (see Revelation 22:16). In other words, the Saints will eventually join with Christ and rule the world through his power. Rome, for all its power and grandeur, for all of its ability to afflict the lives of the Saints at the end of the first century and beyond, was merely a ship passing in the night of eternity. The Lord has always promised that the first shall be last, and the last shall be first (see Matthew 19:30; Jacob 5:63; D&C 29:30). There was hope for the Saints!

The Saints in Sardis are promised that they will be clothed in a white raiment, that their name will not be blotted out of the book of life, and that Jesus will confess them before the Father and the angels (see Revelation 3:5). The significance of the white robes can be both purity and victory—purity from the sins of the world and victory over Satan and his minions. During the description of events during the sixth seal, John sees the 144,000 and a great multitude of people clothed in white who stand before the throne of God. When John inquires about them, the angel declares that "these are they which came out of great tribulation, and have washed their robes, and made them white in the blood of the Lamb" (Revelation 7:14). The robes have become white, once again, because they have made Christ's atonement efficacious in their lives. As a result, Christ acts as their advocate before the Father at the time of judgment. To be enrolled in the book of life means that the individual will participate in eternal life, or "the kind of life that [God] lives."[22]

The Saints in Philadelphia who overcome are promised that they will become a pillar in God's temple and he will write upon the Saints the name of God and the new Jerusalem and God's new name (see Revelation 3:12). The temple is the place where God dwells; therefore the promise of becoming a pillar in God's temple is the promise of becoming a permanent fixture in God's presence. Elder

Bruce R. McConkie described the significance of having God's name. "God's name is God. To have his name written on a person is to identify that person as a god. How can it be said more plainly? Those who gain eternal life become gods!"[23] Likewise, he explains that Christ's "'new name' shall be written upon those who are joint-heirs with him (Rev. 3:12), and shall signify that they have become even as he is."[24] They belong in God's presence in the New Jerusalem because they are gods. It is therefore not surprising that the last promise, given to the Laodiceans, is that they will be enthroned beside Christ and the Father (see Revelation 3:21). They will, as Paul writes, be "joint-heirs with Christ" (Romans 8:17)!

All of these promises are the promises of exaltation for the Saints who "overcome." Later in the revelation John received a glimpse of the time when these promises would all be fulfilled: "Behold, the tabernacle of God is with men, and he will dwell with them, and they shall be his people, and God himself shall be with them, and be their God. And God shall wipe away all tears from their eyes; and there shall be no more death, neither sorrow, nor crying, neither shall there be any more pain: for the former things are passed away. And he that sat upon the throne said, Behold, I make all things new. And he said unto me, Write: for these words are true and faithful" (Revelation 21:3–5).

Revelation gives us a peek into eternity and what it is like. The Lord could have easily told John to write to the Saints and tell them to buck up and endure to the end so that they could then be exalted. The message is the same, but the power of Revelation comes from its detailed description of possibilities. What does it mean to be exalted? According to Revelation, to be exalted means that through the atonement of Christ we can overcome the limitations of mortality, which we all experience because of the Fall; we can rise above the power of Satan and his minions; we can be purified from our sins so that we can dwell in the presence of God and thus inherit all that he has, including the privilege and responsibility of godhood. This indeed is a message of hope for those in the midst of tribulations.

MODERN LESSONS FROM JOHN'S REVELATION

Although Revelation was originally sent to seven specific churches in Asia Minor, the number seven, which symbolizes completeness or wholeness also suggests that its message was for the entire Church.[25] We can understand that symbolism to mean the entire Church at the end of the first century, or we can understand it to mean that its message is timeless: just as important for the Saints today as it was when it was first recorded on the isle of Patmos.

The scriptures teach us that tribulation, in any age, is an integral part of mortality. Lehi taught his son Jacob that "it must needs be, that there is an opposition in all things" (2 Nephi 2:11). Similarly the Lord instructed Joseph Smith that "it must needs be that the devil should tempt the children of men, or they could not be agents unto themselves; for if they never should have bitter they could not know the sweet" (D&C 29:39). In fact, at another time Joseph declared that "men have to suffer that they may come upon Mount Zion and be exalted above the heavens."[26] Tribulation is a refiner's fire, and as Elder Neal A. Maxwell reminds us, although "there are variations in our trials," there are "no immunities."[27] The question then should not be, Why do we have tribulation? but How can we deal with it when it comes? Revelation provides four powerful lessons, regardless of whether the tribulation we experience is global or personal in nature.

First, we have noted that John's understanding of the plan of salvation, particularly his knowledge of the war in heaven, undergirds his message in Revelation. The restoration of the gospel of Jesus Christ has blessed us with the same understanding. The plan of salvation allows us to glimpse eternity and thus allows us to put our mortal tribulations into an eternal perspective. We can have confidence that just as Christ overcame Satan in the premortal existence, so He will also overcome him here in mortality.

Second, despite the turmoil that may encompass us, we can have confidence that Christ is in our midst. The Church of Jesus Christ of Latter-day Saints is his church, and he plays an active role in it—he is, as we have noted, no absentee landlord. That position alone should give us great comfort. On the macro level we can know that the Church is in good hands. On the micro level he is there with us, and we can turn to him in every situation. Alma the Younger learned that at the lowest point of his life he was able to think of Christ and cry out to him for mercy. In doing so, he records, he "could remember [his] pains no more; yea [he] was harrowed up by the memory of [his] sins no more" (Alma 36:19). We should never forget the vivid picture that John paints for us of Jesus standing at the door: "Behold, I stand at the door, and knock: if any man hear my voice, and open the door, I will come in to him, and will sup with him, and he with me" (Revelation 3:20). If Christ is not there by our side, then we can be sure that we are the ones who have moved away. In times of tribulation we should take comfort through turning to Christ. Instead of allowing ourselves to be encompassed about by the cares of the world, we should instead turn to Christ and be "encircled about with the matchless bounty of his love" (Alma 26:15).

Third, we must be actively engaged in the fight against evil. The Lord told the Saints in the seven churches that they must "overcome" in order to inherit the blessings of eternity. Likewise, we cannot afford to sit passively by and watch our society gather momentum on Satan's slippery slide of "eat, drink, and be merry, or tomorrow we die" (2 Nephi 28:7). Edmund Burke captured the essence of Revelation's message when he wrote that "when bad men combine, the good must associate; else they will fall, one by one, an unpitied sacrifice in a contemptible struggle."[28] The Brethren have asked us to be actively involved in our neighborhoods and communities. They understand well the collective power of individuals who unite in promoting the cause of good. One classic example from the Book of Mormon of actively opposing the incursion of evil is found in Helaman 6. Both the Nephite and the Lamanite nations had become very prosperous and, as a result, the Gadianton robbers once again began to infest the land. What is interesting here is that "when the Lamanites found that there were robbers among them they were exceedingly sorrowful; and they did use every means in their power to destroy them off the face of the earth" (Helaman 6:20). In contrast, we read that the Nephites "did unite with those bands of robbers, and did enter into their covenants and their oaths, that they would protect and preserve one another in whatsoever difficult circumstances they should be placed, that they should not suffer for their murders, and their plunderings, and their stealings" (Helaman 6:21). Why don't we read of righteous Nephites using every means to destroy them off the face of the earth, as the Lamanites did? Is it possible that they had been lulled into a sense of complacency?

Perhaps. Notice Mormon's editorial insertion about the results of both approaches to the Gadianton robbers: "And thus we see that the Nephites did begin to dwindle in unbelief, and grow in wickedness and abominations, while the Lamanites began to grow exceedingly in the knowledge of their God; yea, they did begin to keep his statutes and commandments, and to walk in truth and uprightness before him. And thus we see that the Spirit of the Lord began to withdraw from the Nephites, because of the wickedness and hardness of their hearts. And thus we see that the Lord began to pour out his Spirit upon the Lamanites, because of their easiness and willingness to believe in his words" (Helaman 6:34–36).

Fourth, we must preach the gospel. As the last part of verse 37 indicates, "they did preach the word of God among the more wicked part of them, insomuch that this band of robbers was utterly destroyed from among the Lamanites" (Helaman 6:37; see also Alma 31:5). So much of the tribulation we face in this world originates when people willfully or ignorantly break God's commandments. Cecil B. DeMille, producer of the classic film *The Ten Commandments,* speaking at a Brigham Young University Commencement, warned us that "we cannot break the Ten Commandments. We can only break ourselves [and, I would add, those around us] against them."[29] That's why the Lamanites had success against the Gadianton robbers by preaching to them the word of God. If we wish to receive the blessings of eternity described in Revelation, we must resolve to enter into a partnership with Christ. John saw that the Saints of God overcame the red dragon "by the blood of the Lamb, and by the word of their testimony" (Revelation 12:11). Likewise, in his first epistle, John taught that "ye . . . have overcome . . . because greater is he that is in you, than he that is in the world" (1 John 4:4). Christ is the power into which we must tap if we are to overcome the forces of evil which we encounter. That's why the Lamanites were successful against the Gadianton robbers. They understood this principle and then put it into practice. As we encounter Satan's influence in either individuals or institutions in our society, we must also have the courage and conviction to draw on the power of Christ. As we do so we will, in a very real sense, participate in the great millennial and celestial scenes witnessed by John. What a wonderful message of comfort and hope!

Conclusion

The book of Revelation is a timeless masterpiece. Its message is primarily not about the end of the world but rather about the myriad of blessings God seeks to bestow upon his people. It is about what is possible when people turn to God, live his laws, and thus overcome Satan's influence. In all of John's writings, he is interested in showing that the forces of darkness will ultimately yield to the Light of the world. It is noticeable that when he describes the heavenly city that the Saints will inherit, he specifically notes that "there shall be no night there; and they need no candle, neither light of the sun; for the Lord God giveth them light: and they shall reign for ever and ever" (Revelation 22:5). Although Revelation concentrates on the cosmic battle, we should be aware that, as one scholar wrote, "The battle between good and evil takes place not only in the arena of history but also in human hearts."[30] Therefore, the message of hope and comfort expressed in Revelation also provides valid lessons for us during our individual struggles with Satan's influence. Mortality is about learning to deal with tribulations of every nature. But the promise of Revelation is the same as that given to the Prophet Joseph: "Ye cannot behold with your natural eyes, for the present time, the design of your God concerning those things which shall come hereafter, and the glory which shall follow after much tribulation. For after much tribulation come the blessings. Wherefore the day cometh that ye shall be crowned with much glory; the hour is not yet, but is nigh at hand" (D&C 58:3–4).

Notes

1. In Revelation, John does not use tribulation to denote the normal characteristics of mortality such as sickness, accident or death, but rather to denote unfavorable circumstances that arise from Satan's influence. In this paper I do likewise. We should not try to place all tragedies at Satan's door.

2. The Prophet Joseph Smith indicated the seriousness of betraying the Brethren. "O ye Twelve! and all Saints! profit by this important Key—that in all your trials, troubles, temptations, afflictions, bonds, imprisonments and death see to it, that you do not betray heaven; that you do not betray Jesus Christ; that you do not betray the brethren. . . . Yea, in all your kicking and flounderings, see to it that you do not this thing, lest innocent blood be found upon your skirts, and you go down to hell. All other sins are not to be compared to sinning against the Holy

Ghost, and proving a traitor to the brethren." *Teachings of the Prophet Joseph Smith,* sel. Joseph Fielding Smith (Salt Lake City: Deseret Book, 1976), 156.

3. Raymond E. Brown, *The Epistles of John,* vol. 30 in *The Anchor Bible,* ed. William Foxwell Albright and David Noel Freedman (Garden City: Doubleday, 1982), 718.

4. Walter Bauer, *A Greek-English Lexicon of the New Testament and Other Early Christian Literature,* trans. William F. Arndt and F. Wilbur Gingrich (Chicago: University of Chicago Press, 1957), 870.

5. Bauer, *Greek-English Lexicon,* 414.

6. Suetonius writes: "Since the Jews constantly made disturbances at the instigation of Chrestus, he expelled them from Rome." *Claudius,* 25, in Loeb Classical Library, trans. J. C. Rolfe (Cambridge: Harvard University Press, 1979), 53. Here "Chrestus" is generally understood as "Christ."

7. See also Suetonius (*Nero,* 16) and Sulpicius Severus (*Chronicle,* 2.29), in C. K. Barrett, ed., *The New Testament Background: Writings from Ancient Greece and the Roman Empire That Illuminate Christian Origins* (San Francisco: Harper, 1989), 17. Both discuss Nero's persecution of the Christians.

8. *Ante-Nicene Fathers,* ed. Alexander Roberts and James Donaldson (Grand Rapids, Mich.: Eerdmans, 1993), 560. Not everyone accepts Irenaeus' account at face value. Some wish to give it a date before A.D. 70. See, for example, Philip Edgcumbe Hughes, *The Book of the Revelation: A Commentary* (Grand Rapids, Mich.: Eerdmans, 1990), 10; and J. Massyngberde Ford, *Revelation,* vol. 38 in *The Anchor Bible,* 4. Nevertheless, John's use of Babylon as a symbol for Rome correlates with Jewish practices that became popular after the destruction of the temple. That would argue for a date after A.D. 70.

9. Tertullian, *Apology,* in Roberts and Donaldson, eds., *Ante-Nicene Fathers,* trans. A. Cleveland Coxe, 22.

10. Eusebius, *The History of the Church from Christ to Constantine,* trans. G. A. Williamson (London: Penguin Books, 1965), 3.17–20.

11. Leonard L. Thompson, *The Book of Revelation: Apocalypse and Empire* (New York: Oxford University Press, 1990), 95–115.

12. Pliny, *Letters,* 2 vols., in Loeb Classical Library, trans. William Melmoth, rev. W. M. L. Hutchinson (Cambridge: Harvard University Press, 1968), 2:403.

13. For more detailed outlines see Richard D. Draper, *Opening the Seven Seals* (Salt Lake City: Deseret Book, 1991), 249–51, or Wilfrid J. Harrington, *Revelation,* vol. 16 of *Sacra Pagina Series,* ed. Daniel J. Harrington (Collegeville, Minn.: Liturgical Press, 1993), 17–23.

14. Harrington, *Revelation,* 17.

15. Joseph Smith interprets the twenty-four elders as elders from the seven churches who "had been faithful in the work of the ministry and were dead" (D&C 77:5) and describes the beasts as "figurative expressions . . . describing heaven, the paradise of God, the happiness of man, and of beasts, and of creeping things, and of the fowls of the air" (D&C 77:2).

16. Harrington, *Revelation,* 79; Draper, *Opening the Seven Seals,* 45.

17. *Theological Dictionary of the New Testament,* 10 vols., ed. Gerhard Kittel, trans. Geoffrey W. Bromiley (Grand Rapids, Mich.: Eerdmans, 1967), 942.

18. Harrington, *Revelation,* 186–87, 942. For an explanation of the translation here as "bright white" rather than "luminous" or simply "bright" see *Theological Dictionary of the New Testament,* 4:27.

19. Hughes, *Book of Revelation,* 46.

20. Bruce H. Porter and Stephen D. Ricks, "Names in Antiquity: Old, New, and Hidden," in *By Study and Also by Faith: Essays in Honor of Hugh W. Nibley,* 2 vols., ed. John M. Lundquist and Stephen D. Ricks (Salt Lake City: Deseret Book, 1990), 1:504–7.

21. Porter and Ricks, "Names in Antiquity," 510.

22. Bruce R. McConkie, *Mormon Doctrine,* 2d ed. (Salt Lake City: Bookcraft, 1979), 237.

23. Bruce R. McConkie, *Doctrinal New Testament Commentary,* 3 vols. (Salt Lake City: Bookcraft, 1965–73), 3:458.

24. McConkie, *Doctrinal New Testament Commentary,* 3:567.

25. See Harrington, *Revelation,* 45; Hughes, *Book of Revelation,* 25.

26. Joseph Smith, *History of The Church of Jesus Christ of Latter-day Saints,* ed. B. H. Roberts, 2d ed. rev., 7 vols. (Salt Lake City: The Church of Jesus Christ of Latter-day Saints, 1932–51), 5:556.

27. Neal A. Maxwell, *Ensign,* May 1997, 11.

28. Edmund Burke, "Thoughts on the Cause of the Present Discontents," in *The Writings & Speeches of Edmund Burke,* 12 vols. (Boston: Little, Brown, 1901), 1:526. Probably the more famous saying is "The only thing necessary for the triumph of evil is for good men to do nothing" which has been attributed to Burke but, as yet, has not been found among his writings. See *Familiar Quotations: A Collection of Passages, Phrases and Proverbs Traced to Their Sources in Ancient and Modern Literature,* ed. Emily Morison Beck, 15th ed. (Boston: Little, Brown, 1980), ix.

29. Cecil B. DeMille, "Commencement Address," delivered at Brigham Young University, Provo, 31 May 1957; in *Brigham Young University Bulletin,* vol. 54, no. 17 (15 June 1957), 5.

30. Arthur W. Wainwright, *Mysterious Apocalypse: Interpreting the Book of Revelation* (Nashville: Abingdon Press, 1993), 203.

CHAPTER TWENTY

JEWISH HOLY DAYS AND THE TESTIMONY OF CHRIST

DAVID M. WHITCHURCH

The Gospel of St. John has been called by some "the greatest book in the world."[1] Even though for Latter-day Saints such a statement mostly typifies the Book of Mormon, the value and importance of The Testimony of St. John (as it is titled in the Joseph Smith Translation) should not be underestimated.[2] The fourth Gospel manifests its worth through a wealth of knowledge and insight into the Savior and his divine calling. John clearly states that the purpose for writing his Gospel is that his readers "might believe that Jesus is the Christ, the Son of God; and that believing [they] might have life through his name" (John 20:31). It is evident that John furnishes frequent and compelling testimony that Jesus is the "Anointed One" sent by the Father to redeem humankind from their fallen state.

The Book of Mormon contributes valuable insight into understanding the writings of ancient prophets. Nephi taught that the words of Isaiah were "hard for many of [his] people to understand; for they know not concerning the manner of prophesying among the Jews. . . . And there is none other people that understand the things which were spoken unto the Jews like unto them, *save it be that they are taught after the manner of the things of the Jews*" (2 Nephi 25:1, 5; emphasis added). Extending Nephi's admonition regarding Isaiah's writings to those of other ancient prophets, including John, provides a sound foundation upon which to work. The historical background of St. John, chapters 5 through 10, in light of Jewish custom, culture,

David M. Whitchurch is an associate professor of ancient scripture at Brigham Young University.

and tradition as it existed during the time of Jesus, including weekly synagogue scripture readings, known as Jewish lectionary, and the applicable Jewish feasts and holy days are important building blocks in that foundation.

HISTORICAL SIGNIFICANCE OF ST. JOHN

Upon careful examination of the fourth Gospel, it becomes evident that John is well grounded in the writings of the Old Testament. John combines scriptures from Exodus, Deuteronomy, Judges, Isaiah, Zechariah, Ezekiel, and Psalms with his own writings to bear a solemn witness of Jesus' divinity.[3] Evidence argues favorably that John referred to various versions of the Old Testament, including the Septuagint (the Greek version of the Old Testament), the Masoretic Text (the traditional text from which the King James Version was translated), and the Palestinian Targum (local Aramaic translations).[4]

John's writings also reveal a strong cultural, historical, and geographical attachment to the Holy Land. The disciple "whom Jesus loved" (see John 13:23; 20:2; 21:7, 20) demonstrates an intimate knowledge of Jewish holy days, including the Sabbath,[5] Passover,[6] the Feast of Tabernacles,[7] and the Feast of Dedication.[8] He regularly refers to such Jewish rituals as purification (see John 3:25; 11:55), marriage customs (see John 2:1–10); and burial (see John 11:38, 44; 19:31, 40). John displays a vivid knowledge of topography as he talks about going down from Cana to Capernaum and about Jacob's well being deep (see John 4:11). Lastly, he identifies such places as Ephraim (see John 11:54), Aenon (see John 3:23), Mount Gerizim (see John 4:20), Jerusalem (see John 5:1), Cedron (see John 18:1), Bethesda (see John 5:2), Siloam (see John 9:7), and Golgotha (see John 19:17) in a manner consistent with one who has firsthand knowledge of the region. It becomes evident that the more we increase our knowledge of the meridian-day culture, customs, and traditions of the Holy Land, the more likely it becomes that the scriptures will unveil to us their oft-veiled testimony that "Jesus is the Christ, the Son of God; and that believing [we] might have life through his name" (John 20:31).

THE JEWISH LECTIONARY

Public reading of the scriptures dates at least as far back as the time of Moses. Every seven years during the Feast of Tabernacles Moses commanded Israelite men, women, and children, and people not of Israel who lived among God's covenant people to appear before the Lord and "read [the law of God] before all Israel in their hearing" (Deuteronomy 31:11). Near the end of Old Testament times, the people were also reminded of the importance of public scripture reading by Ezra.[9]

Although it cannot be determined for certain when weekly readings of the scriptures began, evidence suggests that the Septuagint was compiled, in part, for the purpose of regular public readings (called lections) in the Jewish synagogues.[10] If that is true, then it would appear that at least by the first half of the third century before Christ, weekly lections were in use.

During the tannaitic period,[11] which includes the time of Christ, the Law had been divided into sections for systematic public readings. This weekly reading, frequently referred to as the Jewish lectionary, meant that on any given Sabbath, a specific scriptural text would be read during synagogue service.[12] The scriptural passages used for these readings in the synagogue came from the Pentateuch, or five books of Moses (*Torah*), with additional readings taken from the writings of the prophets (*Nevi'im*)[13] or the book of Psalms (*Tehillim*). Many have suggested that the reading of Isaiah 61:1–2 by Jesus in the synagogue at Nazareth is evidence of such a practice (see Luke 4:16–21).[14]

Aileen Guilding, in her study, *The Fourth Gospel and Jewish Worship,* maintains that during the time of Jesus textual passages were set up and rotated on a three-year, or triennial, cycle.[15] She contends that many of Jesus' major discourses followed on the heels of an Old Testament Sabbath lection.[16] A prime example of Dr. Guilding's thesis can be seen by examining Jesus' discourse on the bread of life (see John 6). John specifically states that it took place near the time of Passover (see John 6:4). According to Guilding, the three-year synagogical lections near Passover were as follows:

Year 1. Genesis 1–8, with Genesis 2–3 being read on the Sabbaths closest to the feast.

Year 2. Exodus 11–16, with Exodus 16 being read about four weeks after the feast.

Year 3. Numbers 6–14, with Numbers 11 being read on the second Sabbath after the feast.[17]

Knowing that the Savior's audience in John 6 had likely heard at least one of these lections gives us tremendous insight into this message of the Master Teacher. For example, John 6 reflects a theme centered on Exodus 16, the lection of Year 2; yet, it also echoes the lections of the other two years. Some parallels emerge between John 6, Numbers 11, and Genesis 3—the latter centering on the tree of knowledge of good and evil in the Garden of Eden.[18]

When Genesis 3 is compared with Numbers 11 an interesting theme emerges. For example, in the book of Numbers, Moses tells of Israel's contempt for manna. The people openly complain for want of "flesh" to eat. The message and potential application is sobering: those who reject blessings sent from God will be "driven" out of his presence or destroyed if they do not repent. History provides multiple examples of this truth, including Adam and Eve's removal from the Garden of Eden, ancient Israel who provoked God while in the wilderness, as well as many of the Jews to whom Jesus delivered his discourse on the bread of life[19] (see John 6:66).

From such comparisons it seems possible that studying the Jewish lectionary can powerfully augment our understanding of the Savior's teachings. Certainly, a strong case has been made for the bread of life discourse in John 6. As good as it appears at the outset, however, Guilding's supposition has been subjected to sharp criticism.[20] Most scholars agree that weekly Sabbath readings from the Old Testament were in place at the time of Jesus but, to date, no universal reading schedule has been determined.[21] Estimates for completing a reading cycle of the scriptures range from yearly (thought to be used in the region of ancient Babylon) to upward of three and a half years (thought to be used in ancient Palestine). There is also disagreement as to the time of year the reading cycle began. Without this information it becomes difficult to make definitive statements regarding which Old Testament readings may have coincided with Jesus' discourses.

Even though at present it cannot be determined which scriptural texts coincide with a given Sabbath, two conclusions may be drawn from studying the Jewish lectionary. First, assuming that the general populace participated in Sabbath synagogue services at the time of Jesus, most of Jesus' audiences would be well versed in Old Testament scriptures.[22] This meant that as Jesus spoke he could readily make allusions to Old Testament passages in ways that did not demand explanation. Therefore, as we study the teachings and discourses of the Savior, we should familiarize ourselves with the Old Testament and look for the connections and associations they have with the Gospels. Jesus himself bore solemn witness regarding the importance of the Old Testament when he said, "They are they which testify of me."[23] Second, even though scriptural passages from the Sabbath day lections cannot be identified, there is widespread agreement that specific readings are associated with the Jewish feasts and festivals.[24] That allows students the opportunity to pursue careful scripture analysis between Jesus' discourses delivered during feast days and their affiliated Old Testament scriptures.

JEWISH SABBATHS, FEASTS, AND HOLY DAYS

John 5 through 10 includes accounts of the Sabbath, the Passover (with its associated Feast of Unleavened Bread), the Feast of Tabernacles, and the Feast of Dedication.

Chapter 5: The Sabbath. Jesus declares that there can be no Sabbath rest for him because, as the Son of God, he must continue to exercise the powers of life and judgment entrusted to him by the Father.

Chapter 6: The Passover and the Feast of Unleavened Bread. Jesus uses the multiplying of bread as a means to teach that he is the true bread of life who has come down from heaven. His flesh and blood will replace the manna of the Passover of the Exodus.

Chapters 7 through 9: The Feast of Tabernacles. The ceremonies of water and light associated with this feast symbolically represent Jesus, who is the true source of living water and light.

Chapter 10: The Feast of Dedication (also known as the Feast of Lights, or Hanukkah). The Feast of Dedication recalls the Maccabean dedication of the temple and its altar. Jesus, through his discourse of the Good Shepherd, proclaims that he is the one who has truly been consecrated by God.

The extensive amount of information related to these festivals cannot all be discussed here. Instead, the primary focus will be with the rituals and practices as they relate to the discourses of the Master Teacher.

JOHN 5: THE SABBATH

John 5 begins by stating that Jesus went to Jerusalem during a feast. Many have speculated about what feast he was attending; however, John never provides the information necessary to make a positive determination.[25] John may have purposely left out this information because it was not pertinent to his message. Instead, by simply mentioning Jesus was attending a feast, he lets his audience know why the Savior left Galilee, and, more importantly, lets them know that a feast in Jerusalem meant the city and temple would be filled to capacity with people from throughout the region.

The cardinal message and conflict in John 5 revolve around keeping the Sabbath day holy. To fully appreciate this chapter, it is necessary to understand the Jewish Sabbath. The institution of the Sabbath dates from the beginning of the earth's creation. Following the Creation account, the scriptures remain silent regarding the Sabbath until the Israelite exodus.[26] Thereafter, the importance of the Sabbath manifests itself throughout holy writ. Many of the Old Testament prophets, such as Isaiah, Jeremiah, Ezekiel, and Nehemiah, teach and, at times, condemn God's people for desecrating this holy day.[27] Of all the special days identified in the scriptures, the Sabbath is the only one embraced within the Decalogue (see Exodus 20:8–11).

The Jewish commitment and determination to keep the Sabbath day holy can be readily seen throughout rabbinic literature.[28] The keeping of the Sabbath was of such import that a person who publicly desecrated this most holy day was treated as an idolater.[29] Israel was commanded to kill those who failed to comply with God's law. The precedent for such an act came from Jehovah himself, who commanded that the man who gathered sticks on the Sabbath must "be surely put to death" by stoning at the hands of all Israel (see Numbers 15:35).

Upon the death of Malachi and other Old Testament prophets, the interpretation of scripture was taken up by individuals of religious and social influence who lacked the prophetic mantle. Scribes, Pharisees, Sadducees, and the like began to expound on Jewish law. Over time, the Jewish leadership "elaborated from the command of Moses, a vast array of prohibitions and injunctions, covering the whole of social, individual, and public life, and carried it to the extreme of ridiculous caricature."[30] The *Mishnah* itself states that "the laws of forbidden work on the Sabbath are as mountains hanging by a hair."[31] In other words, actual Sabbath laws as revealed in scripture are minuscule compared to the interpretations of those laws.

Thus, it is not surprising that the Savior confronts the Jewish leadership on several occasions regarding Sabbath prohibitions.[32] A prime example is found in the story of the man healed at the Pool of Bethesda (see John 5). After healing the man of a thirty-eight-year infirmity, Jesus commanded him to "rise, take up thy bed, and walk" (John 5:8). The rabbinical interpretation of this act identifies two ways in which the Savior was guilty of Sabbath-breaking. First, Jewish law prohibits the carrying of items from one domain to another on the Sabbath; and second, it specifically forbids the carrying of an empty bed.[33] This supposed abuse of the Sabbath led to a confrontation within the temple, just a stone's throw from the Pool of Bethesda (see John 5:10–15).

The pivotal point in the story comes when Jesus, the Lord of the Sabbath (the one who commanded Moses to put to death the man for gathering sticks), reminded his antagonists that not *all* work ends on the Sabbath. Jesus boldly reminded them that God is required to work on this most holy day, and that he, being God's Son, is only doing the work of his Father (see John 5:17). If the Jewish leaders were angry at Jesus for what they thought were Sabbath violations, this open declaration ignited profuse indignation. Not only had Jesus broken the Sabbath but, in their view, he had now made "himself equal with God" (John 5:18).

In light of the law of Moses, their anger and desire to kill Jesus seems understandable (see John 5:16); however, the Jewish leaders were so steeped in their own tradition that they failed to recognize the individual who had divine prerogative to countermand the excessive interpretations of that law. Ingeniously, Jesus reasoned from their own tradition to support his position. Jewish theologians recognized that God could not suspend all his work on the Sabbath, for if he did, "all nature and life would cease to exist."[34] Rabbi Johanan in the Babylonian Talmud states, "God has kept in His hand three keys that He entrusts to no agent: the key of the rain, the key of birth, and the key of the resurrection of the dead. And it was obvious to the rabbis that God used these keys even on the Sabbath."[35]

Beginning with John 5:19–22, Jesus explained that the work he did—granting life and judging those who have died—was done in imitation of his Father. Jesus' capacity to imitate the Father came because the Father empowered him, through the Atonement, to grant life to those who were in the realm of spiritual death, on account of sin. He demonstrated this life-giving power by finding the man in the temple and telling him, "Behold, thou art made whole [physically and spiritually]: sin no more, lest a worse thing come unto thee" (John 5:14). Thus, the only threat to real life was further sin. Similarly, Jesus became Judge because the Father had "committed all judgment unto the Son" (John 5:22). This judgment is to be taken in the Old Testament sense of vindicating the good (see Deuteronomy 32:36) and delivering him "from the deceitful and unjust man" (Psalm 43:1).[36]

For the remainder of the chapter, Jesus uses the law of witnesses given by Moses (see Deuteronomy 17:6; 19:15; Numbers 35:30) as a means to attest to his unbelieving audience that he is the Messiah (see John 5:32–39). Rather than the required two or three witnesses, Jesus provided a total of four: John the Baptist (see John 5:32–33), his own works and miracles (v. 36), the voice of the Father himself (v. 37),[37] and the holy scriptures (v. 39).[38] By so doing, Jesus powerfully and unmistakably offered to the Jewish leaders immutable evidence that he was the Son of God. Most important, he did it using the very law they claimed brought them salvation. Jesus concluded this confrontation by reminding the Jewish leaders: "For had ye believed Moses, ye would have believed me: for he wrote of me. But if ye believe not his writings, how shall ye believe my words?" (John 5:46–47).

John 6: The Passover and the Feast of Unleavened Bread

John stated that the setting for the bread of life discourse took place near the time of Passover (see John 6:4). This feast (lasting one day) and its closely affiliated counterpart, the Feast of Unleavened Bread (lasting seven days), are integral to the discourse (see Leviticus 23:4–6).[39] Celebration of Passover commemorates the Israelite escape from Egyptian bondage. This spring festival begins the fourteenth day of the Jewish month Nisan (also called Abib). Its name comes from the passage in Exodus in which Moses informs the children of Israel, "For the

Lord will pass through to smite the Egyptians; and when he seeth the blood upon the lintel, and on the two side posts, the Lord will pass over the door, and will not suffer the destroyer to come in unto your houses to smite you" (Exodus 12:23). The sacrificial lamb and shedding of blood saves Israel.

Prior to the destruction of the temple in A.D. 70, the Jews gathered in family groups to keep the Feast of Passover. Part of the feast included slaying a lamb, roasting it whole, eating it with unleavened bread, and drinking wine (see Exodus 12; Deuteronomy 16:1–8).[40] Josephus states that during the temple's destruction, nearly 1.2 million Jews were either killed or taken captive in Jerusalem. Furthermore, most of the people were not from the Holy City but had come for the Feast of Unleavened Bread.[41] Such large numbers traveling to Jerusalem suggests that people throughout the area thought about and prepared for weeks prior to the Passover and Unleavened Bread celebration.

John introduced Jesus' bread of life discourse by reminding his readers that Passover was "nigh" and then telling them about the miracle of feeding the five thousand near the shores of Galilee (see John 6:4–12). It is clear from the exchange of words between Jesus and his followers that more was going on than simply a free meal. This was evidenced in the people's attempt to take him by force to make him a king and to coerce Jesus to prove to them who he was by producing manna (see John 6:15, 25–31). Such actions result from an expectation that the Messiah would appear sometime during Passover and, once again, provide manna for his people.

According to rabbinic and aprocryphal sources, the association between Passover and manna developed during the Israelite conquest of Canaan.[42] The day prior to Israel's crossing of the Jordan was the fourteenth of Nisan. The following morning, after keeping the Feast of Passover, "the manna ceased" (Joshua 5:12). From this, "the expectation grew that the Messiah would come on Passover, and that the manna would begin to fall again on Passover."[43] The Old Testament lections read during Passover reminded Israel of the manna/Messiah relationship, along with other themes found throughout John 6, including the atoning blood of the lamb; escape from bondage; passage through the

Red Sea; King David's deliverance from his enemies; God's miraculous rescue of Jerusalem from the Assyrians; and prophecies
about "the stem of Jesse" (that is, the Christ) and how, in righteousness, he would usher in the millennial reign.[44]

After the feeding of the five thousand, certain participants concluded, "This is of a truth that prophet that should come into the
world" (John 6:14). The key to understanding the Savior's message is
to identify who "that prophet" is. The Old Testament, New
Testament, Book of Mormon, and Pearl of Great Price combine to
reveal the identity of "that prophet."[45] Moses clearly indicated that
at some future date a prophet would arise, similar to himself, who
would speak the word of God. Furthermore, when this prophet
appeared, the people would lack the faith, as Israel did in Moses'
day, to enter into Jehovah's presence (see Deuteronomy 18:15–16; Exodus
19:10–21).[46] This may explain why those who sought Jesus after his
return to Capernaum were so defensive and demanded a sign when
told that to be able to "work the works of God" they must "believe
on him whom [God] hath sent" (John 6:28–29). Thus, Jesus
unabashedly reminded them that they were the ones whom Moses
said would have the same lack of faith as their forefathers who cow-
ered at the thought of seeing Jehovah at Mount Horeb (Sinai).

Moses also foretold the consequences for those who refused to
hear the words of "that prophet": "I will raise them up a Prophet
from among their brethren, like unto thee, and will put my words in
his mouth; and he shall speak unto them all that I shall command
him. And it shall come to pass, that whosoever will not hearken unto
my words which he shall speak in my name, I will require it of him"
(Deuteronomy 18:18–19).

The importance of this Mosaic prophecy is evident throughout the
scriptures. Peter, after healing the lame man at the temple gate,
declared to an astonished audience that Jesus had come in fulfillment
of Moses' prophecy (see Acts 3:19–26). Other references regarding
"that prophet" were made by Stephen before his martyrdom (see Acts
7:37–38) and by the angel Moroni, who quoted to the Prophet
Joseph Smith Acts 3:22–23 and said, "That prophet was Christ"
(Joseph Smith–History 1:40). Nephi declared that "this prophet of
whom Moses spake was the Holy One of Israel" (1 Nephi 22:21).
Then, as if to add a final witness, the Savior himself said, "Behold, I

am he of whom Moses spake, saying: A prophet shall the Lord your God raise up unto you of your brethren, like unto me" (3 Nephi 20:23).

With such powerful declarations regarding "that prophet," certainly, the people's would-be attempt to make Jesus king, demonstrated at least a limited understanding of Moses' prophecy. After he successfully eluded the people for the night, Jesus went to the synagogue at Capernaum (see John 6:15, 22–26, 59). From the ensuing discussion, it becomes apparent that many of the Jews, like their forefathers (see Deuteronomy 18:15–16), were unwilling to comply with the requirements mandated by "that prophet." Indeed, those at the synagogue in Capernaum were more interested in signs and food than in partaking of the nourishment that only the incarnate Redeemer of Israel could provide (see John 6:27–31).

Furthermore, as Jesus declared he was the "living" Passover bread sent from heaven (John 6:51), he bluntly gave notice that if they failed to partake of his flesh and blood, they had no life in them (see John 6:53). Elder James E. Talmage taught that the Jews clearly understood the Savior's intended message: "The utterances to which they objected were far more readily understood by them than they are by us on first reading; for the representation of the law and of truth in general as bread, and the acceptance thereof as a process of eating and drinking, were figures in every-day use by the rabbis of that time. Their failure to comprehend the symbolism of Christ's doctrine was an act of will, not the natural consequence of innocent ignorance."[47]

The Passover meal, with its attendant symbols, became the perfect opportunity for the Master Teacher to testify that "that prophet" of whom Moses prophesied had indeed come to deliver Israel from bondage. When Jesus stated, "Except ye eat the flesh of the Son of man, and drink his blood, ye have no life in you. Whoso eateth my flesh, and drinketh my blood, hath eternal life; and I will raise him up at the last day" (John 6:53–54), he was clearly giving the people an opportunity to choose. As families anticipated and prepared for Passover, the connection between the soon-to-be celebration with its slaying and roasting of the sacrificial lamb, drinking of wine, and eating of unleavened bread with "that prophet," must have been difficult to miss. Yet, because many could not "believe on him whom

[God had] sent" (John 6:29), John told us, "From that time many of his disciples went back, and walked no more with him" (John 6:66).

JOHN 7–9: THE FEAST OF TABERNACLES

Following the bread of life discourse, Jesus could no longer freely travel throughout the Holy Land. Even those in distant Jerusalem, the very heart of Judaism, "sought to kill him" (John 7:1). Yet, Jesus, knowing the risks, would use the upcoming Feast of Tabernacles to once again bear powerful witness of his divine mission. With familial pressure to leave for the feast, the Savior waited, choosing to arrive at mid-festival (see John 7:3–9). His reputation preceded him, for those at the feast already were debating just who this Jesus really was (see vv. 10–13). The Redeemer of mankind would soon give them the opportunity to learn for themselves.

The Feast of Tabernacles is the last of three designated feasts that all males were required to attend (see Deuteronomy 16:16). It began on the fifteenthth day of the seventh month, called Tishri (September or October). The book of Leviticus speaks of a seven-day celebration, with an additional eighth day set aside as a solemn assembly (see Leviticus 23:34–36). This autumnal feast received the name *Tabernacles,* the English rendering of *Sukkot* ("booths"), because people celebrated it out-of-doors in booths made of tree branches. The dwelling in booths was to remind Israel of the care and protection God provided while they journeyed to the promised land (see Deuteronomy 8:7–18).

According to the *Encyclopedia Judaica,* "Tabernacles was from ancient times one of the most important feasts of the Israelites and is therefore called *'the feast of the Lord.'"*[48] Elder Bruce R. McConkie says of this feast, "In the full sense, it is the Feast of Jehovah, the one Mosaic celebration which, as part of the restitution of all things, shall be restored when Jehovah comes to reign personally upon the earth for a thousand years."[49]

The Feast of Tabernacles is celebrated at a unique juncture of harvesting in the Holy Land. Farmers have finished the "in-gathering" of grapes, figs, pomegranates, and dates, but they still look forward to the picking and processing of olives. It is a time of tremendous rejoicing as an agrarian society offers thanks for what they have received and, at the same time, looks forward with anticipation and prayer for the much-needed cycle of rain (symbolizing living water) to once again bring the earth back to life.[50] It is interesting to contemplate the significance of the Feast of Tabernacles in relation to the day of Pentecost (Acts 2:1–13). Even though Pentecost was months away, Jesus' coming to the temple was an important part of the gathering before he concluded his mortal ministry. The soon-to-be olive harvest is a reminder to us all that the gathering of olives (a symbol for the people of Israel; see Jacob 5), and the processing of olive oil (oil being a symbol of the Holy Spirit; see D&C 45:56–57) is an important part of the gospel. During the coming year, the Savior would culminate his mortal ministry by harvesting the righteous in preparation for their receiving the gift of the Holy Ghost. The allegory of the olive tree (see Jacob 5) makes it clear that the gathering of God's covenant people will continue until our Savior once again returns to his temple at the conclusion of the harvest.

Two aspects of the Feast of Tabernacles are critical to the Savior's proclaimed testimony.[51] The first deals with a daily water libation ceremony, which takes place throughout the feast. The *Mishnah* states that a priest carrying a golden pitcher capable of holding three "logs" (one and one-half pints) takes water from the Pool of Siloam (a Hebrew word meaning "sent"), approximately a half-mile distant, and carries it to the sacred altar of sacrifice at the temple. It is timed so that upon its arrival, a trumpet sounds announcing the priest, who then enters the Water Gate, giving him direct access to the Court of the Priests and the sacred altar. Once there, he is greeted by another priest, who holds in his hands a container of wine. Together, they ascend the ramp to the altar and pour the water and wine libations into designated funnels, which empty onto the sacrificial altar.[52] The *Mishnah* asserts that each day, upon conclusion of the liquid libations, the priests "went in procession a single time around the Altar, saying, *Save now, we beseech thee, O Lord! We beseech thee, O Lord, send now prosperity.* [Psalm 118:25.] . . . But on that day [the seventh day of the feast] they went in procession seven times around the Altar" (*Sukkah* 4.5).[53] This seventh day, known as *Hoshana Rabba* or "the Great *hoshana*," exemplifies Israel's need and reliance upon Jehovah. The word *hoshana* means "Save, I pray!" or "Save, now!"

Each day during the feast, the *Hallel* (see Psalms 113 to 118) is chanted by the priests while the people who gather at the temple carry in their hands palm branches and a lemon-like fruit, called a citron, to remind them of their wanderings in the wilderness and the bountiful harvest they received when they were brought to the promised land.

The second aspect of the feast related to the Savior's testimony followed the ceremony of the pouring of the water. At the close of the first festival-day,[54] the priests descended fifteen stairs from their court to the Court of the Women. Located in this court were "golden candlesticks . . . with four golden bowls on the top of them," which, according to the Talmud, rose fifty cubits in height (nearly seventy-three feet). There were "four ladders to each candlestick," which four priestly youths climbed to pour a total of 120 "logs" of oil into the bowls (approximately ten gallons) (*Sukkah* 5.2).[55]

Upon the lighting of the candlesticks, the *Mishnah* states, "there was not a courtyard in Jerusalem that did not reflect the light" (*Sukkah* 5.3). Righteous men then danced before the candlesticks with torches in hand, singing songs of praise. While, at the same time, Levites stood on the fifteen steps playing "harps, lyres, cymbals and trumpets and instruments of music" (*Sukkah* 5.4). Two priests began at the top of the stairs with trumpets in hand. At predetermined places they sounded the trumpet, making three blasts at each stop, until they reached the eastern gate of the Court of the Women, called Beautiful (see Acts 3:2). Once there, they turned about and faced the temple and said, "Our fathers when they were in this place turned with their backs toward the Temple of the Lord and their faces toward the east, and they worshipped the sun toward the east; but *as for us, our eyes are turned toward the Lord*" (*Sukkah* 5.4; emphasis added). All energy was focused on the people's need for and reliance upon Jehovah. The dancing, rejoicing, and spiritual jubilation lasted through the night.[56]

The eighth day of the Feast of Tabernacles was a solemn assembly, and the people were again commanded to "do no servile work therein" (Numbers 29:35). This holy day was considered by the rabbis as a separate festival. It was a memorial dedicated to scripture study and special prayer for rain[57] (see Zechariah 10:1).

It should be noted that the Feast of Tabernacles came just five days after the Day of Atonement (*Yom Kippur*). On this day of reconciliation, the high priest alone was required to "make an atonement" for the holy sanctuary, tabernacle, altar, priests, and people (see Leviticus 16:33). The purpose of this atonement was to prepare a congregation for the upcoming feast, wherein "a people at peace with God might rejoice before Him in the blessing with which He had crowned the year."[58]

To fully appreciate the testimony of Jesus, one must combine the rituals surrounding the feast with the Jewish lections read during the feast. Besides reciting the Mosaic instructions regarding the Feast of Tabernacles (Numbers 7:1–8:4), two additional scriptural events were recounted, one past and one future. The recitation of the past remembered the dedication of Solomon's Temple, which took place during the Feast of Tabernacles. Upon placement of the ark of the covenant in the Holy of Holies, a thick cloud of "glory . . . filled the house of the Lord [Jehovah]. Then spake Solomon, . . . *I have surely built thee an house to dwell in, a settled place for thee to abide in for ever*" (1 Kings 8:11–13; emphasis added). The ensuing dedication linked the arrival of Jehovah at the Feast of Tabernacles.

The other important event associated with and read during the feast anticipated Jehovah's return and "in-gathering" of his people. Zechariah prophesied of Jehovah's triumphant return and reign as king over all the earth (see Zechariah 14:1–9). Even though only Zechariah 14 is read as a feast lection, prophecies such as the "King" coming to Jerusalem, "lowly, and riding upon an ass" (Zechariah 9:9) and "they shall look upon me whom they have pierced" (Zechariah 12:10) must surely be recognized as Messianic. A statement associated with Abba bar Kahana, a fourth century rabbi, says that the Feast of Tabernacles "*holds within itself the promise of the Messiah.*"[59]

With this background in place, the teachings of Jesus become clearer. The Savior began his message at the Feast of Tabernacles by identifying himself as the one sent from God (see John 7:18). He told his audience that if they truly want to know the truth of his doctrine, they must "do his will" (John 7:17) and keep the law of Moses (see John 7:19). Jesus iterates numerous times that he is *sent* from his Father.[61] The Greek word for most occurrences of "sent" in John's writings is *pempo*. It differs from the word "sent" (*apostello*) found in John 7:29. In this passage, Jesus uses the same term that is used to identify the Pool of *Siloam* (see John 9:7). Both words, *pempo* and *apostello,* mean "sent" but a distinction is typically made of the latter when it is God who does the commissioning and/or sending.[62] Just as the "living water" retrieved from the Pool of Siloam was "sent" (*apostello;* see John 9:7) from God, Jesus, too, was "sent" (*apostello*) by the Father to bring life to those who abide in the true law of Moses. It should be noted that "living water" by definition is water that is sent directly from God (such as rain water sent from heaven or spring water flowing from the earth).[63] The significance of the different meanings to the word *sent* is evident in the response made by the Jewish leadership. Upon making the bold pronouncement, "I am from him, and he hath *sent [apostello]* me" (see John 7:29; emphasis added), the Jewish leadership were so infuriated that, "they sought to take him," (John 7:30) presumably to put him to death, but were unable to do so because his "hour was not yet come" (7:30).

The confusion and blindness of the people (see John 7:40–52) provide an ongoing theme throughout the following chapters. On the last day of the feast, Jesus used the background of the water-libation ceremony to proclaim that he was *the* source of water *sent* from God and that "if any man thirst, let him come unto me, and drink" (John 7:37). This declaration echoed the prophetic voice of Zechariah, which was read during the feast to remind the people that when Jehovah returns "living waters shall go out from Jerusalem. . . . And the Lord shall be king over all the earth" (Zechariah 14:8–9).

The day after Jesus' declaration, he arrived at the temple early in the morning (see John 8:2). It is difficult to determine with certainty, but it is conceivable that the celebration from the lighting of the candelabra was either continuing or just concluding. Speaking in the treasury (see John 8:20) located in the Court of the Women, Jesus once again took the opportunity to teach and testify to the people of his divine role. He publicly proclaimed, "I am the light of the world [and] he that followeth me shall not walk in darkness, but shall have the light of life" (John 8:12).

The Pharisees immediately challenged his testimony, claiming that if his testimony were true he would not bear record of himself (see John 8:13). The resulting confrontation furnished Jesus an opportunity to use the imagery that he is "living water" sent from God. He said, "If God were your Father, ye would love me: for I proceeded forth and came from God; neither came I of myself, but he *sent* [*apostello*] me" (John 8:42). The disputation concluded with Jesus publicly and unmistakably announcing, "Before Abraham was, I AM" (John 8:58). A clear statement that he was Jehovah *sent* from God to the children of Israel. The "I AM" expression replicates the Septuagint, or Greek, version of the Old Testament, in which Jehovah directs Moses to tell the children of Israel, "I AM hath *sent* me unto you" (Exodus 3:14; emphasis added). The response from the Jewish leaders led to yet another attempt to take Jesus' life (see John 8:59).

Jesus now confirmed his identify by *doing* (see John 7:17) that which only one *sent* from God could do—he opened the eyes of a man blind from birth.[62] He did this by sending the man to "the pool of Siloam, (which is by interpretation, Sent.)" (John 9:7). The symbolism speaks for itself. Jesus is *the* source of living water *sent* from God to open the eyes of the blind through sacrifice on the sacred altar of fire.

Significantly, the healing of the blind man once again occurs on a Sabbath day (see John 5; 9:14). The *Mishnah* identifies kneading as one of thirty-nine types of work forbidden on this day (*Mishnah Sabbath* 7.2). Because Jesus "kneaded" the soil to make clay with which to anoint the eyes of the blind man, he was, according to rabbinical interpretation, in violation of the Sabbath (see John 9:11–16). The Master Teacher used this opportune time to demonstrate the "ingathering" process that heals those who are blind but believe (see John 9:35–38) but not those who say they see but in truth are blind (see vv. 40–41).

JOHN 10: THE FEAST OF DEDICATION

A subtle but important transition occurs between the Feast of Tabernacles (see John 7–9) and the Feast of Dedication (see John 10). The casual reader might assume that Jesus began his discourse of the Good Shepherd (see John 10:1) immediately after his indictment of the Pharisees at the conclusion of the Feast of Tabernacles (see John 9:40–41), but a careful reading clearly shows nearly three months had passed, fall had given way to winter, and the Feast of Dedication was underway (see John 10:22).[63]

The Feast of Dedication celebrated an event that had its beginnings in 175 B.C. The Greco-Syrian king, Antiochus IV (Epiphanes), in an attempt to subjugate the Jews, pillaged the land of Judah and desecrated the holy temple by setting up an idol to Zeus and sacrificing swine upon the altar of God (see 1 Maccabees 1:21–63). Antiochus followed his destruction with a campaign to eradicate Judaism. Soldiers were sent throughout the land to force the Jews to submit to paganism. A pious priest named Mattathias and his sons stood firm and defied Syria. After Mattathias's death, his sons, with Judas Maccabeus at the lead, continued to wage a grass-roots rebellion that not only defeated Antiochus but eventually gained independence for the Jewish nation.

With the capture of Jerusalem, priests entered the temple, cleansed it, and replaced the desecrated altar with a new altar. On the 25th day, during the winter month of *Kislev,* in the year 164 B.C., the altar was dedicated (see 1 Maccabees 4:36–58). "Judas, and his brethren, and all the church of Israel decreed, that the day of the dedication of the altar should be kept in its season from year to year for eight days . . . with joy and gladness" (1 Maccabees 4:59). The name of this feast comes from the Hebrew word *Hanukkah,* which means "dedication" or "consecration."[64] Celebrations of Hanukkah prior to the destruction of the temple in A.D. 70 focused on the dedication of the altar of sacrifice and the cleansing of the temple.[65]

Flavius Josephus described the Feast of Dedication in his day (A.D. 37–100) as follows: "Now Judas [Maccabaeus] celebrated the festival of the restoration of the sacrifices of the temple for eight days; and omitted no sort of pleasures thereon: but he feasted them upon very rich and splendid sacrifices; and he honoured God, and delighted them, by hymns and psalms. . . . And from that time to this we celebrate this festival, and call it Lights."[66]

The celebration of Hanukkah has close ties to the Feast of Tabernacles. It likely began as a celebration commemorating the dedication of the altar, because the Feast of Tabernacles had been missed on account of the war. Thus, many parallels exist between the two feasts, including the eight-day celebration, the illumination of lights, the carrying of palm branches, the recitation of *Hallel* (Psalms 113 to 118), and a celebration of the renewal of daily sacrifices.[67] Both feasts are clearly modeled after the dedication of Solomon's Temple. The

Old Testament passages associated with and read during Hanukkah describe dedicating the house of God with sacrifice, feasting, thanksgiving, music, and singing.[68]

Of all the feasts identified by John, the Feast of Dedication has the least direct association with the Savior's message. Yet, the background of the feast gives some helpful clues. Throughout the book of John, the Savior used images and events as an aid to help teach and testify of his divine Sonship. For example, at the well in Samaria Jesus identified himself as living water (see John 4:14); after multiplying the loaves and fishes, he proclaimed that he was "living bread" (John 6:51); during the Feast of Tabernacles he testified that he was "the light of the world" (John 8:12); and while healing the man born blind, he again proclaimed that he was "the light of the world" (John 9:5). This pattern suggests that while Jesus "walked in the temple in Solomon's porch" (John 10:23) during the Feast of Dedication, he availed himself of another opportunity to testify of his divinity.

Solomon's Porch, located at the east end of the Temple Mount, sat directly in front of the temple. Its location provided ample opportunity to witness sheep being "shepherded" toward the temple proper and its sacred altar. As mentioned, the Feast of Dedication was a time of tremendous celebration and sacrifice. It seems reasonable to surmise that the bringing of sheep for temple sacrifice helped trigger Jesus' Good Shepherd discourse. If even a fraction of the number of sheep was used during the Feast of Dedication that was used during Solomon's dedication (120,000; see 1 Kings 8:63; 2 Chronicles 7:5), the scenario would provide an ideal teaching opportunity for the Savior.

The Old Testament frequently alludes to God as a shepherd.[69] Thus, Israel saw themselves as God's flock who were under his divine care and protection.[70] Although speculative, Aileen Guilding states that the Sabbath lections surrounding the Feast of Dedication "contain the theme of sheep and shepherds and of God the Shepherd of Israel."[71] Ezekiel 34 furnishes an excellent example of one of these lections. In it, Jehovah denounces the shepherds of Israel who have failed the flock. These shepherds are condemned for their cruelty, mismanagement, and scattering of his sheep (see Ezekiel 34:2–6). As the chapter progresses, Ezekiel describes how in time Jehovah will turn against these shepherds and seek out his sheep that have been scattered, and "will set up one shepherd over them, and he shall feed them, even my servant David; he shall feed them, and he shall be their shepherd. And I the Lord will be their God, and my servant David a prince among them" (Ezekiel 34:23–24).

The association between Ezekiel 34 and John 10 adds weight and meaning to the Savior's statement, "Other sheep I have, which are not of this fold" (John 10:16). True to Ezekiel's prophecy, the Jewish leadership had indeed brought about a spiritual scattering. This, of course, included those descended from Lehi, as well as other lost tribes and branches of Israel (see 3 Nephi 15:11–24). Jesus' testimony at the Feast of Dedication was that he was the "porter," or *gatekeeper* (John 10:3), "the door of the sheep" (v. 7), and "the good shepherd" (v. 14). Jesus, standing at the temple during a feast that commemorated the dedication of the altar of God, provided the ideal opportunity to remind his people that the altar of the temple stood as a symbol of atonement and that only he could ultimately bring "peace between Israel and their Father in Heaven."[72] Rather than accept his invitation to "hear [his] voice" and "follow [him]," however, the Jews (likely meaning the Jewish leaders) "took up stones again to stone him" (John 10:27, 31).

CONCLUSION

Nephi wrote that he labored diligently "to persuade [his] children, and also [his] brethren, to believe in Christ, and to be reconciled to God" (2 Nephi 25:23). He stated, "We talk of Christ, we rejoice in Christ, we preach of Christ, we prophesy of Christ, and we write according to our prophecies, that our children may know to what source they may look for a remission of their sins" (2 Nephi 25:26). Prophets throughout the ages have desired no more, and no less, than to bear this same witness. John's advantage in bearing this testimony came from his personal relationship with Christ and his eyewitness account of the Savior's own ingenious and self-proclaimed testimony that he was and is the "Anointed One" sent by the Father to redeem humankind.

Through careful examination of the Jewish rituals, customs, and traditions associated with the Sabbath and the Feasts of Passover, Tabernacles, and Dedication, John bore a fervent and powerful testimony that "Jesus is the Christ, the Son of God," in hopes that all who read and hear his message might believe and "have life through his name" (John 20:31). True life, then, comes only to those who know these truths. Our testimony of Jesus Christ is central to who and what we are as Latter-day Saints. As we increase our understanding and testimony of the Savior through scripture study, prayer, and hearing the word of God from our modern apostles and prophets, we can then use these truths to bless the lives of those around us.

NOTES

1. Merrill F. Unger, *The New Unger's Bible Dictionary*, ed. R. K. Harrison (Chicago: Moody Press, 1988), 700.

2. Bruce R. McConkie, *Doctrinal New Testament Commentary*, 3 vols. (Salt Lake City: Bookcraft, 1965–73), 1:65.

3. For example, John frequently refers to such Old Testament stories and prophets as the Creation (John 1:1–14), manna (6:31), water from the rock (7:38), the brass serpent (3:14), the tabernacle (references to "dwelt" and to pitching a tent imply the tabernacle, according to *Anchor Bible*, 38 vols. [New York: Doubleday, 1964–], 1:13–14), the law of Moses (1:17, 7:19, 22–23; 8:5, 9:28–29), the prophets (five from Isaiah, two from Zechariah; one from Ezekiel; the last part of Zechariah seems to lie behind John's reflections on the Feast of Tabernacles and on the stream of living water), and Psalms (John 2:17; 4:14; 10:34–35; 19:24, 29).

4. Raymond E. Brown, *The Gospel According to John I–XII*, 2 vols. (New York: Doubleday, 1966), 1:lxi.

5. See John 5:9–18; 7:22–23; 9:14–16; 19:31.

6. See John 6:4; 13:1; 18:28.

7. See John 7:2.

8. See John 10:22.

9. See Nehemiah 8:1–8.

10. *Encyclopedia Judaica*, 16 vols. (Jerusalem: Keter, 1974), 15:1246.

11. *Tannaim* is from the Aramaic *tanna*, which means "to repeat" or "learn." The time period ranges from circa 20 B.C. to the early part of the third century A.D. During this time the unwritten authoritative traditions were transmitted via oral repetition. See H. L. Strack and G. Stemberger, *Introduction to the Talmud and Midrash*, trans. Markus Bockmuehl (Edinburgh: T&T Clark,1991), 7.

12. *Encyclopedia Judaica*, 15:1247.

13. Unger, *Bible Dictionary*, 1297. The readings taken from the writings of the prophets were called *Haftarah*.

14. Brown, *Gospel According to John*, 2:277–78; Aileen Guilding, *The Fourth Gospel and Jewish Worship: A Study of the Relation of St. John's*

Gospel to the Ancient Jewish Lectionary System (London: Oxford University Press, 1960) 6–7; John L. Fowles, "The Jewish Lectionary and Book of Mormon Prophecy," *Journal of Mormon Studies*, ed. Stephen D. Ricks (Provo: Foundation for Ancient Research and Mormon Studies, vol. 3, no. 2 (Fall 1994), 118–22; Unger, *Bible Dictionary*, 1297.

15. Guilding, *Fourth Gospel and Jewish Worship*, 8–20.

16. Brown, *Gospel According to John I–XII*, 1:278–80.

17. Guilding, *Fourth Gospel and Jewish Worship*, 60–61; quoted in Brown, *Gospel According to John I–XII*, 1:279.

18. Some of the comparisons Guilding makes between Genesis and John 6 are as follows: "Gen. 3:3 repeats God's warning from Gen. 2:17: 'You shall not eat of the fruit of this tree . . . lest you die.' This may be contrasted with John 6:50: 'This is the bread that comes down from heaven that a man may eat it and never die.' Gen. 3:22 has God's decision to drive man out of the garden '. . . lest he put forth his hand and take also of the tree of life and eat and live forever.' This may be contrasted with the invitation to eat the bread of life of which John 6:51 says, 'If anyone eats this bread, he will live forever.' Gen. 3:24 'So he drove man out.' In John 6:37: 'Anyone who comes to me I will never drive out." Quoted in Brown, *Gospel According to John I–XII*, 1:279.

19. See Genesis 3:23–24; Exodus 19:17–24.

20. Strack and Stemberger, *Introduction to the Talmud and Midrash*, 263–64; Raymond E. Brown, "Book Review of Aileen Guilding, The Fourth Gospel and Jewish Worship," in *Catholic Biblical Quarterly*, 22 (1960): 460–61; J. Heinemann, "The Triennial Lectionary Cycle," *Journal of Jewish Studies*, 19 (1969): 41–48; Michael L. Klein, "Four Notes on the Triennial Cycle," *The Journal of Jewish Studies*, 32 (1981): 65–73.

21. Marc Bregman, "The Triennial Haftarot and the Perorations of the Midrashic Homilies," in *Journal of Jewish Studies*, 32 (1981): 74–84; Klein, "Four Notes on the Triennial Lectionary Cycle," 65–73; Heinemann, "Triennial Lectionary Cycle," 41–48; *Encyclopedia Judaica*, 15:1246, 1386.

22. This assumption seems quite likely. For example, Alfred Edersheim in his book *The Temple: Its Ministry and Services As They Were At the Time of Christ*, indicates that it was not necessary at the Feast of Tabernacles to read the entire law of Moses as commanded in Deuteronomy 31:10–13 because the "law as a whole [was] sufficiently known from the weekly prelections in the synagogues." (Grand Rapids, Mich.: Eerdmans, 1978) 286.

23. John 5:39; emphasis added.

24. Strack and Stemberger, *Introduction to the Talmud and Midrash*, 262–64.

25. J. Reuben Clark Jr. states that this is a Passover feast. *Our Lord of the Gospels* (Salt Lake City: Deseret Book, 1954) 221. Footnote 1*a* to John

5:1 in the LDS edition of the King James Version of the Bible reads, "The *Koine* Greek manuscripts of the Gospels (Byzantine) read 'the feast,' implicitly the Passover. . . . Some earlier manuscripts do not make this identification." Others such as Brown view this feast as possibly Pentecost or Passover (*Gospel According to John I–XII,* 1:206). Others, such as Guilding, identify it as either Pentecost or the Feast of the New Year, also called Rosh Hashanah (*Fourth Gospel and Jewish Worship,* 47).

26. God took six days to create the heavens and the earth, and on the seventh he ceased from his labors, looked upon what he had done, declared it good, and "rested" (Genesis 1:1–2:2). The word *rest* is used to translate the Hebrew verb *shavat,* meaning "to stop, cease, or desist." Thus, the name *Sabbath* (a noun) continually reminds the faithful that on this day they must "cease" from their weekly labors and worship the Lord. In commemoration of the Creation, God reminded his people at Mount Sinai that he had "blessed and sanctified" the seventh day, making it a day wherein "thou shalt not do any work" (Exodus 20:8–11). Furthermore, upon Israel's receiving manna, God commanded on the sixth day that his covenant people were to gather "twice as much bread" because the next day was the "holy sabbath unto the Lord" (Exodus 16:22–23). Today, Jews continue to honor the double gathering of manna, along with the prohibition against work, by placing two loaves of bread on the table for their Sabbath evening meal. See *Encyclopedia Judaica,* 14:566.

27. See Isaiah 58:13–14; Jeremiah 17:19–27; Ezekiel 20:20–24; 22:8; 44:24; Nehemiah 10:31; 13:15–22. Such admonitions continue through our modern prophets. For example, President Gordon B. Hinckley recently reemphasized the importance of keeping this most sacred day holy (*Ensign,* November 1997, 69).

28. For example, "If Israel keeps one Sabbath as it should be kept, the Messiah will come. The Sabbath is equal to all the other precepts of the Torah." During Jesus' day, Sabbath relevance can be viewed through the writings of Philo, a Jewish philosopher and scholar of Alexandria (20 B.C.–A.D. 50), who saw the Sabbath "as an opportunity for man to imitate his Creator who rested on the seventh day." Quoted in *Encyclopedia Judaica,* 14:562, 565.

29. *Encyclopedia Judaica,* 14:564.

30. Cunningham Geikie, *Life and Words of Christ,* ch. 38 (New York: Columbia, 1891), quoted in James E. Talmage, *Jesus the Christ* (Salt Lake City: Deseret Book, 1915), 215.

31. Quoted in *Encyclopedia Judaica,* 14:564. The word *Mishnah* is from the Hebrew and means "instruction." It is believed that the Mishnah are the oral laws given by God to Moses at Sinai. These collected traditions were collected and compiled circa A.D. 200. Today, they make up a considerable portion of the Talmud.

32. See Matthew 12:1–13; Mark 2:23–28; Luke 6:1–11; 13:10–17; 14:1–6; John 5:9–18; 7:22–24; 9:14–16.

33. Mishnaic tractate *Sabbath* 7:2 states that "carrying things from one domain to another is the last of 39 works forbidden" on the Sabbath, while "carrying empty beds is implicitly forbidden" in *Sabbath* 10:5. Quoted in Brown, *Gospel According to John I–XII,* 1:208.

34. Brown, *Gospel According to John I–XII,* 1:217.

35. I. Epstein, *The Babylonian Talmud,* English ed. (London: Soncino, 1961), Taanith 2a; quoted in Brown, *Gospel According to John I–XII,* 1:217.

36. Brown, *Gospel According to John I–XII,* 1:218–19.

37. This testimony of the Father possibly refers to Jesus' baptism when "there came a voice from heaven, saying, Thou art my beloved Son, in whom I am well pleased" (Mark 1:11).

38. The Savior may have used four witnesses to underscore to the Jews that his testimony goes beyond the Mosaic requirement of three. The book of Amos uses a Hebrew idiom, *"for three transgressions . . . yea, for four"* as a way to produce a cumulative effect emphasizing the strength of his own testimony (Amos 1:3, 6, 9, 11; see also Proverbs 30:15, 18, 21, 29). *Soncino Books of the Bible: The Twelve Prophets,* 14 vols. (London: Soncino, 1966), 14:84. In both Amos and Proverbs the fourth transgression is followed by a prophecy of great destruction. This may be a means whereby the Savior cautions his unbelieving audience regarding the consequence to those who reject his message.

39. During the Feast of Unleavened Bread, all leaven was removed from their homes and from their diet (see Exodus 12:15). The unleavened bread was a reminder to Israel of their swift flight from Egypt (see Exodus 12:39). The Savior also used leaven as a symbol of hypocrisy and wickedness (see Luke 12:1). This usage implies that Israel, Jehovah's covenant people, must remove all wickedness from amongst them and flee spiritual bondage.

40. *Encyclopedia Judaica,* 13:164–68.

41. Flavius Josephus, *Wars of the Jews,* 6.9.3, in *Josephus: Complete Works,* trans. William Whiston (Grand Rapids, Mich.: Kregel, 1978), 587. Such large numbers have also been supported in the Talmud. See *Encyclopedia Judaica,* 13:164.

42. Brown, *Gospel According to John I–XII,* 1:265.

43. Quoted in Brown, *Gospel According to John I–XII,* 1:265. A source from the second century after Christ, Apocryphon II Baruch 29:8, states: "The treasury of manna shall again descend from on high, and they will eat of it in those years." Several Midrashic sources also refer to a second redeemer who will cause bread to rain from heaven.

44. Passover lections include Exodus 12:21–51; 13:1–16; 22:24–23:19; 33:12–34:26; 13:17–15:26; Numbers 9:1–14; 28:19–25; Leviticus

22:26–23:44; Deuteronomy 15:19–16:17; Joshua 5:2–6:1; 2 Kings 23:1–9; 21–25; Ezekiel 36:37–37:14; 2 Samuel 22:1–51; Isaiah 10:32–12:6. See *Encyclopedia Judaica,* 15:1251–52. For more information on Jesus as the "stem of Jesse," see Isaiah 11:1; D&C 113; Bruce R. McConkie, *The Promised Messiah* (Salt Lake City: Deseret Book, 1981), 192–95.

45. See McConkie, *Promised Messiah,* 443–44.

46. According to E. P. Sanders, "The acceptance of the covenant removes the consequences of the sin of Adam and restores Israel to the *Herrlichkeit* [Glory] lost through Adam's fall. The restoration, however, is brief. Because of the incident of the golden calf, Israel loses its restored status: as Adam's fall resulted in the separation of mankind from God, the worship of the golden calf results in Israel's separation from God. Thereafter it becomes the goal of the individual Israelite to regain what had been lost through the fall of Israel." See E. P. Sanders, *Paul and Palestinian Judaism: A Comparison of Patterns of Religion* (Philadelphia: Fortress Press, 1987), 37.

47. Talmage, *Jesus the Christ,* 342.

48. *Encyclopedia Judaica,* 15:496. See also Leviticus 23:39; Judges 21:19.

49. McConkie, *Promised Messiah,* 432–33; see also Zechariah 14:16.

50. "The Feast of Tabernacles and the Holy Spirit," *Neot Kedumim Newsletter,* October 1997, 4.

51. For a more complete discussion of the many nuances associated with Christ's divinity, see Albert Edersheim, *Temple,* 269–87; McConkie, *Promised Messiah,* 432–35; *Encyclopedia Judaica,* 15:495–502; *Mishnah,* trans. Herbert Danby (London: Oxford, 1933), 172–81.

52. *Mishnah,* trans. Danby, 179. See also Unger, *Bible Dictionary,* 419. Upon completion of the water pouring, the people demand that the priest raise his hands to ensure that the water has been properly emptied onto the altar. The reason for this seems to relate to a time in the life of Alexander Jannaeus, the Maccabean king-priest (c. 95 B.C.). On one occasion when he was performing this ceremony he emptied the water on the ground instead of the altar in response to the distrust and hatred the people had for him. The people were so angered by his actions that they threw at him their lemonlike citrons they were carrying as part of the celebration. During the ensuing uproar his armed soldiers killed six thousand people. Flavius Josephus, *Antiquities of the Jews,* 13.13.5

53. *Mishnah,* trans. Danby, 178.

54. This would be the second day of the feast, because the first day was set aside as a holy day or Sabbath wherein no work was allowed, including the lighting of fire. See Leviticus 23:34–35.

55. *Mishnah,* trans. Danby, 179, and n. 16. A cubit is about seventeen and one-half inches.

56. *Mishnah,* trans. Danby, 179–80.

57. *Encyclopedia Judaica,* 15:501.

58. Edersheim, *Temple,* 304.

59. Brown, *Gospel According to John I–XII,* 1:326; emphasis added.

60. *Jeremiah,* trans. H. Freedman, in *Soncino Books of the Bible,* 14 vols. (London: Soncino, 1970), 11:10. See also Jeremiah 2:13; 17:13; John 4:10; 7:38; Zechariah 14:8.

61. See John 7:16, 18, 28–29, 33; 8:16, 18, 26, 29; 9:4.

62. Geoffrey W. Bromiley, *Theological Dictionary of the New Testament,* ed. Gerhard Kittel and Gerhard Friedrich (Grand Rapids, Mich.: Eerdmans Publishing, 1977) 68.

63. The evidence for this is found in the cohesion of the Good Shepherd discourse before John's introduction of the Feast of Dedication (10:22) and the continued theme discussed afterward. Compare John 10:1–18 with John 10:26–27, keeping in mind verse 22 in which John introduces the Feast of Dedication. For a more comprehensive discussion see Brown, *Gospel According to John I–XII,* 1:388–89.

64. *Anchor Bible Dictionary,* ed. David Noel Freedman, 6 vols. (New York: Doubleday, 1992), 2:123.

65. See 1 Maccabees 4:36–61; 2 Maccabees 1:18; 2:16, 19; 10:3, 5, 7.

66. Josephus, *Antiquities,* 12.7.7.

67. 2 Maccabees never calls Hanukkah a festival of tabernacles, but it clearly relates the two occasions. See the following for further support: *Anchor Bible Dictionary,* 2:124; *Encyclopedia Judaica,* 7:1283; Unger, *Bible Dictionary,* 422.

68. See Numbers 7; Deuteronomy 20:5; 2 Chronicles 7:5–11; 1 Kings 8:63–66; Nehemiah 12:27; Psalm 30:1; *Anchor Bible Dictionary,* 2:123–24.

69. See Genesis 49:24; Psalms 23; 78:52–55, 70–72; Isaiah 40:11; 49:9–12; Jeremiah 13:17; 23:1–8; Ezekiel 34; Micah 7:14.

70. *Anchor Bible Dictionary,* 5:1189.

71. Guilding, *Fourth Gospel and Jewish Worship,* 129–30.

72. Rabbinic sources plainly taught that the sacred altar of the temple stood as a symbol of atonement, for it brought "peace between Israel and their Father in Heaven." See *Encyclopedia Judaica,* 2:770.

CHAPTER TWENTY-ONE

THE CELESTIAL JERUSALEM

DENNIS A. WRIGHT

John the Revelator watched as the celestial city of Jerusalem descended in glory from the heavens. Its visionary dimensions filled the sky and stretched from horizon to horizon. Radiant with the glory of God, the city's arrival culminated a thousand years of millennial peace as the terrestrial heaven and earth passed away. With awe, John observed its grandeur as a city of light and glory. The images John recorded, both symbolic and real, testify of the wonders of earth's celestial destiny and of its sanctified inhabitants. The coming of the celestial Jerusalem will complete the earth's temporal existence and reestablish the dwelling place of God with man.

The contributions of biblical scholarship are helpful to our understanding of the book of Revelation, but when they are combined with the unique perspective of the restored gospel, we gain a greater appreciation of the wonderful promises associated with the celestial Jerusalem, the eternal home of the Saints.

THE REVELATION OF JOHN

As an apocalyptic document, John's revelation provides a panoramic view of the history of the earth. It begins with a premortal council in heaven and ends with Christ's final victory over evil and the creation of a celestialized earth, which is reserved for the elect of God. Early in the revelation John witnessed a premortal gathering (see Revelation 4–5). He saw Christ accept responsibility for a sealed scroll representing the plan for the mortal existence of the earth (see Revelation 5:1–7). The seven seals placed on the scroll

---

Dennis A. Wright is an associate professor of Church history and doctrine at Brigham Young University.

signified seven different periods of the history of the earth leading to its becoming a celestial sphere. As the Revelation unfolds, each seal opens and John observes various stages in the continuous battle between good and evil. The opening of the final, or seventh, seal ushers in a millennial era of peace and prosperity as Christ renders Satan powerless and reigns personally on the earth. The Resurrection then begins, preparing mankind for a day of judgment (see Revelation 20:5, 11–12).

At the end of the millennial period, Satan again confronts the forces of Christ, ending the era of peace. This conflict results in Christ's complete victory over evil and prepares the earth for the arrival of the celestial Jerusalem. It is at this time that John witnesses the final restoration of the heaven and earth, made possible by the redeeming power of Christ. He sees the celestialized earth receive the holy Jerusalem as a heaven-sent capital city, completing the transformation of the earth to a dwelling place of God and for the heirs of the celestial kingdom.

The arrival of the celestial Jerusalem occurs at the end of John's apocalyptic vision (see Revelation 21–22). A review of important images from John's vision of the transformed earth and the celestial Jerusalem will give us insight into the meanings John conveys.

New Heaven and Earth

Some consider the creation of a new heaven and earth (see Revelation 21:1) as a renewal or restoration of the earth to its original form.[1] From that perspective, the new heaven and earth are not the result of God's rejecting his creation in favor of a new earth. Rather, he acts to return the existing earth and heaven to its original form.[2] Scholars relate this transformation of the earth to a restoration of the conditions existing at the time of the Garden of Eden.

Restoration sources expand this perspective to include a second transformation that exceeds the paradisiacal, or terrestrial, glory of the garden scene. At the second coming of Christ, the earth will change from a telestial to a terrestrial order. John described this event as a "new heaven and earth" (Revelation 21:1). The terrestrial earth will last for a thousand years, until its final transformation to a celestial sphere. The Lord declared to the Prophet Joseph Smith in 1830 that the "heaven and the earth shall be consumed and pass away, united into one body" as in the days before its division (D&C 133:23–24).[10] From that perspective, it appears that the sea may not cease to exist but will change to accommodate the transformed geographical form of the earth. It is not clear whether Elder McConkie considers this change effective both as a millennial and a celestial phenomenon; however, he does provide a different perspective on the "no more sea" noted by John in his vision.

THE VARIOUS JERUSALEMS

The new heaven and earth will result from God's action upon existing elements rather than being a special, new creation. The celestial Jerusalem is different, however, for it does not originate on earth but descends from heaven as a new creation. It is not a reformation of the earthly Jerusalem but a new city prepared in heaven to complete the transformation of the earth.[11] Standing in sharp contrast to the city Babylon described as a harlot in earlier chapters, the celestial Jerusalem stands as a radiant bride, symbolizing the covenant between Christ and his people.[12] As the earthly Jerusalem with its temple historically provided a symbol of God's covenants with mankind, the heavenly Jerusalem represents the fulfillment of those promises.[13]

The Old Jerusalem. From a Restoration perspective, the celestial Jerusalem is the last of several Jerusalems that appear as part of the history of the earth.[14] The Jerusalem of the Old and New Testament was the first to appear. Existing from ancient times, this city gained prominence as the capital city of King David. Throughout the remainder of the biblical account, Jerusalem continued to hold a special position in the spiritual life of the people.

The New Jerusalem. The second city is the New Jerusalem built on the American continent before the Millennium.[15] As part of the work of the latter-day restoration, a city of Zion, or the New Jerusalem, will be built in the land of Missouri (see 3 Nephi 20:22; D&C 45:66–69; 84:3–4). This city will be a gathering place before the return of Christ. During the Millennium, Christ will establish this city as the capital of his kingdom in the Western Hemisphere.

The Rebuilt Jerusalem. The third city is the original Jerusalem rebuilt by faithful Jews on the foundations of the old city.[16] For this purpose, a remnant of the Jewish people will gather to this Jerusalem and there shall be a new heaven and a new earth. For all old things shall pass away, and all things shall become new, even the heaven and the earth, and all the fullness thereof, both men and beasts, the fowls of the air, and the fishes of the sea; and not one hair, neither mote, shall be lost, for it is the workmanship of mine hand" (D&C 29:23–25).[3] A later revelation described the sanctified earth as "crowned with glory, even with the presence of God the Father" (D&C 88:19). Celestialization, the final state of the earth, will fulfill the purpose of its creation and result in a sanctified and immortal state symbolized by the image of a globe of glass and fire (see D&C 130:7–9).

Orson Pratt, an early apostle, described the final transformation as one initiated by divine fire that will refine the elements to a resurrected form "far more glorious than it will appear, during the thousand years of rest."[4] The final "new heaven and earth" will result from the transformation of the earth from its millennial, or terrestrial, form to an eternal celestial dwelling place for God's exalted children. In a later discourse, Elder Pratt compared the transformation of heaven and earth to that of man's resurrection. He explained that the Lord would "call the scattered elements of this creation from their dispersion, bring them together again, and organize them into a new heaven and a new earth."[5] He understood that the resurrected earth would have a similar size and shape as it does now, but it would be restored to its proper, eternal form. That would fulfill the purpose and destiny of the earth.[6]

No More Sea

The disappearance of the sea (see Revelation 21:1) appears related to Jewish traditions that considered the sea a source of chaos and destruction.[7] Hence, to some, the disappearance of the sea implies the complete victory of Christ over evil.[8] One scholar provides a different perspective as he relates the sea to the "cosmic sea" that separates man from God.[9] For him, the disappearance of the sea symbolized the unification of God and mankind.

Elder Bruce R. McConkie suggests a possible relationship between the disappearance of the sea and a restoration of the ancient antediluvian geographical configuration. "Seas shall no longer separate islands and continents. . . . All the land surface of the earth shall be before the second coming of Christ. Immediately preceding Christ's return, a great battle will rage around this city. Christ's return will end the battle and save the city's inhabitants (see Zechariah 12–14). During Christ's millennial reign, this city will serve as the capital city for the Eastern Hemisphere.

The City of Enoch. Fourth will be the city of Enoch that returns to join the New Jerusalem on the American continent (see Moses 7). This city first existed on earth before the time of Noah. Because of the righteousness of its inhabitants, the city was translated and lifted into heaven. As one of the millennial events, the city of Enoch will return to unite with the New Jerusalem on the American continent (see Moses 7:62–63).

The Celestial Jerusalem. The fifth and final city is a holy Jerusalem that will descend from heaven, after the Millennium, to complete the celestialization of the earth. This is the celestial Jerusalem described by John as the final dwelling place of the elect of God. Of divine origin, it will descend from heaven as a new addition to the earth.

The Latter-day Saints will first build a city of Zion, a New Jerusalem, on the American continent before the second coming of Christ.[17] Then, faithful Jews will gather and rebuild the old-world city of Jerusalem.[18] Christ's return will then initiate a new heaven and earth, or a terrestrial order. During the millennial period, two Jerusalems, one each in the eastern and western hemispheres, will serve as world capitals for the government of God on the terrestrial earth. As part of Christ's millennial reign, the city of Enoch will descend from heaven to join the American Jerusalem, uniting the Zion from above with the Zion from below (see Moses 7:62–64). One apostle considered the millennial Jerusalems as a type for the ultimate celestial Jerusalem that is to descend from heaven at the end of time.[19]

Most accept the idea that the descriptions recorded by John (Revelation 21:2, 10) represent a single holy city.[20] But Restoration sources provide a contrasting insight. A common Restoration view suggests that John saw two different cities in his vision. The first city, described in Revelation 21:1–4, refers to the city of Enoch that will return to unite with the New Jerusalem on the American continent.[21] According to this perspective, John uses the term "new heaven and earth" to establish the arrival time of Enoch's city after the first transformation of the earth from a telestial to a terrestrial sphere. It is during this millennial period that John sees the glorious city of Enoch return to the earth and unite with the New Jerusalem built on the American continent. The verses that follow, Revelation 21:4–9, relate to the millennial period: The first scene describes the effects of Christ's personal reign on the earth (see vv. 4–7); the next scene refers to the Judgment, final resurrection, and second death that will occur at the end of the Millennium (see v. 8). Then, beginning in verse 9, John observes the descent of a second city, the celestial Jerusalem, which arrives at the end of the earth's mortal existence. This perspective considers the city described after Revelation 21:9 as the celestial Jerusalem, which descends after the millennial period when the earth will assume its final form.[22]

An account by Elder Orson Pratt provides another perspective. He suggests that the Lord will lift into heaven the terrestrial Jerusalems (the old and New Jerusalems) at the end of the Millennium.[23] After that, Christ will release Satan, who will muster his forces for a final conflict, which will end with the ultimate victory of Christ as he transforms the earth by fire into a celestial world. The two Jerusalems will then return in celestial glory, as recorded by John in Revelation 21 and 22, to serve as capital cities for the celestialized earth.

Elder Pratt considered that Revelation 21:1–4 referred to the return of the celestialized New Jerusalem originally built on the American continent as part of the latter-day restoration. He taught that the second city noted in John's revelation (Revelation 21:9, 22) alluded to the old Jerusalem rebuilt by the Jews as part of the millennial preparations. Both Jerusalems will return as glorified cities, representative of the celestial order. Elder Pratt viewed the remainder of the revelation as a rich description of the second city, the celestialized version of the old Jerusalem to be rebuilt by the Jews.

While different perspectives do exist, there is general agreement among Restoration sources that John observed two different cities in his revelation. Also accepted is the future unification of the city of Enoch and the New Jerusalem. Most sources consider the celestial Jerusalem, or the second city seen by John, to be a capital city that displays the characteristics of the celestial kingdom.[24] Here the faithful will enter with garments washed clean in the blood of the Lamb, to "the city of the living God, the heavenly Jerusalem, and to an innumerable company of angels, to the general assembly and church of the firstborn" (Hebrews 12:22–23).[25]

A DESCRIPTION OF THE CELESTIAL CITY

John described the second city through symbolic images that convey his insights into the function and destiny of the celestial city as a habitation for the heirs of God's kingdom.

Precious stone, clear as crystal. John stated that he was carried "away in the spirit to a great and high mountain" (Revelation 21:10). From this perspective, he saw a "great city, the holy Jerusalem, descending out of heaven from God, having the glory of God: and her light was like unto a stone most precious, even like jasper stone, clear as crystal" (Revelation 21:10–11). The precious stones appear to convey images of light that emanate from the holy city. It is curious that John would select such opaque substances as jasper (see Revelation 21:11) and later gold (see Revelation 21:18) and compare them to clear glass or crystal. Some suggest that John's description was an attempt to capture the internal brilliance of the holy city.[26] The light and glory appear to come from within the city itself rather than being light reflected from an outside source.[27] The precious stones and gold convey John's understanding that this is no earthly city but one that radiates the glory of God.[28] The stones, metals, and associated light are John's attempt to describe the indescribable.[29] The Prophet Joseph Smith commented on this as he noted man's struggle in finding a way to describe something never before experienced by mortals.[30]

John's observations of the holy city parallel information provided by the Prophet Joseph Smith regarding the celestial world: "The angels do not reside on a planet like this earth; but they reside in the presence of God, on a globe like a sea of glass and fire" (D&C 130:6–7). At another time, Joseph noted that the celestial world was a place of "everlasting burnings," or eternal light and glory.[31] Further revelation explained that the celestial earth would be like unto crystal (see D&C 130:6–9). As a celestial city, Jerusalem displayed the inherent glory of God, symbolized by precious stones and metals that radiated the light or power of God.

Walls, foundations, and gates. There is agreement among scholars regarding the symbolic meaning of the walls, foundations, and gates of the holy city. The "great and high" wall has twelve gates, each named after one of the tribes of Israel. Names also appear written on the twelve foundations of the city, but these are the twelve apostles of Christ (see Revelation 21:12, 14). The two sets of twelve appear to link the Old Testament tribes of Israel with the New Testament apostles. The foundation of the apostles (see Ephesians 2:20) reflects the role of the twelve in governing the twelve tribes of Israel (see Matthew 19:28). The celestial Jerusalem symbolizes the harmony between the covenants of the Old and New Testament made possible by Christ and his apostles.[32]

Each gate of the city is made of a single pearl (see Revelation 21:21). In John's time, the value of a perfect pearl exceeded that of gold or other precious stones.[33] The concept of a single pearl as an entry point does not correspond with the conventional view of the "pearly gates" of heaven. Rather, it presents an image of a portal of light through which the faithful enter. Scholars typically do not comment on the purpose of the angels standing beside each gate.

Restoration sources provide valuable insight into the meaning of the walls, foundations, and gates. The apostolic wall symbolizes security and peace and defines the boundary between the celestial world and lesser orders.[34] As the foundation of the wall, the apostles help determine who is invited to dwell in the holy city. The angels that guard the gates test the worthiness of those desiring to enter.[35] The image suggested by each pearl-gate in the wall parallels the description provided in an 1836 revelation to the Prophet Joseph Smith. In this vision in the Kirtland Temple Joseph saw "the gate through which the heirs of that [celestial] kingdom will enter, which was like unto circling flames of fire" (D&C 137:2). The image of light emanating from the single pearly gate, and of a circling flame of fire, appear to define a portal of light rather than a conventional gate. As before, the images attempt to describe what appears to be almost indescribable.

A foursquare city. An angel appears and measures the city for John. The measurements symbolize the magnificence of the celestial Jerusalem (see Revelation 21:15–17). Using modern equivalents, the city approximates a fifteen-hundred-mile cube. As such, the city would fill a large portion of the present Middle East and extend upward beyond the existing atmosphere. The Greek New Testament text suggests a symbolic interpretation, as the dimensions translate into twelve thousand "stadia." The consideration is that the number twelve thousand represents the number of apostles, or tribes of Israel, multiplied by one thousand. From that perspective, the resulting number represents the innumerable group of worthy heavenly hosts invited to the city.[36] Scholars consider this John's way of saying that the city will have room to spare for all those found faithful.[37]

The shape of the city is also significant. Its similarity to the original Holy of Holies in the tabernacle of Moses and the later temples of Solomon and Herod suggests a commonly accepted interpretation. The Holy of Holies was the most sacred room in the Jewish temples. Although its dimensions varied, its shape remained that of a perfect cube. Here rested the ark of the covenant, and here God communicated his will to the prophets. Only those individuals selected by God could enter this sacred place.

The city's shape as a perfect cube supports the interpretation that it represents a type of Holy of Holies and only those prepared to meet God face to face can enter. The Holy of Holies, anciently limited to a few persons, is now open to all of God's people.[38] Given the shape of the city, Richard D. Draper described the entire city as a sacred sanctuary. He also interpreted the symbolic dimensions of the 144-cubit wall surrounding the city. The number 144 symbolizes a fulness of priesthood authority that rests on the foundation of the apostles.[39] Their authority defines the sacred city and separates it from the profane.

Rivers, streets, trees, and temples. Because the ancient temples served as the center of religious life in Jerusalem, John appeared surprised that the holy city lacked a temple (see Revelation 21:22). Some consider that the absence of a temple reflects the perfected nature of the city.[40] "The city *is* the temple," explains one author, and therefore there is no need for a separate structure.[41] Historically, the temple provided a place for mankind to meet God. Within the celestial Jerusalem, however, God will dwell with mankind as in the beginning, making a temple unnecessary.[42] Also, from a Restoration perspective, the ordinance work assigned to the temple is complete and hence the need for a temple no longer will exist.[43]

John noted that the city did not appear to need light from the sun or moon (see Revelation 21:23). The fact that the city does not require external light implies the effect of God's presence in the celestial Jerusalem. As in the images of precious stones shining forth, the holy city will radiate the glory of those who dwell therein. The glory of God will provide the light of the holy city and the Lamb will be its lamp.[44] Revelations to the Prophet Joseph Smith provide insight to the light of Christ that illuminated the holy city. He learned that the light of Christ is the same light that "proceedeth forth from the presence of God to fill the immensity of space" (D&C 88:12). Joseph learned that this light gives life to all things and provides the governing power that directs all things. This light is also related to the power of "quickening" that enables the resurrection and sanctification of mankind. The revelation explained that light acts upon mankind, preparing him for God's presence. Finally, the light provides the means whereby Christ perfects and sanctifies the faithful (see D&C 88:34). Those accepted into the celestial Jerusalem enjoy the benefits of the light that fills the city. They become "gods" to "dwell in the presence [light] of God and his Christ forever" (D&C 76:58, 62).

John observed a pure river of the water of life flowing through the city (see Revelation 22:1). The account described the river running down the middle of a street that had the appearance of gold (see Revelation 21:21; 22:2). Numerous "tree[s] of life" line the banks of the river, each bearing fruit for the healing of the nations (Revelation 22:2). Most accept that the tree of life image refers to the original tree in the Garden of Eden. After the Fall, God placed an angel to guard the tree of life, so that mankind might not partake of its fruit. In the celestial city, God removes all barriers, and mankind freely partakes of eternal life.[45] For one scholar the word *nations* (see Revelation 21:24) represents the Gentiles who accept a covenant with Christ.[46] From this perspective, the fruit appears to have the effect of healing the Gentiles, who accept the gospel and join in harmony with the rest of Israel.

Lehi's dream in the Book of Mormon (see 1 Nephi 8) gives a Restoration perspective on the trees John observed. The new-world prophet described the fruit as "desirable to make one happy" and "most sweet, above all that I ever before tasted" (1 Nephi 8:10–11).

Later, his son Nephi received instruction from an angel regarding the tree and its marvelous fruit. The angel explained that the fruit represented the "love of God," which is "the most desirable above all things" (1 Nephi 11:22). One Restoration author related the fruit to "eternal life in the presence of the Father." [47] He explained that this gift came because of the condescension of God, who, greater than all, descended to a mortal level to assist his children. The sacrifice of Christ made possible the resurrection of all mankind and the eternal life of the faithful. As the gifts of salvation and exaltation are most desirable, the tree of life symbolized the love of God for his children. John rejoiced as he saw the ban lifted from the tree of life and the healing effect it had on those who partook (see Revelation 22:1–3).

AN ETERNAL HOME FOR THE SAINTS

Turner noted that "the Bible begins with a garden but ends with a city."[48] Although that view is valid from one perspective, John's Revelation suggests a much broader view. In the initial part of the vision, John saw the hosts of heaven as they existed before the creation of the world (see Revelation 4–5). He described his anxiety over decisions related to the plan for mankind's mortal existence (see Revelation 5:4). An angel comforted him by showing him that the "Lion of the tribe of Juda" (Revelation 5:5) would have the power to assume responsibility for the plan of salvation for his Father's children. John understood that this experience of mankind occurred at the foundation of the world, before the garden scene. John saw Christ initiate the plan that would allow mankind to enter a mortal experience, with the opportunity to gain a fulness of joy (see 2 Nephi 2:25). The events that led to the celestial Jerusalem did not begin in the garden. As John witnessed, they began long before, at a time when mankind lived in the presence of God and enjoyed his light and glory.

The celestial Jerusalem promises mankind a return to his celestial home. By following Christ, he will receive much more than he lost in the garden.[49] Drawing upon images of the tree of life and the living waters, John taught that Christ invites all to drink of the waters of life.[50] "Blessed are they that do his commandments, that they may have right to the tree of life, and may enter in through the gates into the city" (Revelation 22:14). For Latter-day Saints who accept the revelations from God, the celestial Jerusalem represents the fulfill-ment of all the Lord has promised through his prophets.

At an appointed time, the faithful Saints will ascend Mount Zion and enter "the city of the living God, the heavenly Jerusalem" (Hebrews 12:22). Here they will join "an innumerable company of angels, to the general assembly and church of the firstborn" (Hebrews 12:22–23). "Wherefore, as it is written, they are gods, even the sons of God. Wherefore all things are theirs, whether life or death, or things present, or things to come, all are theirs" (D&C 76:58–59). They will dwell on a sanctified and immortal earth made like unto a Urim and Thummin, clear as glass, where all who dwell thereon will know all things pertaining to the kingdom of God (see D&C 130:9–10). Of this future reality, the Prophet Joseph recorded, "We saw the glory of the celestial, which excels in all things" (D&C 76:92). He counseled, "Wherefore, let no man glory in man, but rather let him glory in God, who shall subdue all" (D&C 76:61).

John watched as the celestial Jerusalem descended from heaven, knowing that it represented a fulfillment of all things. The plan was complete, and mankind could now return to live with his Heavenly Father. What Christ began in the premortal world, he ended with the arrival of the celestial Jerusalem on a glorified earth.

NOTES

1. T. F. Glasson, "The Revelation of John," *The Cambridge Bible Commentary* (London: Cambridge University Press, 1965), 115.

2. Wilfrid J. Harrington, *Revelation,* vol. 16 in *Sacra Pagina Series,* ed. Daniel J. Harrington (Collegeville, Minn.: Liturgical Press, 1993), 16:206–7.

3. Also see Hyrum M. Smith and Janne M. Sjodahl, Introduction to and commentary on *The Doctrine and Covenants* (Salt Lake City: Deseret Book, 1972), 154.

4. Orson Pratt, in *Journal of Discourses,* 26 vols. (London: Latter-day Saints' Book Depot, 1877), 18:322.

5. Pratt, *Journal of Discourses,* 21:226.

6. See Joseph Fielding Smith, *Doctrines of Salvation,* comp. Bruce R. McConkie, 3 vols. (Salt Lake City: Bookcraft, 1954), 1:72.

7. J. Massyngberde Ford, *Revelation, The Anchor Bible,* ed. David N. Freedman (Garden City, N. Y.: Doubleday, 1975), 38:361.

8. Leon Morris, *The Book of Revelation: An Introduction and Commentary* (Grand Rapids, Mich.: Eerdmans, 1987), 237.

9. G. B. Caird, *A Commentary on the Revelation of St. John the Divine* (New York: Harper and Row, 1966), 262.

10. Bruce R. McConkie, *Doctrinal New Testament Commentary,* 3 vols. (Salt Lake City: Bookcraft, 1965–73), 3:580–81.

11. Harrington, *Revelation,* 207.

12. *The Interpreter's Bible,* ed. George A. Buttrick, 12 vols. (New York: Abingdon Press, 1953), 12:608.

13. David L. Turner, "The New Jerusalem in Revelation 21:1–22:5: Consummation of a Biblical Continuum," in *Dispensationalism, Israel, and the Church: The Search for Definition,* ed. Craig A Blaising and Darrell L. Bock (Grand Rapids, Mich.: Zondervan, 1992), 274.

14. McConkie, *Doctrinal New Testament Commentary,* 3:581.

15. For a discussion of the New Jerusalem to be built on the American continent, see Graham W. Doxey, in *Encyclopedia of Mormonism,* ed. Daniel H. Ludlow, 4 vols. (New York: Macmillan, 1992), 3:1009–10.

16. For further information on the millennial Jerusalem to be built on the site of the ancient city, see David B. Galbraith, D. Kelly Ogden, and Andrew C. Skinner, *Jerusalem, the Eternal City* (Salt Lake City: Deseret Book, 1996), 524–36.

17. Joseph Smith, *History of The Church of Jesus Christ of Latter-day Saints,* ed. B. H. Roberts, 2d ed. rev., 7 vols. (Salt Lake City: The Church of Jesus Christ of Latter-day Saints, 1932–51), 4:541.

18. Andrew F. Ehat and Lyndon W. Cook, eds., *The Words of Joseph Smith* (Provo: Brigham Young University Religious Studies Center, 1980), 6:180.

19. James E. Talmage, *The Articles of Faith* (Salt Lake City: Deseret Book, 1984), 316–17.

20. Morris, *Book of Revelation,* 242.

21. Bruce R. McConkie, *A New Witness for the Articles of Faith* (Salt Lake City: Deseret Book, 1985), 588. A statement by the Prophet Joseph Smith lends support to this perspective; see Joseph Smith, *Teachings of the Prophet Joseph Smith,* sel. Joseph Fielding Smith (Salt Lake City: Deseret Book, 1976), 86.

22. McConkie, *Doctrinal New Testament Commentary,* 3:586–87.

23. Orson Pratt, in *Journal of Discourses,* 16:322–23; 18:346–48.

24. McConkie, *Doctrinal New Testament Commentary,* 3:586.

25. Smith, *Teachings of the Prophet Joseph Smith,* 12.

26. Morris, *Book of Revelation,* 242, 244–45.

27. See T. E. Martin, *John, Jude, Revelation,* ed. William M. Greathouse, 12 vols. (Kansas City, Mo.: Beacon Hill Press, 1983), 12:259.

28. Charles T. Chapman, *The Message of the Book of Revelation* (Collegeville, Minn.: Liturgical Press, 1991), 131.

29. Turner, "New Jerusalem," 276.

30. Smith, *History of the Church,* 6:50.

31. Smith, *History of the Church,* 6:366.

32. Glasson, *Revelation of John,* 118.

33. Ford, *Revelation,* 337.

34. McConkie, *Doctrinal New Testament Commentary,* 3:587.

35. Brigham Young, in *Journal of Discourses,* 2:31.

36. Chapman, *Message of the Book of Revelation,* 130.

37. Turner, "The New Jerusalem," 288.

38. Chapman, *Message of the Book of Revelation,* 130.

39. Richard D. Draper, *Opening the Seven Seals: The Visions of John the Revelator* (Salt Lake City: Deseret Book, 1991), 236–37.

40. Gary G. Cohen, *Understanding Revelation* (Chicago: Moody Press, 1968), 173.

41. Harrington, *Revelation,* 215.

42. Martin, *John, Jude, Revelation,* 263.

43. Conversations with Richard D. Draper, January 1998.

44. Morris, *Book of Revelation,* 247.

45. Glasson, *Revelation of John,* 121.

46. Chapman, *Message of the Book of Revelation,* 132.

47. Kent P. Jackson, "The Tree of Life and the Ministry of Christ," in *1 Nephi to Alma 29,* ed. Kent P. Jackson, vol. 7 of *Studies in Scripture Series,* 8 vols. (Salt Lake City: Deseret Book, 1987), 7:38–39.

48. E. L. Copeland, quoted in Turner, "New Jerusalem," 290.

49. Turner, "New Jerusalem," 290.

50. *Interpreter's Bible,* 12:611.

INDEX

341